On the Rim

The publication of this book was assisted by a bequest from Josiah H. Chase to honor his parents, Ellen Rankin Chase and Josiah Hook Chase, Minnesota territorial pioneers.

On the Rim

Looking for the Grand Canyon

MARK NEUMANN

Minneapolis   London

University of Minnesota Press

The photograph on page 47 is reprinted courtesy of the Museum of Northern Arizona
Photo Archives (#78.0071). The photograph on page 57 is reprinted courtesy
of the Katherine Harvey Collection, Grand Canyon Museum Collection.
All other photographs in the book by Mark Neumann.

Lyrics of "Wand'rin' Star," by Alan Jay Lerner and Frederick Loewe, copyright 1951
(renewed) Alan Jay Lerner and Frederick Loewe. Chappell & Co. publisher and
owner of allied rights throughout the world. All rights reserved. Used by permission
of Warner Bros. Publications U.S. Inc.

Published by the University of Minnesota Press
111 Third Avenue South, Suite 290
Minneapolis, MN 55401-2520
http://www.upress.umn.edu

Library of Congress Cataloging-in-Publication Data

Neumann, Mark.
    On the rim : looking for the Grand Canyon / Mark Neumann.
        p.   cm.
    Includes bibliographical references (p.   ) and index.
    ISBN 0-8166-2784-3 (acid-free paper). — ISBN 0-8166-2785-1
(pbk. : acid-free paper)
    1. Grand Canyon (Ariz.)—Description and travel.   2. Tourism—
Social aspects—Arizona—Grand Canyon.   3. Tourism—Psychological
aspects—Arizona—Grand Canyon.   4. Landscape—Social aspects—
Arizona—Grand Canyon.   5. Landscape—Arizona—Grand Canyon—
Psychological aspects.   I. Title.
F788.N47   1999
917.91'320453—dc21   99-35133

For Janna Jones, David Eason, and Mary Strine

Contents

Acknowledgments

Many people helped me during the long process of researching, writing, and thinking about tourism, leisure, and the canyon. With extreme gratitude, it's my pleasure to mention and remember them here.

First and foremost, I want to thank the numerous park visitors, National Park Service staff, and the Fred Harvey Company employees at the Grand Canyon who granted me interviews, supplied photographs, and replied to my many questions over the years I spent working on this book. Their stories and images fill many of these pages.

Thanks to a University of South Florida Research and Creative Scholarship Grant in 1993, I was able to conduct research at the canyon and at several archives and special collections in Arizona. In particular, my appreciation goes to Colleen Hyde and the staff at the Grand Canyon Museum Collection for continual help and advice in locating documents, photographs, and historical materials related to the park. I found excellent assistance at the Museum of Northern Arizona Photo Archives in Flagstaff; the Bancroft Library at the University of California, Berkeley; the Special Collections Department in the Marriot Library at the University of Utah; the Department of Archives and Manuscripts in the Hayden Library at Arizona State University; the Heard Museum and Archives in Phoenix; and from the always helpful staff at the campus library of the University of South Florida, Tampa. The Coconino County Sheriff's Department and the Coconino County Courthouse in Flagstaff provided me with numerous court transcripts and investigation reports; I am thankful for the valuable help I received from Coconino County Deputy Attorney Camille Bibles. Moreover, the cooperative staff at the Arizona Department of Corrections in Phoenix and the Superior Court of California in San Joaquin County, in addition to the help of San Joaquin County Deputy District Attorney Michael Platt, made the research process go easier.

At the University of Minnesota Press, my editor Carrie Mullen showed unwavering enthusiasm for my project and patience with me on the long path toward bringing this book to press. My gratitude also goes to Robin Moir, Amy Unger, and Adam Grafa for their excellent assistance and expertise with permissions, photographs, layout, and everything that went into the production of this book. I was fortunate to have Wendy Jacobs's sharp and masterful copyediting on the final manuscript. Finally, I wish to thank Janaki Bakhle, who first saw potential in this work.

I am truly grateful for the many good colleagues who offered me their time, help, and interest over the years. Nancy Hewitt went beyond the call of duty by carefully reading several drafts of the manuscript. Her thoughtful ideas and criticisms have made these better chapters, and she offered me a good compass during the many times I found myself lost in the canyon. Elizabeth Bird and Lawrence Grossberg offered useful comments and criticisms during the proposal stages of the project and on several occasions afterward. I owe special appreciation to Douglas Harper for encouraging me to use my photographs in this book and generously allowing me unlimited use of his darkroom. David Payne was always willing to serve as a sounding board for my ideas during our regular front stoop seminars. I also benefited enormously from my ongoing dialogues with Dominique Desjeux, Tim Simpson, and Robert Drew, who all shared with me their experiences and ideas for studying cultural life. Art Bochner and Carolyn Ellis lent considerable support to my research over the years and were fundamental in helping me publish some early essays on canyon tourism. My department chair, Eric Eisenberg, offered regular encouragement and made possible the time and equipment I needed to complete this book.

Apart from these colleagues, I have been fortunate to receive the generous support of my parents, Jean and Albert Neumann, who gave me my first look at the Grand Canyon. Their work, their sacrifices, and their curiosity about the places and people beyond our small town allowed us to travel through much of America during my youth. I also thank Jeanne Travers for everything she provided during the summers I spent in Arizona. And I can only wonder what would have happened to this book, and me, had I not met Ronnie Earl in March 1994, when I was rapidly approaching a dead end. He pointed me to a new path full of promise. I have been fortunate to travel it in good company with the guidance of my friend Richard Bittman.

I am sincerely indebted to my dissertation adviser, Mary Strine, for taking an early interest in my work and helping me give it shape and purpose. Many of her astute insights and ideas remain in these chapters. My mentor, teacher, and friend David Eason first planted the seeds for my thinking about contemporary culture and tourism and, through his example, taught me how to write about them. I am truly grateful for his ideas and wisdom; they have been at the heart of this project and my continuing education.

Finally, my ability to complete this book is largely a result of the good advice and boundless support offered by my wife, Janna Jones. With a kind heart, enduring patience, and incisive comment, she listened to me read every line of every page more than once. Her spirit and imagination are present in this book and are a gift to my life.

Introduction

Beneath clear night sky and towering pines, I sit with nearly a hundred tourists on wooden benches anchored to the ground in a clearing near the Grand Canyon Visitor Center. This is the Mather Amphitheater and tonight—August 25—we've gathered for a park ranger's evening campfire program that will teach us about some aspect of the Grand Canyon's geology, history, or ecology. Today is National Park Service Day, commemorating the 1916 passage of the Organic Act and, consequently, the establishment of the National Park Service. But before the scheduled educational program begins, Ranger Andy—uniformed in Park Service greens, grays, and the traditional crisp-edged brimmer—tells us we're going to have a sing-along. Smoke wisps from the smoldering campfire at his feet as he projects slides with the lyrics from Broadway show tunes on the big screen behind him. *South Pacific. Oklahoma! Fiddler on the Roof.* Amiable, utterly sincere, and with microphone in hand, the ranger calls up melodies supposedly popular enough to transform a reluctant group of strangers into a choir.

"Sunri-i-ise . . . sun-set, sunri-i-ise . . . sun-set," we begin in soft voices, unsure of the risks of singing in public; men, women, and children strain for the key and pitch. Tonight we come here from Iowa, California, Maine, Arkansas, Oregon, Chicago, Salt Lake City, Switzerland, Ontario, Germany, and a little town outside of Pittsburgh. We wear windbreakers and sweaters; the air is chilly and a few drape blankets over their legs. Children unable to read the lyrics are restless, but so are some of the adults. A stringy-haired teenage boy in a Nirvana T-shirt on the bench in front of me flicks a flashlight beam on and off at the ground for no apparent reason. "If I were a rich man . . . ," we sing, this time with a little more gusto. Andy introduces each song with trivia questions about the musicals. Our last number is "Wand'rin' Star" from the 1950s musical *Paint Your Wagon.*

"All right, who wrote *Paint Your Wagon?*" asks the ranger. I hear the crowd murmur; a few of the older couples look at each other, nose to nose, as if the answer might be somewhere between them.

"Lee Marvin!" shouts an enthusiastic man.

"No, it's not Lee Marvin," chuckles Andy. "It's Alan Jay Lerner. Lee Marvin played in *Paint Your Wagon,* though." He sings the first verse and chorus of "Wand'rin' Star" so that we can get a sense of the melody. "Let's all sing it now," he says, "because it's kind of what we're doing here in the park, on our vacations. We're like the forty-niners, movin' on, lookin' for a better tomorrow." And with those words, we sing:

> When I learned to talk, the word they taught me was "goodbye"
> That and "Where's my hat?" are all I'll need until I die
> Achin' for to stop and always achin' for to go;
> Searchin', but for what? I never will know,
> I was born under a wand'rin' star
> I was born under a wand'rin' star . . .

Even though I try to sing the song I've never heard before, I know it's a familiar tune. For more than a century, the American West has been a real and imaginary scene of adventurous wandering.[1] Ranger Andy and Lerner's lyrics sentimentally aim the vacation crowd toward nostalgic images of restless searchers aching for something unnameable. We all know that just a short walk away, down an asphalt-covered trail, the visitor center parking lot is filled with minivans, rental cars, station wagons, campers, and four-wheel-drive sport utility vehicles. About one mile to the west, and a short ride on the canyon shuttle bus, are El Tovar Hotel and Hopi House, both built in the first decade of this century, and perched on the canyon rim. From there, you can walk past the newer Kachina and Thunderbird Lodges to the 1930s Bright Angel Lodge and adjoining Arizona Steak House. Below this cluster of hotels lies the Historic Grand Canyon Railroad Depot; steel rails lead all the way to Williams, some sixty miles to the south. Across the road from the Visitors Center, Babbit's General

Store—selling groceries, books, sporting equipment, hot deli food, compact discs, calendars, T-shirts, and magazines—closed up for the evening just half an hour before our campfire program. Next door, at the Yavapai Lodge and cafeteria, customers move slowly, carrying plastic trays with dinners of spaghetti, broiled chicken, chili, ground sirloin, green beans, carrots, mashed potatoes, and gravy portioned out by servers sweating out their shift behind a glass divider. The cash registers are still ringing in the Yavapai curio shop. Just beyond the store and lodge, aluminum-sided trailers and brightly colored nylon tents fill all the spaces in Mather Campground. Six miles south of the park entrance is the small gateway community of Tusayan, where cars and RVs roll through a commercial strip of scenic airplane and helicopter rides, souvenir shops advertising free tourist information, gas, food, lodging, and an IMAX movie theatre showing "Grand Canyon—The Hidden Secrets" in six-track Dolby stereo on a screen seven stories high and eighty-two feet wide. But on this stage beneath the pines, all of this seems far away as our voices come together, recovering a quixotic tale of the American West. Ranger Andy proposed that we, too, were "wand'rin' stars"; the drift of private journeys brought us to this moment of public performance, one where the moorings of culture, memory, song, and ritual offered a glimpse into a world of shared yearnings and common predicaments. Here, the Grand Canyon seemed a cultural dreamland where, as poet David Bottoms wrote, we find "that place we go to save ourselves, / that place where the object / of the dream is place."[2] And singing along like this at the Mather Amphitheater seemed, at best, to offer us all a dreamy veil of fantasy, to impart a romantic cast to our vacations, and to shroud us from the blunt truth that we were sitting on orderly rows of benches singing Broadway musical numbers for a uniformed man whose amplified voice sounded through the two audio speakers mounted on the permanent screen built in the forest near the edge of the Grand Canyon.

Things were not so different a hundred years ago. In June 1898, Burton Holmes visited the canyon's South Rim and returned to give public lectures and show his audience lantern slides of the marvels he and his party witnessed. "I am afraid that the only pictures that I can show you will not produce upon you the impressions that they should," Holmes told his audience. He feared his pictures were an "imperfect media of revelation," he said. "A soul returned from Paradise would scarcely be at a greater loss for words or similes." But with a mouthful of apologies for the crime of inadequate representation he was about to commit, he eventually gave the audience a look at his pictures.[3]

Holmes said the Grand Canyon "revolutionized" his perceptions of beauty and the sublime. Undoubtedly, he had cribbed for his lecture from geologist Clarence Dutton's 1882 government survey report, which called the canyon "a great innovation in modern ideas of scenery."[4] And, like Dutton, Holmes told his audience that not everyone would be able to appreciate the scenic view. "I believe that when we behold the scene for the first time, a series of new brain-cells is generated, and until they have become sufficiently developed, the canyon withholds its message," he cautioned. "In the average mind there is no place for an impression so unlike any before received. At first sight the mentality is dazzled. . . . No painting, photograph, or sketch can do more than suggest to those who have not seen. Photographers by scores have risked their lives to reach that one elusive point of view where the grand lines of majesty would meet one another at the focal plane, but all have failed."[5]

Betting against the odds of foiled painters and photographers, Holmes and his party arrived in Flagstaff by rail and took the eleven-hour stagecoach ride to the rim, packing nearly a mile of motion-picture film, view cameras, and more than two hundred wet plates. They arrived at John Hance's tourist camp at the canyon's edge and stayed in tents erected on wooden platforms and furnished with dressers and mirrors, rocking chairs, and hammocks. Hance, a former miner who decided that taking copper ore out of the canyon paled in comparison to what he could earn from the tourist business, was not alone on the rim. A few miles to the west, Niles and Ralph Cameron, along with Peter Berry, had built a big log house called the Grand View Hotel. The hotel opened in 1897 and employed a European chef who wore a white apron and white cap. Five years earlier, they had built the Grand View Trail descending to Horseshoe Mesa to mine a rich copper vein, but it had quickly become a popular tourist trail.

Holmes's slide show and lecture reminds us that the Grand Canyon has been a place for weaving stories and fantasies for more than a century. In showing his slides, Holmes framed the canyon as a theater of multiple views and observers, all converging at once in his voice. He spoke in reverential awe of sublime beauty but also confessed he considered throwing himself over the edge into eternity when he first gazed upon it. He wanted to frame the impossible canyon with photographs and motion pictures but, in the end, admitted failure for himself and anyone else who had tried to do the same over the past thirty years. Despite the presence of a burgeoning hospitality industry on the South Rim, he cautiously gave his audience a glimpse of the scenic wonder, as if they were to witness the discovery of a new planet. Holmes seemed to look into the chasm and into himself, a man poised at the brink of a new world full of promise, yet he felt the firm ground shifting around him. His voice spoke from a crossroads of science and spirituality, conceit and humility. He boasted to his eastern audiences like an adventurer but found his bed on the frontier in a hotel at the edge of the earth.

Just thirty years before Holmes and his companions took the stagecoach to what he called "the most entrancing scene that ever dawned upon the eye of man," the Grand Canyon did not exist for the American public. In September 1540, a party of Coronado's conquistadores under the command of García López de Cárdenas, the son of a Spanish nobleman who came to North America in search of wealth and fame, were the first Europeans to see the canyon. Cardenas and his men spent three frustrating and unsuccessful days trying to reach the river below. They reported that the canyon's landscape was dry, difficult for passage, and a place to generally avoid. For more than three hundred years, the canyon area was largely left to the natives who lived in the surrounding region. By the late 1860s, most maps of the United States showed little more than a great blank space for what is now northern Arizona.

All of this changed, however, after Major John Wesley Powell's exploration of the Colorado River. Powell left Green River, Wyoming, on May 24, 1869, with a crew of nine in four wooden boats to explore the canyons of the Colorado River. Just two weeks earlier, dignitaries had ceremoniously hammered a golden railroad spike at Promontory Point, Utah, and linked the nation with steel tracks. A telegraph wire attached to the rails reported the hammer's blows for progress to eastern cities. The Union Pacific tracks linking the nation's east and west had carried Powell's specially built boats for an expedition into, as he described it in his expedition journal, the "Great Unknown." When Powell returned from his harrowing expedition, he toured the United States as a hero, telling of his adventures and reporting the details of the Grand Canyon to the rest of America. If completing a transcontinental railway suggested a taming of the American frontier, Powell's expedition into the uncharted space on the map quickly pointed Americans to a place where the frontier dream would live well into the next century. Over the next two decades, more and more tourists looking for that dream would arrive at the canyon, and lodges would spring up along the rim. By 1901, an Atchison, Topeka and Santa Fe Railway spur coming from Williams brought rail service to the brink of the canyon as well as increasing numbers of visitors. Theodore Roosevelt was elected president of the United States that same year, and he traveled to the canyon in 1903. An active outdoorsman, the president campaigned for the conservation of public lands and sought to protect them from mining and cattle interests. In November 1906, Roosevelt signed a bill to establish Grand Canyon Game Reserve. With congressional approval of the 1906 Act for the Preservation of American Antiquities, Roosevelt had the authority to set aside areas containing "objects of historic and scientific interest" as national monuments. Under the Antiquities Act, he established Grand Canyon National Monument in January 1908. Eleven years later, on February 26, 1919, President Woodrow Wilson signed a congressional bill to establish Grand Canyon National Park.[6]

But during the two decades before the creation of the national park, the Grand Canyon was gaining currency throughout the United States as a symbol citizens might grasp as a source of national pride and identity. Burton Holmes's lectures were but a small contribution to a cultural image of a Grand Canyon that had been circulating since the 1870s and, over the next three decades, continually became magnified in works of art, books, magazine accounts, calendars, stereographs, government reports, postcards, tourist guides, and railroad advertisements. Since the early twentieth century, an image of the Grand Canyon has become etched in the minds of millions who come from all over the world to view firsthand the vast scenes mapping our mythic stories of nature, culture, and history.

"The world's landscapes are but the screen on which the past, present, and anticipated cosmic vanity of mankind is written," notes James M. Houston. "Land is the palimpsest of human needs, desires, meaning, greed, and fears."[7] Houston's metaphor of "written" landscapes invites us to consider how national parks like the Grand Canyon are also symbolically constructed from a variety of narratives telling stories of American nationalism, the majesty of nature, cultural identity, the dramas of westward expansion. In the Grand Canyon Visitor Center, on the lobby wall, hangs a plaque with the words of Theodore Roosevelt: "Leave it as it is. You cannot improve on it. The ages have been at work on it, and man can only mar it. What you can do is to keep it for your children . . . and for all who come after you, as the one great sight which every American . . . should see." Nearly fifty years later, Freeman Tilden, an early proponent of national park public interpretation programs, echoed Roosevelt when he said the purpose of national parks is "to preserve, in a condition as unaltered as possible, the wilderness that greeted the eyes of the first white men who challenged and conquered it."[8] Both men shared a view that national parks were "national museums." Like museums, national parks rescued and saved places and things from becoming lost to the transitory forces of the modern world. And like museums, the parks are modern institutions constructing and sustaining images of nature, history, and culture. Although the parks may seem like enchanted islands frozen in time, they are places of a cultural mythology.

In the Grand Canyon, we find a landscape drawn by people like Powell, Dutton, Holmes, the Cameron brothers, Tilden, and numerous others who have literally and metaphorically inscribed the scene with their visions and values. Yet these acts of inscription seem to disappear over time as a mythic Grand Canyon waits on the horizon. "What the world supplies to myth is an historical reality, defined, even if this goes back quite a while, by the way in which men have produced or used it," wrote Roland Barthes in 1957, "and what myth gives in return is a *natural* image of this reality. . . . Myth does not deny things, on the contrary, its function is to talk about them; simply, it purifies them, it makes them innocent, it gives them a natural and eternal justification. . . . In passing from history to nature, myth acts economically: it abolishes the complexity of human acts, it gives them the simplicity of essences, it does away with all dialectics, . . . it organizes a world which is without contradictions because it is without depth, a world wide open and wallowing in the evident, it establishes a blissful clarity."[9] What may seem at face value a preserved natural environment, a place of cultural tradition, or a national monument is, instead, a reflection of selective *production* where, as Raymond Williams points out, "from a whole possible area of past and present, certain meanings and practices are chosen for emphasis [and] certain other meanings and practices are neglected or excluded."[10] National parks and their surrounding regions exemplify how the forces of tourism are often centered in the manufacturing of cultural images, regions, and people that reveal political, historical, social, and economic relationships among culture, state, and class-based forms of representational power. "Why are certain practices singled out as cultural traditions while others are forgotten or ignored?" asks Wai-Teng Leong. "Who, in particular, links people and practices to the past and for what purposes? Who defines the cultural traditions for which groups? Which group is able to impose its version of the past on other groups and why?"[11]

In June 1988, ninety years after Burton Holmes took a stagecoach from Flagstaff to the South Rim, I packed up my VW bus with camping gear, a tape recorder, a camera, and all the cans of soup, tuna fish, and boxes of macaroni and cheese I could find in my cupboards, and drove from Salt Lake City, Utah (where I was working on a doctorate), to Grand Canyon National Park to begin research for a dissertation about the cultural meanings of tourism.[12] This was not my first visit to the canyon. I had seen it when I was fifteen years old while on a summer vacation with my parents and younger brother in 1976. We drove a 1969 yellow Ford Fairlane from our home in Connecticut to California that summer and spent a night at the canyon on the way back. It was the summer my father taught me to drive by letting me take the wheel on long stretches of open highway, even though I had not yet applied for a learner's permit. The park campgrounds were full when we arrived that August afternoon, so we spent the day hiking along the rim, taking in the views and souvenir shops. After sunset, we drove to the national forest lands near the park's east entrance and set up our tent in the darkness with the help of the Ford's headlight beams. We left at dawn the next morning. My father wished we could have stayed longer, but his two-week vacation from the factory in our hometown where he was a machinist was quickly coming to an end, and he had already extended our trip by a phone call to his boss with a bogus story about car trouble. Maybe we'd come back when there was more time, he said, but this seemed less a plan for the future than a means of reconciling what seemed all too brief a visit to the canyon. Neither he nor my mother ever went there again.

Actually, our family's trip to the Grand Canyon was like many of those visiting today. A park administrator told me the average stay is a little more than four hours, and most of the visitors I talked with were stopping there while on trips to and from somewhere else. During the summer of 1988, I stayed at the canyon for four months interviewing tourists, park rangers and administrators, and park concession employees.[13] I hiked the canyon's inner trails, attended guided ranger walks and evening programs, took commercial tours, went to visitor center programs and museums, made photographs, and traveled through the nearby Navajo and Hopi reservations. Some of my days were spent poring through archival documents in the Grand Canyon Study Collection, and in libraries in Flagstaff and Tempe. At night, I slept on the ground near an old dead tree in a clearing off of a forest service road south of the park. The tree had once been hit by lightning, so it seemed a safe place. In the early hours before dawn, I would often wake up to hear coyotes howling nearby in the forest. Over time, I made friends with some of the park employees, and a few let me stay a night or two in their small government housing units. Other times, I splurged for a week of campground fees and stayed at Mather Campground in the park. At the time I started work on my dissertation, I was twenty-seven and had no idea the great presence the Grand Canyon would hold in my life for the next ten years. I went back to the canyon for a shorter stay in 1989 and then wrote my dissertation. But after taking a faculty position at the University of South Florida in 1990, I found myself returning to the Grand Canyon again in 1992, 1993, and 1994; each time I interviewed more people, found new archival documents, and made more photos.

My initial interest, however, was not so much in the Grand Canyon but in tourism as a powerful metaphor for the broader character and conflicts of modern life. Tourism is a way of moving through the world. What we refer to as modern mass tourism began in Europe during the mid-nineteenth century. Since that time, tourism has become an international phenomenon. In the United States and elsewhere, as Alexander Wilson notes, it is a confusing history, characterized by changes in the landscape with the rise of motel strips, campgrounds, resort communities, and theme parks. It has prompted the development of an industry designed to organize free time and shape desires. And it has blurred the distinction between the rural and the urban, and the ways we conceive of each.[14] In this view, tourism becomes a historical set of social and cultural practices; an aestheticizing of experience, time, space, and people; and a historically and materially based mode of consciousness. What I came to appreciate about the Grand Canyon—and what kept me returning—was that it was a "natural" site where the forces of modern life appeared as a dramatic and contradictory presence. At the turn of this century, on the rim of its great empty chasm, a tourist world took shape that continually sought to affirm itself as a refuge from the modern world. More than anything, the Grand Canyon was a natural scene dramatizing how tourism and modernization went hand in hand. Historically, canyon tourists appear against a backdrop of broad cultural transformations that took hold of America in the last decades of the nineteenth century. The growing accessibility of western regions through locomotive travel and the efforts of railroads to promote the national parks were only part of a larger set of cultural changes facing Americans in the form of new developments in visual technologies, mass transportation, and mass communication systems that put a face on a broader ideology of progress. For many easterners experiencing a sense of alienation in modern cities, the Grand Canyon offered a promise of redeeming spiritual and traditional values through contact with nature and Native Americans living in the "natural" world of government reservations.

Grand Canyon tourists at the turn of the century experienced a world where, as we have been saying since W. B. Yeats, "the center cannot hold." As Jackson Lears notes in *No Place of Grace,* Americans facing the "marriage of material and spiritual progress" in modern America found themselves on the brink of a moral void of a culture that had seemingly "lost sight of the larger frameworks of meaning" and was experiencing a "crisis of authority." While the official optimism of progress thrust America toward the twentieth century, many members of an educated bourgeoisie expressed the terms of an antimodern spirit that left them longing for real life in a world that increasingly felt weightless and sent them seeking authentic experience in a variety of places and practices.[15] Against this backdrop, the Grand Canyon could appear as a place of grace, where people might, ironically, search for some transcendent and transparent image of greater unities in its divided landscape. Contemporary cultural critics—who find the self marooned in a "simulacrum," moving through mediations of experience that never hit the ground, who see a postmodern culture as an exhausted machine feeding off its productions and artifacts, who mourn the "death of the subject" and find the pathology of schizophrenia an apt metaphor of a fragmented consciousness, or who report the tired news that we are experiencing a breakdown of once unifying cultural narratives and that we live in an age of "incredulity toward metanarratives"—would surely appreciate the predicament of the tourists who came to the Grand Canyon during the first decade of this century and have been arriving since.[16] Like people past and present, many tourists experience the character of modern life as a "unity of disunities"; theirs is a struggle to make themselves "at home in a constantly changing world" where, as Marx wrote, "all that is solid melts into air."[17]

There are many reasons nearly five million people left home last year to visit the Grand Canyon they have already seen in magazines, television commercials, brochures, postcards, and snapshots passed across kitchen tables.[18] Like many tourist sites, it is a place where they come looking for experiences they cannot find at home, and it is often an experience centered in vision. But it's more than a common viewpoint or lookout people share at the Grand Canyon; they take and make the scenes of a natural world endowed with the complexity and character of modern life. In a general sense, tourism is a cultural phenomenon reflecting the instability of modern communities, the public and private pursuits of cultural unities and consensus, and how people, governments, and nations try to hold a vision of the world, and themselves, in place. The landscapes of tourism are where people are continually asked to reconcile the incongruities of "home" and "away," boredom and adventure, and self and other. The Grand Canyon is a place where strangers and symbols circulate, mediating experience, knowledge, and memory in collective and momentary performances containing visions of self and culture. At the brink of the canyon, visitors from the nineteenth century to the present come to figuratively embody what James Clifford suggests is a broader predicament of modern life: "a pervasive condition of off-centeredness in a world of distinct meaning systems, a state of being in culture while looking at culture, [and] a form of personal and collective self-fashioning."[19] Clifford could easily be describing someone like Burton Holmes, spinning out a tale of the Grand Canyon as a site of scientific certainties, spiritual affirmation, aesthetic distance, commercial representation, and adventurers' myths. But Clifford renders the predicament of any of us who live in an age where we must often struggle to find a sense of coherency in our experience, or come to grasp a sense of self in the discontinuities of contemporary life. As we work to make sense of ourselves and our world, we do so in places where we confront visions of self and world others have made. We confront models of experience that tell us how we live, how we feel, what we think, and what we want. But these models do not always fit our experience, so we sometimes work against them, trying to find some sense of self and world we might call our own.

To a large extent, these are the conditions tourists face as well. Daniel Boorstin is one of a few early writers who tried to sort out the social significance of tourism.[20] Drawing a distinction between aristocratic travel of the nineteenth century and the democratization of travel in the twentieth century, he argues that the *active* "traveler" of the previous era has been replaced by a *passive,* pleasure-seeking "tourist." The modern age of tourism, says Boorstin, is filled with "diluted, contrived, prefabricated" experiences that transformed travel from an elite form of adventure to a popular act of consumption. In contrast to Boorstin, Dean MacCannell understands tourism as an active response to the difficulties of living in a modern world.[21] MacCannell rejects the notion that tourists are satisfied with superficial and contrived experiences and instead says tourists seek "authenticity." Just as primitive societies made pilgrimages in search of the "sacred," he argues, modern tourists seek authentic experience. Boorstin and MacCannell anchor the debate about the cultural meaning of tourism at opposing poles. At the end of the road, tourists are either shallow, an outgrowth of the superficiality of modern life, or serious, attempting to escape the alienation of modern life and discover the "real." While neither seems to comprehensively address all the possible variations of tourist experiences, the disparity of their views only inflects the broader concerns about the relationship between self and society in a modern world.

Amid the transformations of cultural life in an industrial and postindustrial age, modernization creates and remakes the sites of home and work, the places of pleasure and leisure, and the gaps between them. This book examines the Grand Canyon as an emergent and residual site for the production of the zones of a social imaginary that reflect and contain the geographical and temporal dislocations of contemporary life. The Grand Canyon offers many *theaters* or *stages* for social display, consumption, and production where people seek experiences at a distance from the routines of everyday life. The Grand Canyon holds many geographies that appear at the intersections of lives as they are both lived and imagined—symbolic constructions of public space and private life—where exterior and interior landscapes are dramatized in the interplay of space, time, and social performance. In part, this book contemplates the significance of the Grand Canyon as an American icon and its cultural and historical production, particularly during the last decades of the nineteenth century and the first decades of the twentieth century. But it also examines the Grand Canyon as contemporary cultural theater dramatizing collective and individual pursuits for the meaning of nature, family, self, and freedom. French sociologist Henri Lefebvre warns that monuments should not entirely be "looked upon as collections of symbols . . . nor as chains of signs." Instead, monuments are composed and sustained at a variety of levels such as "bodily lived experience," the "spoken word," the perception of "socio-political signification," and the "dissemination of the written word and of knowledge [that] welds the members of a society into a 'consensus.'" For Lefebvre, the Grand Canyon would not be so much a "monument" but a "monumental space" allowing for a back-and-forth exchange between the private voices of ordinary conversation and the public voices of "lectures, sermons, rallying cries," texts, images, and performances. It is through all of these that monumental spaces become the "metaphorical and quasi-metaphysical" symbolic arenas that serve as the foundations and underpinnings of a society. Monumental spaces, Lefebvre says, are where the realms of politics and religion symbolically and ceremonially exchange power and authority; they are where the "authority of the sacred and the sacred aspect of authority" transfer back and forth and, in the process, mutually reinforce one another.[22]

In this book, I treat the Grand Canyon as a monumental space of public discourses spoken and written by planners, politicians, preservationists, institutions, artists, entrepreneurs, and commercial industries who treat the Grand Canyon as a tourist destination, a spectacle of nature, and a site for an expression of modern representational politics since the end of the nineteenth century. Since that time, commercial, scientific, and aesthetic discourses have framed and tamed the canyon's landscape for tourists. These discourses give meaning, order, and shape to the canyon's landscape through interpretive programs, commercial tours, architecture, guidebooks, and park policies. Taken together, they show how the Grand Canyon is not simply a landscape of nature but a culturally created spectacle unified and divided by the broader dramas of cultural transformation taking place in America since the turn of the century. At the same time, I focus on how contemporary tourists make the scene by making it their own. As a result, the early chapters of the book concentrate more heavily on historical events and texts, whereas the latter chapters focus on the activities and stories of the tourists I encountered.

One difficulty I experienced in attempting to conduct an ethnographic study of tourism was an absence of any stable community of tourists. My efforts consequently became geared toward composing the multiple dimensions of tourists' experiences. I watched and listened to them on trails and observation points. I interviewed them during their stay at the canyon, and after their trips were over and took shape as stories. I wrote to people I met there or whose names I gathered from visitor registers and asked them to respond to open-ended questionnaires. Others responded to a query I placed in a national travel newspaper and wrote me letters describing their experiences. It became impossible to find any unified portrait of the "tourist experience"; instead, I found multiple and incongruous narrative domains where people expressed themselves in a variety of voices and actions. Through all of these observations and accounts, these chapters describe how people appropriate, resist, and reshape the cultural narratives that name not only the Grand Canyon but also characterize and critique dimensions of work, careers, family, home, and the broader desires, disappointments, and vacancies in their lives.

Finally, the Grand Canyon depicted in these pages is a result of my own attempt to "make the scene." As part of that effort, I include photographs in various chapters that are intended not to serve as specific illustrations but to offer a visual counterpart to the written text. Like all images, these photographs find their interpretation in the process of reading and through the context of the historical and lived events, and the stories and analysis preceding and following them. "Photographs quote from appearances," John Berger has written. In many ways, a photograph is a "lengthy quotation . . . whose expressiveness can contain its ambiguity of meaning and 'give reason' to it . . . the length here to be measured not by time but by a greater extension of meaning."[23] I include these images as a means of contemplating the iconography and scenes of travel at the Grand Canyon, not so much to offer empirical evidence but, as Berger suggests, to "instigate" ideas about how people and cultures construct landscapes of meaning and, in turn, how landscapes help refashion the people who move through them. In each of the following chapters I weave together events of the canyon's past and present that manifest a physical, temporal, geographical, and imaginary landscape of the many chasms and divides running through modern life.

Chapter 1 examines how early railroad and hospitality entrepreneurs appropriated Native American cultural traditions and symbols, and popular myths of the American West, to construct and promote a commercial tourist scene at the Grand Canyon. The tourist world that developed along the canyon's South Rim since the turn of the century dramatizes a modern yearning and struggle to recover a sense of cultural tradition, history, and authenticity. By the end of the nineteenth century, warfare and government policy had increasingly devastated and transformed Native American life in the Southwest. Yet it soon reappeared at the Grand Canyon and in the surrounding region through imaginative reconstructions—architecture, souvenirs, performances—anchored by a growing tourist industry capitalizing on native cultural traditions. The Grand Canyon offered early visitors nothing less than a theme-park landscape and a promise of redeeming spiritual and traditional values through contact with nature and people who lived in a "natural" world. Along the canyon's South Rim, they found a theatrical stage where they could playfully participate in an ongoing drama that indulged urban fantasies of indigenous native culture and the American frontier. This chapter also examines how the canyon's commercially created tourist landscape found shape and form through nostalgic and romantic images of Native American culture and a mythos of the Wild West. It is a scene, since the start of this century, dramatizing an ongoing allegory of modern loss and redemption, and the divided face of nostalgia and progress in American culture.

In chapters 2 and 3, I examine the forces at work in another arena of cultural production by focusing on the conflicts and divisions between scientific and spiritual interpretations of the Grand Canyon's natural landscape. As a "cultural abyss," the Grand Canyon offers an image of a great cosmogonic site of rational and spiritual profundity, a place reflecting public and private attempts for coming to terms with questions of universal origins, creation, and being. Since the late nineteenth century, scientific and spiritual interpretations of the canyon have lodged broader cultural and historical divisions between secular and sacred ways of seeing, knowing, and believing, and point to a cleavage between distanced, scientific modes of interpreting nature, which aim for objectivity, control, and certitude, and individual spiritual longings for answers to the mysteries of one's place in the world. Pondering the deep and wide chasm from the rim, visitors are often drawn toward the symbolic domains and discourses of science and spirituality in search of the larger meanings the Grand Canyon may hold. On the one hand, geological explanations, institutionalized through Park Service interpretive programs, museums, and educational exhibits, attempt to solve the mystery of the canyon by quantifying its dimensions and presenting its landscape as a textbook that tells the story of time on earth. This is the "official" story of the Grand Canyon, one dominating public interpretation in the park since the 1920s. On the other hand, many park visitors since the turn of the century have resisted the lessons offered by a geological narrative and see the canyon as an affirmation of supreme spiritual forces at work in the universe. The Grand Canyon is a sublime landscape, where spiritual impulses are stirred in people who hold the spirit of God. Taken together, these two chapters trace the contours of a landscape divided by questions over the meaning of prehistoric fossils and personal faith, a geological formation of sedimented stone and a cultural formation of canonical texts continually marking the history of a chasm between rational and religious views of the world, and a symbolic abyss of origins and authority that begins and ends in the Word.

Chapter 4 considers how the aesthetic proclivities of elites and expanding technologies of vision making Grand Canyon scenes since the turn of the century reveal cultural divisions among broader notions of individuality, alienation, and anonymity in a mass society. Canyon visitors captivated by the promise of an individual encounter with a sublime nature have instead, through a variety of interpretive and mobilizing technologies, found themselves in an increasingly crowded place. This chapter examines how an "appropriate" way of seeing the Grand Canyon has been tied to the perspective of a cultivated upper class. A desire among elites and intellectuals for cultural symbols of a distinctive national American identity and a growing antiquities movement fueled a mid-nineteenth century movement to establish national parks as cultural monuments that could instill national pride. But the Grand Canyon offered more than a counterpoint to European displays of cultural heritage. Early travel accounts and guidebooks suggested that a canyon experience should be equated with the social codes and conduct characteristic of urban cultural settings like the opera, the symphony, and the museum. Such practices not only offered metaphors encouraging visitors to see the canyon as a contemplative text but also set the terms for drawing class-based distinctions between cultured observers and the "average" tourist crowds they deemed a nuisance. However, park promoters argued that the undeveloped masses might be redeemed by the civilizing forces of nature's scenes and designed park plans with an eye toward routing the public through programs designed for their scientific and aesthetic development. Yet, it is the figure of a solitary observer, silently contemplating the canyon from the rim, who endures in the popular imagination, despite the technological, commercial, and institutional development of the park. As chapter 4 shows, this image preserves an ideal of an autonomous observer whose presence in the scene illuminates the contradictions between an exterior landscape and an interiorized set of coordinates plotted for tourists who increasingly receded into a series of preformulated viewpoints.

Chapter 5 is a series of accounts examining how popular images of the Grand Canyon and promises of travel become incorporated in tourists' personal journeys. While cultural arbiters at the end of the last century mapped the canyon as "Celestial City," full of artistic masterpieces, contemporary tourists carry new maps drawn from a variety of mass-produced texts. The chapter also examines a Grand Canyon where the forces of cultural mobility and mass media merge as tourists make the canyon a domain of popular culture that dissolves any clear dichotomy separating fantasy and reality. Contrary to the aesthetic and cultural pieties that envision tourists as hapless crowds caught up in the machinery of mass culture, contemporary tourists find and make the Grand Canyon a complex geography of fantasies that appear at the intersections of places real, remembered, and imagined. It is a landscape of a popular cultural poetics erupting from a vast chasm of desires for location and presence in a modern world of images and discontinuities, a landscape where people stage private and public dramas of culture and self, and where a society of spectacle and a concretely situated observer become integrated and alienated through narratives and performances that mutually energize each other.

Whereas much of this book examines the symbolic production of space, chapter 6 focuses on how Grand Canyon tourists mark time during their vacations. It considers how people assign meaning and significance to their time away from home and how tourism reveals the divisions between leisure and everyday life. The metaphor of performance illuminates the relationship between individuals and landscape, suggesting the concrete vacancies and existential gaps between the lives people lead at home and the selves they imagine and seek during their vacations. Although the vacation is measured by calendars and clocks, chapter 6 explores how people seek to fill their time at the canyon with the depth, significance, and value they cannot find in their daily routines. The canyon becomes a backdrop for personal performances that reveal people attempting to belong to the world in new ways by incorporating a cultural icon into the private dimensions of their lives. Vacations are often a mode of identity production whereby people create, perform, and record imaginative visions of family and friends. The Grand Canyon becomes a symbolic marker in relationships, prompting some to revisit the park annually. Through activities like camping and hiking, visitors seek out risks and challenges, new ways of experiencing their bodies, and forms of work and effort yielding rewards they cannot possess through their jobs. Some go over the edge to seek out the "real" canyon away from the tourist crowds but instead find they awaken hidden dimensions of selves. Others go over the edge as a way of putting an end to time and life. In all of this, the Grand Canyon becomes a public and cultural theater burgeoning with private dramas, a domain where people do not entirely escape but reflectively examine the worlds of work, home, and routine from a distance. Their stories and performances show how tourism is not a time for the passive consumption of information, souvenirs, and scenic views but one of varying depths and dimensions when cultural symbols, images of the past and future, and desires and disappointments move through people's lives as they move through the scenes of the Grand Canyon.

Finally, chapter 7 reconsiders the meaning of the Grand Canyon as a symbol of cultural consensus and iconic authority. Beneath the surface of all the images, interpretive programs, and the custodial policies of the National Park Service, another vision of American life sometimes appears and disappears, as if to shake the foundations of our conventional views of nature, culture, and the pursuits of freedom. While the Grand Canyon appears in the American imagination as a scenic painting drawing together forces of antiquity, time, and tradition, its surface and enchanting spell sometimes crack. In the breaks and gaps, new canyons appear on the horizon, always evasive, and always holding a potential for making other scenes in word and image.

1

The Nostalgic Theater of the West

Every morning, a historic steam train leaves Williams, Arizona, at 9:30 and carries passengers to the rim of Grand Canyon. The Grand Canyon Railway brochure promises a "Wild West journey to the edge of time"; it is a trip that "Departs: 1901 A.D., Arrives 2 Billion years B.C." Traveling aboard a restored 1910 locomotive, passengers can "relive the romance . . . and ride the rails in the tradition of kings, presidents, cowboys and movie stars," says another brochure. "Come back to the Old West Territory and experience a nostalgic ride across northern Arizona's plains and forest lands, . . . Arrive at the historic Grand Canyon Depot, only steps from the South Rim of the Grand Canyon!"

Theme-park caricatures of the Old West appear, seemingly from nowhere. A strolling Mexican mariachi band in matching outfits and sombreros plays guitars, violins, and horns before a small cluster of tourists on benches. Railroad personnel dressed in period uniforms go back and forth from depot to train, preparing it for the morning ride. A turn-of-the-century sheriff, arms folded across his chest, talks with an elderly woman wearing a golf visor. On the east side of the depot, cowboys in chaps, long plainsman coats, vests, weathered hats, and gun belts stand near two saddled horses. The cowboys drink coffee from Styrofoam cups and eat doughnuts.

"This is the train we'll be riding up to Grand Canyon this morning," a man narrates into a microphone built into his camcorder as he makes a slow circular pan of the scene. His camera traces a horizontal arc through the air, collecting everything—rail cars, depot buildings, mariachis, cowboys, and other tourists. He stops to zoom in on a woman and her two year old strapped in a stroller. "And there's Sandy and Hillary . . . wave to Daddy, honey. Come on, wave to me, sweetie," he says, as his wife rubs suntan lotion on the little girl, who stares off into space.

I watch a haggard-looking cowboy called Two Feathers show his pistols to a man and his seven-year-old son. He removes the blanks from the chamber and shows one to the boy. He stares at the blank in his palm and asks to hold the pistol, but Two Feathers won't let him. "See those handles?" says the cowboy, holding his gun by the barrel. "Those are elk horn handles and they cost me a hunnard dollars. If you dropped 'em and broke 'em, well, I guess I'd just have to kill you." Two Feathers grins at the father while the boy stares at the gun. The old cowboy gives them a quick show, spinning the pistols back and forth around his fingers a few times before slipping them back into their holsters. The father asks for a picture. Two Feathers obliges, puts his arm around the boy, and aims his gun barrel at the camera until the shutter snaps.

"So, do you want to be a cowboy?" the father asks. The boy pauses and nods, seeming shy and unsure as he answers "yes." Two Feathers looks at the boy and then squats so he is eye to eye with the tourist's son. "No, you don't wanna be no cowboy," Two Feathers tells him. "You go on and go to school and make somethin' of yourself . . . be somethin' special." The boy nods without saying anything and moves close to his father.

He looks awkward standing in the wide and curious space separating the lives of these two men who ask him about his desires for the future. I remember my own cowboy period as a boy in a Connecticut suburb decades ago. My father often cooked up scenes that had us riding through the movies with John Wayne. "Saddle up, pilgrim," he'd say every now and then in his best Wayne monotone, usually as we were getting ready to go fishing, to church, or the store. This was the extent of his stock John Wayne imitation: a brief but frequent tribute to his fearless western hero always on the move to fix something gone wrong. I preferred the mythic outlaw bank robber and gunslinger duo of Newman and Redford in *Butch Cassidy and the Sundance Kid*. In fact, I so much loved the film that when I was twelve, and my father had taught me to use his 8mm home-movie camera, I amused myself with elaborate plans to re-make the movie as soon as I could save enough money from yard work and odd jobs to buy the film stock, and find someone who would loan me the horses. I spent many days trying to convert the big attic of our house into a set for interior shots of bank robbery scenes. I held script readings with neighborhood kids, privately deciding which of my friends would get to play Butch to my Sundance Kid. This fantasy occupied nearly a year of my young life but quickly faded one night in our kitchen, when my parents asked me if it was realistic to be devoting so much time alone to making a feature-length film rather than playing with the other kids after school. I think it's really just listening to Two Feathers give the young boy (and his father) an honest hint about the cowboy life, breaking the frame of heroic illusions, that leads me back to my own childhood desires to escape suburban boredom. Yet, for some reason I'm unwilling to give in to nostalgia—my own or anyone else's—this early in the day. Instead, I ponder how many times Two Feathers may have told other boys to go to school and "be somethin' special" while their fathers looked on. Cynically, I imagine him in some darkened Williams watering hole, on what, for most tourists, might be a bright afternoon, listening to Willie Nelson on the jukebox warn all those mommas to keep their babies from the romantic loneliness of the cowboy trail. Another private movie scene, no doubt, one that says more about me than anything I know about Two Feathers. The drama is both subtle and grand at the depot, and the skepticism any of us hold for authenticity or sincerity in this mini–Wild West theme park is merely banal.

Traces of backstage realism appear a few minutes later, however, when Two Feathers tells me a little about his supporting role in this tourist attraction. He'd come from Missouri and for years worked as a cowboy on ranches in Oklahoma and Arizona. The mechanization of ranch work, he says, largely accounted for the move into his present occupation. "They don't need cowboys no more," he tells me. "It's all machines and computers now. The machines do the work. They only need ya a few times a year to herd." Two Feathers didn't seem to mind the change at all. "This kinda work's easier," he says, nearly smiling, "and I don't git tired of talking with tourists because it's different people and I don't hafta be with the same ones every day." When he wasn't cowboying at the Williams Depot, he tried to get other acting jobs. Someone was making a movie in northern Arizona, and he would try to get work there. "It's gonna be a chase western and they need guys who know how ta rope and handle a horse," he says. "I never took no acting lessons, but if they want someone who kin rope and ride . . . hell, even walk across the street, at least I'll be workin'." Agriculture and livestock technologies pushed Two Feathers out of one job; the tourist-attraction machinery offered some compensation by turning his former life into part-time work.

"Cowboys are disappearin', that's why people wanna see 'em," he says. "'Specially the Europeans. They wanna see cowboys and Indians. They should hire more Indians here, but they don't wanna come." I ask why he thought people were interested in the depot and old western characters like him. "This is just like the movies. People will go see a western every time one comes out. Back in the eighties, westerns took place in outer space. That's what *Star Wars* was—cowboys in outer space. Now, westerns are makin' a comeback. They're makin' more and more, and people love 'em. I can't say why, but they go see 'em. And they show up everyday to see me and the fellas shoot it out over there," he says. "I dunno, I guess they think a cowboy is free . . . not tied down to nothin', somethin' like that, probably."

The face of a mythic West disappeared and reappeared in popular novels, photographs, motion pictures, and places like the Williams Depot. Two Feathers may have understood this better than most as he watched the meaning of being a cowboy transform before his eyes. He walks over to a roped-off area and joins Snake Eyes, Kit, and Two Aces, three other cowboy characters who have been roaming the depot and talking with tourists. In the half hour before the train's departure, they perform a brief melodrama ending in a gunfight.

I join the crowd of waiting passengers and sightseers around the edges of a makeshift corral and watch the cowboys get a card game underway. They don't need to set up any story for their skit. We already know it. The card game is just a premise for them to accuse each other of cheating. "He's got five aces!" a cowboy shouts, and shoots the deceitful player at close range. A few people in the crowd jump as his pistol cracks in the morning air. As might be expected, the remaining men quickly take cover and begin to kill one another off. One of the cardplayers prevails, but the sheriff soon arrives and shoots him down. The whole thing is over in two minutes. While the audience applauds, the dead cowboys get on their feet, brush themselves off, and begin a brief audience participation routine.

"Who here is from east of the Mississippi?" yells Snake Eyes.

The crowd is quiet. Someone behind me says, "We are," but the cowboys don't hear her. "Alright, then," says Snake Eyes, with an air of exaggerated irritation. "Who's from *west* of the Mississippi?" Silence. "Two Aces, these people don't know *where* they live," the cowboy barks to his companion.

"Whadaya expect?" hollers Two Aces. "They're tourists!" The punchline gets a round of laughs, signaling the end of the show. People move in for more photo opportunities. Snake Eyes and Kit, who, I later learn, works in an antique shop in Williams, lift children onto the saddled horses, from where they search the crowd below for their parents' camera lenses.

I watch Two Feathers drawn into the frames of tourists' cameras. His dusty hat, chaps, and spurs stand out

against the T-shirts, shorts, and tennis shoes worn by those posing at his sides. For every snapshot, he draws his guns and aims directly at the photographer's camera lens. Whoever eventually looks at his picture will be staring into his gun barrel. And each time Two Feathers strikes this pose, it gestures to the Wild West as it was first written in the movies. Taking aim at these tourists' cameras, the haggard cowboy replays the final scene from Edwin S. Porter's *The Great Train Robbery*, in which the train bandit draws his pistol, aims at the audience, and fires right into their faces. Produced by the Edison Company in 1903, Porter's movie was the first narrative film made in America, one in which Orange Hills, New Jersey, served as the first cinematic setting of the Wild West.

Soon, the whistle blows and the ninety-ton engine lurches forward. Those on board wave from windows. Those remaining at the station record the departure with videotape and snapshots as the festive scene at the depot dissolves. The mariachi family walks toward a van in the parking lot. Kit unties the horses and leads them toward a trailer. Two Feathers and his companions get into an old sedan that kicks up dust and gravel as they drive to the main drag in Williams for breakfast. In a few minutes, all I see is the black smoke thrown from the train engine into the clear blue of the morning sky, chugging north to the Grand Canyon.

It's tempting to imagine the old locomotive tunneling backward through time. The steel wheels had run over the same path bringing tourists to the rim since the Santa Fe Railway first opened the Williams–Grand Canyon spur in 1901. Yet, despite its promoters' claims, the train's daily departure is more than a sentimental passage to the innocence of an earlier era. It's also a journey to a place that has, for a century, tried

to remain dislodged from the passage of time. The train dramatizes the forces of progress and nostalgia that have *historically* marked Grand Canyon tourism. From the very beginning of the twentieth century, the locomotive bound for the canyon has been a dual emblem of progress and mobility, transporting tourists into a landscape of romantic cultural memory. The nostalgic Grand Canyon steam train serves as a daily reminder of what Christopher Lasch described as "the ambiguity that was always inherent in the westward movement, alternately conceived as the wave of the future and as a journey into the past."[1]

The railroad, moving west across America since the mid-nineteenth century, embodied the progressive promise of technology, industry, and expansion. In 1902, English traveler James Muirhead described American railroads as a "picturesque" triumph of civilization, "long thin lines of gleaming steel, thrown across the countless miles of desert sand and alkali plain . . . a mighty mass of metal with its glare of the cyclopean eye and its banner of fire illumined smoke, that bears the conquerors of nature from side to side of the great continent."[2] Muirhead only underscored an idea many railway proponents had been arguing for decades. The railroads could unite a segmented America through mobility, collapse its vast distances of space and time, foster a centralized commodity market operated from eastern cities, and overcome regional political and economic divisions that stood as barriers to a national ideology of progress.[3] In addition to being an essential instrument of expanding industrialization, the comfortable and safe Pullman car appeared as "a chariot winging Americans [usually elites] on an aesthetic journey through the new empire."[4] The speed and power of the railroads symbolized the climate of a rapidly changing America, but progress was not without its critics. Those who despised and feared industrializing America, however, often escaped the sounds of civilization on trains headed west.

According to historian Jackson Lears, European and American elites near the end of the nineteenth century recognized that "the triumph of modern culture had not produced greater autonomy (which was the official claim) but rather had promoted a spreading sense of moral impotence and spiritual sterility—a feeling that life had become not only overcivilized but also curiously unreal."[5] For Lears, this "anti-modern impulse" reflected the deeper uncertainties of people whose days were captured in the currents of progress. An increasingly secularized and industrialized society had failed to meet culturally internalized desires for individuality, morality, and spiritual fulfillment. Sensing that something was missing in their world, many nineteenth-century Americans looked for "authentic experience" outside the bounds of their daily lives.

The idea that nature could rejuvenate those dissatisfied with the incessant rhythms of urban life had been popular in America since the mid-nineteenth century. Many sought the natural world of western landscapes and the native people who lived there as a site of relief from the routines, pressures, and anxieties of the city. "Thousands of nerve-shaken, overcivilized people are beginning to find out that going to the mountains is going home," observed naturalist John Muir in 1898. "Awakening from the stupefying effects of the vice of over-industry and the deadly apathy of luxury, they are trying as best they can to mix and enrich their little ongoings with those of Nature, and to get rid of rust and disease."[6] Yet, even as easterners left their urban homes for leisure excursions to the Southwest, they found that the commercial forces of tourism had recast the natural world in the shape of modern dreams.

Beginning in 1876, the Santa Fe Railway and Fred Harvey, an English immigrant who operated a railroad depot restaurant in Topeka, Kansas, began an extensive and lucrative business collaboration developing tourist facilities throughout the Southwest.[7] However, they built more than depots, restaurants, and hotels; they manufactured a vision of Southwest culture. "In commodifying the Indian Southwest as a tourist or secular pilgrimage center," Marta Weigle argues, "Santa Fe/Harvey corporate image-makers transformed it into a mythological holy land of grand natural wonders, inspirational primitive arts, and domesticated, artistic 'natives.'"[8] Rescued from bankruptcy, the Santa Fe began an ambitious campaign under the leadership of the company president, E. P. Ripley, designed to recreate an image of the Southwest and draw tourists. Ripley wanted to shake the Santa Fe's reputation as a company serving greed-driven land speculators, prospectors, and buffalo skinners. The new advertising campaign built on an image of respectability, promoting the desert landscape as a region safe for travel and filled with a compelling display of native life. "The landscape is wholly unlike the East," claimed an early advertisement for the Santa Fe's *California Limited*. "A land of wide horizons, of peaks miles high and titanic chasms. A world of color, too. These four are unique in all the earth: The Grand Canyon, the Petrified Forest, the Painted Desert and the Indian Pueblos. Reached only by the Santa Fe."

Other American railroads were doing much of the same to develop tourism and preserve scenic landscapes in regions where their tracks carried passengers. For instance, in 1871, the Northern Pacific Railway lobbied on behalf of creating Yellowstone Park. The Great Northern Railway championed efforts to develop Glacier National Park in 1885. The Southern Pacific promoted travel in the Sierra Nevada mountain region, and the Union Pacific advertised a circuit tour of Grand Canyon's North Rim, Bryce, and Zion National Parks in the 1920s.[9] The Santa Fe had been promoting the Grand Canyon well before it became a federally designated monument. In the 1890s, the railroad operated stage lines from its Flagstaff depot to the canyon's rim. By 1901, they owned and operated the railroad spur out of Williams that today's tourists take on their nostalgic ride to and from the rim.

Yet, the railroad brought more than transportation to the canyon. In partnership with the Fred Harvey Company, the Santa Fe began developing a leisure retreat along the South Rim. But the canyon's commercial tourist landscape expressed ambivalent cultural attitudes toward modernity. The forward-looking face of progress carried tourists to what seemed like the end of the civilized world, to the brink of eternity, but at the canyon, that face suddenly turned to cast a sentimental backward glance. The steel rails stopped at the edge of the Great Abyss, leaving its passengers to gaze upon nature's unstoppable forces of time and change. On the rim, however, the clock *could* be stopped, and the "weightless" feelings of modern life might find more secure footing in the romance of an imagined past.

"Nostalgia is a sadness without an object," notes Susan Stewart, and like any narrative, nostalgia "is always ideological: the past it seeks has never existed except as narrative."[10] Railroads stretching across the continent surely bridged distances between the country's opposite coasts, but the rapid conquest, expansion, and settlement of the West, mingled with memories of the Civil War, still left many Americans divided about questions of history, tradition, and identity. The Grand Canyon's leisure world developed in a context of such questions—rising around the edges of a geographic and cultural abyss—by deferring the ambiguities of a modern present to romantic and sentimental reflections of the past. As early tourists ventured to the canyon, often hoping to escape an overcivilized and unreal world, they wandered through scenes of a fictional frontier fabricated in the buildings rising along its rim and through advertising copy promoting a dreamscape where an idealized West remained intact. The canyon's commercial tourist landscape created an architecture of experience embodying idealizations and tensions between future and past, home and away, and civilization and a natural world.

Stopping the Clock at the Edge of the World

Like many visitors to the canyon early in the twentieth century, Edwin Burrit Smith described his journey as arriving "at the brink of what at first seems to be the very edge of the world." He spoke of a place beyond the scope of time: "When all the earth has been explored, when the secrets of nature have been discovered, when the field of adventure has been narrowed to the utmost, the Grand Canyon will remain unspoiled by the touch of human hands, as awful in its unique grandeur as it is today."[11] Published in 1902 by the Santa Fe, his account expressed a familiar promise, particularly to members of the upper classes, who lived their days in a steady and rapidly changing America. Smith's visit to the canyon offered a brief respite for the Chicago attorney on a hurried business trip to the West Coast. Life itself seemed to be in a hurry for his generation, but he was not alone in believing that nature could withstand the forces of progress sweeping through America. Yet, his visit was too brief and hopeful. By 1902, with the seeds of tourist development beginning to sprout amid a cultural climate of incessant change, Smith's optimism for an "untouched" canyon was, perhaps, rather naïve. After all, the train carrying him to the "edge of the world" had been in service for a year.

Since the mid-1880s, tourists making the twelve- to thirteen-hour stagecoach trip from Flagstaff to the Grand Canyon could find a few accommodations in tent camps and small hotels. In 1897, John Hance became the Grand Canyon's first postmaster when the post office of Tourist, Arizona, was established on the South Rim.[12] Although late nineteenth-century travelers welcomed the expanding accommodations at the canyon, some feared development might get out of hand. Reporting on an 1895 stagecoach trip from Flagstaff to the South Rim, Mrs. M. Burton Williamson seized the opportunity to criticize plans for coming railroad travel to the Grand Canyon. "Anything that hints at a 'timetable' is entirely out of place in the presence of this solemn, silent and magnificent exhibition of the prodigality of time," she wrote in 1899. Williamson worried that trains might be followed by "trolley cars running down the canyon, claiming the distinction of running down the steepest grade of any electric road in the world, and airline bridges spanning the distance from one dome or spur of granite to another. A railroad indicates progress, yet does it not seem a desecration, an insult to centuries of solitude?"[13] In 1902, John Muir held similar reservations about the wilderness perishing at the hand of progress. "When I first heard of the Santa Fe trains running to edge of the Grand Cañon of Arizona, I was troubled with thoughts of the disenchantment likely to follow," Muir told readers of the *Century Magazine*. But after observing the trains "crawling along through the pines of the Cocanini *[sic]* Forest and close up to the brink of chasm," Muir concluded that the locomotives were nothing more "than mere beetles and caterpillars, and the noise they make is as little disturbing as the hooting of an owl in the lonely woods."[14] The collaboration of the Santa Fe and the Harvey Company, however, did little to abate Williamson's fears. What Muir feared would be "disenchantment," the commercial developers saw as "reenchantment."

Fourteen years after the first passengers arrived at the canyon by train, another visitor's account only seemed to echo Edwin Smith. "There is much to say for the sensations of the present day visitor," wrote Dwight Elmendorf of his 1915 canyon visit. "To step out of a luxurious train, where all modern conveniences have been enjoyed . . . and then after a walk of a few rods, to find oneself gazing into the depths of a marvel that surpasses the most exalted dream . . . is like being brought, when pursuing the path of prosaic daily life, suddenly to face the boundless reaches of eternity."[15] Like Smith, seeing the canyon's tranquil grandeur jolted Elmendorf toward philosophical musings. But eventually he confronted another dream—an imaginative tourist world largely developed and promoted by the Santa Fe Railway and the Fred Harvey Company.

For tourists like Smith, Williamson, and Elmendorf, the voice of eternity might have whispered into their ears thoughts of insignificance, humility, and impermanence. Surely, the canyon could possess visitors this way, and many sought consolation in the eyes of science or the word of God. But the world along the rim struck the chords of another eternity, one carrying a tune of sentimentality, romance, and innocence. On the South Rim, the meanings of time and place imploded, allowing tourists to move through a surreal theater that juxtaposed the progressive comforts of middle-class luxury with an imaginary frontier scene of spectacular nature, cowboys, and Indians. "The more emphatically the modern age insisted on its own wisdom, experience, and maturity, the more appealing simple, unsophisticated times appeared in retrospect," notes Lasch. The American West has been the "childhood of the nation," a place where "ancestral wisdom" deferred to idealizations of "childlike innocence," and the progressive, rapid settlement and expansion of the West "implied nostalgia as its mirror image."[16] At Grand Canyon, the unchanging dream world created by the Santa Fe and the Harvey Company was a concrete response to the anxieties of cultural change and instability. Progress and nostalgia existed side by side, critiquing and reinforcing each other. In the middle, stood the tourist, finding a paradoxical pleasure from the pull of each impulse.

While the Grand Canyon promised an escape from the trudge of the modern city, developers aspired to recreate urban convenience and comfort. Along the rim, they cut comfortable paths through the landscape. In 1915, the Santa Fe described the canyon as a place where visitors were "furnished horses that would grace a city park" or could tour the landscape in "a big auto—the easy-riding $5,000 variety"; it was a place where the "only modern note in the picture is the throbbing, high-powered auto. All else seems to have come from a different world and a different time."[17] To the west of the depot and the tourist hotels, visitors could view the canyon while meandering along Hermit Rim Road. "It is like a city boulevard in the wilderness, wide, smooth and dustless—the acme of engineering skill," a brochure noted. Unlike the rutted stage roads of previous decades, this road was thirty feet wide, surfaced with crushed stone and cinder, oiled and rolled firm. In cars or on horseback, field glasses hanging from their necks, visitors could wander the edge. The road enabled continuous views of the far-reaching canyon with relative comfort, transforming it into a cinematic spectacle.

For the city dweller, nineteenth-century technologies like the stereoscope and the cyclorama brought the distant canyon closer. The Santa Fe's description of the views from Hermit Rim Road conflated the real canyon with a way of seeing acquired at home. More than a means to access the natural canyon, the roads developed by the Santa Fe were continuations of boulevards that began in Chicago or New York and now offered one more spectacle for the eyes of the mobile observer. Canyon visitors were ensured safe and secure passage through a world considered desolate and forbidding only decades earlier. But the visual splendor of the Grand Canyon arranged for tourists was only part of a larger leisure world that captured eastern visions of the mythic West. The eyes that extended outward from cities and over the rim also looked backward.

El Tovar Hotel, the first sight to catch the eyes of arriving rail passengers, simultaneously suggested an atmosphere of modern comfort, Old World tradition, and rustic frontier ambiance. Its style and design exhibited the same set of mixed attitudes toward culture, taste, and tradition that beset many Americans in the late nineteenth and early twentieth centuries. Although the rapid pace of American progress and modernization left many concerned about the creation of distinctive national symbols, traditions, and styles, places like El Tovar reflected, in part, the sustaining appeal and preference for European models of cultural identity. "One might reasonably expect a stronger emphasis upon Americanness in the Western part of the nation," notes historian Michael Kammen, "but the creation of culture and concern for tradition during those years remained very much the purview of migratory Easterners, whose memories were inclined in that direction and whose criteria of taste still came largely from trans-Atlantic images and impressions."[18] Like resorts in the Rocky Mountains modeled after Swiss and Austrian alpine hotels, El Tovar's mix of styles not only aspired to compete with the fashionable resorts of Europe but also played on desires for a frontier experience and hopes for an indigenous symbol of American tradition. But the story of the American West was one of converging cultures, and conveying "Americanness" inevitably meant a bricolage of numerous artifacts moving across a changing landscape.

Named after Don Pedro de Tovar, a soldier in Coronado's army, El Tovar was designed for the Harvey Company and Santa Fe Railway by Chicago architect Charles Whittlesey. In 1902, three years before El Tovar's opening, Whittlesey's Alvarado Hotel in Albuquerque began serving as a way station for Santa Fe passengers, its design reviving the Spanish mission architectural style. But at Grand Canyon, Whittlesey combined stylistic elements of the Swiss chalet and Norwegian villa, using native stone and Douglas fir logs shipped from Oregon to build a hotel costing a quarter of a million dollars. El Tovar's eighty steam-heated guest rooms had hot and cold running water and electric lights powered by a steam generator. With water scarce on the South Rim, the hotel stored a supply arriving daily by rail car from Del Rio more than 100 miles away. In addition to guest rooms, El Tovar boasted a solarium, a music room, a fifteenth-century Norwegian-style dining room, a roof garden, a greenhouse for raising vegetables, and telephones. As if to ease the potential fears of visitors from the East, the Santa Fe offered assurances that a sizable piece of civilized life awaited on the canyon's rim. "Everywhere you are reminded that though away from home this is another home," the Santa Fe told prospective visitors in 1915.[19] El Tovar's "width north and south is 327 feet and from east to west 218 feet," noted an earlier brochure. "Not a Waldorf-Astoria, but more like a big country clubhouse, open to any traveler seeking high-class accommodations."[20] Perched on the "edge of the world," the hotel was more than an outpost on a border between the rugged frontier and familiar urban comforts. It was a place where upper-class tourists, arriving from cities by locomotive, were surrounded by a veil of fantasies about the frontier and idealizations of themselves.

Although Whittlesey grafted Norwegian and Swiss architecture onto American materials and then named his building for a Spanish conquistador, El Tovar's interior gestured toward a rustic, western, frontier ambiance. "Boulders and logs for the walls and shakes for the roof, stained a weather-beaten color, merge into the gray-green surroundings," described a 1909 Harvey brochure. "The inside finish is mainly peeled slabs, wood in the rough, and tinted plaster, interspersed with huge wooden beams."[21] From its very beginning, hotel promoters sought to capitalize on American longings for tradition and permanence. El Tovar seemed to have been on the rim all along. Promotional literature described it as a conspicuous retreat into a fantasy world that blended the adventure of the hunting lodge with the security of home. In The Rendezvous, a sitting room near the entry, prospective guests could contemplate the desires to have both:

From the low roof hang electric lights placed in log squares swinging at the end of long chains. Gray Navajo rugs cover the brown floor. There are cosy tete-a-tetes and easy chairs. On an upper shelf repose heads of deer, elk, moose, mountain sheep, and buffalo, mingling with curiously shaped and gaudily-tinted Indian jars from the Southwest pueblos. An old-fashioned clock ticks off the hours. Several small escritoires remind you of letters to be written to the home folks. . . . What wonder that every morning and evening most of the guests gather in this room—the ladies to read and gossip; the gentlemen to smoke and tell of their latest adventures.[22]

With the Grand Canyon wilderness stretching only a few paces from El Tovar's entrance, it was there, beneath the stuffed heads of wild game and native artifacts, that guests might imagine feeling at home in the remote Southwest. The Rendezvous was a place where visitors could meet nature on their own upholstered terms. "The celebration of rustic felicity was never intended for rustics," notes Lasch. "It could be savored only by people of refinement who did not seriously propose, after all, to exchange the advantages of breeding and worldly experience for a life close to nature, no matter how lyrically they sang nature's praises."[23] In The Rendezvous, only the "old-fashioned" clock marked passing moments of the present while guests lounged in a museumlike parlor infatuated with a manufactured past. The Rendezvous, like the larger tourist world surrounding it, was a scene where contradictions between past and present seemed to settle on the surface. Under electric lights disguised by logs, The Rendezvous celebrated its guests' ability to move freely through the world, escape the present, and have nature and native culture served up to them as an exhibit. Despite the heads of big game mounted on the walls above native pottery, guests were told to expect a cosmopolitan atmosphere at El Tovar. "All paths here intersect," Santa Fe ad men told visitors. "While you are leisurely dining it is pleasant to look around and see who your neighbors are. They have come from every section—perhaps a New York or Chicago banker, a Harvard professor, an Arizona ranchman, an English globetrotter, and a German savant. Pretty women and lovely children complete the picture."[24] Although the canyon drew visitors from diverse locales, El Tovar mostly registered guests who clung to similar manners, tastes, and attitudes about comfort and civility.

As men smoked their adventures beneath trophies from someone else's hunt, women found another reminder that El Tovar could be a "home away from home." Upstairs from the lobby and overlooking The Rendezvous, an octagonal space called the "Ladies Lounging Room" was draped in crimson hangings. "In it the better half of the world may see without being seen—may chat and gossip—may sew and read—may do any of the inconsequent nothings which serve to pleasantly pass the time away," said the Santa Fe.[25] Such descriptions of El Tovar conjured a sense of a stable, Victorian bourgeois life that, by the turn of the century, had become more of a memory than a daily experience. By conveying images of a nineteenth-century "cult of domesticity" that separated the public sphere of men from the private sphere of women, Santa Fe advertisers appealed to residual sentiments for the social order of earlier decades.[26] Although "all paths intersected" at El Tovar, the meeting occurred in a place illuminated by the sentimental glow of a relatively recent past.

Since the Civil War, authoritative models of Victorian life had been eroding in the face of an expanding industrial and bureaucratic society.[27] Cultural elites became preoccupied with a waning sense of individual autonomy, discipline, and moral certainty in a society they feared was becoming "soft" and "overcivilized." In leisure, men looked to athletics and the rugged outdoors to rediscover masculinity and character. Enthusiasm for competitive sports, outdoor recreation, and physical exercise swept through the leisure worlds of the social elites. "Upper-class fascination with prowess was stimulated in part by fears that modern living rendered males intellectually and emotionally impotent," notes Elliot Gorn. "Men emphasized the importance of vigor because, rather suddenly, they were terrified of losing it."[28] Middle-class women increasingly moved outward from the suffocating walls of domestic interiors into the public sphere and became involved in a variety of social reform movements. Women's sports and athletics also developed in colleges, and by the "late 1880s the arguments of physical exercise advocates were beginning to carry the day" as a means to evolving a higher mind and body.[29]

In suggesting that men and women would find distinctively different leisure experiences at the Grand Canyon, the Santa Fe Railway and the Harvey Company only mirrored a larger fiction of the West circulating in popular culture. As described by its promoters, the canyon's commercial leisure world was largely inclined toward male fantasies shaped in mythic stories of the frontier and the Wild West since the mid-nineteenth century. Eastern visitors could not help but carry those visions, popularized and romanticized in magazines and novels, to the canyon. Tourism promoters merely rode the back of a larger symbolic West and galloped toward the East with saddlebags full of promise. The western frontier represented the borders of society, a place long ingrained as a site of male freedom away from the constraints of a modern life. The imagined West captured the values and virtues of a natural, premodern world fostered by decades of frontier mythology. Numerous authors have described the mythic American frontier, continually shifting with westward expansion and rapid settlement, as a contradictory place offering either an escape from society into a wild and violent life, or a peaceful garden awaiting the civilizing hand of modern progress. For James Fenimore Cooper's Natty Bumppo, the frontier was a place for "the solitary hunter unencumbered by social responsibilities, utterly self-sufficient, uncultivated but endowed with a spontaneous appreciation of natural beauty."[30] Henry David Thoreau and Ralph Waldo Emerson each cast their visions of nature with an eye toward pursuits of self-sufficiency and transcendence from modern civilization. Mark Twain's Huckleberry Finn, who decided to "light out for the territory," was speaking to readers for whom the West "had already taken on an identification with freedom and independence in a country that regarded freedom and independence as its peculiar hallmark."[31]

By the turn of the century, Theodore Roosevelt, artist Frederic Remington, and novelist Owen Wister had thoroughly ensconced western regions in a fiction that played into their generation's fears of cultural instability. Each of them largely envisioned the West with the contours of a premodern world where "exposure to the hardships of the frontier was meant to provide a corrective to the demoralizing effects of comfort and overrefinement." Here a patriotic Anglo-Saxon supremacy exerted itself over the threat of Indians, Mexicans, and Chinese who had eagerly come to prosper on American soil, and "the gunfighter still rides off into the sunset when his work is done, unable to bear the constraints that come in the wake of his triumphs."[32] For their audiences, who had been groping for distinctive forms of American heritage since the end of the Civil War, the nostalgic and romantically minded Wests imagined by Roosevelt, Remington, and Wister proposed, at least for men, the elements of a remedy. Amid their preachings on physical fitness and moral rectitude, the Wild West became an alluring context for turn-of-the-century elites constructing and embracing new images of masculinity.

Roosevelt was one of the most famous advocates for the value of the western experience. Consumed with thoughts that "overcivilization" had corrupted American elites, Roosevelt drew upon his own experiences as a hunter, rancher, and soldier to regenerate the lost political and cultural vitality of his class. "He felt he had achieved a 'strenuous' personal lifestyle which appeared to him morally superior to that of the leisured class to which he belonged," notes Richard Slotkin. Recounting his adventures as a hunter and ranchman, Roosevelt told a "story of his own regeneration or self-recreation in the West, which he offered to other members of his class as a demonstration that even the most advanced of the civilized races could reacquire the essentials of spirit and lifestyle that gave their conquering pioneer ancestors their prowess."[33] Roosevelt not only established Grand Canyon National Monument in 1908, he also represented to his generation a therapeutic image of how western excursions could recover a sense of manhood made weary and weak by city life. If the southwestern tracks laid by the Santa Fe and embellished by Fred Harvey offered tourists a palpable route to the romantic West popularized throughout the second half of the nineteenth century, the Grand Canyon was the place to live such stories on their own terms. And El Tovar's Rendezvous room, with wild trophies from the hunt lining its walls, resembled nothing less than the great study Roosevelt had constructed in his New York home.

The early twentieth-century tourist world of Grand Canyon was a place where themes of western freedom offered solace to the anxieties of the Eastern Establishment. The canyon is "more than something stupendous to look at. It is a place for a genuine Out West outing," claimed a lengthy 1915 Santa Fe brochure. Self-consciously capitalizing on regional awareness as well as fears of rapid industrialization and westward expansion, developers assured visitors that something of the Wild West remained intact. Side by side, modern comfort coexisted with the allure of being alone in the natural world of the West. "In magical contrast with the life and sparkle of El Tovar—its fellowships and its democracy—is the nearby solitude," said the brochure. "In a moment you may leave the crowd and become a hermit." The line between civilization and the frontier, that mythic and moving border Frederick Jackson Turner claimed had closed by 1893, when the ideal of pioneer individualism began to shift to an ideal of social control by law, remained preserved in the timeless tourist ether of Grand Canyon. After a day of wandering the rim, fueled with a legacy of frontier fantasies supplied by Cooper, Thoreau, Emerson, Crockett, Twain, Wister, and Roosevelt, tourists could eat delicacies in a Norwegian dining room, retire to private quarters with flowers on the dresser, indulge a hot bath, and slide between cool, clean linen sheets.

Tourism promoters emphasized how the South Rim could restore and renew the spent and tired bodies arriving from cities. "In power to recuperate man's exhausted energies, the Grand Canyon stands supreme," boasted the Santa Fe. "You inhale a pure, thin air, laden with scent of pine and cedar. Your lungs expand, your muscles harden, your face browns. Soon you are 'fit,' in every sense of the word." By 1915, fit bodies and tanned skin marked members of a leisure class who engaged in sports and the outdoor life; pale skin was a sign of a confined life spent in factories. At Grand Canyon, Santa Fe advertisers combined the healthy, status symbol of the suntan with icons of regional attire: "Tan? Yes, and lots of it. The kind that goes with a Stetson and 'chaps' and khaki suit. In a week you will look like a native, and the tan on the native son's face is something worthwhile."[34] As their faces soaked in the northern Arizona sunshine, tourists might also find the warmth of a deeper romance with the West and with themselves. Santa Fe advertisers had their fingers on the pulse of the social elites. Roosevelt had captured that anxious beat ten years earlier when he preached the virtues of a "strenuous life" to Chicago's upper crust in 1905. "You work yourselves, and you bring up your sons to work," he told the audience at the Hamilton Club. "If you are rich and worth your salt, you will teach your sons that though they may have leisure, it is not to be spent in idleness."[35] For Roosevelt's generation, which feared the weakening effects of inherited wealth and material comfort, upper-class leisure pursuits sought harmony with the character-building virtues of work. At Grand Canyon, this credo took on a superficial quality; a tourist could at least *look* like a hardy "native son," yet sacrifice none of the comforts to which he was accustomed.[36] It was, in many respects, a meeting place balancing a mutual pursuit of character and comfort—the essence of the "strenuous life" Roosevelt modeled throughout his own career.

"The imagined West that has gripped American consciousness has been, on the whole, an overwhelmingly masculine West," observes historian Richard White. "But it is an odd masculinity because it reverses the usual symbolism that identifies men with culture and women with nature." Next to the adventurous, risk-taking, often lawless and wild men of popular western stories, women appear as symbols of civilization. The arena of popular western fiction in the late nineteenth and early twentieth centuries offered few narrative spaces giving "white women access to the premodern virtues the West supposedly embodies."[37] The early advertisements for El Tovar paralleled the emblems of civility women carried in western fiction. Despite a tendency to characterize them as spectators or markers of refined culture, women visiting the Grand Canyon did more than sew, gossip, read, or watch men play out their dreams of adventure.

Since the late nineteenth century, women followed the same "masculine" pursuits as men; for instance, they rode and walked to the Colorado River at the canyon's bottom. "Our crowd, ladies and all, made trip from cabin to river, back to cabin and up to head of trail in one day," wrote Mary Smith on July 16, 1892, in John Hance's visitors' register, "according to Mr. Hance, beating the record made by ladies."[38] Lillian and James Upson of Baldwinsville, New York, traveled without a guide to the bottom of the canyon in October of the same year. "If future parties of camping ladies intend going down, would advise them to employ the guide, and go prepared for roughing it," Upson wrote in Hance's register. "The ladies should wear very short wide skirts, and have Hance's burros to help them up from the cabin."[39] Two decades later, El Tovar Hotel was renting women divided skirts for riding and straw hats to screen the desert sun and heat. Apparently, dark skin was not quite so attractive on ladies as gentlemen.

Although Smith and Upson's entries suggest that women travelers were not confined to hotels or viewing areas along the rim, they seem to acknowledge the extraordinary nature of their excursions. Unlike men, who might renew their vitality in the western culture of conquest and "roughing it," turn-of-the-century women had few popular cultural narratives to draw from. Early photographs of women dressed in skirts and shirtwaists at the bottom of the canyon and along the rim seem only to reinscribe the civilizing tendencies attributed to them in popular discourse about the West. Where men donned cowboy hats and chaps, or mimicked the styles of Teddy Roosevelt's Rough Riders, women travelers were embodiments of modern fashions carried from eastern cities. They often brought the image of the Gibson girl model— elite, independent, athletic—into the scenes at the canyon. Unlike men, who could draw from a nostalgic and romantic reservoir of western heroes, the predominant representatives of white women in western fiction were either pioneer wives isolated from civilization or prostitutes. Neither of these types seemed appropriate analogs for upper-class ladies on vacation.

But in the hotels and restaurants at Grand Canyon—in fact, all along the route of the Santa Fe—women of leisure came face to face with another model of white womanhood. These were "Harvey Girls," single women between eighteen and thirty years old, mostly from the East and the Midwest, who responded to newspaper and magazine advertisements for jobs as waitresses in Harvey establishments. "One would like to believe that all the Harvey Girls were adventurers—spirited single women with a vision of excitement and freedom luring them west on their own," argues filmmaker and historian Lesley Poling-Kempes. "But most were prompted by economic necessity and the knowledge that the West has an abundance of single men."[40] Under the patriarchal gaze of the company, Harvey Girls carried an image of civilization into the West; and although many remained in the area after they left the company, they have been largely ignored as a force in settling mining communities and railroad towns. Unlike those who escaped to canyon vacations, Harvey employees occupied a closely regimented world of work and life. "They were expected to act like Harvey Girls twenty-four hours a day," notes Poling-Kempes. "They were told where to live, what time to go to bed, whom to date, even what to wear down to the last detail of make-up and jewelry."[41] Only white women were hired as Harvey waitresses in the early decades, although during World War II, the company did employ Hispanic and Indian women. For women tourists, Harvey Girls may have appeared to embody a dream of living independently in the American West, but it was a life inherently tied to service and the leisure fantasy of a man's West.

When the Harvey Girl appeared on American movie screens in the 1945 MGM musical *The Harvey Girls,* the conflicting themes of frontier independence and domestic civility served as a backdrop for a fairy-tale romance. Judy Garland played Susan Bradley, a young Ohio woman who heads west as a mail-order bride. She chooses instead to become a Harvey waitress in the fictional railroad town of Sandrock, Arizona. The film proclaimed the civilizing force of the Harvey Girls with an opening dedication: "These winsome waitresses conquered the West as surely as the Davy Crocketts and the Kit Carsons—not with powderhorn and rifle, but with a beefsteak and a cup of coffee."[42] With song and dance numbers, the film romanticized the West in a familiar story pitting outlaws, gamblers, and saloon girls against the Harvey waitresses, dressed in puritanical black and white uniforms, who worked the depot's restaurant. By the end of the film, the Harvey Girls have taken over the saloon, cleansed Sandrock of its vices, and sent the dance-hall girls on a westbound train to San Francisco. The symbolic battle between civilization and wildness is embodied in the romance between Susan Bradley and Ned Trent (played by John Hodiak), the saloon owner with a shady past who runs the town. Ned falls in love with Susan and decides to clean up his act. Susan, unaware of Ned's reformed ways and unsure of his love for her, boards the train and tells the departing town's madame she is willing to exchange her prim and proper Harvey uniform for the sassy dress of a saloon girl in order to win Ned's heart. Instead, the madame tells Susan of Ned's change of heart, and he waits for her back in Sandrock rather than going to San Francisco to open another saloon. Susan stops the train, and soon the gambler and waitress, surrounded by cactus and sagebrush, are exchanging marriage vows. On film, the western adventure promised the Harvey Girl was a story of love for men who lived freely at the boundaries of society. But when Susan settles down with the mysterious Ned Trent, he seems less a mystery. When the Santa Fe train leaves Sandrock, with cars carrying the saloon girls and Trent's lawless associates, it leaves behind a more sanitized, civilized, and stable frontier community. It simply wasn't the same *wild* West once the Harvey Girls appeared on the scene.

The appearance of such stories about the American West left women few options for adventure or independence beyond those realized by men. Some critics view the western genre as a male response to the growing presence of women's social reform movements and demands for emancipation in the late nineteenth century. "It is no accident that men gravitated in imagination toward a womanless milieu . . . a social setting that branded most features of civilized existence as feminine and corrupt, banishing them in favor of the three main targets of women's reform: whiskey, gambling, and prostitution," argues Jane Tompkins in her study of Western movies and Western novels.[43] When it came to describing the leisure places of men and women, the early Santa Fe and Harvey advertisements for Grand Canyon often resembled the conventional narrative structure of the western. Their descriptions of the El Tovar exiled women to roles and rooms that recalled a Victorian domesticity and silence. Women appear as pretty, gossipy, needlepoint witnesses to men's adventures. Yet, most often, they are reminders of a civilized presence in an imaginary rugged frontier that tourism promoters retained as an essential element of the canyon's world. In a culture where masculine identities were in question and women were experiencing new forms of independence, the leisure world of the canyon anchored itself in fantasies of male freedom, adventure, and nostalgic visions of female domesticity. The Grand Canyon advertised by commercial developers was built on the ruins of Victorian stability, and their brochures described a fictional leisure world where a former social order, one where men were men and women could watch them being men, remained intact.

Romancing the Ruins

The hotels and paved roads, both divided and connected by progress and nostalgia, were only one facet of a Grand Canyon that materialized a desire to hold on to a disappearing past. Since the turn of the century, the canyon's commercialized tourist world had been shaped by a dramatic allegory of loss and redemption. An "appreciation of the transience of things, and the concern to redeem them for eternity, is one of the strongest impulses of allegory," noted German cultural critic Walter Benjamin.[44] For Benjamin, the "ruin" was the physical symbol paralleling the idea of allegory. The ruin is "an always disappearing structure that invites imaginative reconstruction."[45] And beyond the doors of the El Tovar, tourists found various sentimental and romantic

representations of the frontier and Native American culture in scenes populated by the phantoms and artifacts of an imagined past.

A few days before guests began arriving at El Tovar, the Harvey Company opened Hopi House, directly east of the hotel. From the front porch of El Tovar, visitors could take a short stroll to the stone and adobe building, a small replica of a Hopi

pueblo in Oraibi, Arizona. Next door to the modern hotel, the reproduced pueblo offered tourists another facet of a mythic Southwest. Consistent with the dialectical pulls of progress and nostalgia, Hopi House created an atmosphere where time, geography, and cultural difference collapsed in a disjointed quest for history, tradition, and authenticity. Regardless of its name, Hopi House exhibited an array of cultural artifacts that would never have accumulated in a pueblo at Oraibi. "Several rooms of the Hopi House are devoted to an exhibit of rare and costly specimens of Indian and Mexican handiwork," read an early brochure description. "Here is displayed the priceless Harvey collection of old Navajo blankets, winner of a grand prize at the Louisiana Purchase Exposition. Here, too, is a Hopi ethnolographic [sic] collection . . . and a Pomo basket exhibit, the finest of its kind in the world. And a room filled with rare buffalo hide shields . . . and a salesroom."[46] In addition to these, a totem room displayed carved masks from Northwest native peoples. A Spanish-Mexican room attempted to recreate a scene from a "typical" Southwest dwelling, with a caballero's saddle, spurs, and sombrero placed near a corner fireplace. In a workroom, tourists could watch Hopis make blankets, pottery, jewelry, and other salesroom articles. The distinctive differences between cultures, however, was subsumed by the larger commercial machinery geared toward merchandising non-Anglo cultural artifacts. The Hopi House exhibits and displays were only part of a great enterprise intended to allow visitors to become "anthropologists" and move freely and safely through a strange and mysterious native world. "Go inside and you see how these gentle folk live," reads a 1909 Harvey brochure. "The rooms are little and low, like their small-statured occupants. The floors and walls are as cleanly [sic] as a Dutch kitchen. The Hopis are making 'piki,' twining the raven black hair of the 'manas' in big side whorls, smoking corn-cob pipes, building sacred altars, mending moccasins—doing a hundred un-American things."[47]

By the 1890s, traditional Indian life had all but vanished in America. But as their populations receded, killed by U.S. soldiers or forced onto reservations, they reappeared in imaginative cultural constructions. "To be an Indian in modern American society," argues Vine Deloria Jr., "is in a very real sense to be unreal and ahistorical."[48] For Deloria, anthropology stands behind many modern Indians' ambivalence toward models of cultural identification. "The massive volume of useless knowledge produced by anthropologists attempting to capture real Indians in a network of theories has contributed substantially to the invisibility of Indian people today," he argues.[49] But anthropology was only part of the cultural machinery producing an ambiguous cultural space Indians began to occupy in the early twentieth century. Throughout the Southwest, the collaborative advertising and merchandising efforts of the Santa Fe Railway and the Harvey Company reimagined native culture in ways that appealed to modern desires for tradition, authenticity, and the spiritual associations "primitive" people held with the natural world.

In 1907, the Santa Fe began a general mailing of an annual calendar with illustrations depicting romantic and primitive themes of native life. "The railway's advertising images of the landscape and the Indian were glazed with beauty and picturesqueness, promoting 'a last refuge of magic, mountains and quaint ancestors'," notes writer and filmmaker T. C. McLuhan.[50] The calendar, along with brochures, posters, lithographs, postcards, and maps, succeeded in creating strong interest in native culture. From a place of physical and cultural marginalization, native life was recaptured in a growing economy of images and souvenirs, and generated increased travel through the Southwest. For instance, a 1900 guidebook advised travelers on their way to Grand Canyon that "at the train itself you are likely to see members of the tribe, dignified and dirty and shrewd at a bargain, ready to sell baskets or blankets, perhaps crude but effectively decorated by the aboriginal proprietors of this part of the world."[51] Another early guide complained that the "'simple savage' with his 'untutored mind' does not propose to do anything for nothing; and he will do very little for anything. Why he will even charge you 'two bits' if you take a snap shot at him with a kodak."[52] Even though the commercialization of crafts and souvenirs, and the camera, had obviously transformed native life, guidebooks maintained the claim that an unchanged native culture lay waiting for a visitor's curiosity. "Indians of the Grand Country are one of its most fascinating lures," noted park superintendent Miner Tillotson's 1929 guide. "The district is one of the very few areas in the United States where the 'red' man still lives in his native state, primitive but happy, contented, unchanged by the white man's civilization."[53]

McLuhan suggests that in "assuming the cultural legacy of the American Indian, the [Santa Fe] ad men gave the impression that they were a knowledgeable 'ethnographic authority,' confidently imposing themselves on another culture by encapsulating it in both image and aphorism."[54] The Santa Fe's advertising department recognized that anthropological knowledge of the region carried prestige and could work in the interests of the railroad. For instance, in 1903 the company published an ethnographic account of the region that also served as a travel guide. Those "who wish to know the Navaho intimately should visit the reservation in the winter and should be prepared to spend not days, but weeks or months, roaming from hogan to hogan, where they may always be sure of a welcome," wrote George Dorsey, curator of the Field Columbian Museum in Chicago and holder of the first American doctorate in anthropology.[55]

It didn't take long for the Harvey Company to capitalize on the growing interest in native cultural objects; in 1902, it founded the Fred Harvey Indian Department to merchandise native arts and crafts. From its beginnings, the department synthesized anthropology and tourism to perpetuate the growing market for native works. For instance, a Harvey display of Navajo blankets and baskets won the grand prize at the 1904 St. Louis Exposition. Between 1903 and 1905, the company sent specimens to the Smithsonian's National Museum, the Carnegie Museum, and the Berlin Museum. With good freight rates and eager collectors on the East Coast, the "early 1900s were clearly very favorable for the company and its collection," noted Byron Harvey III, Fred Harvey's great-grandson. "The company's agents, present the year round, frequently were able to purchase items never offered to summer visitors. Winter brings hard times to the Indian or Spanish American farmer and consequently whole wagon loads of irreplaceable *Santos* and Indian arts were brought in for sale."[56] Even before the Indian Department was formally established, the Harvey Company had been making native handicrafts available to tourists. In 1899, Herman Schweizer, a company buyer, commissioned Navajo silver jewelry for sales at Harvey shops along the Santa Fe line. Schweizer's enthusiastic acquisitions and merchandising of native objects fueled the Indian Department's growth, and he was referred to as the "Harvey anthropologist." The expanding native craft market eventually meant providing places for tourists to buy them. The Hopi House at Grand Canyon became one of the earliest buildings designed to merchandise native culture.

Hopi House was designed by Mary Jane Colter, an architect and schoolteacher from Minnesota.[57] She was seventeen years old when she began studying art and design at the California School of Design, and she learned about architecture by apprenticing in a San Francisco city architect's office during the late 1880s. Graduating in 1890, she returned to St. Paul to teach mechanical drawing at the Mechanic Arts High School. The Harvey Company first hired her in 1902 to decorate the salesroom of the newly opened Indian Building in Albuquerque. Impressed with her interior design for the building, the company asked Colter to design a showroom at the canyon for its collection of native arts. Colter was thirty-five when Hopi House opened in 1905. In 1910, the Harvey Company offered her a permanent position. Between 1902 and 1949, Colter's architecture and interior design work for the company gave shape to twenty buildings in Kansas City, Chicago, St. Louis, Los Angeles, Albuquerque, Santa Fe, Gallup, Winslow, and the Grand Canyon. When the Harvey Company initiated a major expansion of Grand Canyon tourist facilities in 1914, Colter designed several buildings aimed toward a nostalgic return to an imagined West.

Hopi House was conceived to stimulate interest in native craft sales and "symbolized the partnership between commercialism and romanticism that typified so much of Fred Harvey architecture."[58] The Harvey Company was convinced profits could be made from tourists who wanted to stroll through a world other than their own. In the first three decades of the twentieth century, the Grand Canyon became a gallery for Colter's designs. The Lookout (1914), Hermit's Rest (1914), Phantom Ranch (1922), The Indian Watchtower (1932), and the Bright Angel Lodge (1935) all blended Harvey commercial interests with her increasingly sentimental images of the West. "She recreated a bygone era, a more tranquil age when time moved more slowly," affectionately notes Colter biographer Virginia Grattan. "She created pleasant sanctuaries that were removed from the noise and rush of the twentieth century, places where people could rest and regain their composure."[59] Indeed, her buildings fixed on romantic themes of "native simplicity" and "pioneer tranquillity" as Colter invented a series of sentimental and fantastic time zones along the canyon's rim. Seeking architectural harmony with the landscape, Colter consistently used local building materials for conveying a primitive and rustic look to hazily recall a "bygone era." But rugged boulders and rough timber soon gave way to dreamier visions. For instance, The Lookout, built with stone matching the surrounding canyon cliffs, was situated west of El Tovar. Its exterior of piled rocks resembled the ruins of an ancient rampart. Weeds grew through the stones of The Lookout's parapet roofline. The porch and lower exterior observation area hung out from the canyon and offered tourists a place to photograph the canyon or roam its depths through a powerful telescope. In a stone and timber interior room art was exhibited; postcards, paintings, and photographs were also for sale. In the case of The Lookout, Colter's sense of "historical romanticism and nostalgia evident at Hopi House had been tempered by fantasy—a metamorphosis away from archeological authenticity and toward pure romanticism."[60]

At the end of the west rim tourist road, Hermit's Rest served as a starting point for overnight mule trips into the canyon. An early Santa Fe brochure described the site as "a new resting place for wayfarers, built in the solid rock of a little hill, like a hermit's cave of prehistoric times, yet furnishing modern refreshments and the warmth of an enormous fireplace when the day is chilly."[61] With Hermit's Rest, Colter blended the idyllic designs of a wilderness mountain man's home with the features of a medieval castle. Its stone porch extended to the canyon rim and was furnished with rustic furniture made from stripped tree limbs and stumps. Bear traps hung from roughly hewn posts that supported the roof beams. Inside, a row of windows looked out on the canyon. An enormous, stone-arched fireplace alcove commanded the center wall, and a bearskin rug lay spread on the flat stone floor. Iron candelabras hung from two huge posts framing the fireplace. Although the building suggested a romantic and secluded dwelling of a wilderness hermit, no one ever resided in it. Like her other designs, Hermit's Rest housed a vague dream world, a material point of departure for visions of rustic frontier life and nature as a sanctuary from civilization. Colter's buildings created an amnesiac atmosphere of history, supplying tourists with enough details and motifs to evoke a past that had disappeared sometime before they ever arrived.

Although she looked to other cultural groups and historical periods for her buildings, Colter's architecture was, in many ways, a response to the broader issues of American cultural identity at the time. During the 1880s, when she trained at the California School of Design, many architects became interested in realizing a distinctive vision of a modern, national architecture design. Rather than be confined to continually reproduce the building styles of England or the European continent, they wanted to declare an independent American style. "Is there any reason why American architects should not be something more than mere copyists of European models?" asked Harold Mitchell in an 1882 issue of the *California Architect and Building News.* "I think they would undoubtedly be more respected by the age they live in, as well as by the ages yet to come, if their works carried more the stamp of originality; in fact more

truly American, unreflected from the other side of the water."[62] That style, claimed
Mitchell in his short manifesto, would be absent of the ornaments, leaves, and animals
honoring the past ages of foreign countries. Instead, architectural design should spawn
from materials found on American soil and reflect the interests of the public who would
use the buildings. For Colter and other designers, notes architectural historian David
Gebhard, "the pristine purity of simplicity was to be found not in their European heritage but in the art and architecture of primitive man. . . . By the late nineteenth century
the only American Indian groups which still possessed an active culture were those of
the Southwest."[63] Colter extended that vision of simplicity into contrived memories of
frontier life and stories of a cowboy West. But her use of American Indian cultural motifs most clearly expressed the contradictory impulses of her era by connecting a progressive vision of American architecture with nostalgic desires for an unchanged past.
"The separation of nonmodern culture traits from their original contexts and their
distribution as modern playthings are evident in the various social movements toward
naturalism," argues Dean MacCannell. "These displaced forms, embedded in modern
society, are the spoils of the victory of the modern over the nonmodern world. They establish in consciousness the definition and boundary of modernity by rendering concrete and immediate that which modernity is not."[64] Colter and the Harvey Company
literally relocated native culture to the Grand Canyon, reconstituting and artificially
preserving its memory in the shape of tourist attractions.

Although the Bright Angel Lodge was the last tourist building she designed for
the canyon, Hopi House and The Indian Watchtower at Desert View are the beginning and endpoints of Colter's appropriation of native design and illustrate her movement from realism toward fantasy. Colter designed the new Watchtower building,
constructed in 1932, to serve as an endpoint for Harvey tours on East Rim Drive and
another place to sell refreshments and native crafts. "The problem was to build a
building . . . as high above [the rim] as possible, and yet make it so much a part of its
immediate surroundings that it would not stick up 'like a sore thumb,'" Colter explained in a manual she wrote for Harvey tour guides. She decided that conventional
styles of modern architecture and contemporary building materials would be inappropriate for a structure created to enhance the view of the canyon and, at the same time,
appear as natural to the landscape. "Then—the idea of the Indian Watchtower was hit
upon," Colter said. "The Tower would give the height we needed for the view rooms
and telescopes; the character of the prehistoric buildings would make possible the har-
monizing of its lines and color with the terrain; its timeworn masonry walls would
blend with the eroded stone cliffs of the Canyon walls."[65]

The Watchtower's facade suggested the ruins of an ancient civilization. Colter
designed the tower after visiting and studying several archeological sites scattered
throughout the Southwest. However, standing seventy feet high and measuring thirty feet in diameter at the base, The Watchtower was larger than any tower she had

seen at the ruins of Mesa Verde, Canyon de Chelly, Hovenweep, or Wupatki. The Watchtower's circular ground floor was styled after the ceremonial kivas found in prehistoric ruins excavated by archaeologists. The term "kiva" signifies "world below," and the kiva is an underground masonry chamber used for ceremonial purposes. A small hole in the floor of the kiva was a symbolic portal to the spiritual Underworld, and a ladder through the roof symbolically led to the world above. But Colter's version of the kiva was built aboveground; it had large windows framing views of the canyon and functioned as a salesroom for native handicrafts. A narrow stairway on the west side of Colter's Kiva Room led into the tower. Visitors could climb the stairs and stand on the circular roof of the Kiva Room or continue to climb the stairway spiraling up to other observation points.

Inside the tower, Colter chose Hopi artist Fred Kabotie to decorate the walls with murals depicting the legendary associations the Hopi people held with the Grand Canyon. For the most part, he was free to paint as he

wished. However, Colter urged him to include a painting of the Hopis' snake legend. "Since the Colorado River at the bottom of the Grand Canyon is the main feature that people see from the Watchtower," Kabotie recalled, "I painted the Snake Legend, showing that the first man to float through the canyon was a Hopi—hundreds of years before Major John Wesley Powell's historic Grand Canyon trip in 1869." Although the building was Colter's interpretation of native culture, Kabotie's *Snake Legend* and other paintings carried clues about other meanings the land and native culture could hold. Yet, in the tourist context of Grand Canyon, they said little of the divided lives Indians like Kabotie experienced. Like a number of other Hopis, Kabotie worked the Harvey tourist facilities during the 1920s and 1930s. At the same time, he was also earning a reputation among art collectors and anthropologists as an important native artist. Drifting between Santa Fe, Phoenix, and the Grand Canyon, Kabotie seemed at odds with his own culture. His autobiography tells the story of a man who at times dressed like John Dillinger, drank excessively, but frequently returned to the reservation, where he slowly became reconnected with his Hopi heritage. Even after the paintings were completed, Kabotie would find himself in The Watchtower for several more years. Following the building dedication ceremonies, Katherine Harvey approached the artist and said, "Now Fred, this is your place. It's really right for you," recalls Kabotie. "As soon as we can arrange it, you'll be working here." And she kept her promise. Two years later, Kabotie was managing The Watchtower gift shop and overseeing a crew of Hopi employees who, he remembered, kept "the tower in good shape, floors mopped and the big picture windows so clean that you couldn't see the glass."[66] With the Hopi reservation nearly a hundred miles away from Desert View, Kabotie became another cultural import. Colter had already been successful in transporting and reconfiguring core samples of native culture when she built Hopi House. Managing The Watchtower gift shop, Kabotie was, in many ways, a reluctant cultural castaway, marooned in a fabricated tourist facsimile of Indian life he had helped to assemble.

The Watchtower separated the complexity of native culture from time only to become appropriated as a timeless monument serving the interests of commercial tourism entrepreneurs. Colter gave clear instructions to Harvey tour guides who described the tower. "This building should NOT be called a 'copy'; a 'replica'; a 'reproduction' or a *'restoration'*. It is absolutely none of these," she wrote. "Someone has called it a 'RE-CREATION'. That describes best the INTENTION of the design." She did, however, *create* rather than re-create a vision of a native past. Although the building simulated a synthesis of different ruins throughout the region, Colter hinted at the historical *possibility* of a structure like The Watchtower standing at Desert View. "In itself a prehistoric Indian building was not inappropriate. One might well have been built on this very finger of rock hundreds of years ago by the ancestors of the Hopi," she imagined for the Harvey guides. "There would be nothing inconsistent in building here as they might have built had they not migrated before the Golden Age when the Tower and the Great Kiva were the order of the day."[67] For Colter, it was merely a matter of suspending disbelief and reimagining native life in the interests of the Harvey Company, and the tourists they wanted to attract.

More inventive in design than Hopi House, The Watchtower became animated by a similar dramatic energy bred from the differences between the culture of American Indians and the world of mostly white, urban visitors who wandered through its "scenes." Reporting on the May 1933 dedication of The Watchtower, Sallie Saunders took stock of those differences. Amid the celebratory dedication activities—native dancing, costumes, a spiritual blessing of The Watchtower—Saunders's interest in the spectators called up the innate lesson of the canyon's tourist world. "The white men in the audience suddenly appear almost pathetic, dressed in the world's common clothes—poor, drab male creatures divested of their heritage of glory," she wrote. "Even the cowboys, part of the intently watching audience, fail to be completely gorgeous in their wild-patterned shirts, neck bands and ornate boots. It is the Indians' day."[68]

With costumed Hopis dancing and ritually sanctifying the building, The Watchtower might well have been seen as a monument to the cultural life of American Indians. But it also marked a deeper modern quest for spiritual and cultural redemption, and for the values of tradition seemingly absent for many, bound as they were to the progressive rhythms of urban life. "These visitors will return to the troubled, throbbing tempo of their days with new thoughts, new visions granted them by this insight into an age-old culture," wrote Saunders. The Watchtower at least suggested a brief retrieval of time-honored cultural traditions, their promises of stability and integrity, often overlooked by the forward gaze of American progress. The sweeping view of Grand Canyon from the tower was "like liberty itself," said Saunders, proposing that the "building stood so concretely for the recognition of an intangible thing—the relation between the white man and the Indian."[69]

As visitors stood on The Watchtower's observation deck, they might have turned away from the canyon for a moment, looked toward the east, and pointed to the Navajo reservation faintly visible on the distant plateau. With the warm May sun piercing the clear Arizona sky, we may only wonder about the feelings of freedom and liberty they found in surveying the surrounding scene. In different ways, The Watchtower (as its name implies) offered an ironic monument to their vision. On the one hand, it was a reminder of the many ways Native American life had become fixed for the visitors'

gaze in a spectacle combining anthropological curiosity with cultural imagination. In a modern building designed to enhance and enlarge perspective, a structure fashioned on the ruins of native life, The Watchtower gazed upon the legacy of difference and division between Indian culture and the modern world only as a nostalgic expression. On the other hand, the tower manifested "liberty" as a form of mobile vision, a chance to look into other centuries and cultures from a single vantage point. Concealed in the mock ruins of an ancient world, The Watchtower testified to the freedoms of modern life given shape through mobility and leisure time. There, visitors stood like princes, as the guitar poets have sung, keeping their view fixed on a way out of their own world, listening for a wildness in the distance amid the liberties of coming and going as they pleased.[70] Yet, it was in many ways an insidious freedom, an interminable search that suggested one keep looking, keep moving, and keep reaching into a hazy past for assurances about an uncertain present and future.

Colter's architecture responded to such yearnings by translating history through

an aesthetic of sentimentality. Today, her buildings stand as memorials not only to the questions of regional identity that have, for more than a century, floated through the West but also as reminders of the longings for history, tradition, and authentic life that have possessed many Americans since the late nineteenth century. In 1882, a few years before Colter began her design studies, Harold Mitchell advised American architects to embrace the meaning and experience of their own time. "The architect must throw the traces around the neck of circumstances, architecture being, like ourselves, very much the creature of circumstances," he wrote.[71] The circumstances facing Colter were also those of a generation who stood poised at the brink of a great cultural abyss, hopeful about the future yet uneasy about its continuity with the past. Nostalgia offered a cultural response to the dramatic transformations Americans experienced at the close of the nineteenth century and the first decades of the twentieth century. The backward gaze of nostalgia was more than a consolatory leisure escape into the simpler times of a "bygone era." For those living in an age of progress, Kammen argues, nostalgia creatively helped "to legitimize new political orders, rationalize the adjustment and perpetuation of old social hierarchies, and construct new systems of thought and values." At the turn of the century, Americans sensed the uncertainties of perpetual change and innovation lurking somewhere behind an ideology of progress;

many "needed notions of the past that would help to define their national identities in positive ways, and required secure traditions to serve as strong psychological anchors. Otherwise, as one momentous century ended and the prospect of a new and uncertain one loomed, they faced the future as culturally displaced persons. Nostalgia . . . provided identity, integrity, and perhaps even a sense of security—however false."[72]

Perhaps no other image of a Grand Canyon visitor would seem to capture so profoundly the contradictions and uncertainties of the twentieth century as the photograph of the man who walked along the edge of the abyss on the last day of February 1931. Returning from a visit to the California Institute of Technology, Albert Einstein and his wife, Elsa, stopped at the canyon for a brief visit. It would be difficult to know what the famous physicist thought as he peered into the emptiness from the South Rim. Then a professor of theoretical physics at the University of Berlin and an international celebrity, the fifty-one-year-old Einstein had spent much of his adult life in transit. Over the past three decades he had lived in Hungary, Switzerland, and Czechoslovakia. Ten years earlier, he had been awarded the Nobel Prize in physics. A week earlier, in California, news photographers clamored for a shot of him with Charlie Chaplin. At the time of his visit, he and Elsa were heading back across America to board a steamer for Europe. In two years, Einstein—a Jew with Swiss citizenship living in Berlin—would again set sail for America to escape the rising heat of anti-Semitism in Nazi Germany, and he and Elsa would make their last home in Princeton, New Jersey.

When tourists, in 1905, caught their first glimpse of Hopi silver artists, weavers, and displays of Harvey craft curios after passing through the threshold into the dimly lit simulacrum of Colter's replica of a Hopi pueblo, the twenty-six-year-old Einstein had been working in a Swiss patent office in Bern, scribbling notes for his special theory of relativity, which became nothing less than his stamp on the twentieth century. Colter was still drawing her plans for The Watchtower when the Einsteins toured the canyon that Saturday in February 1931, but they did visit Hopi House. The couple was photographed there with Herman Schweizer and J. B. Duffy, general passenger agent for the Santa Fe, who had arranged for a brief ceremony to make the physicist an honorary chief. According to an Associated Press report, the Hopis, who lauded presidents and celebrities in a similar fashion, were "puzzled to assign an honorary name to the scientist. 'What's his business?' the redskins asked. 'He invented the theory of relativity,' they were told. 'All right,' was the reply, 'we'll call him "Great Relative".'"[73]

The photograph of Einstein, posed with Elsa, Hopi workers, and Schweizer and Duffy, only seemed an exaggerated staging of the dialectic of progress and nostalgia shaping the Grand Canyon during the first three decades of the twentieth century. The headdress and pipe given to him had nothing to do with Hopi culture. They belonged to the Plains Indians and the movies made in southern California, where Einstein and his wife had boarded a train the previous day. In the photograph, the

feathered headdress covering the skull of the man many called the century's greatest and most complicated thinker did, in fact, suggest that he was a "Great Relative" to the Hopis. Grasping a young Hopi girl's hand, the couple seem like two homeless children of a modern world. If Einstein epitomized progress and science, he also embodied its politics of displacement and exile, the contradictions of a technological age, and an ambivalence toward certainty and spirituality. Just two weeks before his South Rim visit, he had told CalTech students that applied science brought people "little happiness" because they have failed to make "sensible use" of it. "In war it serves that we may poison and mutilate each other," he said. "In peace it has made our lives hurried and uncertain. Instead of freeing us in great measure from spiritually exhausting labor, it has made men into slaves of machinery, who for the most part complete their monotonous long day's work with disgust and must continually tremble for their poor rations." He urged the students to use their creations as a "blessing and not a curse to mankind." In his critique of modern progress, the physicist speculated about the meaning of contentment by drawing on the example of native life. "Just consider a quite uncivilized Indian, [and] whether his experience is less rich and happy than that of the average civilized man. I hardly think so," said Einstein. "There lies a deep meaning in the fact that children of all civilized countries are so fond of playing Indians."[74]

It's impossible to know if Einstein felt happier after donning his new headdress and becoming the "Great Relative" on that Saturday afternoon. On that day, he was a celebrity on a trip home with his devoted wife. We may only wonder if he realized that the young Hopi girl whose hand he gently held in his own was playing Indian, too. In fact, all of the costumed Hopis who stood next to him were part of a performance they had not scripted. When the couple left the canyon, the Hopi workers would stay in their simulated pueblo as part of the display, hammering away at silver, weaving rugs, and dancing in the late afternoons for the strangers who arrived in cars and trains with hopes of entering another dimension of time and space. Like many canyon visitors, Einstein clung to the handrails of nostalgia as he peered into the open space of eternity. Back on the train, the physicist would stop in Albuquerque, where he and Elsa would again be greeted by Indians working for the Harvey Company. Traveling east somehow went against the grain of American progress, the future, so boldly carried in the image of a westbound train. And as they sped on to Santa Fe, I see Einstein running his fingers over the feathers of his new war bonnet and looking at the green mountains to the northwest. It's unlikely he could have known that within ten years scientists working there would create a form of energy to forever change modern life. Their efforts would come to pass largely because a 1939 letter from Einstein urged President Franklin D. Roosevelt to support American scientists in their efforts to build an atomic bomb before Germany did. But in 1931, as the wheels of the Santa Fe locomotive pounded below, he was moving through Indian country and eventually toward Germany. Regardless of the direction, he was pushing through time and space, toward a home he would soon abandon to the forward motion of his life and the inevitable and irrevocable changes wrought by a politicized pursuit of a purified culture. And all of this truly marked his relationship with the Hopis who adorned him in feathers and sent him on his way.

In contrast to Einstein, the Santa Fe Railway and the Harvey Company believed time itself could be brought to a sudden halt. The monumental and sentimental images of native life perpetuated by railroad advertising, Harvey's Indian Department, and Colter's Hopi House and Watchtower literally banked on such an idea. The two companies manufactured an idea of native life that would hold enduring consequences for the Navajos and the Hopis living on the border of Grand Canyon. The picture of Einstein at the Grand Canyon is but one small reminder of how the uncertainties and anxieties rendered by modern progress sought relief in a nostalgic retreat toward an imaginary world where time might seem to stop. The cultural space contemporary Indians occupy today only reflects the deeper relations between the modern world and native life that began to find a *tangible* form in the developing tourist world at Grand Canyon in the first decades of the twentieth century.

Highway Moccasins and Mythic Indians

Fred Harvey's name appears as a signature on the paper sacks of souvenirs tourists carry out of the Hopi House. Today, Hopi House remains devoted to his company's vision of tourism as commodity exchange. Silver and turquoise jewelry, pottery, baskets, serapes, ponchos, western hats, beaded belts (often manufactured overseas), and kachina dolls line the walls of the dimly lit adobe gift shop. Alongside these, the familiar tourist-zone staples—T-shirts, postcards, decals, bumper stickers—sit in piles waiting to adhere the canyon's significance to private lives. As I wander the Hopi House sales floor, I notice a young girl wearing a feathered headdress and carrying a toy tom-tom. She impatiently waits as her mother scans a moccasin "conversion chart" that cross-references men's, women's, and children's shoe sizes for the United States, Europe, Britain, and Japan. I recall a trading-post billboard message on I-40 near Holbrook, Arizona: "Moccasins for the entire family." Walking through the small wooden door of Hopi House, I head for the porch of El Tovar to write out some postcards and carry a straw cowboy hat I bought for a niece in San Diego.

At The Watchtower gift shop at Desert View, an elderly Navajo woman wearing turquoise and silver jewelry weaves a rug. A sign above her reads: IT IS CUSTOMARY TO DONATE MONEY BEFORE TAKING A PICTURE. Occasionally, a few tourists cluster around her to observe, but watching the woman weave each fiber into a rug is an exercise in patience for people whose vacation clocks are ticking away, and they quickly move on to other displays. Near the cash register, I stare at video images of Hopi ceremonial dances on a small television screen. *Grand Canyon: A Journey into Discovery* is one of several videos sold at The Watchtower and other canyon souvenir counters. While the magnetic tape memory of Hopi dancers moves to a sound track of flute and drum, the voice of the actor Telly Savalas narrates the scene. "Contact with the Spanish conquistadors and missionaries, and later the reservation system, has had little effect on the political and religious fears of their life," says the former TV detective. "They [the Hopi] are, perhaps, the most representative pre-contact cultural entity surviving in the United States today." Sealed in the screen behind the cashier, the flickering light images of the Hopis are, ironically, dancing to diminish the idea that progress or time has done anything to alter native ways.

Later, standing on The Watchtower's circular observation deck, a young man with a scraggly beard tilts his head up and down, comparing the canyon mirrored in the viewfinder of an old camera with the canyon his naked eye sees. His new T-shirt bears the picture of Albert and Elsa Einstein in front of Hopi House. He bought the shirt there, he says. Below me, tourists ebb and flow toward safety rails and telescopes on the rim. To the southeast, I see cars and buses rolling into Desert View from State Road 64, the Nava-Hopi Road, connecting the east boundary of Grand Canyon National Park to Highway 89 in Cameron. Many have just traversed the western edge of the Navajo reservation. I, too, have driven the thirty-four miles from Desert View to Cameron. In places the plateau rips open, revealing sheer canyon walls rising above the Little Colorado River. For those headed east, such views are only a taste of what is to come when they reach The Watchtower. But the Nava-Hopi Road holds other scenes that, in different ways, run against the grain of nostalgia tourists find at the Grand Canyon.

At an abandoned roadside souvenir stand, the peeling paint of a plywood sign reads: WELCOME TO NAVAJOLAND. It leans against an oil drum overflowing with garbage. Skeletons of cars rust in the desert. Graffiti covers a set of fly-infested outhouses near another empty souvenir stand. Small shack homes sit at the end of dirt roads that turn off the highway to the canyon. A general sense of poverty in the area leaves me feeling less than "welcome" as I drive through the reservation. I cannot help but notice the thick power lines sagging between steel towers. The towers look like giant metal skeletons marching single file across the desert, or huge Cubist sculptures paying tribute to all the kachina dolls sold at trading posts and souvenir stands throughout the Southwest. The lines running between them carry electricity over the heads of the Navajo Nation to distant cities beyond the horizon. Souvenir stands fly flags from Germany, Japan, Switzerland, and Canada. Between the stands, road signs vie for customers. SEE A LIVE WOLF! TURQUOISE AND SILVER JEWELRY, calls one. INDIAN SILVER—POTTERY—RUGS. DEALERS WELCOME. CHIEF YELLOW HORSE NEXT STOP— YELLOW HORSE LOVES YOU—BANKCARDS ACCEPTED, reads a series of messages for Chief Yellow Horse's merchandise tables. If there is a hint of desperation in these signs, it comes from the difficult task of trying to lure tourists away from a steady path to and from the canyon. A sign near Desert View warns that unauthorized souvenir sales in the park are punishable by fine.

It would be a mistake to believe that the tourist stands sprinkled along the Nava-Hopi Road reflect a larger experience of life on the reservation. Beyond the signs and souvenirs, I often found hints of a world pulled between a mythologized native past and contemporary ideals of American mobility. I tuned in the broadcast signal of Window Rock's KTNN radio station while driving from the canyon one afternoon and listened to recordings of native chanting and drumming. Although I couldn't understand any of it, I listened until the drums and chants stopped abruptly, giving way to more familiar sounds of upbeat

jazzy synthesizers and the driving percussion loops of radio advertising. "Southwest Marketing is looking for you," an excited voice announces over the music. "If you're a Navajo woman between the ages of eighteen and thirty and have always had the desire to model, then here's your chance. . . . Southwest Marketing will hold auditions for its 1993 Women of the Navajo calendar." The auditions, he said, would take place at the Navajo Nation Inn in Window Rock. Other radio ads followed, spoken in Navajo. I couldn't understand these, either, except for a few familiar words and phrases— "Burger King," "mattresses," "box springs," "ninety days same as cash"—that apparently had no direct translation. The call for Navajo calendar models sandwiched between recordings of native ceremonial drums was merely one crack in the reflection of a mythologized West. For more than a century, businesses have been creating new markets and products by harvesting Navajo images. The bilingual radio voices, like the geometric shapes of power cables and towers running along the highway, drew lines through the sweeping desert vistas and distant buttes of the reservation, all mapping modern trails through the Navajo world.

With the sounds of country music playing from a radio on the hood of his truck and the wind beating woven rugs hung out for display, Leon, a heavyset Navajo in his midforties, told me about life along the tourist highway. Dressed in a white shirt, new blue

jeans, and a pressed straw hat, he said he liked his business, the chances it afforded to meet people from different countries, and showed me the turquoise earrings, clay pots, and sand paintings spread out on his tables.

"It must be strange living in a place where so many people just seem to pass through," I offered.

"Yeah, it is, but they're only on the highway," he said. "You don't find them out where the reservation is, like where they're herding sheep or where everyday business is being conducted. You don't see them there. The highway kind of takes care of itself. People don't travel much off the highways." Leon had followed those same roads off

the reservation. He was a Vietnam veteran, worked in Flagstaff for nine years as a deputy sheriff, and sold cars there for three more years. But he returned to the reservation and now lived in Tuba City, about thirty miles from where we stood talking.

"This is where I feel home is," he told me. "You know, this is where I find my mother, my brothers, my sisters. And we lack water and we lack a lot of things that Flagstaff provides, but I'll sacrifice that for living with my own relatives." Part of that life carried a hope of one day running his own trading post. "They're all operated by Anglos," he said. "Their relatives have been here maybe a hundred years. That's where they started, y'know? . . . We just got to the point where we accept that. But one of these days we'll be running it. When they get tired of being here. I think I'm an enterprising individual. I think I can compete with them now. . . . I'd like to get into a store. And maybe within the next couple of years you'll be able to see a Navajo running a trading post. Something that will keep the wind off my back and the rain and things like that."

Leon's departure and return to the reservation was typical, he said, of how many live in the Navajo Nation. People leave because of the poor economy. They go to find work, go to school, and as they get older, many return. Hearing the traces of some vague, liberal guilt in my words, I asked if he was resentful toward the Anglo businessmen who established the tourist economy on the reservation and, more broadly, the historical treatment of Navajos by the U.S. government.

"Well, that was a long time ago," he said, then paused to fix a blanket knocked down in the wind. "I was born without anything and it's my job to go forward. We're all born in certain steps and then one of these days I'll be able to catch the next step. And then, if I do good, I'll go to the next step. Then when I get too old, my kids start from that step, they build from there. We can't always blame the past for what's occurring." Leon's response expressed ideals of upward mobility and economic individualism. He had named the Protestant work ethic as a ladder leading only upward but echoed the terms of traditional Navajo values for hard work, thrift, and the preservation of family possessions.[75]

Before I left Leon at his stand, I asked about a flag I'd seen flying at some of the other souvenir stands on the highway. It was an American flag with a portrait of Chief Joseph superimposed over the stars and stripes. Dispossessed of traditional homelands, Joseph led hundreds of Nez Percé on a two-thousand-mile journey to the Canadian border in 1877. After battling the U.S. Army, and with wounded men and hungry children surrounding him, the chief laid down his gun about forty miles from the border where he hoped to find a sanctuary for his people. For many historians, his surrender marked one of the final battles between Indians and the U.S. government. In the flag on reservation souvenir stands, I saw a sign of division and pride. It was a sad reminder of the fateful hand dealt to native cultures throughout the United States and testimony to their persistence through more than a hundred years of grim history. For Leon, however, it was a banner of unity and loyalty.

"To me, that flag symbolizes a bond between the Navajo, no, not the Navajo, the *Indian* and the United States," he claimed. "We've always supported the United States and I think that's a symbol of us being closer together. Whenever they need our young mens, we're always willing to go. I think that's what that symbolizes." Given his service in Vietnam and the optimism he held for the future, I shouldn't have been surprised by his words. I wanted to think he spoke differently with friends and family in Tuba City, that he experienced some resentment toward a world where a contrived tourist caricature of Indian life had become so firmly rooted that he would spend his days selling it. My drama of modernity pictured Leon facing some modified version of the hard choices Chief Joseph confronted more than a hundred years ago. He was trying to live with dignity in the face of forces that would not retreat and that he could not control, no matter how far he ran toward a place where he might keep them at bay. Leon, however, seemed less distressed and gave me his bottom line in simpler terms. Tourists "want to see an Indian wearing his war bonnet whether he comes from the Navajo reservation or the Pueblo reservation or whatever," he told me. "They still want to stereotype us. It doesn't matter. If that's what they want to see, you know, if I can sell another five dollars dressed up with the war bonnet, I'll dress up with the war bonnet. Money is money."

Leon wasn't the only one who knew how to capitalize on Indian stereotypes. As I drove from the canyon toward Cameron one morning, I saw a man dressed as a warrior standing on a rock in view of passing tourists. I parked on the worn dirt turnout where two teenage Navajo boys were spreading necklaces on a table and setting up for another day of sales. The costumed man was Jake, they told me, and he worked the road. A Sioux originally from North Dakota, Jake had gone to Brigham Young University in Provo, Utah, for a few years but left because, he said, he had "a difficult time fitting into that society." In 1985, he started "working the road," which meant standing on a rock from mid-June until the end of August, dressed in a traditional Indian costume. Tourists would see Jake, stop to take his picture, and he would charge them for posing.

"They use their film, their camera, they take the picture and I pose," he explained. "Three dollars if the picture is of me alone, and it's five dollars if they want to get in the picture."

"But you're in either picture," I noted. "Why charge more for them to stand next to you?"

"Well, it's an added thing. It gives it more of a personal identification," he said. "A single shot of me is just like a postcard. But for them to be in there, with this kind of setting, with this kind of costume, gives it a more personal value. And I guess its what the market will bear, speak in capitalist terms." Behind the rock where we stood talking, I noticed Jake's Honda CX500 motorcycle parked out of view. Jake said he earned nine dollars the day before, but "June was usually a slow month." When business was good, he claimed to make as much as $250 a day. After the busy season was over at Grand Canyon, he worked as a stuntman in a western theme park near Scottsdale, Arizona. "It's called 'Rawhide,'" he said. "I get shot and fall off buildings for tourist shows."

"What do your friends and family think about this kind of work?" I asked.

"Some of them laugh at it, and I guess it is out of the ordinary," he admitted. "I mean, how many people do you see standing all dressed up by the roadside like this? You don't see any." He paused to put a blanket around his shoulders. The wind had picked up and his costume exposed much of his skin. "But I'll tell you something, they've got the wrong idea about these stands here," he said, pointing to the two teenage boys waiting for customers at their table of earrings and necklaces. "If you look, they've got these nice pick-up trucks by the stand there. And they've got on green army fatigues and T-shirts with 'Ted Nugent' and 'Whitesnake' on them. It seems like they're trying to break out of the mold society wants to put them in. Which isn't bad, I guess, but they don't know what they're passing up." Jake pulled the blanket off and waved at a station wagon cruising toward the park. "If I were a tourist coming through here," he continued, "I'd want a little old lady sitting on a rug so I could get a picture of her. And a man with a silver belt, and some turquoise nuggets, and some moccasins and leggings, the whole bit, so he'd look the part rather than try to fit into mainstream society. I wouldn't care what they asked me for a price because that would be an experience you couldn't get anywhere else. I know that must sound like some Harvard Business School deal." He laughed. A van pulled up next to my Volkswagen and a family poured out to look at the jewelry at the stand. A man with camera equipment started toward the rock where we were talking. This could have been a customer for Jake, so I said good-bye.

"Can I give you some money for taking up your time?" I offered, awkwardly. "How much would be appropriate—do you have an interview price?"

"No," he laughed. "Whatever you want is fine." I had a five and a twenty in my wallet. I gave him the five, not really believing it was enough.

"Good luck, man," Jake said, and I looked at his hand shaking my own. We had done business, I suppose, and I started down the rock when one more question came to mind.

"What kind of costume is that you're wearing?" I asked.

"It's a Sioux warrior's costume," he grinned. "It's what General Custer saw for about fifteen minutes." I nodded, feeling privy to an inside joke, as I passed the man with the camera who was breathing heavily as he lugged his tripod up the rock to where Jake stood waiting.

More than anyone I met on the reservation, Jake replayed the role of the iconic Indian warrior and actor who has occupied the stage of the West since Buffalo Bill's Wild West shows of the 1890s. What Buffalo Bill created—a spectacular restaging of an inverted frontier history, a reenactment of westward expansion with Indian aggression and white victimization—"now seems a postmodern West," suggests Richard White, "in which performance and history [are] hopelessly intertwined."[76] As with Two Feathers, Kit, Snake Eyes, and Two Aces, who enact the classic gunfight at the Williams Depot, Jake's costumed appearance by the roadside needs no introduction or setup. The drama surrounds him, staged and running for more than a hundred years. Jake's and Leon's stories express the hegemony of the imagined frontier narratives that so wholly and historically integrate them into the structure of Southwest tourism. Behind the nostalgic veneer of Indian life found in and around Grand Canyon lay a history of cultural divestment, betrayal, and marginalization that leaves many Navajos, Hopis, and others lodged in a universe of fantasies about native life reimagined and remade since the late nineteenth century. I can only wonder if either imagines a different dream world, one where weeds grow through cracks in the highway, tumbleweeds dance across empty souvenir stands, and the wind carries no sound of camera shutters clicking. With a seemingly requisite sadness, some might say Leon and Jake live *inauthentic* lives. The commercialization of native tradition leaves them in a world resembling little of the intact societies that appear in museum dioramas, old anthropology texts, tourist brochures, or national park exhibits. However, a sentimental mourning for a lost "authenticity" only denies their experience of modernity and perpetually binds their world to a standard of "tradition" reflecting an irrecoverable past. "The cultural other that would occupy the site of 'authentic tradition' would be condemned to a kind of historylessness," argues MacCannell, "a flat existence in which past, present, and future are essentially similar . . . in which everyone lives in the space between two deaths: the death of their culture, now beautifully preserved and presented, and their own physical death."[77] I think of Jake on the rock by the highway, waiting for the tourist with his camera, as standing in the shadow of a mythic Indian cast long ago. Undoubtedly, his picture—the proud warrior solemnly surveying the desert landscape or standing next to some stranger in khaki shorts and sunglasses—rests in the pages of numerous vacation photo albums. The seemingly free and open space of the plateau around him betrays the subtle burdens of tradition he carries. The split-second exposure of his costumed body reveals little of the many decades such images have been absorbed by the longing eyes of tourists.

A National Register of Cultural Memory

Sifting through the Grand Canyon Study Collection's archival photographs one afternoon, I look at the faces of men pulled toward the adventurous myths of the West. Wearing Stetsons and bandannas, pants tucked into high leather boots, they appear as hybrids of Hollywood cowboys and Roosevelt's Rough Riders waiting for something to happen. Among this pile of pictures, I find Katherine Harvey's photo album of a visit to the canyon made sometime between 1900 and 1920. Titled "The Canyon Trip," its brittle pages of snapshots offer a glimpse of how Fred Harvey's granddaughter and her friends indulged the canyon's western fantasy space. Like any photo album, the story of its images rests with its owner who, in this case, is dead. The study collection holds little information about the acquisition. Yet, it is difficult to overlook the outward appearance of the scenes and themes she chose to remember.

Some of the photos capture how the natural world of the canyon translated into a leisure stage dramatizing the imposition of modern civilization. A woman kneels on the brink of the canyon, playing cards fanned out in her hands, as two men look at her. A group takes their lunch on the rocky Hermit Trail. A couple strolls down a wooden boardwalk to the canyon's rim. There are pictures of men racing on horses and pictures of men racing on foot. Other images silently suggest the common laughter of vacation stories about hardships endured there by Harvey and her companions. A woman drinks water from a trough at Indian Gardens. Three men shave in a mirror hanging in a camp. "Early morning proceedings at Hermit Creek," reads a handwritten caption. A man stares into his palm and picks at the skin of his hand. "Port and Gene, cactus troubles," another caption explains. A few pages later, I gaze at Anglo women costumed in Indian headbands and fringed buckskin dresses that apparently inspired them to strike comic poses. One of them leans forward, arms folded across her chest, and looks solemnly into the distance. Another shields her eyes with a flattened hand while her other arm points to something on the far horizon.

Turning the page, I find the most memorable of all these photographs. An Indian boy, perhaps eleven or twelve years old, stands on the canyon's rim. The study collection report notes that he is a Navajo, but the collection administrator, Ed, thinks he is a Hopi. Though no date appeared on the photograph, Ed estimates the year is 1915. In the picture, the boy doesn't look into the camera but to the west, at something out of the frame. His squinting eyes, the sun on his face, and the shadows on the rock suggest that it is afternoon. With a strap slung across his shoulder, he uses both arms and his left leg to manage a weight he carries for someone else.

I never could find out if whacking golf balls off the rim into the Great Abyss was a popular pastime during those years. But I notice the young caddie is grasping the lower shaft of a driver as though ready to pull it from the bag. Although no one is certain about who the boy was or who snapped the photograph, the image offers some evidence of their relationship. At a time when the Harvey Company and the Santa Fe Railway were packaging and promoting a theme-park world on the ruins of centuries-old native traditions, the young caddie was of a generation who would come to know the world through a new set of tourism rituals. I imagine the boy putting down the golf bag and receiving a tip for his efforts, a new Indian Head nickel, one minted about the time this photo was snapped, a profile of Iroquois Chief John Big Tree on one side, a charging buffalo on the other, and the word "Liberty" rising from the coin's shiny surface.[78] Jake and Leon might see an ancestor in the young caddie, one who, from the very start, came to understand his place in a world populated by strangers from the East bearing cameras and money. I realize it is their trail I follow with my own camera.

Looking at the tourists today, I see them wearing Indian turquoise and silver, cowboy hats and bandannas. Grown men and young boys sometimes wear new bolo ties and belt buckles made of copper and cheap silver. Women wear thunderbird earrings and bracelets; some wear beads made from shells. They, too, might look into the faces of the archival photographs of early tourists for ancestral ties. Seeing Katherine Harvey and her friends dressed and posed like Indians only suggested that they lived in a tribe far from the Grand Canyon. Clearly, Harvey's photo album is only a partial glance at a vacation trip whose private meanings escape us. Yet, in different ways, all of her pictures find a meaning that stems from a class who believed the Southwest was, as D. H. Lawrence noted in 1924, "the great playground of the white American."[79] For Lawrence, self-described as a "lone, lorn Englishman tumbled out of the known world of the British empire," the West seemed a strange and confusing theater. "All the wildness and woolliness and westernity and motor cars and art and sage and savages are so mixed up, so incongruous, that it is a farce and everybody knows it," he wrote.[80] Indeed, Harvey's photographs read like a series of performances ironically beckoning toward some audience of family and friends that lay to the east of Grand Canyon. Eastern cities were the places where yearnings for the virtues of the frontier life and the Wild West had been invented and, for at least half a century, seemed most at home.

Of course, not everyone at the canyon—then or now—donned the stereotypical attire of the Southwest. In the archives, plenty of pictures show moderns who seemed to be picked off the streets of Chicago or New York and dropped down on the edge of eternity. In suits and bowlers, dresses and umbrellas, they walked and rode along the rim, looking for (and at) something they could not find in the east. Surely, the spectacle of the canyon might have been enough for their eyes. Given the elaborate

descriptions of the Harvey and the Santa Fe advertising men, however, the canyon was much more. It was a place that captured a mood of modern discontentment, uncertainty, and yearnings for tradition with promises for a genuine western experience, a therapeutic salve of nature and physical fitness, and a nostalgic theater where the images of the past fortified faith in contemporary progressive ideals.

The plaques attached to Whittelsey's El Tovar, Colter's Hopi House, The Watchtower, and several more of her Grand Canyon buildings indicate that these structures are listed on the National Register of Historic Places. I suppose such designations are appropriate, more so if they help us remember that from their inception, the buildings were designed to be historic places. Ironically, they are in many ways buildings of an abandoned historical narrative, emptied of past conflicts and politics that still bear on the present. What they preserve today is an early twentieth-century cultural history of progressive and nostalgic impulses materialized in a western leisure landscape that became less and less remote. More than anything, the buildings register the dreams and visions of restless easterners who spent their leisure days soaking up romantic memories. "Easterners, . . . despite their enthusiasm for progress in general, did not want the West to change," observes Kammen. "They hoped that somehow it could remain an 'oversized museum' for nature lovers and historically minded individuals."[81] In a region where, until the late 1800s, Indians were viewed as a threatening obstacle, tourists rode in the comfort of Santa Fe trains named *The Navajo* and *The Super Chief*. At the Grand Canyon, they could gaze on the scenes of commercially produced past and strike a pose as if they were at home in its polished surface of history.

Sitting in the Bright Angel cocktail lounge, I hear the whistle of the historic Grand Canyon Railway train calling passengers for the sixty-five-mile return trip to Williams. The steam train, like a ghost ship wandering the same sea, begins pounding the waves of time every afternoon at four. A weary young couple gets up to leave. The man gulps what is left in a beer glass while his companion pulls an Instamatic from her pocketbook and puts away the postcards she's been writing. I think they're relieved to be advancing toward their air-conditioned cars and motel rooms. But fifteen miles out of Williams, the train will suddenly stop, and they'll again meet up with Two Feathers and his pseudo-cowboy gang. This time, they'll be dressed as bandits, robbing the tourist train as they do every afternoon on its return run.

Except for me and a bartender rinsing glasses between pulls on a cigarette, the lounge is empty. Suspended beneath the bar's golden shellac surface, I find photographs and souvenirs of earlier days at the canyon—John Burroughs, John Muir, old Fred Harvey postcards, rusty horseshoes, and bent shoe nails. There is a picture of Fred Harvey, too. Confidently posed in a tailored suit and sporting a distinguished goatee, he is the quintessential entrepreneur of the Gilded Age. His eyes look out from the 1880s toward some future space beyond the photographer's lens. Such portraits pursued the vanity of timelessness which, in other ways, Harvey achieved here at the canyon. I can't help but wonder if he could have envisioned, on the day that picture was made, the head of the jackalope (a surreal concoction of a taxidermist who attaches deer antlers to the head of a desert hare) hanging on the wall above the taps for Heineken, Michelob, Samuel Adams, and Budweiser. Fred Harvey died in February 1901, seven months before the first train carried passengers to the Grand Canyon, and saw little of the canyon developments still bearing his name. But the empty lounge, filled only with sounds of a jukebox randomly shuffling through songs, might have left him uneasy.

On the lounge walls, murals painted by Fred Kabotie in 1958 silently render a common life of native culture found in the old pueblos. In Kabotie's panorama of a lost era, women weave rugs, men haul corn, two natives bargain over a rug while a woman watches their dealing. The middle panel shows the center of a plaza, where villagers dance frantically in a circle. A group of masked kachina dancers are entering in the background. Another panel shows a women load a pan of dough into a clay oven. From where I sit, she appears to be loading the bread into the top of the jukebox. On the opposite wall, across the rows of tables, Kabotie painted a panel showing another plaza, the one right outside the Bright Angel Lodge, which overlooks the Grand Canyon. In this scene, a man studies a map while a woman drinks a soda. Another man sleeps in a chair while his wife scans the canyon with binoculars. A young woman films the scene with a home-movie camera while her husband looks at the scenery. Two lovers lounging in chairs have turned away from the canyon and stare into each other's eyes. A park ranger points out a distant sight to a cute pony-tailed woman wearing tight shorts and a sleeveless midriff. Behind them, a family of three strolls toward the plaza. The father slings a camera tripod over his shoulder like a lumberjack carrying an axe. I see an Indian wearing a red shirt, red bandanna, and brown pants. Perhaps this is the artist, Kabotie, taking in the scene he is going to paint in this lounge.

The murals, commissioned by Byron Harvey Jr., were the last works Kabotie painted for the Harvey Company. Seeing them today, covered with protective glass, I find a familiar formula where the present is held up for comparison with the imagined serenity of the past. Obviously, the arrival of Spanish soldiers, the conquest of the pueblos, and the Grand Canyon before tourism are absent from the painted panels. After all, a bar is sometimes a festive place, and Kabotie's tourists are fittingly comic. Kabotie saw many of the changes brought by tourism as he moved between the canyon and his own Hopi homeland. It's appropriate that his final paintings at the canyon would recognize those transformations, although he, too, seemed seduced by the glow of sentiment. Across from panels depicting native people oriented around a communal life of work, ritual, trade, and farming, Kabotie's painted tourists look tired, anxious, and disinterested. Wandering in from different directions, they circle the plaza wall; strangers in their own orbits around a common spectacle. I cannot know if Kabotie intended any of what I see when he painted these walls in the late 1950s, but his scene becomes a living tableau every summer afternoon outside the Bright Angel Lodge. On the plaza now, in fact, people are aiming their cameras and studying the depths of the great geological clock; the spectacle changes so slowly it feels timeless. Only the slow shadows, stretching behind its buttes and temples, mark the movement of a day. What landscape could better sanction the building of a nostalgic theater but a place where, under the heat of the summer sun, people have been busily at work trying to freeze time.

In the lounge, the bartender, having finished washing bar glasses and restocking the cooler with beer, stares off into the drifting smoke of her cigarette. The dinner crowd will be arriving soon, and some will wait in the lounge until a table is ready. For now, the place is calm. The jukebox has shuffled to a live recording of Janis Joplin's "Ball and Chain" while I have been writing notes about Kabotie's murals. Near the end of the song, I notice that the Full Tilt Boogie Band has stopped playing and Joplin is ranting to her audience. "Honey, when everybody in the world wants the same damn thing," she screeches, "when everybody in the world needs the same lonely thing . . ." She launches into a scattered speech about desire and living for the moment, and I listen closely to all of her plaintive wailing. By the end of her speech, I'm thinking she's talking to me, telling me the time of this tourist world. "If you got it today, you don't wear it tomorrow . . . , cause you don't need it," she says. "'Cause as a matter of fact, as we discovered on the train, tomorrow never happens, man, it's all the same fuckin' day."

2

A Cultural Abyss

Walking the paved Rim Trail west of the Yavapai Point museum, I follow a National Park Service interpreter and a group of about twenty visitors from New Mexico, California, New Jersey, Oklahoma, Florida, Washington, Greece, Singapore, Switzerland, Taiwan, and Germany. This one-and-a-half hour guided walk is called the "Awesome Chasm," and according to the *Guide* (an information newspaper published by the Grand Canyon Natural History Association), it will help us discover "the Canyon's true magnificence." Ranger Karen, our leader, has written out a series of statistics and analogies on index cards. This information is designed to relate the canyon to "some of our own personal experiences," she says, and at several stops along the rim we will take turns reading the cards to others in our group. Before we begin, she gives us a few tips on public speaking and how to "talk like a ranger."

"I want you to read with a big voice. Stand so you face most of the people," Karen tells us. "Take a deep breath, bring that air from your diaphragm, and then emphasize the important words." The recitations begin with some basic measurements: The average viewing distance from the rim to river is 3 miles. You can't see more than 25 percent of the canyon from the developed view points. The canyon averages 10 miles across, 1 mile deep, and is more than 277 river miles long. For the most part, our group does a good job of reading with "big ranger voices." But Karen tends to repeat the information after it's read off the card. Occasionally, she'll quiz us on what we've just heard.

"Got that? How deep is it?" she asks.

"A mile," we say, in unison like elementary-school students.

"How wide is it?" asks Karen.

"Ten miles," repeat a few people in our group.

"How long is it?" she says.

"Two-twenty-seven," says one reluctant voice.

"Got it," affirms Karen, and turns to a boy who hasn't been listening. "Don't throw rocks, there's a trail right underneath us." We move on to a set of analogies intended to put the canyon's dimensions in more concrete terms.

"Before the Glen Canyon Dam was built upstream, the Colorado River carried an average sediment load of five hundred thousand tons per day," reads a man wearing a Los Angeles Lakers hat. "This is equal to one hundred thousand five-ton dump trucks going less than a second apart." I'm not the only one whose eyes appear a bit glazed trying to understand this.

"That's a lot of dirt," says the ranger. "Now it averages about eighty thousand tons a day, but I don't know how many dump trucks that is." As others read, we learn that the Colorado River is as wide as the length of a football field. We could stack ten Washington monuments on top of each other to equal the distance from the rim to the river. The state of Rhode Island could easily fit inside the canyon. And it would take eight Golden Gate Bridges to span the distance from rim to rim. The image of Rhode Island dropping from the sky into the canyon with room to spare, and crushing a fleet of bumper-to-bumper dump trucks, transforms the canyon into a reel of cartoons. Our efforts this afternoon caricature the mapping and surveying expeditions carried out in the American West, including the Grand Canyon, following the Civil War. Like the surveys that paved the way for the U.S. military, railroad companies, land developers and settlers, our tour is, in a different way, taming and transforming the canyon into a *social* space. Gathering here and there along the rim, with our index cards as blueprints, our voices erect observation towers of language that order the canyon's impossible emptiness. From the perch of analogy, we throw anything into the abyss—monuments, bridges, trucks, football fields, Rhode Island, nearly twice the population of the planet, ice cream—all in search of more familiar though some times slippery footing.

"In one sense, such statistics are tourist trivia, similar in their appeal to the weight of the fat lady at the circus," notes John Sears in his study of nineteenth-century tourist attractions. "More significantly, they function, paradoxically, both as a means of bringing extraordinary phenomena within a rational framework and of certifying that tourists are in the presence of something which transcends their familiar world."[1] On this tour, that paradox takes the fantastic form of reconciling the canyon's magnitude with the terms of everyday life. Gigantic images are figures on "the interface between the natural and the human," says Susan Stewart, and culturally function as a space for social and bodily projections.[2] But unlike legendary images of gigantic landscapes holding mysterious and supernatural powers, this narrative domesticates the canyon. Reading Karen's index-card passages, we recite coordinates of space and time that socially produce the canyon as a text of measurement, science, consumption, technology, nationalism, and the property lines of daily life. Although billed as an occasion for education or discovery, the tour is a performance of our relationship to nature, one in which the disorder and extreme proportions of the canyon serve to magnify the dimensions of our lives. Throughout the tour, we've been hovering over the canyon, suspended by scientific authority, and drifting on everyday metaphors and analogies provided by the ranger. Nearing the end, she moves us down the trail toward one final group reading.

"I have an analogy here to bring this all into focus," says Karen, passing out our lines. This set of cards is numbered, and we must read them in order. "I'll read the first and last cards," and she begins. "Imagine a seven-volume set of average size books, each containing roughly two hundred pages. Let each book represent six hundred million years of geological time." She finishes and reiterates what she has just read to us. "So get this in your head now, we've got a seven-volume set, two hundred pages each, each book represents six hundred million years. Okay, number two," she says, and a man reads to pick up where the ranger left off.

"At the start of volume one, Earth was formed. Sometime early in volume three, the first life stirred on the planet," says Number Two.

"We've already jumped up to volume three before we get any life," adds the ranger emphatically. A few people glance around the crowd, looking for the next card holder.

"In volume five, the ancient rocks now exposed at the very bottom of the Grand Canyon were formed," reads a woman with a shaky voice.

"Volume five, we're already up to volume five!" spouts Karen.

A young boy tells us, "A little more than halfway through the last book, volume seven, the rocks on the rim of the Grand Canyon are laid down." His mother pats him on the shoulders for doing a good job.

"Get that?" says Karen. "Halfway through our last book, volume seven, the rocks at the rim are laid down." It's my turn to read.

"About three quarters of the way through volume seven, about page 150, the sandstone strata at Zion were formed," I say. As soon as I finish, I hear the next voice quickly tell us the rocks found in southern Utah's Bryce Canyon were formed on page 180 of volume seven.

"By the top of the last page of the last book, the first apelike hominids had appeared," says a heavy man who seems to have trouble with the altitude.

"Last page of the last book, okay?" Karen reminds us, marking our place in the imaginary stack of books we've been describing to each other.

"Modern man, however, didn't evolve until the beginning of the last line, of the last page, of the last book, nearly a hundred thousand years ago," a man from Oklahoma tells us.

"*A hun-dred thou-sand yeeears,*" says Karen, before reading the last card to wrap all of this up. "And because each single letter in our books represents about fifteen hundred years, all of recorded history is contained in the last three characters of the *very last sentence.*" She pauses, then solemnly echoes, "All of human history." We stand quiet and still on the canyon's edge. If this is true, the time these vacationers spend at the Grand Canyon won't amount to a speck of ink. A few people fall away from the group and look out into the walls of the abyss as if searching for the value of the analogy we've just gone through. Karen collects the index cards and breaks the quiet by reading the words of Mrs. Mary E. Hart, a Los Angeles physician who signed a canyon guestbook on June 5, 1895.

"There is a certain malady, commonly termed 'Big Head,' with which a large number of otherwise healthy people are afflicted," reads Karen. "Prescription: Stand upon the brink of the Grand Canyon, gaze down and still farther down into its awful depths and realize for the first time your own utter insignificance." We say nothing. Karen's call for humility is a bit hard to muster, considering we've just been able to collapse all of earth's history into a handy analogy. It is we, after all, who stand on the last page telling ourselves this story of the earth's origins and all of recorded time. Now, we are asked to acknowledge we don't amount to a whole sentence. Perhaps it only suggests how geology provides the authority to survey a world in which we have no sense of place. I watch a man climb a boulder a few yards away. He throws out his arms like wings to keep balance, then snaps a picture of our group "insignificantly" gathered on the Big Period, that imaginary punctuation mark closing the last sentence on the final rocky page of The Great Stone Book Stack.

Standing on the edge, reading these passages, laying claim to the wide expanses of earth history and human knowledge, our group renewed an image of the Grand Canyon historically embedded in its landscape. The idea of stone pages recording the history of the earth may help simplify the abstractions of geologic time for this group of tourists, but it is also an occasion to recover a view of the canyon as a textual production in operation for more than a century. Indexing millions of geologic years from the rim, our group echoed the voices of those who have been reading and writing the canyon's walls since 1869.

The "abyss" has been an enduring symbol that marks a cosmogonic site of intellectual challenge, spiritual profundity, and existential gravity and weightlessness. The Grand Canyon has been all of these to people since John Wesley Powell followed the Colorado River into what he called the "Great Unknown." Since that time, the canyon has been a symbolic space cleaved between distanced, scientific interpretations of nature that claim objectivity and control, and spiritual longings for answers to questions over one's place in nature and the cosmos. Today's "Awesome Chasm" tour, emphasizing geologic measurements and explanations, attests to a scientific gaze deeply encrusted in public interpretations of Grand Canyon. However, like the geologic strata exposed in the canyon's walls, the stacked volume analogy of the "Awesome Chasm" tour reveals many layers of meaning. As with any formation (geological, textual, historical, cultural), it has fault lines, cracks, and cleavages marking shifts, changes, and transformations. The uneven walls of the Grand Canyon are but a physical metaphor for the discursive discontinuities and changing meanings that, historically, have continually remade the natural world into a cultural contest between science and spirituality.

Interpreting the Grand Canyon has meant confronting broader cultural and historical divisions between rational and spiritual ways of seeing, knowing, and believing. These divisions were, in part, indicative of America's progressive age at the end of the nineteenth century. The growing importance of geology, natural science, and evolutionary theories rocked traditional religious foundations, and in different ways, the tensions between them have vibrated in the Grand Canyon from the first scientific expedition down the Colorado through today's institutionalized park interpretation programs. Seeing the canyon as a magnificent textbook of geology or a shrine of spiritual exhilaration and practiced humility belies a history of unresolved conflicts over creation, origins, and enduring questions of one's place in the world. These conflicts and questions appear in a wide range of narratives that have figuratively and material-ly mapped the canyon. The texts of scientific explorers, geologists, surveyors, guide-book authors, artists, tourism promoters, spiritual leaders, clergy, and the accounts of nineteenth- and twentieth-century tourists all reveal how the landscape has been a palimpsest of American culture. The Grand Canyon is a cultural icon and tourist landscape of sedimented meanings and ambiguities, and like most stories of creation, its genesis is a textual terrain of many passages that begins and ends in the word.

The Mythic Adventure of Natural Science

Before 1869, the Grand Canyon appeared as empty space on government maps of what is now known as the Colorado Plateau. At the time, the Colorado was the only un-navigated and unmapped river system remaining in the country. Reports of trappers and military expeditions approaching the Grand Canyon area from the east and the west provided vague accounts of an impassable canyon, dangerous rapids, and legends of the Colorado River disappearing underground for miles. That year, Major Powell, a thirty five-year-old, one-armed Civil War veteran and self-taught naturalist, led the first scientific expedition through the Grand Canyon. Numerous historians have called his famous 1869 survey expedition the last great exploration into a little-known region of the United States.[3] In four specially designed wooden boats, Powell and a crew of nine men left Green River, Wyoming, on May 24, 1869, with the financial backing of little more than a thousand dollars donated by the Illinois Natural History Society and the Illinois Industrial University, and with scientific instruments donated by the Chicago Academy of Sciences and the Smithsonian Institution. Congress authorized Powell and his crew to draw rations from western army outposts, and the expedition set out to study the canyon's geology, collect samples, and chart the unknown river. The three-month, thousand-mile journey caught the attention of the public through Chicago and New York newspaper accounts (which, in July, falsely reported the party met their deaths) drawn from (sometimes unreliable) witnesses and through letters sent from Powell via outposts along the way. What began as a meager scientific survey soon became a struggle for survival. A lost boat, depleted provisions, an early departure of one crew member, and the loss later of three more men offered the makings of an ex-citing story that Powell took to the lecture circuit as a national hero.

Two years later, Powell took another crew—this time with more funding, equip-ment, scientists, and a photographer—down the Colorado to continue his study of the region. His government report on the Colorado and its tributaries, published in 1875, combined the events of the first expedition with the second and reads more like an adventure story than a scientific survey. First appearing as a series of popular arti-cles by Powell in *Scribner's Monthly,* the report included a series of engravings by Thomas Moran, who traveled with Powell's survey on the canyon's North Rim in the 1870s. The articles brought the canyon's landscape to public attention and enlarged Powell's public image as a scientist-adventurer. Read in the context of today's Grand

Canyon visitor, Powell's expedition offers a starting point for understanding the scientific gaze that looks out over the park's tourist landscape. As Powell and crew floated between the canyon's walls, placing names on landmarks and rivers that still hold, their accounts formed a cultural allegory of men riding the currents of shifting philosophical attitudes toward the natural world. Their story dramatically superimposes the mythic adventure epic onto the scientific expedition and captures the declining authority of religion and the growing authority of science.

In a famous passage from his account of the first expedition, Powell and his men prepare to enter the Grand Canyon's inner gorge. With rations severely depleted and boats so battered by rapids and rocks they needed repairs almost daily, they stand on the rocky shore of the Colorado River. "We are now ready to start our way down the Great Unknown. Our boats, tied to a common stake, are chafing each other, as they are tossed by the fretful river," wrote Powell. "We are three-quarters of a mile in the depths of the earth, and the great river shrinks into insignificance, as it dashes its angry waves against the walls and cliffs, that rise to the world above; . . . We have an unknown distance yet to run; an unknown river yet to explore. What falls there, we know not; what rocks beset the channel, we know not; what walls rise over the river, we know not. Ah, well! we may conjecture many things."[4]

Powell didn't write these words in August 1869 while sitting in shadows on the rocky banks of the Colorado. They came to him instead a few years later, and as Wallace Stegner notes, Powell was either "unconscious of the growing sullenness among the men, or for literary effect, writing at a later time, he suppressed that detail."[5] He had long dreamed of exploring the Colorado, and despite his party's grumblings about quitting, he appears throughout the account as a man of unwavering determination. Powell needed to follow the river to the end, and his narrative captures the mood of an ancient epic adventure tale. While he and his crew stood waiting to risk their lives at the brink of the Great Unknown, Powell presents himself as a nineteenth-century Dante: nothing "could drive out of my mind the lust to experience the far-flung world."[6] Below the earth's surface, canyon walls surrounding them, they stand on nothing less than a supernatural stage, where he and his men will encounter uncertain obstacles of fate. "Between the adventurer and his goal, there is only distance to be traveled," writes Paul Zweig in his study of adventure narratives. "The loftiness of the gods, the prodigious magic of unknown races, the fields of blessed isles and the shadow beings of Hades, the aura of beginnings and the desolation of endings: all are enmeshed in the vast contemporaneity of the cosmos." Yet, in the face of it all, "the adventurer's most serious obstacle is himself," says Zweig. "The world extends before him like a fabulous text. Only his ability to 'read' it is in doubt."[7]

For Powell to embody the heroic adventurer, reading the canyon as the Great Unknown also meant writing himself into a landscape modeled on mythic epics. The one-armed warrior, a weary crew at his command, voyaging through a dark abyss in a boat named after his wife, was bound to a classical lineage of men who only became unshakable adventurers through a head-on confrontation with trouble, risk, and uncertainty, and then survived to tell their tale. Yet, Powell's story played out in a landscape where battling a fearful Cyclops or an ascent from Hades had been replaced by quests, literally, of a different nature. The sword and crossbow appeared now as a sextant and barometer, and the timeless wanderings of the mythic voyage were guided by a geologic imagination charting millions of years. Perhaps what Powell most shared with the ancient adventurer was a search for origins, and in the canyon's walls, he found a "fabulous text" full of promising clues. The struggle and endurance required to explore the canyon's forbidding terrain become, for the nineteenth-century man of science and philosophy, an exegetical adventure.

"All about me are interesting geological records," wrote a rain-soaked Powell, recounting an August day when he climbed above the marble of the inner gorge. "The book is open, and I can read as I run," but his enthusiasm was plagued by worries of dwindling rations, rain, and the difficult river. "The lesson of the rocks, and the glory of the scene is but half seen," he noted.[8] In other entries and under better conditions, he commented with great hope about the possibilities for the secrets he sensed waiting in the geologic text. "One might imagine that this was intended for the library of the gods; and it was," he said, describing the canyon's stratified walls. "The shelves are not for books, but form the stony leaves of one great book. He who would read the language of the universe may dig out letters here and there and with them spell the words, and read, in a slow and imperfect way, but still so as to understand a little, the story of creation."[9]

The son of a Methodist minister who refused to follow in his father's footsteps, Powell instead chose a secular path of scientific inquiry. His blend of scientific observation with biblical creationism reflected the ideals of many mid-nineteenth century philosophers who valued empirical observation for the evidence of God it could supply. "Relations between science and religion were cordial, since it was taken for granted that the findings of natural scientists would reinforce the revelations of Scripture," notes American intellectual historian Cynthia Eagle Russett. "Transcendentalists similarly looked to nature to provide them with a symbolic incarnation of divinity."[10] Powell, and men like him, looked at nature for clues to the order and origins of earth history. Although he may have characterized a harmonious meeting of science and religion as "one great book," his impressions came from two very different cultural maps that many mid-nineteenth century philosophers and ministers had been trying to reconcile since Darwinian ideas reached American shores in 1860. The geologic record of places like the Grand Canyon challenged Powell's generation's "ability to read" the text of nature in the hope of resolving deep struggles over certainty and doubt in the late nineteenth century.

Jack Sumner, one of Powell's crew on the expedition, drew the lines of scientific and spiritual debate more bluntly in one of his accounts. If anything could be true, "geology is true," wrote Sumner, and the "testimony of the rocks cannot be impeached.

I think Moses must be mistaken in his chronology as recorded in Biblical history." The entire length of their journey, from Green River, Wyoming, to the Virgin River below the canyon, was "one continuous geological book," Sumner said. "You can turn leaf after leaf from the Quatenary to the Archean. Whoever can read it is a master for sure."[11] Before he joined the expedition, Sumner was a mountaineer who operated a trading post and, like Powell, a self-taught naturalist. Although he didn't have the educational background to read the geologic record with any specificity, Sumner voiced in simple terms a fearful conclusion geologists had uncomfortably been reaching since the Enlightenment: The books of the Old Testament, their stories of creation, destruction, Moses, and the Great Flood, were an inaccurate account of the earth's origins. Generations had been looking at the wrong book for a cosmography.

In the geologic record, scientists classified time in millions rather than thousands of years. In the early nineteenth century, many geologists heretically challenged the idea of creation by claiming that the forces of nature could be viewed in the world people presently occupied. Sedimented rock, erosion, volcanoes, and glaciers "linked the visible natural forces to the invisible abysses of time, the present to the past," notes historian Eric Leed. "The accuracy of biblical chronologies was irrevocably discredited," and this "shattered the Christian notion of time as a moral journey narrating the story of salvation and damnation." Divine acts of creation and destruction "which bracketed human history as a moral progress or a corruption" were lost to a science that found empirical evidence carved in stone.[12] In the 1830s, Charles Lyell's *Principles of Geology* rejected "catastrophic" theories that claimed the earth was in a period of stabilization after a time of great earthquakes and floods. Instead, Lyell proposed a more orderly and structured understanding of gradual geologic change. Lyell viewed incremental changes in the earth's constitution—a minor shift in the rock, a landslide, an erosive stream, and a receding ocean, rather than great catastrophes rupturing the earth—as accounting for the lay of the land over millions of years.

Apart from Lyell's specific scientific propositions, he and other geologists offered evidence for their ideas in the landscape. Geology empirically dislodged the authority of scriptural accounts with the rational and imaginative eye of the scientific observer. "The world of forms which the geologist inhabits, the slow phantasmagoria of oceans and continents interchanging, rising and falling as if earth were waves," suggests literary critic Gillian Beer, "makes for a tranquil elemental view of the universe in which time implies an extended scale of existence beyond the span of our minds."[13] As an imaginative science, geology conceptualized a vision of a world in which man was not present but could see evidence of that world nonetheless. Undoubtedly, this is the image Jack Sumner had in mind when he said whoever could read the great geological book "is a master for sure." Confidently reading the earth for clues of movements and shifts, the geologist saw for himself what generations had believed only God could have seen. This, of course, was the baton geologists passed on to theorists and natural scientists like Herbert Spencer and Charles Darwin, who found in Lyell's *Geology* a framework for a study of human origins and left the pages of nineteenth-century Bibles fluttering in their wake.

Spencer's unified theory of cosmic evolution and Darwin's ideas of biological determinism confused the century's "hard-won affirmation of moral freedom," leveled traditional religious reliance "on the works of nature as evidence of the hand of God," and cracked "the transcendentalists conduit of divinity," argues Russett. "The serene cosmic pattern was replaced by the blind movement of mindless forces eternally sifting and shaping all living things, men as well as the lowliest mollusk, toward ends unperceived and perhaps nonexistent."[14] Nineteenth-century theologians set out to reconcile the growing popularity of Spencer and Darwin with renewed energy for scriptural interpretation. The incongruous worldviews were joined in a seam of "evolutionary theology" that sought to mend the social and moral fabric of a spirituality torn by science. "The Holy Scriptures were given to reveal moral and spiritual truth," wrote Presbyterian reverend James H. McIlvaine in 1877, "and it was no part of their object to the truths of science, upon which consequently, they are no authority."[15] Evolutionary theology meant a nonliteral reading of Scripture and redistributing the intellectual domain of the minister and scientist. Rather than rule over the world like a cosmic king, God existed closer to humans as an inherently creative presence on earth. "God is the one Resident Force, that He is in His world; that His method of work in His world is the method of growth," claimed Congregationalist minister Lyman Abbott in 1897, "and that the history of the world . . . is the history of a growth in accordance with the great law interpreted and uttered in that one word evolution."[16]

For the most part, Powell believed the principles of evolutionists, and he assumed a record of human history lay waiting "on the leaves of the book of rocks."[17] Yet, he could not entirely swallow the notion of mindless chaotic forces indifferent to humans, plants, and animals. Nature may be full of chaos, but man had choice, energy, and dreams of order. "Man, so far as he is superior to the beast, is the master of his own destiny. He adapts the natural environment to his wants, and thus creates an environment for himself," Powell told an 1883 American Philosophy Society meeting. "By his arts, institutions, languages, and philosophies he has organized a new kingdom of matter over which he rules. The beasts of the field, the birds of the air, the denizens of the waters, the winds, the waves, the rivers, the seas, the mountains, the valleys, are his subjects; the powers of nature are his servants, and the granite earth his throne."[18] By the time Powell had spoken those words, he had, among other things, led a second expedition down the Colorado River and been appointed both director of the U.S. Geological Survey and of the Smithsonian Bureau of Ethnology. In those positions, "Powell had in his control a good part of the Science of Man and the Science of the Earth, and he envisioned both in the broadest possible terms," notes Stegner. Since his boyhood years in Wisconsin, Powell had collected specimens and assembled museums; a "curator was precisely what Major Powell wanted to be."[19] At the helm of two Washington bureaus, his consistent impulse to collect and classify—

to realize and materialize a dream of order—was at the core of his life. As specified in his will, when Powell died in 1902, his brain was donated to the Smithsonian, where it remains today, soaking in the preservative of a specimen jar. To the Grand Canyon, Powell had already left his eyes.

Powell didn't invent the idea of a "geological text," but he was the first man to inscribe a geological order on the canyon's walls. With his obsessive interest in mapping the Colorado Plateau, Powell was carried by the intellectual currents of his times. His expeditions of 1869 and 1871–1872 were part of a more extensive exploration that became known as the "Powell survey," which involved numerous other scientists, photographers, and artists who helped establish a deep imprint of the Grand Canyon in American minds. To this day, Powell's legacy and his vision of natural science are cemented in the canyon's landscape. In 1918, a plaque attached to a stone monument dedicated Powell Memorial Point on the South Rim. With his image engraved in bronze, the moving shadows of his memorial daily survey the "granite throne" over which Powell believed man could rule. The marker, however, only formally recognized an already well-established way of seeing the Grand Canyon. Nearly every travel account and guidebook from the late nineteenth century onward retrieves the rational and ordered essence of Powell's initial gaze. In 1908, Charles Holder asked *Country Life in America* readers how one should look at the Grand Canyon. "I would be a geologist when I stand on the edge of this abyss eternal," said Holder, answering his own question. "Some poetic, artistic, color-loving student of geology, such as Powell, who combined all these graces with the nerve of the true man who followed the great gulch from beginning to end."[20] More than a decade later, a U.S. Railroad Administration guide to Grand Canyon underlined Holder's homage to Powell by simply stating, "Not only was he a pioneer, but his daring was for the sake of scientific knowledge."[21] Others who followed Powell, assigned by him to survey the Colorado Plateau, would amplify and expand upon his geological theories of the canyon region and create detailed maps that name buttes, monuments, rivers, and side canyons. But it is the image of an adventuring scientific explorer most often remembered today at the canyon.

Tonight, a one-armed Powell paces and barks, coat sleeve dangling, beneath the stage lights at the Shrine of the Ages next to the visitor center. Three evenings each week during the summer months, he appears here for an hour, portrayed by Earll Kingston, an actor and writer from Berkeley who performs alone in a production entitled "Down the Great Unknown." In a two-act monologue, Kingston resurrects the Powell who had become thoroughly ensconced in his role as director of the Geological Survey. The scene is the antechamber of a Los Angeles convention hall, where he is about to address the International Irrigation Congress on the night of October 10, 1893. Arriving onstage, he carries a rolled-up map of the West. He talks to himself, complaining of the madness in plans to irrigate the entire "Arid Region" and pours himself a glass of water from a pitcher. Turning to the audience, he's startled to see us here.

"Oh, my dear friends. I am so very glad to see you and so very embarrassed that you should see me in this agitated state," says the major. "Do forgive me. I have not forgotten my promise to tell you the story of the '69 expedition." It is to Kingston's credit that he reminds the audience of the life Powell led beyond his voyages down the Colorado. The explorer before us is now approaching sixty years of age, an outspoken advocate of responsible irrigation and land use in the West. Powell's warning to the meeting that night will be simply that "there is not sufficient water to supply the land."[22] It was a vision that has, to this day, largely been ignored. Yet, the story Kingston tells quickly turns away from the politics of irrigation and back to the drama of the adventurer who conquers the canyon. This is what the audience has come to hear. Waiting for the performance to begin, a man from San Diego told me that he and his eleven-year-old son would float the Colorado River tomorrow with a commercial rafting company. He had just booked the tour at the Bright Angel Hotel desk and was happy to get on, thanks to a cancellation.

"I thought he'd like seeing this before we go. He's gettin' into scouting right now and we've been on a campout," said the father. "We're only going for a day, but they say it's a good trip and they give you lunch. It'll be good for him to get this history." I noticed both of them were wearing new hiking boots. Watching Kingston portray Powell tonight may, in fact, give them a model of the wild explorer they can recall tomorrow while sitting, bound in lifejackets, on the pontoons of a huge inflatable raft. The story Kingston tells *is* one of adventure. It is a tale of men dangling from cliffs, battling rapids, collecting fossils, fending off starvation, and returning to civilization only to do it all again. All of this in the name of scientific discovery. When he is finished recounting his first expedition, Powell returns to the immediate purpose of his speech. We hear the sound of a knock on a door out of our view. "Time, Major Powell," says a voice offstage, and the major is ready to make his exit.

"Time, indeed! I shall not need the map, my friends," he tells us. "Keep it to remember me by, if you will, and let your children study it, study it well. Remind them that however they should define this wondrous land, nature too has a definition, and we must heed Hers, for willy-nilly, she will have her way. And I, tonight, shall have mine! Down the river then, and damn the rapids!" And, with that, Powell marches off into the Irrigation Congress to face an audience we hear murmuring offstage. Although the performance has ended, Powell will ultimately abandon his prepared speech, and after telling the Los Angeles audience that there isn't enough water to irrigate the arid western desert, he will get booed from the stage. Our audience, however, enthusiastically applauds the performance. As we leave the Shrine of the Ages, Kingston stands at the door to greet us. His jacket is off now, and two healthy arms extend to shake our hands. The father and son take their turn and say something about their raft trip to Kingston, but all I hear is Powell's hearty laugh. I cannot say what history lesson they take away tonight; maybe Powell's image will accompany them tomorrow on the Colorado. Throughout the summer, Powell will tell other canyon visitors to "keep the map" in remembrance of him.

When the major addressed the Irrigation Congress, his name and voyage through the canyon was already a staple in tourist guidebooks. For any visitor, it would be nearly impossible to look into the canyon's landscape without at least acknowledging some aspect of the geological vision first written down by Powell. "The [geologist's] theory is fortified by many evidences supplied by examination of the district, where, more than anywhere else, mother earth has laid bare the secrets of her girlhood," wrote Charles Higgins in an 1893 guide published by the Santa Fe Railway. "The layman is apt to stigmatize such an assertion as a vagary of theorists, and until the argument has been heard it does seem incredible that water should have carved such a trough through solid rock."[23] In one form or another, geological explanations; cross-section diagrams of the canyon's layers, geologic eras, and names; and depths and ages of limestone, sandstone, shale, and granite formations appear in a multitude of popular publications describing the Grand Canyon. Today, the majority of the National Park Service's interpretive programs focus on the region's geology, archaeology, and paleontology—all beckoning back to the objectives Powell had in mind when he first launched his boats in Green River, Wyoming. The signs in park hotels, restrooms, and campgrounds on the South Rim pleading with visitors to conserve water serve as one reminder of Powell's vision of the "Arid Region." There is not a natural water supply on the South Rim; it must be piped across the canyon from Roaring Springs just below the North Rim.

However, I find a more subtle reminder of Powell daily in the visitor center, where children pick up copies of the *Young Adventurer,* an eight-page information sheet that contains exercises like the "Fossil Match-Up," "Fossil Detective," and "Forest Scavenger Hunt." All are introductions to the adventure of scientific exploration at the canyon. "Tell your own story about the Anasazi Indians who lived in the Grand Canyon 1,000 years ago," read the instructions above nine drawings for an exercise called "Story Squares." "Use the events in these squares, in any order, to make up your story," continue the instructions. "Use all of the squares. You may tell your story out loud, or write it on paper."[24] On the back page of the *Young Adventurer,* I find a set of activities, "How to Become a Junior Ranger," which ask children to fill a bag with litter, to join a park ranger on a guided walk, and depending on their age, complete one or more of the other exercises listed in the publication. When they have accomplished this, a ranger in the visitor center lobby will announce over the public address system: "Ladies and Gentlemen, can I have your attention? This is Stephanie, and she has successfully completed the activities required to make her a Junior Ranger at Grand Canyon National Park." The child is then awarded a Junior Ranger certificate, and the tourists milling about the visitor center usually applaud. Keep the map "to remember me by," Powell's ghost tells the audience in the Shrine of the Ages, "let your children study it, study it well. Remind them that however they should define this wondrous land, nature too has a definition." And as the children put their pencils to the exercises in the *Young Adventurer* and tourists retell the story of stacked volumes on Ranger Karen's "Awesome Chasm" walk, their definitions of nature come to resemble those of Powell, reproduced continuously in these and other texts that hark back to the great stone book the adventurer first began to read and write in the summer of 1869.

The Scene of Split Vision

Unlike many contemporary scientific reports with elusive equations, specialized jargon, and arcane methodologies, nineteenth-century scientists often employed a language that most educated readers found accessible. Scientific writers engaged philosophic questions with a poetic and metaphoric tone, identifying more closely with literary prose than the insular language of today's scientific journals. For many readers, geology came to assume a kind of mythic status for cosmological explanation. With the growing authority of natural science at the turn of the century, Sears argues, geology "seemed most capable of yielding conclusions about the ultimate nature of the universe."[25] The ordered and rational vision of natural science typified in the geological record was both humbling and empowering. Rather than envisioning humans as a transitory presence in an eternally transforming physical world full of struggling species, the natural world was a domain to be conquered by expeditions and ruled by intellect and reason. However, the grand narratives of geology and evolution did not erase the residues of older romantic ideas about nature for the educated elites traveling to places like Grand Canyon.

Enticing as its power may be, natural science did not offer the romantic views that nature had conjured since the late eighteenth century. Romantics found that nature stirred "feelings of awe before the greatness of creation, of peace before a pastoral scene, of sublimity before storms and deserted vastness, of melancholy in some lonely wooded spot," observes philosopher Charles Taylor. From the end of the eighteenth century on, nature seemed to have an inner resonance that was "in some way attuned to our feelings," reflecting and intensifying those we already felt or awakening those that had been dormant.[26] Side by side, a decidedly neutral, outward gaze of science coexisted with an emotional, inward gaze of spiritual ecstasy. As generations looked into nature, their descriptions reflected an era of divided minds. Since the late nineteenth-century confrontation between natural science and an earlier romanticism, we have confronted a "split-screen vision of nature," argues Taylor. "On one side is the vast universe which scientific discovery continually reveals" as "gigantic and minuscule; indifferent to us and strangely other," he says, and on "the other side is the nature whose impulse we feel within, with which we can feel ourselves out of alignment and with which we can aspire to be in attunement."[27]

At the Grand Canyon, this divided vision appeared prominently in Captain

Clarence Dutton's 1882 *Tertiary History of the Grand Canyon District.* A protégé of Powell who went to the Colorado Plateau in the mid-1870s, Dutton's *Tertiary History* was one of three monographs he produced for Powell's survey. His report greatly amplified general theories of fluvial erosion by describing "the Great Denudation"—a slow process of laying bare the geography of the plateau region through erosion. The Grand Canyon illustrated this process in penultimate form as the Colorado River revealed, in spectacular proportion, the stratified depths of a geologic record. But Dutton is more memorable, perhaps, for the aesthetic interest he brought to his survey. His *Tertiary History* offered a unique combination, a dual vision of "geological aesthetics"; as Stegner notes, Dutton "never quite made up his mind whether he was literary traveler or sober scientific analyst."[28] While Dutton's report clearly echoed the progressive values of scientific investigations of the canyon region, he ultimately outlined and cultivated an idea of the Grand Canyon as picturesque scenery—the cultural and economic resource it eventually became. Unlike other survey reports of the region, Dutton's monograph appealed to tastes and romantic inclinations of individual spectators who gazed into the abyss in search of the sublime.

The Grand Canyon is "a great innovation in modern ideas of scenery," claimed Dutton. "Great innovations, whether in art or literature, in science or in nature, seldom take the world by storm. . . . They must be understood before they can be estimated, and must be cultivated before they can be understood."[29] Dutton's government report serves as a benchmark for mapping the aesthetic contours of Grand Canyon and cultivating the sublime stance of an idealized observer. His description of the canyon appeared extensively, as lengthy quotations and nearly plagiarized paraphrasing, in travel accounts and canyon guidebooks well into the twentieth century. While he articulated a vantage point for the leisure traveler who would, in a decade, view the scenery from the South Rim, his vision projected inward to an imaginary, interior landscape of beauty, sensation, and power.

It is notable that the *Tertiary History* describes the canyon from a vantage point opposite the one most tourists would occupy when they came searching for scenery in the 1890s. Dutton looked into the canyon from the North Rim toward the south. When he named Point Sublime in 1880, where the earth suddenly dropped to "illimitable depths" and "in an instant, in the twinkling of an eye, the awful scene is before us,"[30] Dutton could also look across the canyon to the South Rim, where travelers would soon stand reading guidebooks quoting from his survey report. But the specifics of the view were inevitably less significant than the process of viewing and, more important, also knowing what to look for inside oneself while standing at the brink of the abyss. Gazing into the canyon, Dutton animated both landscape and viewer in a manner that inextricably bound them in a quest for cultural and individual autonomy.

In part, cultivating the canyon as a "great innovation in modern ideas of scenery," Dutton called on familiar images of civilization and culture to orient observers to the landscape. He often squares himself in the scene with metaphors and analogies that imposed aesthetic order on nature's chaos. "A curtain wall 1400 feet high descends vertically from the eaves of the temples. . . . The curtain wall is decorated with a lavish display of vertical moldings, and the ridges, eaves and mitered angles are fretted with serrated cusps," wrote Dutton of one scene. "Though exact symmetry is wanting, nature has here brought home to us the truth that symmetry is only one of an infinite range of devices by which beauty can be materialized. And finer forms are in the quarry [t]han ever Angelo evoked."[31] In another passage, he compares the numerous buttes he finds in the canyon. The "nobility of form, beauty of decoration, and splendor of color," he says, are comparable only to a few buttes he's seen in southern Utah at the "Valley of the Virgen." "The comparison [between the Utah scenery and the Grand Canyon] would be analogous to one between a fine cathedral town and a metropolis like London or Paris," notes Dutton. "In style and effects their respective structures differ as decidedly as the works of any well-developed and strongly contrasted styles of human architecture." Eventually, Dutton's pen decorated the canyon as a vast and magnificent display of Eastern architecture. "Hindoo Amphitheater," "Ottoman Amphitheater," "Brahma Temple," "Vishnu's Temple," and "Shiva's Temple" are only some of the names he gave to canyon buttes and towers spread out before him, and he set an example others would follow for naming the landmarks at the Grand Canyon and other national parks such as Bryce Canyon and Zion in Utah.[32]

Dutton's images of great temples, decorative arts, sculpture, and symmetry were, in many ways, consistent with reports from earlier western explorers. Since the early nineteenth century, observers of the American West had described the landscape with images of ruins. The remnants of cities, castles, temples, masterpieces, and a lingering sense of a non-American past metaphorically captured western geography and geology with an eye toward Europe. "Ruins were evidence of the great wheel of time, invoking images of classical antiquity, and confronted human consciousness with a time stream of sublime cyclic flow in which empires grew, flourished, and decayed," writes Paul Shepard.[33] Seeing geological formations as the ruins of buildings, observers lent themselves to dreams of ancient civilizations that had vanished centuries earlier. In descriptions of western landscapes, geological observation allied with the aesthetics of classical architecture to salve the anxieties of Americans who still held tightly to European models of culture, heritage, and tradition. The erosive processes of nature's elements marking the ruins of ancient Athens also left an imprint on the walls and temples of places like the Grand Canyon. "Natural ruins and man's ruins met in the same arena of time, victims together of weather and climate," suggests Shepard, "so that the American West could display as much evidence of time's wheel as could Europe."[34]

Although he was a self-taught geologist, the romantic and literary side of Dutton conveyed an aesthetic vision of the canyon that could resonate with the social ranks of his Yale graduating class, the scientific clubs and the Philosophical Society he belonged to in Washington, and the Cosmos Club he founded with Powell. While his *Tertiary History* emerged out of a progressive vision to map the west, Dutton also expressed a desire for a civilized past. "Scenery is no scenery without the right cultural baggage," Shepard suggests.[35] For Dutton, this inevitably meant carrying those bags west and unpacking their contents on a rim of the Grand Canyon. Travelers who read his report and went west to write their own could anticipate a place where America had its own temples and ruins resembling the antiquities of Europe and Asian civilization, only far more magnificent.

Dutton described the canyon's scenery effusively, as though he was encountering it for the first time. Yet, by the time his *Tertiary History* appeared in 1882, images of the canyon's landscape had been circulating among Americans for nearly a decade. Powell had employed John K. Hillers on his second canyon expedition to photograph the survey region, and Hillers spent months arduously documenting the Grand Canyon and collecting views of the terrain and native tribes in northern Arizona and Utah. Like other photographers of the great surveys, Hillers and Powell supplemented their income with the sales of stereographic views made during their expeditions. By 1873, they had produced nearly 1,500 stereographs and sold about 650 sets commercially. Powell distributed other sets to congressmen and influential associates in Washington.[36] When Powell launched an extensive lecture tour in the East and the Midwest in 1874, he hired Hillers as a projectionist for his views of the canyon territory. In 1876, thousands of spectators viewed Hillers's survey photographs in the Government Building of Philadelphia's Centennial Exhibition. In Hillers's photographs one also finds the faces of others who traveled the canyon and sent images of the landscape back to the American public. For instance, an 1873 photograph Hillers made on the North Rim shows James E. Colburn, a reporter for the *New York Times,* and Thomas Moran, a nationally renowned landscape artist, standing above an impatient or bored-looking Kaibab Paiute boy. For eight days, the reporter and artist traveled the Kaibab Plateau with the Powell survey and viewed the canyon at Toroweap, a place located near what is now the western boundary of Grand Canyon National Park. Colburn's impressions of the journey appeared in a September 1873 *Times* report and, the following year, in *Picturesque America.*

Moran's view of the canyon, however, had a more lasting impact. A year earlier, Congress had paid him ten thousand dollars for a seven-by-twelve-foot oil canvas, *The Grand Canyon of the Yellowstone,* painted from sketches made while accompanying Ferdinand Hayden's 1871 government survey of the Yellowstone territories in Wyoming. His trip to the Grand Canyon in Arizona provided a starting point for another canvas of similar proportion, *The Chasm of the Colorado.* Unveiled in 1874, *The Chasm* fetched the thirty-six-year-old artist another ten-thousand-dollar commission and hung in public view at the Capitol building opposite the Yellowstone landscape. By 1875, the year Dutton headed west to join the Powell survey, a woodcut version of Moran's *Chasm of the Colorado,* along with twenty-eight other wood engravings of the canyon region, had appeared in a three-part article written by Powell for *Scribner's Monthly.* They also illustrated Powell's official report of his expedition down the Colorado. Anyone who might have missed any of these canyon images found an ample supply when they looked at Dutton's *Tertiary History.* The report was illustrated with Hillers's photographs, nine Moran woodcuts, and nine panoramas painted by William Henry Holmes.

In Dutton's *Tertiary History,* it is Holmes's large, double-paged, panoramic paintings in the accompanying atlas that most capture the spirit of a scientific survey. Alongside Dutton's descriptions of stratification and erosion, Holmes's crisp lines seem drawn with an absolutely clear eye, unshakable hand, and razor-sharp pencil. Nothing obscures the artist's penchant for detail. Expansive in the scope of their views, his images serve well a government document aiming to map the region. Yet, Holmes offers a view that not even a photograph could capture. The sky above the canyon holds no clouds or haze, and Holmes's vision extends transparently all the way to the horizon. Everything is seen with the same clear eye. Perhaps what is most obvious, and what lends more clarity to this vision than a photograph, is the absence of a sun to cast any shadows across the sharp landscape. While the panoramas suggest that an assured painter had omnisciently extracted a perfect vision of the canyon, they also reveal a scientifically idealized view of the canyon no one standing on the rim could ever see.[37]

Compared to Holmes, Moran created canyon scenes with an entirely different philosophy. Only one of Moran's large paintings, *The Transept,* based on a sketch by Holmes, is actually reproduced in the *Tertiary History* atlas. But unlike Holmes, whose work primarily found a home as illustrations for government reports, Moran was already a nationally recognized landscape artist by the time Dutton's canyon report was published. Where Holmes stretched the eye in an aim for realistic clarity, Moran assembled entirely different views of the canyon—a set of Romantic scenes where the viewer often looked from an imaginary and impossible vantage point. For instance, Moran's *Chasm of the Colorado* renders a hellish and desolate canyon. The sun dramatically lights distant monuments and patches of foreground, but a thunderstorm is breaking and vapors rise from the dark canyon below. Above the chasm, traces of a rainbow appear in the lingering storm clouds. Like many of his paintings, the scene is built with elements of the canyon he sketched at various place and times.[38]

Finding these two artists meeting in the pages of Dutton's *Tertiary History* means more than seeing them as illustrators for the divided allegiances and dual vision of Dutton's "geological aesthetics." Although Holmes largely remained unknown as a painter, Moran would continually return to the canyon, often bringing other artists, to re-create its scenes until his death in 1926. Both Holmes and Moran had invented their viewpoints, and they often referred to Hillers's photographs in their studios as they composed a canyon to suit the inclinations of a scientific or romantic observer. In the end, it didn't matter that people had previously seen or held before them pictures and photographs of the canyon by the time Dutton's *Tertiary History* was published. Dutton's descriptions provided a literary rendering of the scene but also instructed viewers toward an *interior* landscape that could neither be painted or photographed. It was Dutton's "romantic side" that most captured the attention of later travelers. He was a government scientist who saw the geological landscape with an expansive scientific vision but, in the end, claimed the scene as a place of spiritual yearnings.

The *Tertiary History* synthesized a scenic vision of the canyon made by artist, photographer, and writer together. The text created and claimed the scene as a set of practices that both produced and affirmed an autonomous, educated, and contemplative observer. Feigning the quintessential explorer of terra incognita, Dutton's narrative not only carried the reader along on a journey of constant and sudden discoveries of the canyon but also celebrated the patient and careful practices of observation that aim for revelation through nature. "The lover of nature, whose perceptions have been trained in the Alps, in Italy, Germany, or New England . . . would enter this strange region with a shock, and dwell there for a time with a sense of oppression, and perhaps with horror," he warned. Anyone expecting immediate rapture at the canyon would be disappointed he advised, noting that any scene disclosing its "full power, meaning, and beauty" instantaneously was a superficial experience. Instead, a process of slow acquisition revealed the meaning and spirit of the canyon. "The study and slow mastery of the influences of that class of scenery and its full appreciation is a special culture," he wrote, "requiring time, patience, and long familiarity for its consummation."[39] Reiterating a sense of shock and surprise at the unfamiliar, and expressing a desire to cultivate an understanding of the "innovative scenery," Dutton's instructions to canyon observers fit well with the aesthetic propensities of many nineteenth-century artists and elites. Noting the "class of scenery" and the "special culture" that could most appreciate its meaning, Dutton's gaze into the abyss looked into the heart and mind of an ideal observer who contemplated the canyon like a great landscape painting for a revelation of nature's power, magnificence, and beauty.

In many ways, the observer Dutton envisioned was nothing less than the person who looked at the canyon landscape paintings of Thomas Moran. Moran's early appreciation for the philosophy of John Ruskin, perhaps one of the most influential critics of the nineteenth century, points to a common aesthetic ground he shared with Dutton. "Anything which elevates the mind is sublime, and the elevation of the mind is produced by the contemplation of greatness of any kind," wrote Ruskin, "but chiefly, of course, by the greatness of the noblest things."[40] For Ruskin, the highest forms of art seized and enhanced "that faultless, ceaseless, inconceivable, inexhaustible loveliness, which God has stamped upon all things."[41] Quite simply, Ruskin believed the highest forms of art reflected God, and those who possessed the proper state of mind could find the divine through art, architecture, and music. Moran, however, diverged from Ruskin's call to literally transcribe nature through art and favored, instead, a transcendent relationship between the individual and nature. "My personal scope is not realistic; all my tendencies are toward idealization," said Moran. "The motive or incentive for my Grand Canyon of the Yellowstone was the gorgeous display of color that impressed itself on me . . . and while I desired to tell truly of nature, I did not wish to realize the scene literally but to preserve and convey its true impression."[42] Moran apologized to no one for moving scenery around to suit his purposes. Art, he argued, was an emotional expression of the individual who looked upon the scene, and this was equally true for both the artist and those who looked at the space in the frame.

Moran's philosophy as well as his paintings of the Grand Canyon merely anticipated the canyon viewer Dutton would describe in his 1882 monograph. For both men, the truth of the canyon lay in the aesthetic and spiritual experience of the individual. In arguing for a slow and careful study of the canyon's landscape, Dutton provided not so much an image of the canyon but an outline for how the viewer should locate himself or herself in the scene. In an age when canyon scenery already circulated into homes, and despite his own effusive efforts to convey the shock and surprise of a first view, Dutton clung tightly to an idea that the true canyon rested somewhere inside the patient man or woman standing on the rim. His advice appeared later in guidebooks that quoted directly from his *Tertiary History.* "A visitor to the chasm . . . must necessarily come there (for so is the human mind constituted) with a picture of it created by his own imagination," said Dutton in a 1901 guide. "He reaches the spot, the conjured picture vanishes in an instant, and the place of it must be filled anew. Surely no imagination can construct out of its own material any picture having the remotest resemblance to the Grand Canyon. In truth, the first step in attempting a description is to beg the reader to dismiss from his mind, so far as practicable, any preconceived notion of it."[43] Surely, not even Dutton could live up to this ideal. When he stared over the rim, he found cities of architectural beauty that Ruskin would have appreciated. Dutton reinforced the ideas and practices of an individual observer, particularly one who understood the terms of a "special culture," to remake the scene in his or her own contemplative efforts. Naming a promontory "Point Sublime" was, perhaps, an auspicious starting place—whether at the canyon or in the mind—for later writers who aspired to both Dutton's eloquence and sensibility when they described their own view. Dutton's *Tertiary History* placed the canyon within the scope and vocabulary of a nineteenth-century aesthetic that attracted many for its sense of individualism, morality, and the authority of a culture that could recognize both.

Dutton's split vision of geological aesthetics carries traces of Ralph Waldo Emerson's 1836 *Nature* essays. Emerson's transcendental philosophy read the "language of Nature" as a direct route to a universally interconnected and ultimate unity. "Words are signs of natural facts," wrote Emerson in the "Language" chapter of *Nature.* "The use of natural history is to give us aid in supernatural history. The use of the outer creation is to give us language for the beings and changes of the inward creation. . . . Every natural fact is a symbol of some spiritual fact." For Emerson, describing nature exercised and illustrated moral virtues "so that picturesque language is at once a commanding certificate that he who employs it, is a man in alliance with truth and God." The factual languages of natural science, botany, and geology deadened the spirit of nature's unity, he argued; science lacked an ample sense of humanity and overlooked the eternal connection between man and world. "When I behold a rich landscape, it is less to my purpose to recite correctly the order and superposition of the strata," he wrote in the *Nature* essays, "than to know why all thought of multitude is lost in a tranquil sense of unity." For Emerson, restoring the world to its "original and eternal beauty" meant redeeming the soul. No one could be a naturalist until he had satisfied "all the demands of spirit."[44]

Emerson's philosophy of self-reliant and divinely sufficient individualism offered nineteenth-century American readers a model for breaking free of their European heritage. "We have listened too long to the courtly muses of Europe," Emerson wrote in his 1837 essay "The American Scholar." In 1844, he again argued for a spiritual relationship with nature wherein truth could reveal itself as a celestial city inside the hearts and minds of individuals. "Nature is loved by what is best in us. It is loved as the city of God. . . . And the beauty of nature must seem unreal and mocking, until the landscape has human figures that are as good as itself," wrote Emerson in his second *Nature* essay. "Our hunting for the picturesque is inseparable from our protest against false society."[45] Three years later, Ruskin's *Modern Painters* was published in the United States, and it seemed to validate a set of attitudes about nature, individualism, and morality that Emerson had outlined in the previous decade. Emerson and Ruskin had each found their inspiration in the English essayist Thomas Carlyle, who feared the technology of industrial society, attacked excessive materialism, and romanticized the power of the individual.

For Americans steeped in Emersonian philosophy, Ruskin's aesthetic theory provided a route to God through a nature expressed as culture. Ruskin's view of painting, sculpture, and architecture—in short, his sense of an exterior culture that displayed an internalized spirit—offered possibilities for inward individual perfection that ultimately redeemed social hierarchies, social order, and privileged the worldview of an educated class. Ruskin's contemporary Matthew Arnold, who defined culture as "the best which has been thought and said in the world," suggested personal cultivation would ultimately bear greater dividends for a progressive society. "The culture we recommend is, above all, an inward operation" that "places human perfection in an *internal* condition," wrote Arnold in his 1867 *Culture and Anarchy*. However, Arnold was quick to point out that the cultural apostle could not remain in isolation and charged those who saw the internal light "to carry others along with him in his march towards perfection, to be continually doing all he can to enlarge and increase the volume of the human stream sweeping thitherward."[46] By 1867, Emerson seemed to share a similar view and reformulated his charge to break free from European culture. In a Harvard lecture on the progress of culture, he expressed confidence in the "few superior and attractive men" who could embody a "knighthood of virtue" and become moral models of guidance in a "barbarous age," notes Alan Trachtenberg. Emerson "gave heart to an attitude . . . that inheritors of New England culture now represented a minority of virtue, intelligence, and cultivation," and their mission was to "preserve civility in public life."[47]

Among nineteenth-century critics and social theorists, the idea of culture, whether manifested in a canvas or a canyon, served as a means toward such perfection. The grim face of industrialism already sowed lines of class division and discontent. An appreciation for civilized culture could redeem individuals and, eventually, ideals for a democratic and progressive society. In the end, however, culture was a matter of *individual* taste and education, and idealizing the canyon in the terms of architecture, painting, sculpture, and music inevitably meant sorting out those who had the chance of seeing and feeling its power from those who did not. Despite the distance observers sought from the Old World, their accounts tended to recapitulate a vision of culture that carried the philosophical foundations set in motion by nineteenth-century Romantic poets and British social critics. A dominant meaning of the term *culture,* as Raymond Williams argued, arose amidst nineteenth-century debates over industrialization and democratization. "The positive consequence of the idea of art as superior reality was that it offered an immediate basis for an important criticism of industrialism. The negative consequence was that it tended, as both the situation and the opposition hardened, to isolate art, and specialize the imaginative faculty to this one kind of activity."[48] This specialization meant elevating the artist, the cultivated observer, and placing culture above a broader, conflicted arena of social life—class, politics, and work. Believing that high art and literature expressed divine perfection, social critics thought culture—and its elite official arbiters—could serve as a source of redemption for the social corruptions leveled by industrialism.

For a Gilded Age literary scholar and self-taught scientist like Dutton, the circulating philosophies of sublime experience and individualism became intertwined in the ideas of Emerson, Ruskin, and Arnold. In different ways, their ideas echoed in the rhetoric of preservationists who sought to transform natural landscapes into American culture. Natural scenery offered individual enlightenment, cultural redemption, and an affirmation of one's social identity. Emerson died the same year the *Tertiary History* was published. Neither Emerson, Arnold, nor Ruskin ever traveled to the Grand Canyon. If any of them saw it, it was through Moran's paintings or engravings. Yet, the three of them had provided Dutton with the foundations of an aesthetic and spiritual vision that is evidenced in his composition of the landscape from Point Sublime. This was the "cultural baggage" Dutton carried west to dress the canyon. For those who followed in his tracks, the canyon was continually a place where observers found evidence of God's city, a metaphor that spoke to their desires for spiritual rapture and affirmation but also to their quest for an indigenous monument of American culture.

Soul Shocks in the Imaginary City

Dutton's *Tertiary History* had obviously influenced Charles Dudley Warner, an essayist, editor, and novelist from Hartford, Connecticut, who devoted two chapters to the Grand Canyon in his 1891 *Our Italy.* "Human experience has no prototype of this region, and the imagination has never conceived of its forms and colors," wrote Warner of his own journey to the canyon. "It is impossible to convey an adequate idea of it by pen or pencil or brush."[49] Even as he offers a proviso that his account "deals only with a single view in this marvelous region," Warner's canyon echoes with Dutton's voice. When he is not mimicking Dutton's literary style, he quotes directly from the *Tertiary History* to the point of calling for a "popular edition" of Dutton's government report. He affirms Dutton's propensity for "Oriental nomenclature to bring [the canyon] within our comprehension" and expands upon Dutton's architectural sensibilities. "I was continually likening this to a vast city rather than a landscape," wrote Warner, "a city of no man's creation nor of any man's conception . . . yet everything reminds us of man's work."[50]

Finding a city in the depths of the canyon was more than an act of literary imagination or hallucination. Since the late eighteenth century, Romantics had taught Americans how to appreciate wilderness, observes Roderick Nash, and "by the middle decades of the nineteenth century wilderness was recognized as a cultural and moral resource and a basis for national self-esteem."[51] In his own way, Warner recapitulated Dutton's desire to cultivate an understanding of the canyon as a "great innovation in modern ideas of scenery." Although Warner and later observers acknowledged their impressions could never quite capture the canyon, it was really more than the canyon they were after. Their accounts reflected a larger quest, an American errand into the wilderness, where nature would undergo a transmutation into culture that recuperated images of an idealized democratic society sanctioned by God.

"We had come into a new world," wrote Warner of his first sighting of the canyon, and the city below him—surpassing artists' visions of the New Jerusalem, Heaven, or his first impressions of Rome—registered the spiritual and cultural promise of America.[52] The emotions called up as he faced the Grand Canyon created a "shock so novel that the mind, dazed, quite failed to comprehend it." Despite being caught in a whirl of surging emotion and mental paralysis, Warner saw his "city of the imagination" as an overblown bricolage of European imagery. "There was a castle, terraced up with columns, plain enough, and below it a parade-ground; at any moment the knights in armor and with banners might emerge from red gates and deploy there, while the ladies looked down from balconies. But there were many castles and fortresses and barracks and noble mansions," he wrote. "In time I began to see queer details: a Richardson house, with low portals and round arches, surmounted by a Nuremberg gable; perfect panels, 600 feet high, for the setting of pictures."[53] Clearly, Warner had dutifully followed Dutton's lead and let his imagination roam in endless directions. But nearly everyone who described the canyon to the public seemed to wind up in the same imaginary city, effusively conveying images of magnificent architecture and testifying to the "soul-shocks" that ran through them on the rim.

"Instead of being filled with air, the vast space between the walls is crowded with Nature's grandest buildings, a sublime city of them, painted in every color, and adorned with richly fretted cornice and battlement spire and tower," John Muir told *Atlantic Monthly* readers in 1898. "Every architectural invention of man has been anticipated, and far more, in this grandest of God's terrestrial cities."[54] Nearly two years later, poet and journalist Harriet Monroe told an *Atlantic Monthly* audience, "The souls of the great architects must find their dreams fulfilled" at the canyon. Yet, this was not earth, she said, rather "heaven itself was across there," and it was "as though to the glory of nature were added the glory of art; as though, to achieve her utmost, the proud young world had commanded architecture to build for her."[55] In 1902, Muir resurrected his architectural assessment of the canyon for readers of the *Century,* noting lavish castles, huge cathedrals, and pyramids. The canyon depths displayed a "vast extent of wild architecture—nature's own capital city—[and] there seem to be no ordinary dwellings," said Muir. "All look like grand and important public structures" with "every radiant spire pointing the way to heaven."[56] To a Protestant nation steeped in a rhetorical legacy of biblical imagery, Warner, Muir, and Monroe sounded like visionaries seeing a landscape of divine providence. Their voices carried strains of John Bunyan's *Pilgrim's Progress,* in which Christians flee to the "celestial city," and Puritan leader John Winthrop, who told his company in exodus across the Atlantic, "we shall be a City Upon a Hill, the eyes of all people are upon us." More significantly, however, they echoed Emerson's romantic individualism. "Emerson stressed that America's communal attempt to found in history itself a holy City on a Hill could succeed only if each American's soul searched for a Celestial City that transcended history," observes Michael Cowan. "In order for the eternal City of God to manifest itself on earth in the form of a New Jerusalem, Americans first needed to discover citizenship in this eternal City."[57]

By the late nineteenth century, imagining a perfect and heavenly city in the canyon's depths could appeal to deeply inscribed American visions of social harmony and divine order that had yet to materialize in the New World. Despite plans for democratic community and architectural beauty, the rapid growth of eastern urban centers often left their denizens feeling oppressed by industrial smoke and muddy streets, and anonymous among the swarming crowds. For many, nature not only offered a retreat from the harsh realities of city life but also a place to reimagine its uncorrupted possibility. Assigning these images to the canyon's landscape, writers simultaneously preserved the ideal of God's city in America and bore witness to their own idealized inner landscape. Faced with the increasing chaos of expanding industry and recent memories of a divisive Civil War, imagining a city of God in the canyon below called up an undying optimism for a divine and harmonious community on American soil.

Writers reporting "soul-shocks" after gazing into the canyon testified to a relationship between the observer and God that confirmed their own spiritual leanings and aimed toward claims of *cultural* maturity. If the canyon was viewed as holy ground, it was not only because Americans felt God's presence stirring their hearts but also because many felt a need to push something monumental and distinctively American before European eyes.

Wandering along the edges of this imaginary city, their accounts were maps of their desires for a civilized culture. The Grand Canyon "flashes instant communication of all that architecture and painting and music for a thousand years have gropingly striven to express," boasted Charles Higgins in an early 1892 Santa Fe guidebook. "It is the soul of Michael Angelo and of Beethoven."[58] Six years later, John Muir rejoiced over a canyon where "every rock temple becomes a temple of music; every spire and pinnacle an angel of light and song, shouting color halleluiahs."[59] Recording their spiritual reveries from the rim, writers also suggested the canyon possessed a historical and cultural depth comparable or superior to any work of human civilization. Although many drew comparisons with antiquities of the Old World, it was a symbol of culture and heritage in the New World—a superior and distinctively *American* cultural shrine—each sought to define and affirm for this offered an avenue to a stable national identity.

The landscapes of the Grand Canyon, like Yellowstone and Yosemite, could help fill what many Americans feared was a void of American culture. The Grand Canyon offered another shrine of national pride to help soothe those Americans haunted by feelings of cultural impoverishment. Yet, the accounts of canyon travelers also suggested an internal instability. Writers who sought spirituality and sublimity could not quite give up the geological vision Powell and Dutton had both endorsed. Both of these visions inform the descriptions of Grand Canyon travel stories and guidebooks at the turn of the century, which suggest how people managed the scientific and spiritual conflicts of the period as they wrote themselves into its scenes. "The scene is one to strike dumb with awe or to unstring the nerves," wrote Warner. "One might stand in silent astonishment, another would burst into tears. . . . Turning suddenly to the scene from another point of view, I experienced for a moment an indescribable terror of nature, a confusion of mind, a fear to be alone in such a presence." Several paragraphs later, Warner has settled down, calmly explaining how the "process of creation is here laid bare through the geologic periods."[60] The emotional chord struck by the canyon becomes a controlled and measured assessment in Warner's description. In 1899, Mrs. M. Burton Williamson conveyed a similar experience of the scene. "The mind is not prepared to appreciate the infinite variety at first, it is too colossal," she wrote. "Its immensity is felt immediately, but the grandeur of these jasper cities grows more majestic as the mind becomes accustomed to the unfamiliar vision." Although the scene first grew as a set of feelings, she eventually came to a tamer description oriented in a vocabulary of God and science. "We are filled with reverential awe as we see before us the work of a thousand centuries of physical energy exhibited in the dynamic power of stream and rain erosion."[61]

As travelers described the canyon, they negotiated broader conflicts regarding evolution, geology, God, nature, and self. For instance, John L. Stoddard's account of an 1897 visit to the canyon expresses a vision of the landscape that poetically addresses theological and scientific issues regarding the place of humans in the scheme of nature. "These wrecks of Tempest and of Time are fingerposts that point the thoughts of mortals to eternal heights," he said, "and we find cause for hope in the fact that, even in a place like this, Man is superior to Nature; for he interprets it, he finds in it the thoughts of God, and reads them after him."[62] Stoddard's God was celebrated in nature, and the canyon was a "sermon in stone." The message of that sermon, however, found meaning through the language of evolution and geology. The Grand Canyon showed evidence of "Nature's patient methods; a triumph of the delicate over the strong, the liquid over the solid, the transitory over the enduring," said Stoddard. "To calculate the aeons implied in the repeated elevations and subsidences which made this region what it is would be to comprehend eternity. In such a retrospect centuries crumble and disappear into the gulf of Time as pebbles into the Cañon of the Colorado."[63] In the canyon's landscape, Stoddard observed a world informed by the ideas of a natural theology that reconciled nature's God with the eyes of science. As a popular travel lecturer, he could appeal to audiences of both believers and nonbelievers who were sorting out the period's bewildering views on spirituality and science for themselves. In the end, Stoddard's account seemed to conjure more uncertainty than wonder. "Even thought had no existence in that sunken realm of chaos," he told his audience. "I felt as if I were the sole survivor of the deluge. Only the melancholy murmur of the wind ascended from that sepulchre of centuries. It seemed the requiem for a vanished world."[64] The lone survivor listening to the wind chant for vanished ages in the canyon's tomb is, indeed, a melodramatic scene. But was Stoddard mourning the canyon's layers of worlds come and gone, or his own world where spiritual authority had been ruptured by natural science? Clearly, his own place in the canyon's cosmic landscape still vibrated from the collision of two disparate world views only a few decades earlier. Like any survivor of the changes and transformations of a progressive age, he adapted to his circumstances with a species of discourse—what Kenneth Burke called a "linguistic gargoyle"—that mixed and blended the incongruities of spiritual and scientific orders of classification.[65]

Stories like Stoddard's revealed another installation of the dividing line between a progressively minded modernism and a sentimental antimodernism that valued the return to nature. Although Stoddard's interpretive powers rested just below those of nature's God, he may have found some hope and security in Darwin's idea that "natural selection works solely by and for the good of each being, all corporeal and mental endowments will tend to progress toward perfection."[66] For others, however, evolutionary ideas carried such a powerful message of insignificance that the canyon became a stage for deep existential and philosophical conflicts. Wrestling to give the canyon meaning, visitors found a symbolic site to wrestle with the meaning of their lives. Harriet Monroe, for example, simply couldn't take it anymore and felt the urge to throw herself over the edge. "The strain of existence became too tense against these infinities of beauty and terror. My narrow ledge of rock was a prison," she wrote in 1899. "I fought against the desperate temptation to fling myself down into that soft abyss." Monroe said she would have taken the plunge if it were not for the "trill of an oriole" in a nearby pine tree. The bird's song brought the message of "a friend who would save me from intolerable loneliness, from utter extinction and despair" and "seemed to welcome me to the infinite." God spoke to Monroe through the oriole, through nature, and her story captures the canyon as a site of a mystical experience. "In nature's innermost sanctuary, man must be of the elect," she concluded. "It is not for nothing that the secret is hidden in the wilderness, and that the innermost depths of it are inaccessible to our wingless race."[67]

Monroe's story affirmed the unknowable forces of nature, but with a twist that turned away from increasingly logical arguments of natural theology and *toward* a theology of experience. At the turn of the century, reports of mystical experience were not an uncommon response in a culture deeply investing itself in rationality and order. "Mystical states of mind pointed to the inadequacies of positivism," notes Jackson Lears. "The mystic's vivid experience of eternity preserved some supernatural meaning in a secular world, some vestige of gravity in a weightless universe."[68] The weight of an oriole's song was enough to keep Harriet Monroe from going over the canyon's edge and lead her into the sanctuary of the infinite. But it could have been just about anything—a blade of grass, a grain of sand, Niagara Falls, a walk in the hills with the dog, observed William James. James, for one, took reports of mystical experiences seriously in his Gifford lectures on natural religion in 1902. Although he admitted his own constitution shut him off from enjoying such experiences, he studied the accounts of people who claimed to know "mystical states of consciousness" firsthand. "Mystical truth exists for the individual who has the transport, but for no one else. . . . It resembles the knowledge given to us in sensations more than that given by conceptual thought," James argued. "They have been 'there,' and know. It is vain for rationalism to grumble about this."[69] After all, those who claimed mystical encounters relied on the same evidence as those who interpreted nature through "'rational' beliefs," he said. As scientific explanations claimed more of the universe and the arguments of natural theology began to lose force, "the appeal to experience offered an impregnable shield against naturalism," notes Russett.[70] Nonbelievers may have scoffed at Monroe's idea that the "innermost depths" of "the secret hidden in the wilderness" were "inaccessible to our wingless race," but they would have approved of her understanding that "man is the elect" of all the species.

Mystical experiences retained the idea of "chance," the possibility of cosmic forces beyond the scope of scientific description, and retained the place of the individual in a drama of nature. At the turn of the century, numerous canyon visitors indulged the occasion to testify about mysterious forces of nature claiming their bodies and minds. For instance, Charles S. Gleed told of being possessed by the sight of the canyon. "Helplessness wound about us and the hypnotism of wonder took our faculties captive," wrote the Topeka attorney in 1902. "The mystery fascinated, the void beckoned. We scarcely know why we did not obey the summons—why we did not abandon the present and, by following the big stone, escape to the future."[71] Despite the flourishing descriptions of the canyon's supernatural power, some feared the canyon was getting lost in melodrama.

Annoyed with the incessant sensational testimony of canyon visitors, James MacCarthy could not pass up an opportunity to supply a few of his own adjectives as he scolded writers. "Shrive yourselves, ere you approach, of all your little, vainglorious conceits, of all your pretty, gabbling rhetorical formulas of exclamatory ecstasy," MacCarthy warned. Although he named the canyon as a "deep pre-Egyptian grave of Nature's patient digging, gorgeous, mysterious and solemn, where Time, the mother of worlds, has sepulchered her dead children, the centuries and millenniums of the past"; he claimed (and with no hint of irony) that the Grand Canyon was not a place for rhetoric. "Rhetoric is something worse than a presumptious and profitless vanity; it is a profanation," he said. "Come and interrogate your soul in this gorgeous and appalling presence, and then you will realize (as I now painfully realize) how inadequately I have in this lame sketch suggested to your imagination its stupendous glories and its divine pathos."[72] MacCarthy's noisy disavowal of rhetoric is, perhaps, forgivable only in light of his eagerness. He did seem to understand his contradictory impulses for silence and speech. "Pray spare me, in this mysterious and subduing presence, from the categorical inquiries that will naturally rush to your tongue," he said. "I cannot answer them; my emotions, this day, are in thrall and I wish to reflect on 'the thoughts that arise in me.'"[73] Despite urging others to see the canyon for themselves, he wanted them to know and see *his canyon*, and preserve the *idea*, at least, of a personal, intimate, and emotional experience with nature.

The enthusiastic poetic portraits of visitors and the sober, precise, technical language of scientific experts not only crowded the landscape with rhetoric, they also inevitably reduced nature's silent mysteries to individual dramas of intense spirituality, adventure, conquest, and vanity. "Both the poet's metaphors and the scientist's abstractions discuss something in terms of something else," observed Burke,[74] and in his own awkward way, MacCarthy suspected this, too. The uneasy and unspoken truth about the canyon was that it had become a dumping ground for rhetoric, an empty space that poets, scientists, journalists, painters, and everyday visitors filled with anxious images of themselves and their culture. Not only could the Grand Canyon be whatever one wanted it to be, it was also a stage for people to narrate visions of themselves in the larger dramas and conflicts of their times. By 1901, one guidebook had even recast Powell's scientific expedition down the Colorado into a Judeo-Christian allegory for life's journey. George Wharton James dedicated his *In and Around the Grand Canyon* to Powell, whom he called a "Scholar, Warrior, Scientist, Gentleman, [and] Friend," and whose "explorations of the Canyons of the Colorado in the interests of Science confirm him one of the bravest, most heroic, and daring explorers of the century." At the end of his guidebook, however, Powell's expedition modeled a spiritual voyage. As with the explorer on the river, James noted, "life flows on, passing through canyons and rapids, dashing by the cruel, hungry granite and over dangerous waterfalls; but just as surely as the river flows on and enters the Great Pacific, so will man enter the unfathomable ocean of the heart of God."[75]

In books and magazines, the canyon's scenes generally chattered with voices that had been untethered in the cosmos by the eyes and minds of natural science but now experientially rediscovered their place in a landscape by claiming nature's silence for spiritual nourishment. In various accounts, the Grand Canyon divided more than the Kaibab and Coconino plateaus; it symbolically recognized an enduring gap between the secular and the sacred, scientific and spiritual knowledge, objective certainty and subjective emotion. "I see now that none of the accounts that I have read fully reflect the spirit of the Canyon. Most of them simply describe the author's own feelings," travel lecturer Dwight Elmendorf's companion told him in 1915. "Now this does not appeal to me in words at all. It impresses me first of all as a Great Silence. . . . What I want is information—not someone else's emotions. I have my own feelings—and they are strong enough." Elmendorf concluded that his friend's attitude was probably typical of most canyon visitors. "They want to be told *about* the Canyon, not what they are to *think* about the Canyon," he said. He clarified this murky distinction in favor of a geological explanation. "As the copper surface of an etching plate is eaten by acid, the earth's surface has here been etched by water and weather," Elmendorf explained. "The geologist finds the story in the layers of rock laid bare in the course of erosion. He reads it in chapters of limestone, sandstone, shale and granite."[76] This disagreement between the value of subjective knowledge (revealed in personal sensation and emotion) and objective information (revealed in scientific explanation) suggested that more than the meaning of the canyon was at stake. Objective knowledge, carrying the authority of conquest, power, and certainty, settled the meaning of the canyon with a rational order that extended into all facets of daily life. Personal impressions of the Grand Canyon, filled with emotion and exaggerated poetic metaphors, kept the door open to a God, an unknowable cosmos, and a sense of mystery about the world. Testifying to sublime experience was a momentary escape from the rationalized orders of daily urban life, but more important, it also produced an image of the autonomous individual who, after reveling in ecstasy, regained a sense of self-control and spiritual renewal.[77]

In 1927, John C. Van Dyke discussed the emotional impact of the canyon by recreating what had by now become a familiar scenario: a visitor who feels compelled to jump over the edge. "But does not that way lie madness? Is it the fear of the gulf so much as the fear of self—the fear that you may yield to an irrational impulse?" Van Dyke asked his readers. "The terror of the abyss is not in the Canyon but in your oversensitive nerves. Civilization has keyed you up to the snapping point, and here in the presence of a great sensation you feel the strain." As far as Van Dyke was concerned, nature was life, and civilized people had lost sight of this fundamental truth. There is "possibly some madness in both the building and the street that spurs on [their] own incipient mania," he claimed. "But there is no madness in Nature and no terror in her precipices once we have the fumes of civilization out of our brain and have returned to the normal life."[78] Like earlier writers who found the canyon (and, more generally, in nature) a place to lodge their complaints against urban life, Van Dyke saw the canyon as site for spiritual redemption. The soul-shocks earlier writers experienced on the rim had been a result of nature's chaos, which hit them like a thunderbolt. They were overcome by the scenery, where an invisible, ineffable force penetrated them. In the face of this exhilarating and awesome experience, they regained themselves by resisting an urge to fling themselves into the canyon. Van Dyke's hypothetical tourist, however, arrives at the canyon already out of control, a victim of psychological strains induced by daily life, and prey to "irrational impulses." It is not the supernatural force of Nature's chaos that prompts thoughts of leaping into what Harriet Monroe had, decades earlier, called the "soft abyss." Instead, the terrifying abyss is internalized in a self divided between the constraints and anxieties of rational self-control. In this example, sublime experience is a critique of modern individualism. Chaos is not in nature, but in the fumes and streets of the modern city. For the man or woman internally divided and fragmented by the rationalizing forces of urban life, it is the Grand Canyon, a geographically divided landscape, that Van Dyke says will offer spiritual unity.

Despite providing more than two hundred pages of descriptions of his own, Van Dyke concluded the canyon was a place where language failed. For him, nature was God, and the canyon could not be "ploughed or plotted or poetized or painted," he said. "It is too big for us to do more than creep along the Rim and wonder over it. . . . Some things should be beyond us—aspired to but never attained." The canyon should "remain a mystery," Van Dyke claimed, believing that wonder and awe were "a natural inheritance." The ending of his book attested to this spiritual understanding, but not without him taking one last stab at rational certainty. "With definite knowledge one abandons interest," he concluded. "The world becomes commonplace."[79] Traveling through Van Dyke's canyon, readers found a broader critical commentary on civilization, nature, representation, and scientific knowledge. His final sentences warn against a certitude that could pry people from a spiritual mystery and leave them walking through a world as narrow, flat, and ordinary as a yardstick. Van Dyke shared these sentiments, I think, with many earlier writers, who looked into the canyon for something more than either the instruments or theories of geologists could register. However, at the time Van Dyke was writing his book and calling for a deeper appreciation of nature's canyon, railroad advertisers, preservationists, entrepreneurs, and legislators had been at work for three decades trying to establish Grand Canyon as a "common place" of American culture. By 1927, the voices of scientists, promoters, and travelers had produced a textualized canyon sedimented in reports, articles, paintings, photographs, and stories. In this textualized canyon, autonomous and sovereign observers reappeared continually, searching for a scientific education, spirituality, and cultural affirmation while escaping from the realities of urban life, and serving always as the object of cultural discourses written for and about them.

Framing the American Masterpiece

"There is but one thing to say: 'There it is; go see it for yourself,'" Charles F. Lummis told readers of his 1892 *A Tramp across the Continent*. "It is a crying shame that any American who is able to travel at all should fail to see nature's masterpiece upon this planet before he fad abroad to visit scenes that would not make a visible scratch upon its walls."[1] Such words were indicative of Lummis's fervent nationalism and promotion of the Grand Canyon and the Southwest. In the 1890s, Lummis told American tourists to "see America first," and the idea launched a campaign that carried into the first decades of the twentieth century. The Grand Canyon, he wrote, simply topped the list of the great wonders of the world, and he smugly brushed away the legacy of European monuments by urging Americans to see the sights at home. "As a people we dodder abroad to see scenery incomparably inferior," he wrote in 1895 as editor of *Land of Sunshine*. "It is the greatest chasm in the world, and the most superb. Enough globe-trotters have seen it to establish that fact. Many have come cynically prepared to be disappointed; to find it overdrawn and really not so stupendous as something else. . . . But I never knew the most self-satisfied veteran traveler to be disappointed in the Grand Canyon or to patronize it. On the contrary, this is the very class of men who can best comprehend it, and I have seen them fairly break down in its awful presence."[2] The Santa Fe Railway reprinted his essay "The Greatest Thing in the World" well into the twentieth century, and the railroad's advertisements included brief testimonials from "the very class of men"—businessmen, industrialists, attorneys, clergy, politicians—Lummis said could "best comprehend it" and who, he believed, could endorse its legitimacy as a scenic wonder. The Santa Fe, perhaps more than any single force, capitalized on the idea of the canyon as an aesthetic experience. For the railroad's advertising department, what made the canyon worth seeing depended on framing it as a site of culture and less on the geological interests that first drew observers to the region. They saw the landscape's value reflected in the eyes of writers and painters who claimed the canyon for an observer of great art.

"It is old, old, this Grand Canyon, and yet so new it seems almost to smell of paint," wrote American poet Joaquin Miller in a 1901 issue of the *Overland Monthly*. "Take the grandest, sublimest thing the world has ever seen, fashion it as if the master minds from the 'beginning' had wrought here, paint it as only the masters of old could paint, and you have El Cañon Grande del Colorado!"[3] When the Santa Fe advertisers reprinted his testimonial in 1902, their own image-making of the Grand Canyon had been strategically in force for more than ten years. At the time Warner told readers it was impossible to adequately convey the canyon with a "pencil or brush" and Lummis admonished Americans to see "nature's masterpiece" firsthand, the Santa Fe Railway had secured rights to Moran's *Grand Canyon of the Colorado* for chromolithographic reproduction. "These it framed in handsome gilt frames and then sent them out, first by the hundreds and then by the thousands," noted Edward Hungerford in an article on railroad advertising. The Santa Fe "placed them in offices, in hotels, in schools, even in homes—almost anywhere that there was a fair chance of the picture bringing in business."[4] Moran agreed to give the railroad the copyright for his canvas in 1892, after the Santa Fe subsidized a summer trip through the West for the artist, his son, and photographer William Henry Jackson. If Joaquin Miller smelled paint at the canyon in 1901, it was only because the railroad, now with a spur that went all the way to the South Rim, had become a patron for Moran and other artists such as Louis Akin, Oscar Berninghaus, William Leigh, Elliot Daingerfield, Gunnar Widforss, and Carl Borg. They spent weeks at the canyon and the Santa Fe underwrote their travel, accommodations, and even provided some with studio space. In return, the artists either sold their canvases to the railroad or exchanged them for advertising and promotion.

More than any of them, however, Moran revealed the conflation of the canyon with the painter's canvas. In the early decades of the twentieth century, visitors could see the canyon from "Moran Point" at Grand View, venture to "Artists View" off the

Rim Road or see Moran chatting with fellow artists at the El Tovar Hotel. In its great lobby, The Rendezvous, was a spot known as "Moran's Corner." For the painter who had first seen the canyon on the North Rim with the Powell survey in the 1870s, the canyon had become a resource for launching a career of cementing the landscape in American culture. On an 1882 trip to England, Moran finally met Ruskin and showed him sketches of western landscapes. A 1915 article in the *Mentor* recounted their meeting: "Ruskin scrutinized them with an interest that amounted to awe. 'What a horrible place to live in!' he exclaimed. 'We don't live there,' answered Moran. 'We keep places like that for scenic purposes only.'"[5]

Although Ruskin was critical of Moran's work and urged the painter toward a less flashy and more simple study of nature, he respected Moran and bought some of his sketches. Moran, however, was as fervent about his romantic idealizations of the nature as he was about the American artist's role in creating a national culture. "That there is a nationalism in art needs no proof," wrote a sixty-four-year-old Moran in 1902. "Before America can pretend to a position in the world of art it will have to prove it through a characteristic nationality in its art. . . . On a recent visit to the Grand Canyon of Arizona I was more than ever convinced that the future of American art lies in being true to our own country, in the interpretation of that beautiful and glorious scenery which nature has so lavishly endowed our land. . . . [The Grand Canyon] offers a new and comparatively untrodden field for pictorial interpretation, and only awaits the men of original thoughts and ideas to prove to their countrymen that we possess a land of beauty and grandeur with which no other can compare."[6]

Moran's "manifesto" inevitably translated Lummis's "See America First" movement into a call for artists to "paint America first." Both reflected a sense of anti-European nationalism that could boost Americans' pride in their scenic monuments. Investors and tourism promoters enthusiastically supported Moran's and Lummis's pursuit of national cultural symbols and parlayed American cultural anxieties toward an economic advantage. The Santa Fe Railway saw this truth early on. Picking up the tab for artists at the canyon and collecting their paintings not only provided an ample supply of advertising images for promoting the canyon but also symbolically forged a relationship between the observer and the landscape as an experience endowed with artistic vision. The colors of the painter's palette blended on the canvas in images of a landscape that reflected in the eyes of Americans who hungered for cultural security and ideas of unity, and who would also spend money to possess the experience for themselves. "We of the United States arrogate to ourselves the sole right to be called 'America,'" wrote Albert Bushnell Hart in his 1916 "See America First" article for the *Outlook*. "Native Indians, frosty Eskimos, descendants of Spanish and Portugese who arrived decades before the Pilgrim Fathers—all these are set aside in order that we may be 'The Americans.'" Dismissing the roots and realities of racial and ethnic diversity, Hart noted that only the "native modesty" of Americans kept them from "openly boasting of the natural beauties of our land." Hart, however, was quite blunt about the matter. "To apply a commercial term to natural beauties which are beyond any valuation in currency," he said, "'we have the goods.'"[7]

For all of the colors that might bend through the canyon's scenic prism, promoters reaffirmed the singular and distinctive light that would penetrate the eyes of an individual observer. Lummis's "The Greatest Thing in the World," reprinted in a 1915 Santa Fe promotional pamphlet, *Titan of Chasms: The Grand Canyon of Arizona,* still spoke directly to readers and boasted the primacy of personal experience: "There is no preparation for it. Unless you had been told, you would no more dream that out yonder amid the pines the flat earth is slashed to its very bowels, than you would expect to find an iceberg in Broadway. And as you sit upon the brink the divine scene-shifters give you a new canyon every hour." By this time, however, the American public had been told all too well what to expect. The two pages of Lummis's overworked article reprinted in *Titan of Chasms,* however, seem antiquated compared to more than eighteen pages of lodging and tour information, photographs, and maps. For those preparing to visit, the Santa Fe advertising department acted as the first "scene-shifter" of the canyon. Nearly every page is full of photographs showing canyon visitors driving along the rim on newly built roads, the Hopi House, inner canyon tourist camps, trail parties on horseback, auto parties leaving El Tovar Hotel, the canyon railroad depot, and a new automobile garage.

See it for yourself. *See it for yourself.* Lummis chanted this in nearly everything he wrote about the canyon. After Congress established Grand Canyon National Park in February 1919, Lummis's call to Americans took on biblical proportions: "The Grand Canyon Bids You! Come, all ye Peoples of the Earth, to witness God's boldest and most flaming Signature across Earth's face! Come—and penitent—ye of the United States, to marvel upon this chiefest Miracle of our own land! . . . It is a matchless cross-section of Earth's anatomy, to the geologist. To all, it is a Poem; History; an imperishable Inspiration. Words cannot over-tell it—nor half tell. See it, and you will know why!"[8] Like P. T. Barnum and an American Moses, Lummis spoke these words from the opening pages of a 1920 U.S. Railroad Administration pamphlet. With the federal government now guarding the canyon, his proselytism for the Southwest finally had become an official shrine of science, culture, history, and God. Despite his constant objections to those who effusively expressed their passion for the canyon in travel accounts and poetry, it was impossible for Lummis to overstate the case for a personal visit. For Lummis, the Grand Canyon spoke for itself—the mouth of God in the American Southwest—and called the people of the world, especially those living in the United States, to make their pilgrimage.

Despite Lummis's religious rhetoric, the establishment of Grand Canyon National Park, as a place preserved and owned by a democratic public, had become a secular shrine. The Santa Fe advertisers had no trouble printing Lummis's gospel, or anyone's testimony to God, in their literature. In fact, railroad advertising copy, guidebooks, and personal travel narratives were the place to find public accounts of

God's presence at the canyon. All of these texts retained an idea of the canyon as a place for a spiritual experience, but feeling God's presence was always cast as a solitary, internal, and private affair. Under federal supervision, specifically the National Park Service, the common culture of Grand Canyon became marked with the institutional rationalism of natural science and government management strategies. As museums, interpretive programs, and a visitor center were built along the rim, they formalized and materially inscribed the landscape with a public language of scientific education aimed at a democratic public. Geology, paleontology, and evolution became the official story of Grand Canyon, which spoke of a unity in nature that could be read in the canyon walls and that visitors could read to themselves in park service exhibits and designated observation areas.

In 1928, the National Park Service opened the Yavapai Museum and Observation Station on the edge of the South Rim. This stone building became the first formal interpretive station at the park. The building primarily functioned to convey a geological story of the canyon. The museum displayed rock, plant, and small animal specimens, but its most striking feature was a large window looking out onto the canyon, framing the buttes, temples, and inner canyons. Below the window, a huge topographical map provided names corresponding to the sights beyond the glass. A battery of binoculars, fixed in position, with a card below describing each view, was aimed at specific landmarks. "The station is in effect a window through which one may look into the canyon and into the realm of science pertaining to this natural wonder," wrote Ned Burns, the National Park Service's museum division chief. The museum's planners wanted to provide visitors with a structure for interpreting the canyon *on their own*. According to Burns, the museum encourages "the visitor to see and interpret the thing itself from the best viewpoint rather than lead him away from it to see fragments or artificial explanations."[9]

The light reflecting through the great glass panels into the dim stone building illuminated a unified approach to the canyon and to nature, one dominated by a scientific gaze. The canyon was an awesome piece of evidence supporting what many scientists believed to be a neutral and indisputably correct explanation of geology and evolution. For visitors, seeing "the thing itself" was a process of referencing their views to a set of captions for a larger story. The Grand Canyon was not only "a perfectly marvelous expressioning of the earth's physical history, but evidence of the successive steps of life on earth and its distributions at the present time," John Merriam of the Carnegie Institute told the 1928 annual meeting of the National Academy of Sciences.[10] Merriam had directed the planning and construction of the Yavapai Museum. The museum, he reported, represented not only an effort to further geological study at the canyon but was also a place to educate tourists.

Equating public education with national parks had long been an important strategy for preservationists and tourism developers alike. With Congress reluctant to fund national parks solely for their recreational benefits, and with commercial interests ready to exploit natural resources, both preservationists and commercial entrepreneurs campaigned for total park protection by claiming the parks' value for public education and scientific research.[11] In the press, park education advocates looked to the Yavapai Museum as a model for merging two ideals.

"Such museums and nature trails are a logical development in making the parks as useful as possible. In their dual role as recreation grounds and sanctuaries of conservation they can be made to serve admirably in nature education," argued a 1928 *New York Times* editorial. "This truth has been recognized by educational and other organizations which, like the Laura Spelman Rockefeller Memorial and the American Association of Museums, have taken an active part in encouraging the work referred to."[12] Robert Yard, a former editor of the *New York Herald* and then head of the National Park Service information office, seized on the editorial as providing a chance to proclaim that the Yavapai Museum handled "popular interpretation" of nature "in a manner destined importantly to affect the future of outdoor educational methods." He urged Congress to "realize its responsibilities to the national welfare." Yard said that national parks offered "by far the greatest educational opportunity, constituting together an extraordinary super-university of nature, every unit of which may be conceived a special school in one of the many departments of world creation."[13]

There may have been "many departments of world creation," but the National Park Service interpretive program at the canyon tended to teach from a singular text of natural science. Merriam called the Grand Canyon "the cinema of earth history" illustrating "the unity of nature." The canyon expressed "continuity through time and action" and the "presence of moving events of history, with the reality and order of occurrence so visualized that one sees, as it were, the whole panorama of action," he said. "At the Grand Canyon a vastly longer series of ages, or of different times, is visualized at the same moment in the same place."[14] Embedded in Merriam's description of canyon-as-cinema was an enthusiasm for the singular vantage point of the canyon observer. Powell had expressed a similar view a half century earlier as he transcendently gazed upon the "library of the gods." Merriam updated the textual metaphor and imagined the idealized canyon spectator as a moviegoer. Surely, the Yavapai Museum's glass panel could conjure a movie screen, but Merriam's analogy also recognized something else: the organized vision of the spectator, the stationary subject in a darkened room who sees only what the camera sees. Of course, this could not ensure that all visitors would necessarily interpret the canyon's scenes through a geologic lense. They did, however, confront an elaborate and complex mechanism of organized public vision ordering and framing the canyon for them.

Merriam was nothing short of a film director, and the canyon museum was his rough cut of nature's movie. With binoculars and telescopes aimed through the glass panel, visitors found a sequence of edited scenes. They could take in a wide-angle shot of the canyon, then zoom in for a close-up through the binoculars. The explanatory cards below each fixed scene provided the lines of script that became audible, whether read silently or aloud, in the visitor's own voice. A park naturalist stood by as either a narrator in a formal presentation, or what those in the film industry call a "technical adviser," would answer questions as visitors moved from scene to scene. Tourists might feel as though they were learning about the canyon on their own terms, but all the scenes had been blocked out in advance. Someone else chose the story visitors would rehearse. Binoculars were *already* positioned and focused. Maps and labels not only provided answers but also asked the visitor's questions in advance. The place of the visitor (who was assumed to be both hungry for information and insufficiently educated) was prepared and waiting.

Whatever it might be called, a cinema, a schoolroom, or a super-university, the park service interpreted the Grand Canyon as an enormous collection of exhibits. The Yavapai Museum combined all of these as an ideal for the public dissemination of natural science. "In a sense the park as a whole may be regarded as an exhibit and the museum as an explanatory label," suggested Ned Burns. "This concept underlies all park museum work."[15] The Yavapai Museum was only one aspect of a broader institutionalized plan that built on the premise that visitors needed to be educated about the park.

The presence of the tourist body—individually and as a crowd—prompted earlier planners to develop management plans that gave order to both the exterior and interior views of the canyon. "A governing principle of our study is that we should circulate tourist visitors as widely as possible along the canyon rim," wrote U.S. Forest Service ranger Frank A. Waugh in his 1918 plan for canyon development. Describing a rim trail that would lead to Yavapai Point, his report offers a glimpse into the mind of a government planner who rationally calculated the movements of visitors and packaged the potential impacts of sublime experience. "In its final location this walk should touch the rim in about ten points only. These points should be carefully chosen to give the best views of the canyon and secure the greatest variety of prospect," Waugh advised. "The intervening sections of the walk should fall back from the rim, and should run on easier ground among the pinon and cedar trees, thus supplying the desirable intervals of visual and emotional recovery between excessively stimulating views into the canyon."[16] Although regulating traffic for the increasing canyon crowds was his priority, Waugh's plan tried to account for the overwhelming aesthetic experiences visitors often reported. His attention to the tourist's emotional constitution, however, is somewhat anomalous among park management plans that increasingly offered scientific educational lessons to visitors. Waugh's proposal appeared ten years before the construction of Merriam's museum, but it was an early indication of what would come.

In the decade following the opening of the Yavapai Museum, the Field Division of Education head, Ansel Hall, submitted a study for museum development in the park to Superintendent Miner Tillotson, a 1902 Purdue University graduate with a degree in civil engineering. For Hall, the Grand Canyon *was a museum,* and he proposed to label its exhibits. "The educational features of Grand Canyon National Park all support the main feature, Grand Canyon," wrote Hall. "This story is primarily geological, but the configuration of the canyon influences life as well."[17]

Although he rarely mentions tourists, Hall's forty-page report configures tourist life as a set of observation points to integrate spectators with the scene. At Cape Royal on the North Rim, Hall indicated where sighting tubes should be placed to locate and identify "the principal features in the geologic story." Below the tubes, "waterproof exhibit cases are to be installed to hold the exhibits and labels pertaining to the detailed story of each view." At Lipan Point, he wanted to build a lookout shelter "where formations of all five major geological eras can be seen at a glance." Honoring the name given to Point Sublime, Hall saw little need for an exhibit. "It is believed this place should be reserved for inspirational and esthectic *[sic]* reaction on the part of the visitor," he wrote. However, Hall made an exception for an "unobtrusive finder for those who desire to locate and know the names of features seen from here." At the bottom of the Bright Angel Trail on the Colorado River, Hall wanted an educational display at "the exact point seen through the telescope from Yavapai Station." This meant that visitors in the Yavapai Museum could peer into the canyon and observe people educating themselves at information displays on the shores of the Colorado River. The river itself, he said, also held untapped display potential: "At this place we have a wonderful exhibit in place,—the Colorado River; it needs interpretation for a full appreciation of its place in the Grand Canyon story." In addition to explaining the erosive forces of the river, Hall suggested a "study should be made as to the possibility of installing an underwater microphone to bring to the visitor's attention the sound of moving rocks bumping along the bottom, grinding, pounding and cutting downward."

Hall's development plan reflected more than the secular educational ideology of park management; it inscribed the canyon with a visual technology centered on order, control, and the necessity for a public acquisition of official knowledge. Tourists were written into the canyon's scene as a circulating body that required expert management, but it was also a body that could bring legitimacy to park preservation funding requests. Above all, Hall's plan revealed how the touring public's leisure became an object that could be integrated into a rationalizing framework of American culture.

An "exhibitionary complex" originating in the nineteenth century was a "response to the problem of order, but one which worked differently in seeking to transform that problem into one of culture—a question of winning hearts and minds as well as the disciplining and training of bodies," argues cultural critic Tony Bennett. Exhibitory technologies rendered "the forces and principles of order visible to the populace," allowed people to "see themselves from the side of power, . . . knowing what power knows," and organized "a voluntarily self-regulating citizenry."[18] At the Grand Canyon, public education facilities offered visitors a similar vision of an ordered landscape, a chance to align themselves with the knowledge of natural science and submit to the orders of public life. Management plans for roads, trails, and exhibits gave visitors a route to otherwise inaccessible places. But viewing the canyon from observation points and on developed trails meant the journey had been plotted. Such access to the canyon inevitably directed visitors to the geological record, and the names of landmarks, plants, and animal life. Focusing attention on the details of displayed species or the erosive rub of the Colorado River, organizing individual bodies and crowds, and labeling it all with uniformity and confidence left little to doubt or imagination. The information exhibits were simply there, waiting. The power of these plans not only promoted a canyon tamed by natural science but they also tamed the crowd. Providing visitors with a means to internalize a scientific gaze on paths, and at a pace they might feel was their own, park service interpretation expended an incredible amount of energy framing canyon views through a scientific view that was increasingly becoming a *natural* feature of a secular society.

Dusting for Fingerprints of an Almighty

"We used to have a permanent cross out on the West Rim Worship Site," the pastor of the Grand Canyon Community Church told me in the backroom office of his home one afternoon. "But there are enough people who don't like the presence of Christianity that somebody took it upon themselves to just tear it down, destroy it." The West Rim Worship Site is a level area, off the Rim Trail, where natural ledges serve as benches facing the canyon. "It was a wooden cross; I wouldn't want to put a metal cross up there. It was replaced after the first one was vandalized with another wooden cross. That one was vandalized, too," recalled the pastor. Every effort to restore the cross met with the same fate. "Each time it's destroyed, we have to go over to the park service for permission to put another one up," he said. "The only thing we could do that would be permanent, would be to put a metal cross up. But it wouldn't look right. It should be something more natural, something that fits into the setting."

The interdenominational Community Church carries a brass cross up and down the trail every Sunday morning. The cross has a pedestal, and it rests on a concrete and stone slab built to anchor the wooden ones that kept getting torn down. The church makes do, and people worship together on the rim every Sunday morning during the summer months. "There are no church buildings because nobody owns property here," the pastor said. "Churches would love to have their own buildings, would love to have a chapel built somewhere here, but they can't get permission. It's simply not allowed." The Grand Canyon Community Church, along with the Roman Catholic church, the Assembly of God, the Baptist church, and the Church of Jesus Christ of Latter-Day Saints also share worship space in the Shrine of the Ages building. It is a building owned and administered by the park service where, in addition to religious services, public events take place. The single building means that the church groups face constraints in scheduling worship times. In a larger sense, however, "fitting into the setting" has been an issue facing several decades of congregations at the canyon.

Since 1917, planners, senators, and a growing population of permanent residents of Grand Canyon Village have expressed interest in erecting a chapel. Not until 1952, when Protestant, Catholic, and Jewish lay members formed the Shrine of the Ages Chapel Corporation, did the idea seem more than talk. The August 1955 issue of *Arizona Highways* solicited contributions and ran an eight-page article on the proposed Shrine of the Ages chapel planned for construction on the canyon's rim in 1956. The idea of an interfaith worship building gained National Park Service approval, where standing policy was to deny permission to individual groups. The park service's policy simply stated that if one group had permission to build a church, then all groups could demand the same permission. Although the permanent canyon population approached four hundred residents, it was unlikely the small community would be able to support several churches. The collective effort of various faiths under one roof offered a solution. In the summer of 1955, many believed workers would soon begin pouring a concrete foundation for such a church. The park service required that the chapel's design conform with regulations acknowledging respect for the natural scenery and reflect the spirit of a Native American ceremonial kiva. "In order to protect the very primitiveness of the Canyon rim, the building will spring from the rocks and shrubs in complete harmony with its surroundings," reported Ken Parks in *Arizona Highways.* However, the planned building held a remote resemblance to a "kiva." The plans and sketches for Philadelphia architect Harold Wagoner's modern parabolic building gave the impression that a huge spacecraft had landed on the rim. No crosses, tablets of the Ten Commandments, or specific religious symbols appeared in the plans. Inside, pews faced a huge curved window view of the canyon. The building was planned to accommodate different faiths with three separate altars. "These altars will be mounted on hydraulic lifts which are to be operated from the basement below the chancel," said Parks. "Thus, within a matter of minutes, the Protestant altar can be lowered and replaced by [a] Jewish altar with a masonry receptacle for the Ark, or by a Catholic altar."[19]

The spectacular church, however, never was constructed. Individual and church donations were never sufficient to realize Wagoner's plans. But the problem was more than a matter of funds. A 1956 issue of *National Parks Magazine* published a piece by Sierra Club member H. C. Bradley expressing resistance to a church on the rim. "Any edifice on or near the rim of Grand Canyon is out of place and a distraction," wrote Bradley. "I can see no objection to providing Grand Canyon's service village [back from the rim] with a modest church designed primarily for the local population and not as a tourist attraction."[20] This is exactly what happened. With the help of federal funds, another version of a worship building was built away from the rim, near the visitor center. Once government funds entered the picture, it "meant there was going to be a substantial amount of government control in the building," a canyon minister told me. "Somehow, over the years, the intent of the building changed. It became a park service building and they own, operate and administrate the use of that building. So, all of the churches that use it rent space to worship there, but I don't believe the churches are given preferential thought as to renting it. Anybody can rent it for any purpose. They have aerobics in it."

Most of the churches tend to focus on reaching out to people in a largely transient community and mutually affirming the other ministries active in the park. In a place developed with hotels, souvenir shops, and federal buildings for park administration and interpretation, the churches at Grand Canyon appear to visitors as listings in the local information guides. Their congregations appear and disappear on Sunday mornings as different groups enter and leave the Shrine of the Ages. Against the secular thrust of park service interpretation, churches pose little, if any, formal alternative to understanding one's place in the canyon landscape, and for some ministers, that's not really the issue. "My job as a worship leader is not to try to interpret the canyon," the community church pastor told me, adding he wanted people to appreciate the canyon, and "if they sense a special closeness with the Creator during that appreciation, that's great. Let's worship. Let's not see it as an opportunity to confront other perspectives or to engage in debate. I know some people do that. Some are very adamant about the Creationist point of view."

Apart from the interests of community-building and worship, the churches of Grand Canyon Village are islands of spirituality for people who make the canyon their home or spend time there on vacation. However, other religious groups, who appear in the park with federal permits allowing them to exercise their constitutional rights and distribute informational materials, reach out to the steady stream of canyon visitors as a potential audience for spiritual growth. For instance, Ganapati Swami of the Hare Krishna movement travels in a small recreational vehicle from his base in Denver, Colorado, for a few weeks each summer and sets up an information table outside the visitor center. Dressed in an orange robe, sunglasses, and bicycle cap, he sits for hours beneath an umbrella at a table stacked with copies of the Bhagavad Gita, pamphlets, and articles. His objective at the canyon is "to raise people's consciousness," he told me. "It's too bad. A place like the Grand Canyon has the ability to do that to a certain extent, but even though it descends something like a mile to the river, it goes over most people's heads," he said. For him, all of the tourists armed with video cameras were a sign of people alienated from experiencing and enjoying the present. "They're basically living in the past and the future," he said. "While they're here, they don't appreciate it because they're shooting all the sights and scenes so they can take home and show their neighbors and grandchildren in the future."

I asked him how the Bhagavad Gita might help people understand the canyon or themselves in a different way. "There's a whole chapter in which Krishna describes different ways in which one can understand the presence of the supreme within different objects or representations of material nature," he said. "So, in this way, anyone can become, can spiritualize their consciousness just in daily action by remembering God's presence in all of these manifestations." Although Krishna never mentioned the Grand Canyon, Ganapati Swami said the canyon embodied this philosophy. "I found out Clarence Dutton, the man who named most of these rock formations, was also a student of Indian philosophy about a hundred years back," he told me. "Mr. Dutton named the foundation of the whole thing 'Vishnu Schist,' the rock at the bottom of the whole canyon. That also corresponds to Vedic literature where, in the Gita, Krishna says, 'I as Vishnu am the foundation of the source of all spiritual and material things.' It's kind of interesting how he's done that." Ganapati Swami suggested I read the Bhagavad Gita, and I donated ten dollars for a hardcover copy. He also gave me a copy of "Escaping the Reality Illusion," an article written by Kundali Dasa. Western science and Eastern spirituality are essentially oriented toward the same end; both recognize a world filtered by images and illusions aspiring toward cultural consensus about reality, said the article, but neither view quite gets beyond a prison of illusions fed by the imperfection of sensory data and interpretation. The way out of the prison house of illusions lay in Vedic culture, argues Kundali Dasa, because it "trains its adherents—man, woman, and child—to penetrate the relative world to the plane of absolute reality, the spiritual world."[21] For the student of Krishna who spoke with me outside the visitor center, scientific views describing the canyon formation were merely other mirrors. "They have a couple of different theories and the theory now could be yesterday's theory a couple of years from now," said the swami. "That's the way of material science, you know? It's always changing, they never really know. So I don't take that too seriously."

The Grand Canyon opens to spiritual philosophies seeing the power of a creator in nature. For the most part, the minister and the swami view the explanation of origins offered by the park service as provisional, relative and changing theories holding little consequence for spiritual growth. In the canyon's landscape, these divergent approaches don't draw the sides of a public debate as much as they represent the factioned dimensions of spiritual philosophies gathered around a natural and cultural hole where there is no center. Ironically, it is often through park service programs that advocates of different faiths and interpretive paradigms come face to face.

"Most of those people don't challenge a ranger in front of a crowd," one ranger told me when I asked about conflicts between scientific and creationist perspectives on the canyon. "They'll come up quietly after and say, 'Well that's a nice little lecture, but you don't really believe that do you? . . . We know you are a good Christian girl, and we know the government's making you say this.' Our point is not to change their minds, our point is to get them to enjoy the canyon. . . . We tell them we leave the scientific explanation to man and leave it up to a higher authority to tell you why." Another park interpreter said this how-and-why response was one of her "favorite phrases to use, and to get out of [the situation] pretty quick." Although some rangers might suggest a harmony between science and creation, or avoid the discussion altogether, other park service interpreters hold stronger views. "We know most about [the geological view]," claimed another ranger I spoke with. "As far as I'm concerned, it does deserve the higher priority because—with the number of people we have coming through here—it's the one easiest to defend and it's the one we know most about." Another told me seeing the canyon as a site of science rather than a place of "creativity, creationism, or beauty or anything like that" was a more practical approach. "It's easier to look at the scientific side of it and explain that because it is more clear-cut," he said. "It takes less creativity in a person to try and explain the technical side of it. What we have is fact versus what we come up with as a personal experience."

There is really little public debate between creationist and scientific understandings of the canyon, but visitor comments tell a different story. For instance, a register placed in the visitor center by the park service in 1981 asked visitors what they wanted from the park. Among the numerous comments, some tourists criticized the park service's commitment to scientific interpretations of the canyon. "Dear Park Officials: I would like to see stated in your visitor centers that evolution is a theory and not a fact," wrote one person. "Your Indian legend was closer to creation than evolution." Another visitor listed several requests: "(a) Proof that life of a Cambrian was actually 600 million years ago. How is anyone supposed to believe that?! There is a mighty God who created mighty beauty for the people whom he loves so *very* much; (b) For you to show the God who created this beautiful canyon and not the baloney about 600 million years ago; (c) Why do you have to have a theory of Evolution as a way of life. God did it and I believe it." A Danish visitor suggested that the canyon reflected a larger historical shift in American culture. "When U.S. was a Christian country, based on the word of God (Bible), you would not find the words 'plant/animal life,' 'millions-billions years ago,' because the word of God says something other," the entry reads. "The Earth may be so old, but life first began about 6,000 years ago. God Bless you." For two tourists, the comment book became a place for a quick exchange of conflicting views. "Regardless of Evolutionists' theories, No Body But God could ever make anything as Grandeur as this National Park," reads one comment. Beneath it, someone else wrote: "Bullshit. Stand under a dripping faucet for 50 years and you'll see its effects." The meeting of these views was likely only a textual meeting—two strangers in a visitor center, one in front of the other, separated by seconds or minutes, and their respective orders of belief. While they point out the divisions beneath the surface of institutionalized interpretive programs, their exchange is recorded in a register that ultimately makes its way to the shelves of a study collection where it gathers dust. Writing down their thoughts in a visitor register provides a moment of confirmation for one's own beliefs regarding scientific and spiritual matters, but for others, conflicting stories of scientific and spiritual origins told at the canyon are the seeds of confusion.

"This is such a cosmic place," Matt told me one evening at the bottom of Grand Canyon. We were listening to a ranger explain canyon geology in a campfire program near Phantom Ranch. A thirty-six-year-old warehouse worker from San Mateo, California, Matt was on a weeklong vacation with his old friend from high school. After the ranger finished her talk, Matt sounded frustrated. "You've got guys like Christ, Joseph Smith, Mahatma Gandhi, Buddha, and they were all talking about the same kind of thing, but they didn't talk much about geology back then," he complained. "Last Thursday, the ranger told us about the Indian story of the canyon, and there were these spider women . . . or widow women, something like that, and tonight she tells us about fault lines and erosion. I'd like to get it all just put together once and for all, you know?" Even though Matt sensed some common thread linking his list of religious figures, he had difficulty sorting between them or reaching any conclusion other than his sense of a "cosmic" canyon. Listening to the same ranger tell the story of a Hopi legend and explain canyon geology, he heard an official voice of a canyon expert laying out the pieces of a puzzle he couldn't assemble. "All I know is that we've got to hike out of here tomorrow morning," he told me, getting up from our wooden bench. With flashlight beams bouncing on the trail ahead of us, we walked to the banks of the Colorado River and looked up at the same celestial bodies that hovered over Powell and his men in 1869.

At least one group, however, systematically disputes the facts of an established geological view of Grand Canyon. "There's kind of a secular mentality these days that's taken over," Steven Austin of the Institute for Creation Research (ICR) in Santee, California, told me. "So for a theory to be scientific, it must be secular. . . . Now wait a minute, who ever said that science equals naturalism?" Austin, who earned a doctorate in geology from Pennsylvania State University in 1979 and heads the geology department at the ICR Graduate School near San Diego, has been studying the canyon's geology and leading tours at Grand Canyon since 1980. Geologist, teacher, and tour guide, Austin, along with several others holding doctorates in geology, geological engineering, and biochemistry from Harvard and the universities of Texas, Oklahoma, Sydney, and California-Berkeley, have gathered a body of evidence from canyon research trips supporting a neocatastrophic view of the canyon's origins. In other words, *their* scientific evidence from the canyon turns geology back to the biblical story of creation and the Great Flood.

In a video documentary, *Grand Canyon: Monument to the Flood,* and a companion book, *Grand Canyon: Monument to Catastrophe,* produced and distributed by the ICR, Austin and his colleagues argue that evolutionists and creationists analyze the same Grand Canyon rock strata and fossils but interpret the evidence through differing interpretive frameworks. Evolutionists, they say, use a "uniformitarian framework of interpretation," leading them to conclude that the canyon formed during millions of years. Calm oceans advanced and retreated, and rock strata and fossils are the result of erosion and sedimentation occurring slowly through the geologic ages. Creationists, however, use a "catastrophist framework of interpretation" to conclude that rock strata and fossils reveal a rapid depositing of sediment, the kind that could occur with the advance and retreat of a single flood. Since no human witnessed the canyon in the making, its rock strata and fossils *"do not* dictate or determine the conclusions of geologists." Instead, members of the interdenominational ICR emphasize how geologic data is *"used* by geologists to build their interpretations of history."[22] With these interpretive assumptions laid out, the "neo-creationist" geologists methodically debate established evolutionary-based theories about the canyon. Their most striking departure from the views of mainstream geologists is their idea of a fast-flowing ocean covering the continent. Conventional scientists read the canyon walls as evidence of a calm ocean, one whose sediments were slowly deposited over the ages. ICR geologists dispute this idea in their analysis of canyon fossils, instead suggesting that strong water currents quickly killed and buried marine organisms. In other words, the Great Flood described in the Old Testament set off a catastrophic chain of events whereby the canyon formed over a period of weeks rather than millions of years. Austin also disputes previous attempts to determine the age of lava formations in the canyon. Discrepancies among radioactive-isotope dating methods lead him to question whether anyone has successfully dated the canyon's rocks at nearly two billion years.

In their video documentary, I watch as a geologist stands inside the canyon at a place where different strata meet. He points to canyon layers as though identifying a specific passage on the page of a book. "Here I am at The Great Unconformity in the canyon; it corresponds to this line between the darker sediments below and the lighter sediments above," says Kurt Wise, who holds a doctorate in geology from Harvard. Most geologists agree that the "great unconformity," the meeting place of the Dox formation and the Tapeats sandstone formation, is one of the most important single geological sites in the canyon. This is because the Dox formation is more than one billion years old. The Tapeats sandstone, however, directly above the Dox formation, is estimated to be about a half billion years old. "If that is right," Wise explains, there is "a half a billion years missing between the deposition of the Dox and the deposition of the Tapeats sandstone." The great unconformity, he argues, is evidence of the canyon eroding quickly, requiring less time than the assumed chemical erosion many geologists claim, and "what we believe is that the erosion event here corresponds to the erosion event at the beginning of the Flood."[23] Such interpretive disagreements run throughout the documentary.

Austin told me that the park service has been extremely cooperative in providing him with research permits to collect samples and fee waivers for his educational tours. His laboratory at the ICR holds one of the largest collections of canyon rock samples outside of the canyon itself. Yet, he finds that his philosophical and religious assumptions hit a wall when it comes to reaching larger audiences with the ICR's conclusions about the canyon. The Grand Canyon Natural History Association bookstore, housed in the visitor center, declined to sell the ICR book after submitting it to the park superintendent's office for approval. That bookstore doesn't carry any geology books with a creationist perspective. "What is interesting is they want to be multicultural *and* secular at the same time," Austin told me. The interpretive discrepancies between Austin's group and other geologists, and a park service that supports ICR research and tours yet remains reluctant to facilitate public distribution of their views, are clearly matters of authority and judgment. But for Austin and his colleagues, the Grand Canyon itself is a monument to the same.

Watching the final scenes of the ICR documentary, I note each of the five geologists standing at the canyon and taking turns at putting their scientific findings into a larger interpretive context. "The more I study the evidence here, the rocks and the fossils and the erosion pattern . . . the more I come to the conclusion that a flood must've done it," says geoscientist John D. Morris. "But then, when we think about that, we've got to recognize that Flood in scripture was really a judgment of sin. . . . God hates sin. God always judges sin and this is the grim reminder of the hatred that he has for sin . . . and what he does. He punishes sin." Morris says the beauty of the canyon is "really the destroyed remnant of the world before the Flood" and asks the viewer to "imagine how beautiful that pre-flood world must've been so that the destruction of it would look like this." Andrew Snelling, a geologist with a doctorate from the University of Sydney, similarly sees the canyon as a place where God first judged the world by sending a great flood. "We see abundant evidence of that here in the canyon," he says standing on the Colorado River shore. "The next time he is going to judge by fire, and personally, that challenges me to be ready to meet my creator, but it also challenges me to be able to share this information with others." For the other three geologists, the canyon also stands as a sign of God's potential to draw the line but, says Austin, of his "provision and redemption" as well.

Many may bristle at such words coming from geologists reporting from the canyon's rim. Collapsing scientific and theological beliefs, however, has a history dating back to Powell's first expedition. Since the late nineteenth century, advocates of these two positions have argued with one another. "All this our ancestors would have called natural religion; and our ancestors, like modern detectives, would have gone around the grand canyon [sic] with microscopes looking for a little fingerprint of the Almighty," Rev. Charles W. Gilkey told an afternoon session of the 1917 National Parks conference. Gilkey, a minister from Chicago, was speaking on behalf of preservationist efforts to make the canyon a national park. "It may or may not get anywhere to trace the connection between cause and effect or to try in any literal sense to make these the handiwork or the finger marks of the Almighty," he said, "but we can not afford to lose out of our lives . . . the natural religion that comes not so much by process of argument by nature as by process of investigation into the mysteries and secrets of the human soul." Gilkey, the final speaker of that day's session, saw in the canyon something he found absent in modern America. "The sense of depth, that is what everybody misses in our American life," he said. "In becoming so tremendously up to date, we are at the same time getting unusually shallow." He concluded by remarking that the awe-inspiring stars over the canyon only moved people to "a keener awe for that moral light within us, which, after all is said and done, is the only indispensable thing for the future of our nation."[24] In light of the geological, evolutionary, and theological interpretations that had preceded and would eventually follow Gilkey's speech, perhaps he had come upon a single truth about the Grand Canyon: whether one thought of it as a scientific or a spiritual abyss, in the end, it was a *moral* canyon that opened onto a larger American cultural landscape unsettled by secularizing and rationalizing forces.

Compared to the pervasive and "neutral" voices of science and park service interpretation, the pronouncements of contemporary creation-geologists issuing warnings
of God's judgment may seem a harsh, moral imperative, symptomatic of a growing
American neoconservative force. In contrast, the natural sciences—geology, biology,
botany, paleontology—rarely suggest that anyone is so directly implicated. The disci-
plines of natural science resemble wandering tributaries many believe will eventually
empty into a tranquil sea—a common reservoir of slowly deposited knowledge about
the origins of earth and life. John Merriam, who directed the design of the Yavapai
Museum, saw a natural unity embedded in the canyon that "strikingly illustrated" the
interlocking elements and linkages of biology and geology as an unknown story "for
those who will come to chart these wildernesses of the past."[25] Yet, it may be useful to
remember how the charts based on natural science were also used as moral guideposts
to map the chaotic wilderness of a transforming culture at the turn of the century, and
how Darwin's and Spencer's ideas became a foundation for social Darwinists of the
Gilded Age, who leveled ruthless judgments about race, rights, and human welfare.[26]
Of course, natural scientists believed they were innocent of such interpretations. The
larger picture would have to be drawn elsewhere. What distant scientific or moral
linkages, for example, might a *New York Times* reader find on November 22, 1928,
when she turned to page eight and noted that Dr. C. B. Davenport of the Carnegie
Institute had just reported his conclusions about inborn mental differences between
races at the same meeting at which Merriam reported the canyon was a source of "evidence of the successive steps in the history of life on the earth and its distributions at
the present time"? Davenport told the National Academy of Sciences that "negroes
show a superiority over the white in at least certain parts of the field of sensory discrimination . . . but in tests involving some organization, foresight and planning, the
negroes seem to be inferior to the whites."[27] Was there any connection between these
findings and the history of life at Grand Canyon? Was the National Academy of
Sciences or the Carnegie Institute merely a group of scientists asking unrelated questions? Why did these two studies come together in the same meeting and appear in
the same article? Was the answer to such questions found in a "unity of nature"?

Whether one sees a creationist or scientific canyon, the moral dimension in either
view reaches into worlds far beyond the depths of the great abyss in northern Arizona.
The Grand Canyon, however, *is* a place where public discussions of scientific and spiritual issues have long been divided by uneven lines of authority expressed in regimes of
language sedimenting, calcifying, and eroding. When Powell first saw the canyon region, he thought it to be a "Book of Revelations" in the great "rock-leaved Bible of geology." Those who came later walked the rim negotiating but not quite reconciling
the antagonistic terms of naturalism and theology. Today, visitors equally embrace the
canyon's uncertainties with a faith grounded in texts carried from other places and
times. I see this division mirrored in the publicity blurbs on the back covers of two
Grand Canyon books: "Your personal tour of the Grand Canyon by the folks who

know it best!" from the back of *The Grand Canyon: Intimate Views,* a collection of essays by natural scientists; and, on the back cover of *Grand Canyon: Monument to Catastrophe,* "Your personal tour of the Grand Canyon brought to you by the creation scientists who know it best!" Two books, two sets of experts on parallel journeys to different places; side by side, each traces their scientific paths over the same geography.[28] The well-worn path first traveled by Powell ultimately led away from the idea of a "Bible" and answered questions of creation with the long pencil of rationality and reason that increasingly dominated a secularizing society. Creationists discovered they could pick up that same pencil and use it to recopy the pages of an Old Testament Bible on the canyon's walls. Each tries to claim the silent space between the canyon's rims with a distinctive voice, but it is really the space between the canyon and the men and women who stand before its vast landscape that they are after. Encouraging them to read nature's text from different sides of the canyon's broken landscape, each aims to mark a trail through a larger world.

Hunting Fossils in a Divided Landscape

"I studied geology as an undergraduate years ago," I hear a man tell the couple walking next to him. "This is the Superbowl of Geology."

"You start in nature, you return to nature," responds the other man.

"Maybe sooner than you think," says the woman holding his hand, craning for a look over the rim. I listen to them—three friends on a vacation—as we walk with about thirty others on a ranger program called the "Fossil Hunt." Our ranger, Fred, a fifty-seven-year-old teacher who works summers in the park, leads us by the West Rim shuttle bus interchange on a paved section of the Rim Trail. We pass a crowd of visitors, self-assembled in single file lines and waiting to board a shuttle. Everyone carries a photocopied sheet with sketches of fossils we'll be looking for on the rim. Several yards up the trail, I hear the group laughing. Ranger Fred, standing in a small ravine that runs down into the canyon, is finding out how much our group knows about fossils.

"What is a fossil?" he asks. No one answers. "David?"

"They look old," shyly offers David, a twelve-year old whom Fred already knows by name.

"Old?" says Fred. "Old like me? Am I a fossil? Hm . . . not yet, anyway." The group laughs as he jokes with the boy.

"No, you have to examine them. Is it a mollusk or coral or whatever? . . . And then see how old it is," says David.

"*Examine* them. . . . Well now," Fred grins, "we've got some budding paleontologists about." The ranger treats him like a friend with common interests and the boy glows over being considered an "insider." Fred tells us "a fossil is something that had been alive and got buried in mud and silt, it got solidified, and bingo, you have a fossil." His simple summary is much more palatable than the page he gave us listing the temperature tolerances, salinity tolerances, and feeding categories of the crinoid, bryozoan, brachiopod, peniculauris, and other names that I couldn't easily pronounce on the first try.

"About 250 million years ago I would have been standing in the muck of shallow sea," Fred says, standing below us in the ravine. "*Geographically,* we'd be near the equator in central Africa. Some of the fossils we find here are 'index fossils,' and they tell us we are *not* where we would be geographically 250 million years ago." He says this section of the canyon was part of the continent of Pangaea, part of the ancient shifting continental geographies geologists describe with theories of plate tectonics. My imagination tries to picture our group—with our running shoes, loafers, sunglasses, and cameras—standing knee deep in an ancient ocean sometime before humans even walked the earth, but I can't quite make the mental leap that places northern Arizona in Africa. The words "250 million years" reach my ears like the latest figures of the federal deficit. I only hear the sounds of a loaded shuttle bus grinding up West Rim Drive. "This is the Bright Angel Fault and it runs clear across to the North Rim," says Fred, tracing the ravine he's standing in. I follow his arm and pick up the distant lines of the Bright Angel Trail running down to the Tonto Platform. The trail disappears into the Inner Gorge, but I can see the fault line all the way up Bright Angel Canyon to the North Rim. "The Bright Angel Fault exposed the fossil field on the West Rim. The uplift of the west side created an elevation that rain could run down, wash away the soil, and expose the fossils," he explains. "This canyon is fantastic for fossilization!"

These are the extreme ends of the geological and evolutionary record so many researchers have been assembling since the mid-nineteenth century; all the little fragments add up to big pictures of the planet. The remains of clams, sponges, and corals, frozen in stone, are small clues accumulated in this enormous file cabinet of natural science. Many researchers have been piecing together this puzzle, cross-referencing fossils off the coast of Africa with those of Grand Canyon and coordinating all of it with a massive geological clock. The whole enterprise, with its enormous scope of time, detail, classification, certainty, consistency, and faith runs out of Fred's mouth as if he were reporting today's weather from a newspaper.

On the wide, steplike cliffs of the West Rim, Fred leads us off the trail. He quickly locates some fossils, tells us their names, and places coins on the rock so that we can find them ourselves. The children in the group quickly huddle around the pennies and nickels to look at the specimens. Their heads block my view. By the time I get to see them, I'm having trouble finding anything resembling what's on my reference sheet. The kids are moving the coins, I think. Later, I see a few outlines of ancient mollusks, sponges, and sea fans, but I'm mostly taking the ranger's word on all of it. After Frank locates several more fossils, he turns us loose to find our own. The hunt is on, and the children scramble toward the prospect of making discoveries that Fred will come over and certify. I watch three of them scrape the dirt off a rock. Others roam the stone field, bent over like a crowd looking for a lost contact lens. Many of the adults have retreated to the shade of pine trees. I follow Fred and some others to a slightly elevated area, and he shows us a species of clam.

"This is an index fossil, and it tells us this was once a sea," he says. David asks a question about a species of bryozoan, and Fred asks him for his address so he can send some information. I hear a father tell his daughter to ask the ranger to autograph her photocopied sheet of fossil illustrations. Two young girls, wearing identical Bart Simpson T-shirts, ask Fred to look at something they think is a dinosaur fossil, and he happily follows them to their find.

Finding one for myself is really the issue now, but I have neither the eyes, patience, luck, or whatever to locate anything vaguely corresponding to my photocopied page of fossil sketches. But I notice something else and walk a few paces up to an open area on the rim. I immediately recognize the place as the West Rim Worship Site, where a Grand Canyon Community Church service took place a few days ago. The block of boulders and cement, covered with four stone slabs, looks like a piece of an old foundation. The church used it as an altar that crisp and windy Sunday morning when I stood under the trees and watched a sunrise service. The stone ledges behind it became pews, where people in windbreakers and sweaters were singing hymns. The place is quiet now, and I leave after seeing two hikers veer off the Rim Trail and head in my direction.

I sit down on a rock next to the stone imprint of an ancient clam that Frank had marked with a nickel and put the fossil sheet in my day pack. A few people linger, scanning the rim, but the rest of the group has started back down the trail. Below me,

Frank darts around picking up the coins he had used to mark his examples. Above me, a hiker stands on the Worship Site altar and takes the telephoto lens off of his camera. "This canyon is fantastic for fossilization," Frank had said; however, his words carried beyond these traces of prehistoric marine life. The "Fossil Hunt" tour and the Sunday-morning sunrise worship service site shared the same field with remains of age-old mollusks, sponges, and sea fans. Now a hiker, aiming a wide-angle lens, stands on the Worship Site altar making his own fossils with light and emulsion.

"Fossils are where you find them," I once heard a man from Utah say. He would spend weeks at a time wandering the canyonlands in southern Utah looking for the signs of old Anasazai roads, but I knew it was the search for the lost and forgotten remains of the dead, hidden in the rocks, that brought him pleasure. On the rim of the canyon, it was much the same. People searching the stones were calling up a pleasure of discovery in their lives. The same canyon of fossils that prompted the certainties and speculations of the scientist was for others a canyon continually calling forth a spirit. "I used the image of how dark the canyon can be, you know just prior to that sunrise," a canyon minister told me one afternoon, describing his sermon for an Easter sunrise service at Mather Point. "And then when that sun starts to come up, the light starts to really filter down and every little side canyon is touched by that glory and that light and I relate that to our lives." It was all a matter of reading and translation.

"Tell me the landscape in which you live and I will tell you who you are," said philosopher José Ortega y Gasset, but he believed that the cartographies of cultural and social life are best drawn by the hands of an elite.[29] At the canyon, many descriptions suggest the variety of ways people anchor themselves in its landscape well mapped with the conflicts of a modern world. "Man knows he is something more than an organism in an environment, because for one thing he acts like anything but an organism in an environment," wrote Walker Percy. "Yet he no longer has the means of understanding the traditional Judaeo-Christian teaching that the 'something more' is a soul somehow locked in the organism like a ghost in a machine. What is he then? He has not the faintest idea. Entered as he is into a new age, he is like a child who sees everything in his new world, names everything, knows everything except himself."[30] At the canyon, people have, for more than a century, looked into The Wonder with awe and inquiry, excitement and ambivalence. Casting the stratified layers of its walls as a Book of Genesis or Revelations, a bible of geology, or the stacked volumes of human knowledge, an urge to speak and write is, perhaps, an inevitable reaction (and consequence) for those impatiently confronting a great space of emptiness and silence. The language of science and spirit echoing through the canyon for more than a century has always opened onto other canyons of time and space, linking past and future, metaphorically bridging a distant outward gaze toward nature and an inward gaze into heart and mind. For more than a century, the Grand Canyon has led people to probe such depths and distances, as if doing so might help solve or offer some relief to what Burke called the "eternally unsolvable Enigma, the preposterous fact that both existence and nothingness are equally unthinkable." It is in the space between the Kaibab and Coconino Plateaus that people have gazed, measured, revered, and confronted "an occasional shiver of cold metaphysical dread," for it is here the "eternal enigma" appears etched into the earth in absolute clarity. The Grand Canyon retains an image of a world where uncertainty precedes, persists, and stretches beyond the minor routines and dramas that absorb modern life. Above all, as Burke reminds us, the canyon is a place where we dramatically face a "staggering disproportion between man and no-man," and where we remember that people "build their cultures by huddling together, nervously loquacious, at the edge of an abyss."[31]

An Awesome Canon

"The value of the canyon is not in how man can change the canyon, but how man can be changed by the canyon," says Ranger Karen, reading an index-card quote from the nature writer W. J. Breed. Nearing the end of her "Awesome Chasm" walk, we stop near Grandeur Point, as she once more invites us to feel humbled before the immense canyon. "This is a value of the canyon," she continues. "What it can do to us. It's big. You can't see it all from the developed viewpoints. You can't see it all from a plane. You've got to go up in a satellite to see all of Grand Canyon at one time. . . . We feel insignificant even as a species when we realize our little piece in all of earth's history. We think we're such big dogs. . . . We do so much in the world. But we can stand a little bit of humility. . . . The Grand Canyon is a good place to come and be faced with these things, and I haven't even talked about the cosmos and the universe and all that." Our "newfound" feelings of humility and insignificance can help us focus our attention to the significance of nature, Karen tells us. This is a moment to pause and learn about geology, biology, plant life and animal zones, climate changes, and even ourselves. Karen says that she finds inspiration and clarity on the canyon's rim and comes here often when she needs to sort out some problem or just think. This afternoon, we'll have a similar opportunity, and she asks the children in our group to help hand out pencils and sheets of paper.

"Sit still for a few minutes," she says, "and then just write down your thoughts about the canyon, what this walk has stimulated in your mind. You can write it in poetry, you can write it in prose, you can write it in a letter, however you want to write it; draw a picture if that's your way of expressing yourself." I glance at our group seated on the rocks; most are either looking off into the canyon or staring at their white sheet of paper. I sense the spirit of the exercise but want to say something witty or sagacious even though I can't come up with anything. For about ten minutes, I watch the others jot down thoughts and hand them to Karen. A little girl shows her mother a picture she's drawn of a park ranger standing next to a cone-shaped tree. With time running out, I decide to follow her lead and sketch a V-shaped cross-section of a canyon. I span the rims with a set of McDonald's arches and add balloon-shaped clouds spelling out "McCanyon" across the sky. I scan my juvenile doodling and decide it's more embarrassing than humorous. As Karen collects pencils and papers, I crumple the drawing into my pack and turn on my tape recorder, again.

"Okay, here are *your* thoughts," announces Karen, her back to the canyon and facing us. "The Grand Canyon shows each individual how small they really are," she reads from the first paper on the stack. "Increase the size a trillionfold, make each butte, plateau, and rise a planet or a star and now see how small we really are." The group stares at her, and a few nod. One woman claps her hands, thinking we're supposed to applaud, but no one joins her. She looks a little embarrassed as Karen shuffles to the next paper.

"Shakespeare has Hamlet say: 'What a piece of work is a man, How noble in reason, how infinite in faculty, in form and moving how express and admirable.'" I scan the crowd trying to decide who in our group looks most like an English professor. "He must have visited the canyon for this next sentence: 'And yet, to me, what is this quintessence of dust.'"

"Now *that's* nice," someone says, as Karen turns to a new page.

"The canyon gives me the awareness of time and how short our lifetime is," she reads, "glory to God for all this," and shuffles to another page. "What a nice thought it would be if we as humans would have as long as the Grand Canyon has to reach such a magnificent state of being. If we could all reach such a state, to give the kinds of feelings the Grand Canyon gives us here, this very moment, what a wonderful world this would and could be," reads Karen, nodding her head with approval. "For myself, from this very moment, I will be all I can be to this human race. Perhaps that is why God gave us the Grand Canyon." The theme of the readings quickly becomes predictable with nearly everyone affirming Karen's thoughts about humility. Only one or two attempt to restate (with understandable error) the "important facts" we'd read earlier from index cards.

For the most part, the last hour spent on geology and measurement has been left back on the trail. Instead, most respond with serious and amusing expressions about the meaning of life, nature, and reminders of God. "The magnitude of all the dimensions boggles the mind," offers someone else. "Even though this is all explainable in scientific terms and facts, I think the hand of God is also present." Others echo the ranger's earlier words. "As we walk through life, a pause at Grand Canyon challenges our concept of ourself and the world. Live life to the fullest. Harm no one or any life put here," wrote one person. "Because my life is so short as to be insignificant, I should worry not about my own accomplishments in the present. Instead I should learn what has come before and how to protect and nurture our environment for the future," wrote another.

Karen holds up the little girl's drawing of a ranger standing next to a tree. "I guess that might be me," she says, and the little girl next to me smiles as her work is put on display. One participant jotted down a poem:

> The Grand Canyon is mighty big
> it makes one feel like a little pig.
> It's so far down to the lowest part
> walking down will break my heart.
> So it's up on the rim I'll stay today
> and just look down and all around.
> To see the awesome wonderful place
> that caught my heart and makes it race.

A few people laugh politely, but the laughter stops when she reads the first line of the next comment.

"This trip through the Grand Canyon has thoroughly disgusted me. The way it is presented makes one feel suicidal." Karen stops reading for a moment, and I hear a few nervous chuckles. Karen continues. "If its theme states that man is totally insignificant, then why don't we jump off the cliff that is about ten feet in front of us? Who would really care, and just how significant would the loss be? Hey, we're only human, who cares?" A long pause suggests that Karen is uncomfortable with the news that someone has decided not to be part of this little pageant. I notice a man in cutoff denim shorts and a woman wearing a white sundress, probably in their late twenties, standing apart from our group. His arms are folded across his chest, and a video camera hangs over his shoulder. I guess that he must have written this critique.

"I don't have time to address these, but I should," Karen says, obviously put off by the comment that broke the spell. "Actually, I will be speaking to that in a minute," and returns to the stack. "The Grand Canyon is not an object to be owned by one country. Rather it is a testimony to the vastness of time and life to be enjoyed by all people," she reads. The man in the cutoffs is grinning and saying something to his companion. She picks up their day pack and they walk down the trail, but the group keeps their attention on Karen. When she completes the last of twenty-seven reflections, she pauses before trying to bring some closure to all that's taken place on our walk.

"I spent most of this walk making you feel like dirt. I made you feel small. I made you feel insignificant. It's true," she says, with all of our eyes on her. "But this last part, I like to use to make you feel significant. Maybe to the rocks at Grand Canyon, we don't matter. But to each other, our individual lives are important. I just went to a memorial service yesterday for a person who had worked here in '85. She was killed in a car accident. So these thoughts on how life is short and we should live it to the fullest and we should make each day count and some of your thoughts as to realizing our responsibility toward the future are important. Her life didn't matter beans to the squirrels at Grand Canyon, but it mattered to those that she touched, to those in her family, to those there, to those who couldn't come. And so to answer that one question, that's what I'd say. Each life is significant. Each person can do an incredible amount of work toward saving nature, toward appreciating it, towards sharing it with someone else. Those are the sorts of goals that—if each person thought how to be a better person—that would really just solve everything in the world. . . . Wouldn't it now?"

Ritualized public performances often legitimize and recreate "myths of modern enchantment," argues Donald Horne, by symbolically joining people "in a common enterprise, calling attention to their relatedness and joint interests in a compelling way, [and by] promoting conformity and satisfaction in conformity." The visitors who fortuitously assembled themselves for the ranger program walked for an hour and a half on common and culturally sanctified ground. The walk commemorated the canyon's monumental status and allowed each person to imagine, project, and engage in a transparent endeavor of unified and shared purposes. This wasn't an obligatory social ritual but a matter of making a choice from a park service menu of interpretive programs. Traveling together along the rim, we remained strangers but shared a language of science that clocked the canyon's creation in millions of years, geologic upheavals, and shifting plates of lithosphere. By journey's end, we had entered a landscape marked with dreams of social erosion and utopic societies, internal fault lines, and spiritual integrity. Like many who have come to the canyon's edge, we stood betwixt and between worlds—known and unknown, physical and spiritual, real and imagined, familiar and foreign—anchoring ourselves with lines that had been written for us and that we wrote ourselves.

Perhaps Ranger Karen's call to abase ourselves before the canyon had set the tone for the writing exercise and charged many in the group with equal currents of modesty and pretension. We spouted personal philosophies, renounced individual accomplishments, quoted Shakespeare, and promised to live full lives and protect nature. A few celebrated their faith in a God and confronted the ranger's scientific certainties with skepticism. How far into the day the glow of these proclamations would linger, I do not know. But within the context of the walk, each avowal collaborated in a performance exalting both canyon and observer. With all of the reading, writing, and listening, our group contributed to a collective drama; we retrieved the canyon as a significant geologic wonder and a cultural shrine where the practices of scientific and aesthetic observation became palpable.

The "Awesome Chasm" walk was literally and metaphorically a rite of passages and a performance of paradoxes. Both culturally animated and alienated, we moved along the rim in a zone of transformation and exaggeration, ambivalence and certainty, and solemnity and playfulness. Pausing at viewpoints to share in a reading of Karen's script, our physical passage followed a trail of textual passages. Index-card inscriptions. Voices in rote recitation. Geological facts and analogies that redeemed the canyon as an object of rational measurement and poised our group as scientific observers. However, Karen's thoughts on the canyon's inspirational powers and the writing exercise that followed aimed us toward resurrecting the canyon as an object of aesthetic experience. Like nineteenth-century Romantics, many of the remarks mimicked the conventions of a sublime discourse—soul searching, poetic verse, emotional display, internal enlightenment—rooted in desires to grasp something unnameable, the transformative power of nature, and even desires for internal perfection. The canyon could change us, Karen suggested. Many said they needed to change and promised to live differently, humble ourselves, and treat others well.

For Karen to say she'd *made us* "feel like dirt" and then *restored in us* a sense of significance was, indeed, a bit dubious. Yet, this was her interpretive program, and there was some evidence that she could, in fact, make us bark and wag our tails on command. In the end, however, a less conspicuous display of power rested in our complicity to collaborate in this collective fiction; one that recognized consensus and conformity as an expression of our own choices. Perhaps this is why the singular comment criticizing all the talk about "insignificance" was the only moment Karen interrupted her otherwise straightforward reading of our words. For a group of people concertedly orienting themselves in a landscape of humility, this one doubtful voice was a trespasser, as is often the case in dramas of sovereignty, carrying news no one really wanted to hear. The "Awesome Chasm" walk was a vehicle for seeing the canyon and displaying the visitor, albeit not with the harsh transparency of a cynic's remark. On the one hand, parroting canyon facts, proclaiming transformative and transcendent experiences seemed an enactment of a cultural memory none of us possessed on our own. We redeemed a history of discourse that had long endowed the landscape with significance and inspired many to respond with their own "great thoughts." Venerating the canyon helped prevent against its disappearance amid ever-present vacation hassles: traffic, parking, reservations, children, shuttle buses, hospitality services that were not always hospitable, and crowds of tourists. On the other hand, properly appreciating the canyon was a way of relishing one's presence in the scene, a way of not disappearing into the crowd and of amplifying the meaning of a personal encounter with nature. "As I sit here overlooking the canyon I realize that this walk has helped me to lose the feeling of being part of the human tourist mass," wrote a person on this *guided* walk. "Thank you." While the "Awesome Chasm" walk ensconced the canyon in a collective fiction, it was also an occasion to lodge any one of us in a private drama of social and moral elevation. Feeling good about feeling small, especially when mutually reinforced by "insignificant" others, traded the routines of the average tourist, even while following a ranger in a group along the rim, for loftier heights of proclamations and a sense of presence.

Listening to our group reach for the landscape's higher message by quoting verses from a poet's distant dramas, delivering passages derived from earlier visitors who looked into the canyon and pondered matters of life and spirit, or even feeling obliged to produce some form of sage wisdom in a writing exercise on a guided walk, all summoned the canyon as a site of citations invested with profound questions, provisional answers, and public postures. Nearly everyone had dropped a line into the canyon and pulled up some sentiment or ideal that had been swimming through the great abyss for more than a century. No matter what dangled from the end of our pencils, it all reaffirmed the authority of the canyon as a consecrated text. These were the purification, transformation, and incorporation rites of our territorial passage. "A canon provides the rule by which to distinguish proper from improper and gives the standard against which to judge anomolies and measure transgressions," argues philosopher Mark C. Taylor. "Though tradition can, at least for a time, remain oral, a canon tends to be 'fixed' by writing. . . . In short, the canon constitutes the masterpiece that rules the tradition." In our case, recomposing the canyon as a *masterpiece* was inextricably bound to the narratives of scientific and romantic observers who first anointed the scene with their ink. Like the park ranger who led us, we could briefly become custodians of the canyon's historical, scientific, and aesthetic meanings by demonstrating a competent interpretation through reading and writing. "The masterpiece must express its power by extending its influence," notes Taylor. "The masterful work governs effectively by holding out the promise of 'The *mastery of meaning.*' No simple artifact of the *past,* the masterpiece confronts one as a *present* reality by projecting *future* possibilities." The act of reading is more than an acknowledgment of appreciation for a great work. "The masterpiece 'reads' its subject," he argues. The work "is gripping and captivating; one feels 'caught up in its world.' . . . The masterpiece works by bringing together two contrasting movements of translation: reader is born(e) in(to) text as text is carried over (in)to reader."[32] As with a masterpiece, our guided walk urged us to become engaged in a dialogue of interpretive traditions that framed an "Awesome Chasm." "Like the line(s) of a book, the line of tradition is intended to fill holes, close gaps, and span distances," says Taylor. "The goal of conversation with tradition is nothing less than a 'communion' that realizes the fullness of presence. The masterpiece strives to keep tradition alive through a process of repeated representation. This strategy seems to be successful as long as subjects are willing to recognize 'the superior claim that the text makes.' "[33]

The "Awesome Chasm" walk helped secure the cultural sanctity of Grand Canyon by creating a context wherein each person was asked to treat the landscape seriously, often solemnly, and assume the duties of interpretation. "The power of a landscape does not derive from the fact that it offers itself as a spectacle," argues Henri Lefebvre, "but rather from the fact that, as mirror and mirage, it presents a susceptible viewer with an image at once true and false of a creative capacity which the subject (or Ego) is able, during a moment of marvelous self-deception, to claim as his own."[34] The canyon's power, as landscape and text, materializes in the efforts of the individual to exercise this creativity and bring it closer. Yet, the comments of the "Awesome Chasm" participants ultimately recognize a distance and absence that cannot be fully overcome or filled. The canyon continually eludes the possibility for definitive answers, but remains a powerful presence to be reckoned with. The implication is that the visitor *should* be looking for meaning. This search rests on an "ideological presupposition," as literary critic Lennard Davis says of the novel, "that such aesthetic objects are endowed with meanings . . . and the interpretive process of arriving at those meanings will somehow release that secret as well as other secrets about life in general."[35]

Some of these secrets, of course, came to us in a written script that Karen provided and asked that we recite to each other. Pondering the canyon on our own, however, incarnated another historically endowed discursive tradition reaching back to the nineteenth century, when Dutton called the canyon "a great innovation in modern ideas of scenery." Our moment of reflection was an occasion to bear witness to an individual capacity for properly appreciating the scene. Waiting to channel a message onto our blank sheets of paper, we raised the phantoms of earlier canyon observers whose accounts, poetry, and painting often testified to a confrontation with a seemingly infinite source of power. While the poetic and philosophic texts of nineteenth-century Romantics objectified a divine authority that made their authors creative agents of nature's transcendent powers, interpreting the Romantic's text is "ultimately a divinatory process," as Hans-Georg Gadamer notes, "a placing of oneself within the mind of the author, an apprehension of the 'inner origin' of the composition of a work, a recreation of the creative act."[36]

This mood of literary romanticism pulsed through our writing exercise as a way of worshiping the canyon and absorbing visitors in a powerful legacy of reading and writing the landscape. Here is another poem written by someone on the "Awesome Chasm" walk:

Out of Chaos

A mist hangs about mystiriously *[sic]*
as we fathom the depths
of time and nature
in awe we stand
as we stare into a microcosm of unreal reality
The sereness of its winds
whispering through the canyons
carrying sounds unheard
no more of a time that is
unyielding and all ways in the move
Perception unfolds with dawns
light as all is unveiled
Nature, its naked truth revealed
dazzling us with a beauty full
view which makes us realize
the frailty + perfection of
Life.

The themes of transcendent and "naked" truth, perfection, and the revelatory power of nature could easily cast this writer in the pages of a late nineteenth-century guide-book or travel account. At that time, travel writers often criticized such efforts as mere "word pictures" that inevitably failed to capture the canyon's ineffable qualities. Perhaps such criticisms could also be leveled against the preceding poem. But reading these lines put down by a late twentieth-century visitor on a guided ranger walk suggest the persistence of cultural forms across time and space. Sitting with our group near Grandeur Point. I listened to Karen recite these lines, one example of *our* thoughts. The poem gave voice and substance to the "fusion of horizons" Gadamer envisioned between interpreters and texts, and linked the July vacationers with earlier observers who chronicled their experience of the canyon. Reading from these pages, Karen voiced the traces of so many other authors and discourses that locating any single point of observation would, in many instances, be pointless. Instead, these comments revealed a range of cultural reference points moving through visitors as they moved through the canyon.

"A Brave New World, a symphony of the ages. What awe-ful wonderment!" another visitor had written. "What sense could any a man make of it? Emergent from the mud of the river-bed, how triumphant now, and then, at the rim, to see how far he has come and, at night, to reach out to touch the stars. A bright blue planet with a big hole in it! A Grand Canyon of what we don't know!" These sentences mark the landscape through multiple and converging references, observation points, and authors: Shakespeare's "Miranda" in *The Tempest* (or is it Huxley's satiric voice commenting on collective passivity?). An ecstatic canyon visitor calling from the turn of the century. A poet of the evolution. A weightless astronaut orbiting over the Western Hemisphere. And finally, a visitor on a guided walk who, gazing into uncertainty, wanders the canyon through textual *passageways* hearing voices drift through distant open doors.

Perhaps one of the most awesome aspects of the "Awesome Chasm" tour was to watch a group of strangers recuperate and celebrate the canyon's discursive authority through this self-contained, intertextual literary seance. Yet, their comments suggest that the exercise was more than a vehicle for reproducing a legitimate and privileged set of meanings outlined by the ranger. These were not passive and obedient tourists simply consuming packages of information or occupying positions staked out for them in a ranger program. Clearly, many gravitated toward timeworn expressions of Romantic sentimentality and sublimity. But many participants acknowledged and foregrounded a desire, agency, and authority to make the scene their own. "Let us glory in it and know that were we not here, it would not exist," wrote one person. "Though the Canyon is large and elegant, it is I who give it life; for it is I who can can contemplate it, can embrace it and reflect about it," wrote another. "Man is the essence, it [the canyon] is there, immovable, unfeeling, barren from thought. It needs the I as much as I need it!" Although the ranger walk placed the canyon at the center of our vision, these responses reciprocated by centralizing the interpreter. "I feel insignificant, yet grand," wrote someone else. "For I am here and can witness this beauty with my own eyes, [and] try to capture it on film and remember it forever." Far from the one-dimensional images of tourists, so often the objects of critics, these writers express degrees of self-consciousness and ambivalence recognizing their own contemplative presence. They are inclined to capture and anchor a fleeting experience even as they acknowledge that questions of significance, meaning, and value vacillate between the scene and the seer.

Pausing to reflect and write under the auspices of a formal ranger walk meant literally *coming to terms* with the space of both canyon and observer. In part, the terms, quotations, themes, and literary genres they drew from and reassembled affiliated them with a powerful legacy of textual production that had marked the Grand Canyon for over a century. For many, writing about the canyon evoked public postures of literary erudition and philosophical rumination. Some seized the opportunity to disassociate themselves from the tourist crowds for a formalized and officially certified appreciation of the canyon's "higher" meanings. All of these efforts, even Karen's personal story about the loss of a friend, eventually coalesced in an unfolding narrative designed to elevate the canyon's monumental status as a site (and sight) of cultural consensus. Of course, the "Awesome Chasm" walk did not entirely stabilize the meaning of the masterpiece. The walk only lasted an hour and a half, and they would see and feel more of the canyon on their own. Instead, the tour located the production of the canyon as an act of writing and reading. Composing the canyon meant putting down lines, extending its authority and tradition in awesome visions of science and spirit that have been remaking the scene since the end of the nineteenth century. From Powell to these visitors on Karen's walk, the origins of the canyon appeared in sentences stretching toward a future to be spoken and remembered. This group of tourists, strangers to the canyon and each other, had set out to discover an "Awesome Chasm" full of secrets about the earth's beginnings and deeper mysteries of the soul. Along the way, they uncovered the secrets of a cultural canyon. As their eyes gazed into the abyss from Grandeur Point, searching for evidence of beginnings, the origins of the canyon's spectacle rested in each voice and sentence, collectively rejuvenating and recomposing the great text that cast an American cultural formation in stone.

4

Managing a View

" I think this one looks flatter on top, don't you?" I hear the woman tell her husband, pointing to something in the distance. Not far from the visitor center, Joe and Kaye, a couple in their early sixties, sit on a fallen log off the Rim Trail, discussing the canyon spread out before them.

"No, I don't think it's any flatter. It just looks that way from here," returns Joe. His eyes follow two ravens rising out of the canyon on a current of air.

"Sure it is," Kaye tries again, this time a bit louder. "Look at those flat tops on those mountains out there, and look at how flat it is across the way." Joe sits silent, either giving up or giving in to Kaye's sense of the flatness.

"Is this your first time here?" I ask, walking a few steps toward their log bench. It is, Joe tells me. I learn they are a semi-retired couple from Hull, Massachusetts, pulling a camping trailer around the country, and seeing the West for the first time in their lives. Back east, Joe had worked for Polaroid, packing cases of film for shipping.

"I still use the 250 [Polaroid] model because that's the kind of film I was packing at the plant," he says. "But I've got the SX-70 model, too. All color. We go first class. As a matter of fact, I was back at the plant before we left on this trip, seeing some of the mechanics and supervisors and people I used to work with. I said to Dave, the old manager there, 'Hey, I'm going on this trip in a couple of weeks. What are the chances of me getting some film?' He says, 'Wait one minute,' and he comes back with ten boxes, and says, 'Here you go.' Top-shelf stuff, too. Right out of the machine and into the box. Not stuff that's been sitting around."

"I've been taking pictures with a Kodak," Kaye interrupts. "But we don't know how they'll come out. With the Polaroid we can see them right away, and he's really taken some good pictures." We sit quietly for a moment; all three of us stare into the canyon. "You don't know how lucky you are to see this when you're young," says Kaye. "We bought the video of Yellowstone and Yosemite, and we may get this one. We want to show our children what we've been seeing. It gets to the point where the only way to understand it is to show them. You just can't find the words to say what you see, so we bought those videos and they can get an idea of where we've been." She uses a folded pamphlet, *Life on the Canyon Rim,* to brush away a fly buzzing in front of her face. "Have you been on the plane? We took the plane and it was marvelous. It was a six-seater, so each person had their own window, and they flew us all around the canyon," she says, tracing a flight path with her finger. I tell them I have not viewed the canyon from the sky.

"It was just short of an hour," adds Joe, "but you really should see it. I mean this is nice seeing it from here, but you really get a different sense of the grandeur from the air. You can see the whole thing from up in the air. It's just stupendous. This is nice, though. Have you seen the IMAX?" Actually, I had been in a sightseeing plane and the IMAX Grand Canyon Theater in Tusayan, six miles south of the canyon rim, but I wanted to get their impressions. The 525-seat theater gives thirteen daily showings of *Grand Canyon—The Hidden Secrets,* a thirty-four-minute film projected on a seventy-foot-high screen with six-track Dolby sound. "Is it good?" I ask. "Oh, yes," says Joe. "You should've seen that before you came here. It's really an experience. For one thing, they go back to prehistoric times, well, not *pre*historic. But they tell the history of the first people living here. It's all done with modern photography, of course." Kaye nods, agreeing with everything Joe says. "They go back to when the first people were here and they were all nude and running around on the rocks . . . and that was nice," he grins and winks at me. "And then they've got you up in a plane and going down through the canyon on the river in a raft. Really exciting."

"I was getting a little queasy," Kaye confides. "How big was that screen?"

"A coupla stories high," he answers, now framing the canyon through his Polaroid viewfinder. "But you shouldn't miss the IMAX, and the plane, too. I mean, it doesn't matter if you take the flight for half an hour, an hour, or two hours. Once you get up there, you really see the grandeur of the canyon." Joe presses a button on the Polaroid; a tiny motor whirrs and spits out its plastic film.

"That's what they told us to do when we got here," says Kaye. "Go to the IMAX first, then take the plane. But we took the plane first, then went to the IMAX, then here."

"Oh, really," I say. "Who told you to do it that way?"

"The people at the KOA camp where we're staying," she says. "They've been around here a few years so they knew the best way to do it. That's what you should have done before you came here. . . . This is nice, but . . . it's better from the air. It's just different to see it like this." Kaye stops speaking, and we watch the colors and contours of the Grand Canyon slowly appear between the borders of white plastic Joe holds carefully between his fingertips.

Those who yearn for an "authentic" experience of nature may find Joe and Kaye's adventures a story of loss or alienation. A national park captured in a video package. A window view from a scenic air tour. A seat in the IMAX theater simulating flight over and through the canyon. A Polaroid snapshot instantly resurrecting a facsimile of the scene in front of them. All of these are the markers of the familiar laments for *the tourist* who seems to be missing something, who is out of touch, who, as Daniel Boorstin notes, is a "shallow" figure superficially satisfied with "diluted" and manufactured "pseudo-events."[1] Although some may chuckle at Joe and Kaye's lack of discrimination in choosing among a spectrum of canyon views or express regret for all those caught up in the canyon's commercial tourist machinery, the truth is that those seats in the scenic plane, the IMAX theater, and on the fallen log at the canyon's rim have been long in the making.

The vacationing couple from Massachusetts are part of a legacy of canyon observers who find themselves enticed by the promises of a unique and individual encounter with nature but instead confront a canyon landscape populated through and by modern transportation and visual technologies. Both have coexisted at the Grand Canyon since the turn of the century; they mark a landscape divided between the aesthetic conceits of a Romantic observer who searches for solitude and the sublime, and the "average" tourists circulating through the routes and ruts of mass-produced views. This paradox lies at the heart of modern American culture: a pursuit for individual freedom and autonomy in places where a crowd eventually appears.

Disparaging the contemporary tourist for seeing the landscape through some artifice has been a commonplace at the canyon since Clarence Dutton, who noted that fully grasping the scene was the province of "a special culture." Observers who followed Dutton similarly equated the canyon with the great art, architecture, and music of a "civilized" world and continued to claim the scene for the independent observer possessing the aesthetic training, taste, and social decorum to properly appreciate the view. Canyon travel accounts symbolically marked the landscape as a segregated social space that "average" tourists failed to comprehend. Although everyone rode the same trains to the South Rim, writers marked "the tourist" as a threat and a disruptive presence in the scenery. He—and the image usually was masculine—often appears in such accounts as an uncouth and uneducated figure who erodes the "unique" view and serves as a symbolic reminder of the city crowds that prompted the best and brightest to retreat into nature in the first place. However, the great masses could be redeemed, park promoters argued, and scenic landscapes could provide the necessary civilizing force.

These ideas established a tradition that reappears in park management plans in the first decades of the twentieth century and continues today. In a supposedly democratic landscape, the tourist is received as a "visitor," a silent stranger and spectator, and a body circulating through trails, museums, and interpretive programs. At the same time, against a historical backdrop of commercial development and official interpretive and management strategies, the image of an autonomous and sovereign observer persists.

Listening for the Others' Great Silence

As writers and promoters elevated the Grand Canyon into a national shrine and a scenic wonder for all Americans, their accounts, guidebooks, and brochures staked out the terrain as cultural property not everyone could appreciate in the same ways. Fearing that tourist crowds would infringe on the sanctity of their personal experience with nature as culture, writers offered instructions marking the scenery with prescribed lines of taste, propriety, and social decorum. They quite frankly suggested that tourists should either learn a few manners or stay at home. The canyon offers "dreamy landscapes quite beyond the most exquisite fancies of Claude and of Turner," Charles Warner claimed in 1891, and "when it becomes accessible to the tourist it will offer an endless field for the delight of those *whose minds can rise to the heights of the sublime and the beautiful.*"[2] Warner's estimation of the canyon's scenery over the canvases of renowned French and English landscape painters surely expressed a desire for American cultural superiority. Yet, he did more than refract the canyon's beauty through a seemingly unshakable European aesthetic sensibility. While anticipating the tourist crowds who would arrive on the rim, he reinforced a notion that sublime experience had long been reserved for a select group.

"The power of scenery to affect men is, in a large way, proportionate to the degree of their civilization and the degree in which their taste has been cultivated," wrote landscape architect Frederick Law Olmsted in 1865. "This is only one of the many channels in which a similar distinction between civilized and savage men is to be generally observed. The whole body of the susceptibilities of civilized men and with their susceptibilities their powers, are on the whole enlarged." Olmsted prepared these remarks for the California legislature to advocate the preservation of Yosemite for the benefit of "the great mass of society." Those who did not appreciate beautiful scenery, he said, were "either in a diseased condition from excessive devotion of the mind to a limited range of interests, or their whole minds are in a savage state; that is, in a state of low development" and "need to be drawn out generally."[3] Four years before the

Powell expedition pushed offshore to first explore the Colorado River, Olmsted's plan to preserve another American wilderness scene as a *public* sanctuary aimed at redeeming the lower classes through the natural power of civility and beauty. For Olmsted and others, scenic areas offered a moral and didactic landscape—a nineteenth century "outreach" program—for building the character of the "vulgar" and "uneducated" American masses.[4] Scenery, like art and literature, could ideally educate the American public in matters of taste and proper social conduct. Acting as superintendent of New York's Central Park, Olmsted complained about a "certain class" of visitors who believed "that all trees, shrubs, fruit and flowers are common property." Such visitors "are ignorant of a park," he observed in 1857, and "will need to be trained to the proper use of it, to be restrained in the abuse of it."[5] Surely scenic wilderness might have benefits for a greater public, but it was an orderly public Olmsted and others imagined wandering through America's sacred scenery. Among nineteenth-century aristocrats, reformers, and members of a rising middle class, the term *culture* became "synonymous with the Eurocentric products of the symphonic hall, the opera house, the museum, and the library," argues Lawrence Levine, "all of which, the American people were taught, must be approached with a disciplined, knowledgeable seriousness of purpose, and—most important of all—with a feeling of reverence."[6] The same divisions of class, hierarchy, and public order developing in America's eastern cities soon became applicable to the scenic vistas of Grand Canyon and other preserved landscapes. Employing metaphors of high culture to characterize the canyon's cultural magnificence, writers also elevated visions of themselves.

"We know that in order to appreciate the best music the ear must be trained to distinguish musical harmonies; the rhythm appeals to us naturally, but the soul of music comes to us through musical training as well as natural endowment," wrote Mrs. M. Burton Williamson in 1899. "The eye must be educated in order to appreciate art in its highest sense. I was reminded of this when viewing the canyon. Each view of it only enhanced my admiration of it."[7] Admiring the scenery equals an encounter with an objet d'art. For Williamson, it is also a way of honoring and displaying her own *naturally* endowed qualities of perception and aesthetic education. However, aesthetic appreciation was more than a matter of training the ear or eye. It also meant that a properly educated visitor should approach the wilderness as though approaching the symphony, opera, or art museum—by practicing the rules of appropriate social conduct, and self-restraint. Like the well-mannered museum or opera patron, some guides suggested that properly "attending" the canyon involved an ability to control the emotions in an environment best comprehended through silent and distanced contemplation. "Speech is inadequate and uncalled for, at least until the scene familiarizes itself; and the nervous haste with which at first one is prone to glance from object to object gives place to a calmer and more critical mood," noted P. C. Bicknell's 1901 canyon guidebook. "A chattering man or woman would have ruined our pleasure in that brilliant panorama, just as such empty-headed creatures mar the rendering of an opera for those who are there to enjoy the music."[8]

A requisite silence in the face of the canyon attended to both a bourgeois desire for worshiping an internal City of God and practicing the codes of public conduct and reserve appropriate for nature's great hall of culture. The testimonials of observers in the pages of magazines, guidebooks, and promotional literature had so frequently captured the canyon as a stage of personal drama—a place where the greatest forces of heaven and earth would strike the soul like a lightening bolt, and women and men would be reduced to tears "in a tremble of ecstatic fear"; and Bicknell devoted a short chapter in his guide to reigning in all the uncontrollable emotions. "Now, if it were really as bad as all that, it would require a certain amount of moral courage to visit the canyon at all; for most sensible persons shrink from the idea of 'making a show of themselves' in public; but the reader may reassure himself," he wrote. "I have been there a number of times, and I do not hesitate to assert that a man or woman with only an ordinary amount of self-control, may visit any portion of the region and come away again without having in any way made fools of themselves—except, perhaps, by cutting their visit too short."[9] Bicknell's canyon advice parallels the sentiments espoused in nineteenth-century popular etiquette manuals, which preached inconspicuousness and private reserve as a code of conduct for public places. Directions for managing emotion in public were part of a larger concern for "how to establish order and authority in a restless, highly mobile, rapidly urbanizing and industrializing democracy," argues John Kasson. "Etiquette manuals nurtured not the autonomous self-made man, but the intensely disciplined self-contained man and woman." In these early directives for "impression management," he notes, the "conflicting claims and attachments of a differentiated pluralistic culture" pulled people in different directions and they quietly responded by pushing "their deepest convictions further and further within, away from public utterance and display."[10] A silent public posture also conveyed an aesthetic disposition Pierre Bourdieu describes as "a distant, self-assured relation to the world and to others which presupposes objective assurance and distance. . . . Like every sort of taste, it unites and separates." For Bourdieu, the contemplative posture of artistic appreciation is one of "aesthetic distance" and indicative of a privileged class. It is a product of educational and social conditioning that inevitably serves to distinguish some from others who do not possess the necessary "cultural capital." Elites see "the world and other people through literary reminiscences and pictorial references," he argues. "The 'pure' and purely aesthetic judgements of the artist and the aesthete spring from the disposition of an ethos" that becomes "a sort of absolute reference point in the necessarily endless play of mutually self-relativizing tastes."[11]

Far away from the public life of cities, genteel notions of propriety, decorum, and taste translated into a set of practices that were often mapped out in personal accounts of sublime encounters with the canyon. If a visitor demanded contemplative quiet, it was in part because the Grand Canyon described in the pages of popular texts seemed noisy with directions for silence. For instance, readers opening the September 1913 issue of *Scribner's Magazine* found Henry Van Dyke hushing a geographically dispersed congregation with his own poetic testimony. "How far beyond all language and all art / In thy wild splendor, Canyon Marvellous, / The secret of thy stillness lies unveiled / In wordless worship!"[12] Van Dyke's poem carried what had become an all-too-familiar and contradictory message for *individual* canyon observers who, despite strikingly similar pronouncements of aesthetic and moral conviction, loudly wrote the landscape as space of sacred silence through ebullient prose and poetry, and paeans to art, architecture, and music. The pages of guidebooks, magazine travel articles, newspapers, and Santa Fe Railroad promotions became the place to publicly display emotion and rapture and, at the same time, admonish visitors to be silent. Van Dyke's call for "wordless worship" carried two distinct but interconnected meanings for canyon goers. On the one hand, it called for an individual and internal pursuit of a sublime canyon. Here, the great silence of nature's God could also dwell in one's soul. On the other hand, it meant maintaining, even for those not among the self-chosen, a code of conduct appropriate for a culturally sacred space. Maintaining a contemplative silence in the face of this artistic and spiritual scene became a regularly stated demand, regardless of whether one belonged to an educated elite or the "uncivilized" and "uncouth" masses.

This dual function of silence appeared throughout published accounts into the twentieth century. Those who had been taught to pursue a text's deeper meaning staked a similar claim in their ecstatic reports of the canyon. Feeling one's own emotions bubbling under the skin but maintaining self-control was a paradox at the heart of sublime discourse. As writers projected this fantasy into the pages of popular magazines and guides, they also projected a code of bodily discipline onto themselves and others. Imagining the canyon's great silence placed the autonomous observer at the center of a discourse based on distinctions and hierarchies of taste. And in these scenes of spiritual emotion and social decorum, tourists often appear, lurking at the edges of observers' solitary encounters with nature. In these texts, the tourist appears as a noisy threat to the Great Silence. Although nineteenth-century museums, libraries, theaters, symphony halls, and parks were understood to be public places, "they were meant to create an environment in which a person could contemplate and appreciate the society's store of great culture *individually*," argues Levine. "Anything that produced a group atmosphere, a mass ethos, was culturally suspect."[13] Legislators, preservationists, and planners could argue that scenic areas offered educational and cultural salvation to a general public, but popular travel writers often loathed the ever-growing crowds. Even as their articles helped popularize the canyon to an American public, they were often reluctant to welcome the masses who then came looking for the scenes framed on their pages. For instance, Harriet Monroe complained about the two visitors accompanying her on the stagecoach from Flagstaff to the canyon's rim. They were "armed with cameras and possessed of modern ideas," she wrote, despairing over their plans for "improving" the canyon with a big hotel, a railroad from Flagstaff, a water pumping system to bring water up to the rim, and a tram to bring tourists down to the river. "I rose up and defended the wilderness," she countered, "rejoiced in the dusty stage ride, in the rough cabin that rose so fitly from the clearing, in the vast unviolated solitudes,—in all these proofs that one of the glories of earth was still undesecrated by the chatter of facile tourists."[14] John Muir, patron saint of the Sierra Club, equally scoffed at the "scenery-hunters" who "splutter aloud like waterfalls" when gazing at glaciers or scenic vistas in Yosemite or the White Mountains. Compared to those places, he said, the Grand Canyon at least offered some momentary relief. "There is silence, and all are in dead earnest, as if awed and hushed by an earthquake—perhaps until the cook cries 'Breakfast!' or the stable-boy 'Horses are ready!'" he wrote. "Then the poor unfortunates, slaves of regular habits, turn quickly away, gasping and muttering as if wondering where they had been and what had enchanted them." He advised readers to get off the beaten track to avoid the tourists. The canyon would entice them "beyond their wildest dreams" regardless of where they took in a view, he noted, and they "need not go hunting the so-called 'points of interest.'" Muir celebrated the fact that a few of the canyon's landmarks had been named by people like Dutton, Holmes, and Moran rather than the "bewildered, hurried tourist," whom, he said, "would be as likely to think of names for waves in a storm."[15]

Simultaneously promoting the canyon to travelers and disparaging the tourist crowd that actually showed up, magazine articles and guidebooks epitomize and expose a dilemma of the canyon as a *public* space. From the 1890s to the 1930s, tourism promoters and preservationists eagerly invited everyone to witness the natural wonder, yet they continually exalted an eighteenth-century vision of a solitary encounter with nature's sublime. Enthusiasm for a divine city conjured in the canyon's depths was, after all, a play of the literary imagination, and silently *reading* travel accounts best seemed to encapsulate the experience of canyon solitude authors described. As testimonials proclaimed the divine raptures of canyon solitude while their authors feared it would soon disappear in the chatter of tourists, an even larger number of promoters were calling crowds to the rim. Up until 1901, when a railroad spur reached the South Rim, annual visitors numbered fewer than a thousand. In 1915, more than a hundred thousand people visited. This was six thousand more than the combined numbers of visitors to Yellowstone, Yosemite, and Glacier National parks that same year.[16] In 1919, approximately forty-four thousand people arrived by rail alone. The automobile, which first arrived on the rim in 1902, surpassed the railroad as the most popular form of travel to the canyon in 1926. By 1929 visitors numbered two hundred thousand; six years later, that figure had increased to three hundred thousand. To meet the increasing visitor demand during this period, the park service rebuilt the West Rim road, constructed a new road along the East Rim extending to Desert View, and paved a road from Williams to the park's south entrance. In 1933, the Civilian Conservation Corps built trails and campgrounds in the canyon. Officially contracted as the park's primary concessionaire in 1920, the Harvey Company began enlarging its tourist facilities over the next two decades with the construction of Phantom Ranch, The Watchtower, Bright Angel Lodge, and men and women's dormitories on the South Rim. The park service opened a visitor information room and began daily lectures in 1922. Ten years later, the Grand Canyon Natural History Association was founded to work with the park service in fostering visitor appreciation for the canyon's scenery, history, and scientific significance. By 1931, Grand Canyon Airlines was making scenic flights over the canyon.[17]

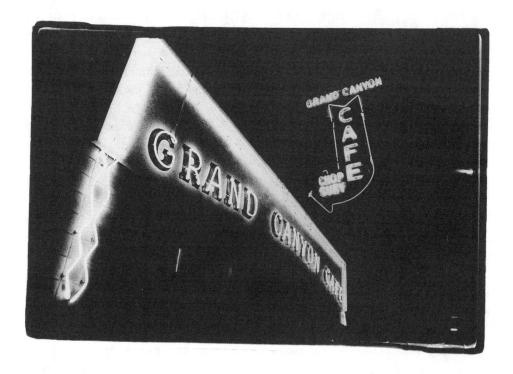

At the 1917 National Parks Conference in Washington, D.C., where legislators heard testimony for establishing the canyon as a national park, Enos Mills, a conservationist and owner of Longs Peak Inn in Rocky Mountain National Park, argued that "scenery is the most profitable resource that we have." Mills noted that before Americans were cut off from Europe in 1914 because of war, they spent more than fifty million dollars traveling abroad. "They spent most of this for scenery, and they spent it chiefly because the American scenery was not ready for the traveler," he said. "If we want Americans to see America, we simply have to think of the development of our parks and get ready for travelers."[18] Development was also on the mind of Ford Harvey, who told the conference that the increasing numbers of visitors to the canyon were in need of services. "There must be some sort of a program for those people; there must be something conventional for them to do," he argued. "To expect them to seek their own entertainment and take care of themselves is to expect the impossible, except in a very small number of cases." He pointed out that the Santa Fe Railway had already spent upward of two hundred thousand dollars to build a nine-mile-long road on the West Rim, and the Harvey company was planning to put in some cottages "accessible to people of moderate means." The situation at the canyon, he said, was simply getting out of hand. The government needed to step in, designate it as a national park, and allocate federal funds. "People will go there if there is not another dollar spent there," warned Harvey. "But it is not a fair thing to the people of the United States that the situation remains as it is."[19]

Undoubtedly, the Harvey Company and the Santa Fe investment in the Grand Canyon could only profit from increased government appropriations aimed toward preserving its scenery and developing tourist facilities. In his address to legislators, Harvey didn't emphasize corporate profits as much as the public benefits that would come from increased access and accommodations at the canyon. "Take your school-teaching class; there is no more desirable class to have visit the canyon than that," he told the conference. "And take the many scientists that are not wealthy, men of letters and artists—we should arrange that those people may have a cottage that they can rent for a very moderate sum; they can keep house there, we providing them with some sort of a store that will sell at moderate prices the particular things that will lend themselves to that mode of housekeeping. We should provide the water and provide the people to care for the premises, leaving the occupant, as much as possible, independent."[20]

Amid these plans for federal funding and commercial development, the image of the unencumbered and independent American standing before the country's nationally endorsed scenery was what ideologically propelled the "see America first" campaign. Harvey's concerns for people unable to "take care of themselves" and his organized plan for their independence was, perhaps, only consistent with the logic of a mass tourism campaign that equated individualism with the consumption of commercial tourist services. Foremost in the public debate over funding national parks and the incessant calls to "see America first" was, as Albert Bushnell Hart had stated, "to raise one's own standard of might and majesty of our own beloved country." For Hart, the individual experience mattered the most. "Every American may still have the thrill of seeing great things for the first time—for him," he claimed. "Everybody who stands on the ledge at Bright Angel may discover for himself the awful grandeur of that chasm, as though it had never before been seen by mortal eye." Although the wonders of America's Far West are "at last being revealed to the plain and humble tourist," he reassured readers that this would not become a place of crowds. "Though we all have a low opinion of 'tourists' in general, we except our own touring and appreciate the easy access to nature," wrote Hart. "One of the splendid things about the grandeurs of America is that they are open to the democracy. You may fence in the seashore at Bar Harbor, but not the prism of the Grand Canyon. Nobody need be afraid that the number of travelers will ever overwhelm the available pleasure grounds of America."[21] Translated through the cultural machinery of western tourism, the ideals of spiritual redemption and self-reliance in nature had become a contradictory image of the individual consumer of nature—the American citizen whose pursuit of natural wonders had become a source of national pride and convenience.

Locomotives pounding the rails, automobiles coughing through the pines of the Coconino Plateau, and airplanes growling above the tree tops toward the chasm carried the multitudes who had finally decided to see America first. Although national park lands encompassed more than a thousand square miles, nearly everyone who personally answered the canyon's call found themselves following the same roads to the same places on the South Rim. Anticipating a solitary meeting with nature and God, those who complained about the crowds only seemed to sense what Walter Benjamin would later describe as a "withering aura" accompanying an age of mechanical reproduction. Of course, Benjamin's well-known 1936 essay examined the reproduction of works of art. The "aura" of an art work, he said, is "its unique existence at the place where it happens to be"; its reproduction collapsed the distance and time characterizing its genuine and authentic quality. "The desire of contemporary masses to bring things 'closer' spatially and humanly," Benjamin argued, "is just as ardent as their bent toward overcoming the uniqueness of every reality by accepting its reproduction."[22] Since the turn of the century, the canyon had, literally and figuratively, become an established work of art. If anything, the growing crowds brought to life another dimension of Benjamin's observation: the circulation of lithographs, stereographs, tourist brochures, and postcards cultivated a desire for the original. As reproduced images popularized and dispersed the canyon to people and public venues throughout America, tourists gathering at the rim aggregated the anonymous consumers of reproductions en masse. Tourists were not only a living reminder of the urban crowds people hoped to escape in their retreat to nature, many believed that they eroded the unique quality of individual experience so often romanticized in travel literature. "The distinction between 'high' and 'low' (or 'mass' or 'popular') culture," notes Susan Sontag, "is based on an evaluation of the difference between unique and mass-produced objects."[23] Along the rim, this translated into social distinctions between people who had hoped to gaze into the canyon alone but found themselves in the middle of a crowd.

As writers mocked tourists and chose to slip away from the swelling crowds in order to "really see" the canyon, the exclusion and debasement of tourists served to uphold a sanctified image of the canyon and the culturally (and "naturally") endowed observer who could truly appreciate the view. The derision of tourists in travel accounts is an instance of what Rob Shields describes as a form of "symbolic exclusion" that appears when geographical and social space is represented through binary oppositions of high and low cultural membership. "The politics of symbolic exclusion" is "one which puts the High in a whole series of possible relationships with the Low without ever losing the upper hand," argues Shields. "The social 'Other' of the marginal and of low cultures is despised and reviled in the official discourse of dominant culture and central power while at the same time being constitutive of the imaginary and emotional repertoires of that dominant culture."[24] By bolstering the writer's private drama (printed for a reading *public*) in the imaginary topography of a sacred retreat—America's equivalent of high culture—the tourist functions as a foil, a paradoxical character who exists on the periphery but is often symbolically central in maintaining the fantasy landscape as well as its codes of meaning, conduct, and observational techniques. The tourist often appears in these accounts as a potential threat to Romantic solitude, silence, and aesthetic appreciation. The "empty-headed creatures" Bicknell saw ruining the opera were merely synonyms for the contemptible and common tourist who violated the canyon's contemplative atmosphere.

Despite Hart's assurances that tourists who chose to "see America first" would never "overwhelm the available pleasure grounds of America," travel writers looked into the multiplied faces of tourists at the canyon and longed for a remote and unique silence. In the presence of the canyon, "one is lifted out of his narrowness of life and into a fuller realization of the majesty and sublimity of the Eternal," noted Leroy Jeffers in a 1919 *Motor Life* article. While aiming to celebrate the opening of the new national park for tourists, Jeffers instead admonished them with instructions. "The spirit of the canyon never is revealed to the noisy tourist who jokes upon its brink and who rides a mule to the river," he warned. "True impressions come only with sympathy and with silence."[25] Noting that the canyon's sunset conveyed the "richness and power as to suggest a Wagnerian opera," Jeffers recounted a solemn and spiritual experience shaped by the aesthetic propensities of legitimate "culture." Writers like Jeffers helped draw the lines of a segregated social space the tourist either disrupted or failed to comprehend. The contemptible tourist regularly appears in travel accounts and guides as an abstraction, a figure of difference or opposition whose uncultivated taste and conduct threatened the sanctity, intensity, and privacy of one's personal experience. Although tourists were close enough to be a noisy nuisance in a writer's narrative of the canyon, they revealed the greater distances separating the people who occupied a common viewpoint. "The Canyon itself is wide here and the circle of vision corresponding great," wrote John Van Dyke of the scene at Grand View Point. Yet he also noted, "The view is much too comprehensive for the five-minute tourist who gazes while his car hums and his chauffeur smokes a cigarette."[26] The idling car motor, sputtering its exhaust, and an indifferent tour guide, smoke drifting from his mouth, were only subtle reminders of the machinery reproducing the views and visitors at the canyon.

Appearing alone or in groups, the five-minute, unthinking, chattering, and anonymous tourist—rather than the development of canyon rail service, hotels, paved roads, guided tours, or souvenir salesrooms—became a source of anxiety for canyon commentators, who feared the crowds were dragging the worst of eastern cities to the canyon's rim. "From the heat and hammer of America's restless factories we came to the Grand Canyon and abased ourselves before the great silence," declared Annette Thackwell Johnson, reporting to the *Independent* in a 1922 article appropriately entitled "Silence." Johnson recounts slipping away from the crowds to "salute the silence of the Canyon" in solitary contemplation, but even in these moments, she cannot fully escape her disdain for the disillusioned tourist. "Dreamily I recalled the complaint of a disappointed girl the afternoon before. . . . 'It's so quiet—so horribly, horribly quiet!' she wailed. 'Why, a tremendous thing like that *ought* to be noisy. You ought to hear the river roaring. Think of the noise of Niagara. That is greatness, terrific, roaring greatness. But this fearfully quiet gap in the earth's surface seems uncanny. . . . It makes one feel like a fly. . . . It seems to be lying there waiting . . . ' she shuddered," wrote Johnson, as she is left pondering the girl's dilemma. "What was the psychology behind her plaint? Was it not that noise may be harnessed—used? Men have set Niagara to work turning power machines for breakfast food. But who can harness silence? Before it busy little man stands helpless, conscious of his mortality." Johnson's depiction of the young visitor not only served her own yearnings for silence but also reiterated her distance from those who saw the landscape as a site of physical production rather than aesthetic and spiritual contemplation. The girl's outspoken passion and disappointment over the power of a nature that was quietly "waiting" only affirmed Johnson's conviction that neither the canyon nor the observer should do anything at all. Throughout her article, she aimed barbs at canyon tourists' apparently blasphemous comments: "don't much care for it"; "awfully disappointed in the colors"; we would "rather spend what extra time we have at Los Angeles beaches."[27] Johnson had as much regard for them as for the cereal boxes churned out in some eastern factory. If a young girl was disturbed at "feeling like a fly" before the canyon's fearsome quiet, perhaps it was because she sensed an obligation to feel as special as those—like Johnson—who filled the pages of magazines with their personal testimonies to silence.

Johnson might have found an alternative reading of the tourist's psychology in John T. McCutcheon's 1909 *Doing the Grand Canyon.* In his nineteen-page essay illustrated with cartoons, McCutcheon depicts canyon tourists as social actors in a comedy of manners staged daily along the rim, on trails, and in the hotels. His tourists are satiric and self-consciously absorbed with maintaining the conventions and manners of canyon spectatorship: "The casual tourist approaches the Canyon with some dread. He fears that he will be disappointed. Surely nothing in nature can equal the expectations of one who has read what great writers have written about this wonderful place. He also fears that if he is disappointed, it may probably be his own fault rather than the Canyon's. It would hurt his pride to be considered as lacking in capacity to appreciate the great beauties of nature, and so, to play safe, he resolves to do full justice to the occasion if it costs him all the adjectives at his command."[28] McCutcheon's "casual tourist" is thoroughly absorbed with self-doubts about his own ability to see the canyon. The orders for experience and rapture preceding his visit exert an authority that ultimately makes him look foolish for trying to live up to them. For all that McCutcheon's cynicism perpetuated the social artifice he saw in canyon tourists, his caricature also evoked a sympathy (typically lost among his contemporaries) for the internal conflicts of an individual who strives to be anything but an anonymous member of a crowd. McCutcheon's tourist confronted a version of class hegemony comparable to what John Berger recognized in August Sander's photograph of three peasant farmers on their way to a dance wearing poorly fitted suits. The burly farmers willingly donned the garments designed for a sedentary class in an appeal to the "standards of chic and sartorial worthiness" that were not their own, observes Berger. Accepting such standards and "conforming to these norms which had nothing to do with either their own inheritance or their daily experience, condemned them, within the system of those standards, to being always, and recognisably to the classes above them, second-rate, clumsy, uncouth, defensive."[29] Wanting so much to appear at home at the canyon, McCutcheon's tourist missed seeing the canyon because he was trying to look at it through someone else's eyes. Those eyes, however, only turned back on him in judgment and rendered him a comic spectacle.

Reconstructing and Rationalizing the Tourist

Twenty years after the publication of McCutcheon's book, Norman Rockwell's cover illustration for the *Saturday Evening Post* was a caricature of the tourist as an overweight, overdressed, cigar-smoking, city dweller descending into the Grand Canyon on a mule. A copy of the *Brooklyn Times* visibly tucked into his jacket pocket, this hapless character is oblivious to the scenery in front of him because he is reading a book titled *See America First*. The image only reiterated the idea that the great American public was out of place, if not unwanted, in the national parks set aside for their benefit. Inside the magazine, a petulant Struthers Burt expressed disappointment over the increasing numbers of park tourists who could not properly appreciate the federal lands they owned. "It is necessary to educate the average tourist, even the stupidest, to some approximation of the point of view of the nature student and the outdoors man," wrote Burt, a dude rancher from Jackson Hole, Wyoming. He applauded, however, the National Park Service's efforts to educate the public. The park service "is as stealthy as an Indian in its approach. In a score of ways it creeps up on you and teaches you something unawares. All about you are opportunities to learn and if you are gently urged toward them it is completely under the guise of having the time of your life." This need to disguise plans for the public's education was echoed by Dale King in a 1940 government report regarding public interpretation at Southwest monuments. "We must lead . . . so [visitors] do not know they are following," wrote King. "We must not herd our charges like a group of cattle. We must present our wares so enticingly that the visitor himself desires to partake of them, and so subtly is he influenced that he does not realize that his action is drawn out by a carefully laid plan."[30] King allows the public more intellectual latitude than Burt, but both writers are identifying an educational philosophy that only became increasingly present in later government publications on park interpretation, and reveals the elaborate and carefully drawn blueprints for visitors' experiences. For instance, one publication offers park interpreters an inventory for managing their interactions with the public. It tells them how to handle visitors' questions, choose the proper music for an interpretive program, and lead people in a sing-along. One section offers a description of creating the ideal conditions for staging an evening campfire program that will bestow the ideals of parks and their otherwise "intangible" values. "If the feature of the program is an illustrated talk, it is well to time the starting of the fire and to use an amount of wood that will reduce the fire to glowing embers by the time projection begins," advised the guide, warning prospective program leaders that a blazing fire could distract attention from the screen. "Programs should end on a quiet note with which the dying embers harmonize." Orchestrating the lighting, sound, and setting in advance would help inspire an atmosphere of fellowship and a spirit of participation in a rustic setting. "With minimal artificial intrusions, the informal setting can come closest to re-creating the traditional American wilderness campfire," notes the guide. "The speaker's goal should be to maintain a spirit of informality and spontaneity without giving the impression of disorganization."[31] This formulaic organization of spontaneous experience was a way of smuggling valuable experience into tourists' leisure time.

Such efforts, Burt had argued in 1929, not only made national parks a place to teach people about nature's beauty but also educated them toward broader ideals of citizenship and "Americanization." The park service educational philosophy always "advances this preference by the democratic method of tactful persuasion and encouragement. It tries to teach people better; it does not argue with them," he wrote. And since there wasn't enough great scenery to meet public demand, "the idea of what a national park is must be clarified in the public mind, refined, and not only preserved but to some extent reconstructed."[32] At the Grand Canyon, a desire to instantiate park ideals in tourists' minds took the form of a broad educational program based in natural science. But the institutionalization of education programs at Grand Canyon in the 1920s and 1930s also gave new weight and meaning to the terms *citizenship, Americanization,* and a "democratic method of tactful persuasion" that people like Struthers Burt believed could be realized in the nation's parks. By 1929 Burt had already given up on the public, and his ideas strayed from the ideals park proponents advocated. Enos Mills, a conservationist considered "father of Rocky Mountain National Park," had told the 1917 National Parks Conference that "within a few years the American people will insist that the people must not only own their parks, but they must run them absolutely themselves."[33] Since that time, however, the park service had come to interpret this ideal as running people through federal lands in *their* custody.

Despite the idea that national parks are the common property of each American citizen, park interpretation programs have largely "convinced the owner that he is not the owner," argues Kenneth Nyberg, "and having provided him with a new title ['the visitor'], the interpreter then proceeds to convince him that he is ignorant, as well."[34] Historically, government publications for training park interpreters lend support to his criticism. For instance, one 1976 training pamphlet suggests that park rangers should "Think: *My* service to the visitor can increase his pleasure in *my* park." Another training guide offers a psychological assessment of the interpreter-visitor relationship. "If the visitor comes to an interpretive talk, a nature walk, or some other activity, they are likely to be in what is termed a 'dependency' situation," suggests the guide. "They look to you, the interpreter, for parental functions: providing guidance, protection, entertainment, giving something to them."[35]

Of course, the extent that Grand Canyon rangers and interpreters subscribe to the views of these early guides varies. But a proprietary attitude toward the canyon and an insolent impatience toward tourists often came up in my conversations and interviews with them. "They want fast-food information," a seasonal ranger told me after finishing a shift at the visitor center information desk. "I get to the point where I think you can give 'em all the literature in the world and they'll never read it. You know, it's like I told you one day, it's like they leave their brains at the front gates some days. It's just that some of the questions are real common sense. But maybe it's common sense to me because I've been here so long."

During the busy summer months, visitors repeatedly ask rangers the same questions about hotels, tours, campsites, shuttles, roads, and trails. The lines at the visitor center information desk do, in fact, resemble the lines at the McDonald's in Tusayan. Park rangers work the desk in shifts, usually no longer than a few hours, to alleviate the frustration, monotony, and anxiety that can accompany saying the same things over and over. The interpreter's training manual counsels rangers with performance strategies for dealing with the "incredibly obnoxious, overly irate, truly tedious visitors who make our blood pressures soar, our armpits sweat and our vision blur" by urging them to practice a sense of calm akin to Eastern meditation techniques. "Let their harsh, unreasonable words flow over you like the surf on a beautiful beach in Mexico. . . . Remain serene. Listen to the drift of their meaning but don't let their anger infect you. Don't change the serene expression on your face either. Breathe evenly," the manual advises. "Don't interrupt them. Let them get out all the poison. . . . When you do answer, speak quietly and with an even, soothing tone. Sound as if you have taken voice lessons from the Dalai Lhama. Never raise your voice or allow emotion to creep into your tone. This is incredibly hard to do."[36] Anyone whose job requires facing a seemingly endless, revolving-door confrontation with customers might identify with the gripes of an aggravated ranger or appreciate the manual's urging for self-control. Yet, listening to the off-duty ranger and reading this advice on the arts of impression management inevitably suggest a "backstage" reality of conflicts and job tensions. Behind the official scenes of the visitor center or interpretive programs, the practices of managing and informing the visitor recede into rituals, stories, and anecdotes revealing familiar, derisive, and comical images of the naïve and contemptible tourist.

"You keep your eyes open for the weirdest tourist outfit, and keep it in mind for the party," one ranger told me, describing a forthcoming "tacky tourist party." Exchanging official uniforms for the attire of the visitors they served daily, their theme party discarded the conventions of the workplace and transformed the tourist's leisure into a carnivalesque ritual of comic critique. Other rangers I interviewed similarly enjoyed relating amusing questions they heard while on the job. "Every once in a while we get several questions about 'where the president's heads are carved on the walls,'" recalled one. Another remembered the time he was at a canyon overlook and listened to a woman tell her children: "This is the place where Lewis and Clark took George Washington across to the other side." Such anecdotes, however, are not confined only to park service personnel.

Employees who work the canyon hotels, restaurants, lounges, and gift shops confront the same tourists who show up in the visitor centers and on ranger interpretive programs, and hold an equal disregard for the crowds and their questions. This was notably expressed by a grounds maintenance worker I met one afternoon. I had just snapped a photograph of him on the esplanade near El Tovar and he asked me why I wanted to take his picture. I told him I was trying to document the tourist world at the Grand Canyon, collecting stories and images of people who visit and work here. He told me he'd also been working on a documentary and proceeded to lay out the storyline. "It's a behind-the-scenes look," he said casually, putting his weed whipper in his maintenance cart. "I have one of the employees who dresses up like a tourist and he throws a piece of trash on the ground. Well I go after him in my maintenance cart, and when I catch him, he says, 'I'm sorry.' I say, 'Too late for that. Look at that beautiful canyon,' and I toss him over the wall. Then, there's a guy in Hopi House who answers tourists' questions. A tourist says, 'Where's the lodge?' and the guy behind the counter points out one door. Another one comes in and asks, 'Which way to the canyon?' and he points to another door. Then, the questions start getting weird, like anything . . . chemistry equations, the names of presidents, just anything stupid like that." He laughs for both of us at these scenarios. Making his video documentary is a way to have a little fun with fellow employees on the off-hours, he tells me. His tourists are disrespectful and without answers, aimless and lost in the landscape he trims and waters on a daily basis. His documentary expresses the fantasies of revenge I hear from many workers who grow tired of the tourists who outnumber them by nearly twenty-five thousand to one each day of the busy summer months.

Undoubtedly, these anecdotes magnify some of the employees' disdain for the park crowds. If anything, they are instances of coping in a heavily institutionalized environment; servicing the vacation escapes of strangers may only exacerbate the routine and monotony of work in the service sector. Park rangers know well how institutional frameworks can bear on a person's life. Officially, the ranger is a GS-25 in the federal government's General Schedule occupational classification code. Entry-level rangers earn less than twenty thousand dollars annually. Those with higher seniority, based on

years of training and service, make less than thirty thousand dollars a year. First-time seasonal rangers, who usually work the peak summer travel periods, make substantially less than full-time government personnel. Everyone is subject to furloughs, and the number of rangers working during a particular season is contingent on budget allocations. At the Grand Canyon, rangers are often provided with low-income housing, based on availability, and they often share a residence with other workers. For many, housing facilities amount to portable government trailers placed away from the village tourist facilities.

It is not surprising that living and working under such conditions would prompt many of the interpreters to find the canyon's tourist population a target of private jokes. Their backstage views of tourists differ little, in fact, from most workers who regularly service people in vacation locales. But the idea of the "unthinking tourist" is not merely a matter of Grand Canyon employee subculture. I found that many park rangers tended to characterize canyon visitors with an air of paternalism. "Most folks come and they don't know what they want, they really don't," one interpretive program administrator said. "We've tried programs as nebulous as, 'all right, the ranger will be here, you meet, you ask the ranger whatever you want to know.' We'll get people showing up, but no one even knows where to begin. They don't have anything in mind. They want us to lead them through some sort of experience." Another similarly described her experiences with visitors as a form of dependency and instruction. At the visitor center information desk, people frequently ask, "'What is there to do?' and 'How do I see the Grand Canyon?'" she said. "Well, the obvious snip answer to that is, 'Well, just open your eyes!' But most of them have a very short amount of time . . . [and] what they're really asking is, 'What I want, from an experienced person who works here, is to know where the best views in the park are.'" In each of their comments, the ranger appears as a source of instruction, knowledge, and enlightenment ("you ask the ranger what you want to know"). But to the rangers, visitors seem as if they "don't have anything in mind," have nothing to say, and haven't opened their eyes.

Reading the interpreter's training manual, I found the dimensions of this teacher-student relationship amplified in an essay by a senior park ranger. He begins by recounting his experience of seeing Michelangelo's *Pietà* for the first time. "I saw the inspiration and genius of Michelangelo who was given to us to release this sublime form from the marble," he recalls. His story, however is an allegory for the park service interpreter who, like the sculptor, can see and release something greater from the canyon's stone. "Whether you are an artist or interpreter (I think interpretation is an art), I believe that there must exist an internal creative force that cries to be unbound like Prometheus," he tells trainees, whose jobs presumably will now be to unleash the essence of the canyon by unleashing their own creativity and shining light into the hollow visitor. "If artists (interpreters) are able to communicate what went through their mind, heart and eyes to mannequin-eyed visitors," the ranger proposes, "and help them think new thoughts and see, maybe for the first time, this quintessence of things, [then] that is what our job is all about."[37] Like the worlds they have left behind for a vacation, canyon tourists remain objects of an institutionalized logic that renders them waiting to receive the views and visions of experts. "I know that I am meeting my objective when visitors come up after the program and say 'You should put that on tape!'" writes the ranger. "The success is that *they* have already done it."[38]

Deciding what visitors want to know, or how successful a program will be, inspires varied approaches from the interpretive staff. A new interpreter, in her first summer at the canyon, told me that people were most interested in trivia. "Do they want to know that this point is 6,800 feet in elevation or do they want to know that ten trillion mosquitos would fill the Grand Canyon?" she said. "I think they'd rather hear about the mosquitos. So, it's just [a matter of] trying to figure out what people want to hear." I asked another ranger, one with more seniority, how she knows what the public wants. "With some scientific studies [of the visitors] as well as with some professional knowledge of things that we know from years of working with the public in national parks," she replied. "I think we're pretty much hitting the nail on the head. . . . We'll experiment, we'll try new things. And if it doesn't work, maybe it was the way we marketed it, or maybe people just weren't interested." However, another ranger who had worked at the canyon for ten years suggested otherwise and said the park service was less than encouraging of visitor feedback. "The management is very afraid of that," he said. "They're shy of feedback as though they're afraid they might get something negative. We kind of go out of our way not to ask for any kind of responses. So the management doesn't get a real good idea of what's going on, of what's happening out there, which is a shame."

"Enlightened" individuals celebrate their appreciation for the canyon, conveying the great unity of nature as expressions of science or art; they necessarily divide themselves from the "tourists," "visitors," "masses," or "general public" they imagine cannot, or do not, see and feel the same when they arrive. It is for the tourists' ears that they testify to their awe. It is in the tourists' interest that guidebooks are written, that ranger programs, tours, museum displays, and trails are planned. These resources can keep them on an educational path, potentially transform them into scientists and aesthetes, remake their leisure into productive time, and inherently guarantee they will not graduate from the course.

Perhaps these are merely the features of contemporary public life reconstituted in a national park. These glimpses of how Grand Canyon tourists appear in discourse suggest how ideals of democratic freedom, often based in an egalitarian philosophy of speaking, listening, and debate, were transformed by the technologies of vision and rational order in American culture. Struthers Burt chastised tourists in 1929 for being uneducated and recommended the reconstruction of their minds. With that mission in mind, a new National Park Service headquarters was then being built on the South Rim. That same year, John Dewey pondered the meanings and ideals of individualism, culture, and civilization in an industrialized America. Quantification, standardization, and mechanization, Dewey noted, were the marks of an "America-By-Formula" many cultural critics (both European and American) saw as a corrosive force in the modern world. The American "type," according to critics, was a superficial, uncritical, suggestible, and homogenous product of a rationalized society whose sense of individualism had become sublimated in a machine age. Dewey, however, saw the problem differently. Such critics were clinging to an old, European ideal of individualism, one that preceded industrialism and the possibilities for a democratic society that technology could create. For him, a modern American individualism required "equality and freedom expressed not merely externally and politically but through personal participation in the development of a shared culture" rather than the continued acceptance of stereotypes "formed in old and alien cultures."[39]

Dewey's philosophy aimed toward the active participation of all in the creation of a culture in which each could exercise imagination and creativity. Although he didn't specifically address the tourist, the idea of remapping the public mind with nostalgic images of spirituality, art, and aesthetics, he argued, was only a way of running from problems that kept America divided. "Many American critics of the present scene are engaged in devising modes of escape," observed Dewey. "Some flee to Paris or Florence; others take flight in their imagination to India, Athens, the middle ages or the American age of Emerson, Thoreau and Melville. Flight is solution by evasion."[40] Such efforts did not confront the challenges of a machine age to create new ideals of the moral and the spiritual, he said, nor did they recognize individual tastes and choices as occasions for personal growth. Instead, a fear of the machine age was what prompted people to "build places of refuge in which man could live in imagination, although not in fact," Dewey argued. "There is no need to deny the grace and beauty of some of these constructions. But when their imaginary character is once made apparent, it is futile to suppose that men can go on living and sustaining life by them."[41]

Although Dewey reminded everyone that "the free working of mind is one of the greatest joys open to man," these images of unthinking tourists and the pervasive techniques for managing people on lands endowed to a free and democratic public may have been troubling to him. I imagine him disappointed had he perused the guidebooks and magazine articles telling people to behave themselves at the Grand Canyon as they would if they were in the Louvre or attending the symphony, or listening to writers chastise tourists, or employ techniques to train their eyes and bodies. For Dewey, perhaps it would be the tourists themselves, leaving home on their own, coming to affirm a national symbol, and seeing nature for themselves, who would sustain some glimmer of a democratic public and his ideals for a common culture.

"Intellectual and literary folks who conceive themselves devoted to pursuits of pure truth and uncontaminated beauty overlook the fact that . . . they too become monopolists of capital," he wrote, and "the monopolization of spiritual capital may in the end be more harmful than that of material capital." Americans dreaming their vacations through brochures and guidebooks, or finding themselves replaying a romantic drama of sublime experience on the canyon's rim, may have been unsettled by Dewey's warning that "to assume the uniform of some dead culture is only another means of regimentation."[42] Whether they looked into the abyss with a crowd of strangers, stood back to claim a distance from the crowds, or even imagined their own sunburned faces as dollar signs filling someone else's bank, tourists found that the new national park offered a vision of freedom far removed from their everyday lives. What mattered most then, as today, were the views, the air, and a world in stark contrast to the clocks that ticked away the days at work and home. Popular audiences did not have to read Dewey to hear a commentary of the machine age; they had their own critics. In 1936, two years after Ansel Hall proposed a comprehensive plan for educating tourists through visual technologies and museum displays, movie audiences watched Charlie Chaplin's *Modern Times* depict a machine age gone awry. Chaplin's assembly-line worker, whose body is caught in the gears of industry and who is under constant surveillance, offered American workers a comic critique of management principles that organized their bodies as sites of rational efficiency and production. More important, they also knew from experience that freedom had not been technologically perfected. Industrial America increasingly defined and institutionalized individual freedom as a set of political, aesthetic, and consumer choices. But could the working public imagine that canyon planners and promoters had also cast their leisure in the logic and strategies of a mass market? At Grand Canyon, their leisure was transfigured into a scientific and aesthetic education aimed toward a common version of American culture. The canyon planners' texts, terms, and turns of the trail aimed toward the cultural redemption of an American public. Yet, even as Americans' wages paid for these programs, tourists were continually asked to be silent recipients of a cultural map plotted by experts they did not know.

To be sure, Dewey's critique and idealization of public life may evoke images of absence and loss bordering on sentimentality. His call for people to actively and collectively participate in determining the meaning of their culture seems a lost whimper compared to the din of mass communication and consumption technologies. "Dewey's notion of public life is naive because in retrospect he seems so innocent of the role of class, status, and power in communication," writes media critic and historian James Carey. Although it may be difficult today to find either comfort or a realistic vision of society in his ideas, Dewey "saw more clearly than most the decline and eclipse of public life, [and] the rise of a new breed of professional experts."[43] Despite the tendency of park proponents to trot out the image of the great American democracy when they testified before legislators in hearings on the establishment of federal lands, it's doubtful that Dewey's ideas for restoring democratic participation would have offered any guidance for those who developed Grand Canyon National Park. His ideal democratic public was already a phantom at the time park boosters were roping off the land, staking a claim in the name of all Americans, and handing the citizens a deed to lands where, since the 1890s, they had been invited, but were less than welcome. More often than not, the spectacular landscape entitled to the great democracy left each person a stranger who was encouraged to see rather than speak. Faced with the rationalizing and standardizing forces of a culture that sacralized independence in an atmosphere of anonymity, asking tourists to straighten up and look quietly into the canyon through the eyes of dead artists, poets, and scientists could, at least, offer some route toward interior fantasies of individuality. Lodging the Grand Canyon in the spectator's imagination could allow each visitor to silently affirm the dream of a common culture. For this privilege, however, tourists were asked to become invisible, remain controlled and reverent, and erase any traces marking their passage through the canyon. Perhaps these unspoken conventions are most apparent in those moments when tourists sought even the slightest recognition of their place in the scene.

"The canyon so dwarfs the human minimus that he simply must express his ego in some manner as a sort of psychological counterattack," observed a distraught Edwin Corle in 1946, noting the messages tourists left on canyon benches. Fearing the wooden benches would be carved into kindling by tourists, the Santa Fe and the Harvey Company covered them with heavy canvas. In response, tourists put away their pocket knives and pulled out their pencils. "Every bench along the South Rim is written on over every available space," wrote Corle. "People sign their names or print them, and usually give the date of their visit and their home town. When the canvas is sufficiently autographed by visitors, and shows signs of wearing out, it is taken off and put in the incinerator, and a fresh canvas is put on the bench." For Corle, recording one's presence at the canyon is an "instinctive" and "natural" urge; yet, he remains curious about the tourist's impulse to register their names on the benches. "The psychology of the hundred million is not strange at all. It is natural," he says. "Among the thousands of inscriptions on the canvas-covered benches there are many that run something like this: 'Joe and Josie Doakes, 227 Wotta Street, Paterson, N.J., Here 3/7/28—Write to us and we'll write to you.' But what for, Joe and Josie?" Corle asks. "What for?"[44]

The couple from Paterson knew others would sit in the same place when they looked at the canyon one day in early March. The crowd they helped comprise was not a problem for them. Their invitation for correspondence was, perhaps, only a small gesture to mark their place in a nameless public sphere—a message in a bottle thrown into the currents of an anonymous public life with a hope it might wash up on some stranger's shore. If the canyon had left them feeling dwarfed, recognizing themselves as only two more inconsequential faces in the crowd was not so deflating. It may be that Joe and Josie Doakes wrote to stand out from the crowd and give their moment on the bench a name. Corle, who published 312 pages of his canyon experiences in *Listen, Bright Angel,* hears their silent message as an opportunity to distance himself from tourists and comment on their egos. Perhaps the Doakeses only differ from Corle in that they had little more than guest books and benches to publicly register their experience at the canyon. Photographs, postcards, and vacation stories shared at home was where an individual encounter with the canyon usually found a recognizable shape.

In the end, the canvas bench cover and the guest register are much the same. Each lists the traces of individuals circulating through public space. Their place in the scene is necessarily anonymous, and recording one's name is, perhaps, an exercise in overcoming this particularly hollow version of insignificance. In the Grand Canyon Study Collection, there is a guest register from January 1980 that was part of an exhibit celebrating the seventy-fifth anniversary of the opening of El Tovar Hotel. Visitors were invited to write their impressions in the register, but the book only remained part of the exhibit for a few weeks. The last three inscriptions appear on January 26, 1980. "Here one finds the true meaning of peace. A place of silence and refuge from today's turmoil and hate," wrote the first person to sign page 142, "Thank you, KY." The two names following KY carried no ambiguity. "Richard Nixon—San Clemente, California" and "Bebe Rebozo—Jan. 1980" are the final two tourists to log their names. On the following page, I found this brief explanation: "On January 26th 1980 Richard Nixon signed this book on his visit to Grand Canyon. We removed this book from the exhibit so that someone would not take the book or tear out the page." Had Rebozo toured the rim without Nixon that day, perhaps the book would have remained and continued to receive visitors' comments. The instant the visitor became something more than an anonymous tourist, the book disappeared to the museum shelves, where Nixon and KY share a page in the history of America's great monument to common ground but remain strangers to each other.

Images of canyon tourists as objects of educational redemption and social disdain have been inscribed in the scene since the end of the nineteenth century and catalog how the tourist's presence has been contradictorily marked by cultural equations of power, privilege, and status. Composed from a series of disconnected views—sighting devices, observation points, exhibits, and guidebooks—a dual image of the tourist floated dreamily through a thoroughly textualized canyon, anchored by promises of cultural belonging and autonomy, yet regularly cut adrift by critics for collectively exercising their freedoms. "When you speak it is in the hushed respectful tone you would use at funeral," McCutcheon's guide told tourists in 1909. "Any loud exuberance of speech would be irreverent."[45] And while the obedient strolled onto the all-consuming canyon viewpoints, silent behind veils of democracy and prepared for an inner journey, they might have noticed a trail of smoke drifting over the trees and disappearing in the breeze over the canyon. Somewhere out of their view, a worker was sweeping up the ashes from canvas fed into the flames of a company incinerator—a funerary pyre of old public bench covers worn out by names and addresses, scratched in pencil and ink, and now drifting over the landscape like a quiet ghost.

Finding a Seat on Cyclorama Point

For all the disparagement "common" tourists may have suffered in the pages of popular texts, everyone looked through some figurative or literal device for their vision of the canyon. Guidebooks, advertising, travel articles, painted landscapes, and stereographs not only shaped the canyon into a marvelous spectacle and distributed it to the public, their pages and images traced a path for the spectator's retreat into the interiors of a subjective landscape where image and experience became powerfully entwined. The empty space of the Grand Canyon became absorbed in the metaphors of art, spirituality, history, and science that anxious visitors had carried to the edge of the abyss and into the pages of their accounts. These accounts located the canyon visitor in a vast landscape of intertextualized references where the conflation of geographical terrain with images, names, codes of conduct, and experiential narratives energized the dislocated and mobilized practices of modern observation. As various textual portraits of the canyon celebrated an individual observer's capacity (or lack of) to possess the scene, that observer disappeared into a series of established and legitimated viewpoints.

When Mary Jane Colter completed The Watchtower at Desert View in 1932, she had "reflectoscopes" installed on the observation deck of the Kiva Room's rooftop. The reflectoscopes—open wood boxes with rectangular black mirrors—were adapted from an invention of the seventeenth-century landscape artist Claude Lorraine, who used the device to frame and enhance the colors in the views he painted. Mirroring the canyon from The Watchtower, the reflectoscope's black glass absorbed the intensity of natural light while intensifying the canyon's colors. For Colter, the devices enhanced a tourist's ability to manage and personalize the expansive canyon scenery. The reason the images "in these reflectoscopes have so much individuality and charm is due to the *framing* of individual views," wrote Colter in her manual for Harvey tour guides. "The general view of the Grand Canyon is so *overpowering* that separating a section of it for a moment [and] making it a *'framed picture'*—brings it better within one's comprehension."[46] Colter's description of the reflectoscope offers but one instance of a whole body of visual technologies—public telescopes mounted at view areas, stationary binoculars at the Yavapai Museum, scenic roads and trails—that expressed the contradictions of an individual freely empowered by a mobilized gaze and a view that had been prepared for an anonymous eye. When the Grand Canyon became multiplied and organized as a set of images, scenes, and ideas that circulated through culture, the personal testimonies of canyon observers recounting their rapture in the pages of magazines and books, or Charles Lummis's call to "see it for yourself," all conveyed a sense that an individual confrontation with the Grand Canyon mattered.

"The guide books, the advertisements, even our enthusiastic conductor had all failed," wrote Benjamin Brooks of his first canyon view in a 1905 report for *Scribner's*

7519. Near Head of Hermit Trail, Grand Canyon, Arizona.

7507. THE LOOKOUT, GRAND CANYON, ARIZONA.

7516. Hermit's Rest, Grand Canyon, Arizona.

Magazine. "So we both fell silent and stood in the one spot—quite forgetting we could see just as much sitting down—for I have no idea how long, looking, and looking, and looking." Even as Brooks attempts to retrieve a real canyon from all of its representations, he also suggests how closely his journey is bound to the mass-produced canyon of images and travel directions organizing experience for visitors. His story was an occasion to redeem the canyon through the individual eye with the capacity to see beyond reproductions and find the landscape in a studied gaze. "Hamilton I could see was thinking hard and feeling much over it," Brooks noted, as he watched his companion finally reach a conclusion. "A fellow can look at this a long time and not see it," said Hamilton. "I hadn't seen it yet myself, you know." In all of their looking, both visitors lost track of time, and it wasn't until the final paragraph of his account that a secure image of the canyon appeared. Having left the scenery behind, and while on the train crossing the desert, Brooks notes for the reader, "We carried with us clear and vivid in our mind's eye the gorgeous picture of the Grand Canyon."[47] Such accounts, stubbornly affirming the value and authority of the individual's gaze, only veiled the deeper foundations of a culture in which new experiences of time, space, and visual perception brushed away the tracks of any particular observer. In contrast to Brooks's personal story of finding the canyon for himself, the numerous photographs accompanying his article shape the canyon for any (and no particular) reader or visitor. Included with his account, venerating an *individual* traveler's perceptions, are pictures of tour guides and mules, ready and waiting for the tourist. On other pages, a pack of mules carries visitors down the Bright Angel Trail, and a train arrives at the canyon depot. There is a view of a hotel on the rim, several pictures of scenery, and a final image of a man standing alone and looking into the abyss.

Those who sought views of the Grand Canyon through guides, travel accounts, or journeying to Arizona found themselves part of a technological ensemble giving order to tourist experience while simultaneously valorizing their independence. Tourists occupied a terrain of overlapping discourses and images that all circulated around them, vying for their time, attention, and currency. The tourist, too, was literally part and *parcel* of this circulation. The trains delivering tourists to the Grand Canyon were more broadly responsible for the spread of industrialization that restructured the meanings of time, space, and perception in the nineteenth century. "The panoramic view from the compartment window can be understood not only as a result of physical acceleration but also, and simultaneously, as a consequence of the new economic relationships which made the railroad journey a commodity to a relatively new extent," observes Wolfgang Schivelbusch in his study of railroads and the industrialization of consciousness. "The realization that one no longer felt like a person but like a commodity indicates some awareness that one had been assimilated not only by physically accelerated speed but also by the generally accelerated process of the circulation of goods."[48]

Art historian Jonathan Crary argues that by 1840, modern forms of institutional and discursive power had also redefined the status of an observing subject. While railroads collapsed temporal and spatial distances, visual technologies—from the stereoscope of the 1850s to early forms of cinema in the 1890s—had relocated vision from a material site of observation, which depended on the bodily presence of a viewer, to the subjectivity of an observer "that depended on the abstraction and formalization of vision." Nineteenth-century visual technologies dislocated, extended, reassembled, and mobilized images and knowledge and aimed toward "multiple affirmations of the sovereignty and autonomy of vision," argues Crary. At the same time, the autonomous viewing subject engendered by this shift became inseparable from "the increasing standardization and regulation of the observer."[49] Commodifying, regulating, and standardizing tourist experience was an inevitable feature of the Grand Canyon by the first years of the twentieth century. Yet, as the landscape became a place of mass-produced visions and experiences, it continually manufactured images of an autonomous and sovereign observer—an individual figure who surveyed a geography dislodged from time and space but who also served as its point of coherence. By the last decades of the nineteenth century, "any significant qualitative difference between a *biosphere* and a *mechanosphere* began to evaporate," notes Crary. "This disintegration of an indisputable distinction between interior and exterior became a condition for the emergence of spectacular modernizing culture."[50] The tourist world on the canyon's rim was a place where bio- and mechanospheres converged.

McCutcheon may have found humor in tourists anxiously reciting the pretensions of preformulated canyon "awe," but he, too, saw pleasure in willingly suspending himself in a canyon of fantasy. "The [canyon's] sense of unreality is so strong that one imagines himself standing in the middle of a cyclorama building looking at a painting of highly colored mountains and mysterious gorges," wrote McCutcheon in 1909. "The silence aides in this delusion, and one half expects to go down some steps out into the noise and reality of a street again."[51] Like so many others, McCutcheon's view of the canyon was an inside job. Its enjoyment issued from a sense of "unreality" comparable to the technological illusion of the cyclorama, a city building where he could recede from the flow of everyday life and "imagine himself" at the center of a spectacle designed for his consumption.

Visitors to Chicago's 1893 World Columbian Exposition might have sensed something similar as they stood in the middle of the cyclorama of the Grand Canyon painted by Walter Burrage. Seven years later, Bicknell's 1900 guidebook would direct tourists to Cyclorama Point at the canyon, a rocky extremity on West Rim near Monument Creek, where Burrage had framed the view for his Chicago exhibit. With scenery surrounding his party like a curved painted canvas, Bicknell both recalls what his tourists saw and directs the reader. "Very striking, too, is the scene spread out below us," he writes. "Studying the prostate landscape with our field-glasses we were enabled to pick out some of the monuments that give the stream its name."[52] Standing at this observation point, named after a mechanical representation of the Grand Canyon, becomes a circular search for points of reference that serve to remake the view. Binoculars study geological formations to identify specific *monumentalized* landscape features that, in turn, bestow a name to Monument Creek, which can be seen from Cyclorama Point—a point of observation found in both Arizona and Chicago.

Technologies of vision not only suspended the coordinates of a lived time and space, they equally implicated the spectator in a real and fictional landscape of successive images effortlessly moving across their eyes. For instance, the Hermit Rim Road advertised by the Santa Fe in 1915 was more than a surface for transportation; it was a monument to enhanced and unconstrained vision. "No other roadway in the world is built along the brink of such a tremendous abyss. While whirling along in an El Tovar yellow coach, or standing on one of the 'points,' you have some of the sensations of an eagle winging the abyss unafraid," claimed a Santa Fe Railway brochure. "In places there is a sheer drop of 2,000 feet within a rod of the rim. Yet you are as safe as in an easy chair at home. Along the entire route the gigantic panorama of the Grand Canyon unfolds for miles and miles."[53] Visiting the canyon promised a cinematic spectacle for a spectator whose vision reached the heights of an eagle from the perch of a comfortable chair. In cars or on horseback, field glasses hanging from their necks, visitors were promised they could see the canyon as if sitting at home or in a theater.

In fact, the canyon did offer tourists a cinematic experience. Ellsworth and Emery Kolb, two brothers from Pennsylvania who came to the Grand Canyon in 1901, began operating a makeshift photography studio in a tent on the South Rim in 1903. They used an abandoned prospecting hole below the rim as their darkroom. Where mineral claims had largely failed at the canyon, the Kolbs developed a good business of mining the tourist population for images of themselves. By 1906, they had built a permanent studio at the head of the Bright Angel Trail. As tourists descended into the canyon on mules, they would photograph them from a studio window overlooking the trail. By the time the tourists returned, the Kolbs had developed prints of each party to sell as souvenirs. In 1911, the brothers made a motion picture of a harrowing journey in a wooden boat down the Colorado River. By 1915, they had added an auditorium to the east end of their photography studio, which hung over the rim of the canyon. On the front of the building, a sign read: "Kolb Bros: Shooting the Rapids of the Colorado River Canyons in Motion Pictures." Since the studio stood next to the trailhead, tourists could descend the stairs into the studio's auditorium rather than hike the trail. Once inside, Emery Kolb would give a lecture about his adventures exploring the canyon. Then, he darkened the room and projected his movie of the Colorado River.[54] With canyon and river just beyond the wall behind the screen, the Grand Canyon appeared silently before each seated tourist in a flow of black and white images chattering through the sprockets of a projector.

Yet, even before the Kolbs' movie collapsed the arduous hiking distance from the rim to the river, people at home were told that gazing at stereographic images of the canyon carried a freedom of vision that surpassed an actual visit. "Tourists often lose half the meaning and half the pleasure of a journey because of their nervous way of scampering from one sight to another without stopping to think about what they see," suggests a 1904 guide. "But when you are looking at the country through stereographs, you can take your time about it. You can linger long enough in any one spot so that the beauty and meaning of what you see may be mentally digested." Finding the canyon through the device was nothing less than an exercise in monasticism, a retreat into a solitary space of studious contemplation. Here are the guide's methods for using the device: "Hold the hood of the stereoscope close against the forehead, shutting out all sight of your immediate surroundings. . . . Read what is said of each place in this book. Refer to the map and know exactly where you are in each case. Read the explanatory comments printed on the back of each stereograph mount. Go slowly. Do not hurry. Go again—and yet again. Think it over. Read all the first-class books and magazine articles that you can find bearing on the subject of the Cañon." Following these instructions, the viewer could, ideally, become seduced by their intensity. After locating themselves on maps and perusing expert testimony in books and magazines, they focused the cards to find the hypnotic drama of a mechanically reproduced Grand Canyon. The whole affair, the guide suggested, would lodge them in a fiction of *realism:* "Does it not make you almost draw back with a shock of surprise? You feel the dizzy space below that perilously overhanging shelf from which the men are looking off; you almost hold your breath as you peer down towards the invisible bottom of the gorge."[55] For home viewers looking at an image of men looking into the canyon, perhaps there was no place where the Grand Canyon hit bottom. Instead, the canyon revealed itself and became comprehensible through a repetitive, interiorized orientation to a larger realm of reference points and disjointed images. As the canyon receded into this discourse, so too did the viewer.

"The stereoscope signals an eradication of 'the point of view' around which, for centuries, meanings had been assigned reciprocally to an observer and the object of his or her vision," argues Crary. He points out that students of visual perception and physiology found the stereoscope rendered natural vision of a thing or place obsolete. "We get the impression, when we actually do see the object, that we have already seen it before and are more or less familiar with it," wrote German physicist Hermann von Helmholtz in the 1850s. "The actual view of the thing does not add anything new or more accurate to the previous apperception we got from the picture." Although parlor stereoscopes were a popular leisure pastime since the 1850s, they engaged their users in a tangible production of "forms of verisimilitude," says Crary. "What the observer produced, again and again, was the effortless transformation of the dreary parallel images of flat stereo cards into a tantalizing apparition of depth. . . . And each time, the mass-produced and monotonous cards are transubstantiated into a compulsory and seductive vision of the 'real.'"[56]

As an early visual technology that dispersed the canyon's scenery into a series of views and voices, the stereoscope is an emblem of a broader approach to seeing the

landscape whereby exterior and interior images and discourse converge in the specta-tor. In the stereograph cards accompanying the 1904 canyon guide, home viewers may have found a pleasure and promise as they pressed the hood of the scope against their forehead. Inside the chamber placed over their eyes, they shut out everything that sur-rounded them. In this space, the dual images of the card appeared as a single picture of reality that became joined in the mind of the viewer. On more than one card, they found pictures of a visitor or a couple—like themselves—alone, gazing into the abyss. It was a view that reimagined a fantasy of the canyon and nature before tourists began arriving on the scene, an image that found its antithesis in the crowds of noisy and contemptible tourists who had become a source of managed vision since the turn of the century. Stationed behind a metal shroud and focused on the surface of the stereo-graph cards, they could silently contemplate a place they held in their minds and con-trolled with their hands. It was a place shut off from the crowds, a place of depth and dimension. And although some of the cards showed the Colorado River rolling through the canyon, the stereoscope, like images since that time, proposed to the viewer that there was no bottom in sight.

Kodak Sunset

In the visitor center courtyard, I stand with a group gathered near a cardboard sign balanced on an easel: PHOTO TALK BY A KODAK PHOTO SPECIALIST. PLEASE JOIN US. For six weeks every summer, Vinnie Carone from the Eastman Kodak Company in

Rochester, New York, leads a free, daily, one-hour clinic designed to teach visitors how to take better photographs on their vacation. This afternoon, about twenty of us form a semicircle around Vinnie. He wears a white knit sport shirt with a Kodak insignia on his chest, and a 35-mm camera hangs from his neck on a bright yellow strap covered with Kodak logos.

"When we're learning how to take pictures, where does everyone tell us to put the sun?" he asks, in a high-pitched and fast-paced voice. "The sun has to be at my back, right?" he says, answering his own question. "That's what everybody told us, right? Not anymore. We're going to be artists. We're going to write with light. We're going to do things like this," he says, holding up enlarged photos of sunsets and sunrises over the Grand Canyon. We watch Vinnie shuffle through a series of landscapes he's assembled as examples of what we can do once he teaches us to better use our cameras. I look at our group—people from Iowa, Pennsylvania, Florida, California, Germany, France, and a couple from Africa. Several wear clothing bearing the coordinates of their workplaces—a printing company, a livestock feed store, an insurance company, and a tire store. It has been rainy and cold today. A few people in T-shirts rub their arms for warmth as we listen to Vinnie anticipate the images we'll see in the canyon.

"Tonight, when you go to Hopi Point for sunset, there's going to be side-lit canyons," he continues. "You're going to see silhouettes, and you're going to see dramatic pictures there that now—after talking to me—you'll be able to take. Instead of going out there and *wondering* how you could do it, I'm *telling* you how." In less than an hour he's given us the power to refashion the world through our viewfinders. He tells us how to eliminate the haze that can reduce visibility. Make the sky appear bluer with polarizing filters. Saturate the colors of the canyon. Frame photographs in new ways by "moving the horizon around." Create drama in our images. Go beyond the limits of vacation photographs. "How do we show how big the canyon is? What do you have to compare it with?" Vinnie asks, only to answer for us. "People. A person. We all know how big our family is. And you're saying to me, 'I didn't come all the way from Zimbabwe to take pictures of my back,' right? You want to go back home and show your face in that picture, show people you were at Grand Canyon." He quickly shuffles through his pile of enlargements to find another example but holds off from showing it to us. "After you've taken those vacation pictures, why not get somebody, sit 'em down on the rim, and just take a peaceful, artistic type of picture where they're looking into the canyon." As he speaks, Vinnie reveals a picture of a woman seated on a rock and looking into a canyon sunset. "And now, we all look at this young lady and say, 'What is she looking at?' . . . She's looking at what we want the viewer to look at, which is the Grand Canyon," says Vinnie. "So after we've taken all those 'smiling-faces-at-the-camera' pictures, turn somebody around and take a picture of them looking into the canyon."

That evening, I ride a standing-room-only shuttle bus to Hopi Point. The *Guide,* a park service information paper, lists Hopi as the most famous and most crowded place to see the sunset. When I arrive, more than a hundred people are already assembled. They stand shoulder to shoulder against the rail, many with cameras and video recorders on tripods, lenses pointed like artillery toward the western horizon. Vinnie is here, too, still dressed in Kodak regalia and showing a man I recognize from the afternoon photo clinic how to adjust the aperture on his Minolta. The sun is still high, and although some remain stationary so they won't lose their place at the front of the railing, the air is filled with voices. I listen to a man tell a couple how he didn't think he would make it out of the canyon while hiking this afternoon. They all laugh over his ordeal. "Go find your brothers and tell them to get back here," I hear a mother command her daughter. Another full shuttle appears, and the new arrivals spill out onto the flat-rock viewing level enclosed by guardrails below the parking area.

Seated on the wall above the crowd, I spot Mike, a nineteen-year-old passenger loader for one of the commercial helicopter tours in Tusayan. "I load 'em up, buckle 'em in. They go up, they come down. I take off the buckles and help 'em out." This was how he described his job when I picked him up one afternoon a few weeks ago, hitchhiking in the rain. His friends had deserted him the previous night in Flagstaff while carousing the bars. He woke up the next morning in the woods near Route 180 after trying to thumb a ride for the seventy-three miles back to Tusayan. He'd already smoked four joints before I stopped, he told me. "Do a lot of people ride the helicopters? They seem pretty expensive," I asked, as we drove. "Well, you always see 'em in the air, that tells ya somethin'," he said. "Gettin' up there costs, like, a hundred for half an hour. It's a rip-off for the tourists, but I understand 'em wantin' to see it from the sky. The canyon is up there, though, even when you're on the ground. When I first got here, I couldn't catch my breath. I came from New Orleans where the highest point is like four feet above sea level. . . . It's okay there, but I really like these higher elevations," he said, staring into a place beyond the wiper blades.

"Mooooo . . . Mooooo," Mike is making the sounds of cattle in a holding pen when I walk over. "Mooooo . . . fuckin' tourons, heh-heh-heh." Tonight, Mike and two friends are sitting on the wall at Hopi Point amusing themselves with the tourists while waiting for the sun to go down. His buddies snicker and they cup their hands around their faces to contribute more of the same to the milling tourist scene below.

"What's up?" I say, wondering if he'll remember me. Surprisingly enough, he does.

"Oh, just havin' some kicks, watchin' the show," he says to me. "This dude picked me up that night you guys ditched me in Flag'," he says, identifying me for his friends, then turns back to me. "Quit the choppers. Bussin' tables for Fred, now. This is my weekend. Just partyin', and raggin' on the tourons." We talk for a few minutes, but we really don't have much to say. So I wander down the steps into the holding pen, join the cattle, and listen as Mike and his friends resume their game. Everyone else seems oblivious to their sound effects and cackles. Between Vinnie, now talking to three men fondling their cameras, and Mike's weekend crew, laying their comic sound track over this social scene, a swelling crowd of tourists mingles between the safety rails on Hopi Point, breathing in the setting sun.

For the ex-helicopter loader, who now picks up dirty dishes after vacationers, having some fun at the expense of those he serves probably offers a small catharsis or even a minor revenge. As he watches tourists leave their restaurant tables to feed on scenery, he knows well how the Grand Canyon tourist machine feeds on them. Out in Tusayan, below whirling chopper blades, Mike had strapped them in and locked the door. Every passenger got a window seat and a headset. With a prerecorded tour narration and the classical sounds of Dvorak, Wagner, sound tracks from *Chariots of Fire* and *2001: A Space Odyssey*, and the New Age synthesizers of Kitaro playing through their headphones, passengers were carried over the trees and past the rim, in thirty and forty-five minute loops that lassoed the canyon from the sky. Those with video cameras, wanting the cinematic experience to last beyond the vacation, could use patchcords to dub the audio pumping through their headsets onto their own videos filmed from window seats. On their return, Mike would unlock the hatch, help the angels out of their wings, and reload with eager bodies from the waiting room.

The implicit message of the photo specialist's daily clinic was much the same: Display images to instill an idea that canyon vacation photographs could hold values of a "higher" art, teach techniques to restore a sense of creative autonomy, and elevate the tourist from the crowd. With earphones and window seats, passengers who fly over the canyon absorbing themselves in the scenery cannot see the spinning blades that carry them. The tourists Vinnie instructed at the park visitor center also would not see the helicopters or scenic airplanes cutting through their view. With passage of the 1987 National Park Overflights Act, Congress "aimed at maintaining the natural quiet . . . frequently frustrated by the audio and visual disruption caused by low-flying aircraft." In an effort to preserve the aesthetic experience of a "natural" encounter with the canyon, federal law established "flight-free" zones over portions of the national park.[57] Man-agement plans for air-space, however, meant more than an effort to ensure public safety. Legislating silence and scenic purity rein-forced an ideal image of the scene, a setting for the solitary specta-tor constructed at the canyon over the last century and, now, re-composed daily in Vin-nie's photo clinic.

But tonight I don't see anyone on Hopi Point framing a lone spectator con-templating the can-yon. It is too crowded for that. Instead, some focus on the shadows bleeding out of side canyons. Others aim at the sun, waiting for its descent. Vinnie told us about the pictures we'd see tonight. Yet, whether anyone here had listened to his photo talk, or even carried a camera to Hopi Point, matters little. The man next to me, now using the tiny flash on his Instamatic to capture a naturalized drama, doesn't need to be re-minded that the sun is some ninety-three million miles away. Gathering like this in the dimming glow of sunset is a communion of sorts. On Hopi Point, it is an event conspicuously symbolic and public. The multitudes are here, yet for many the mo-ment retains private desires for a connection to something greater, perhaps even sa-cred. As the sun creeps behind the horizon, the crowd grows still for a moment, and bodies turn toward the west. The quiet is soon scratched by a flurry of clicking camera shutters, film advancing over sprockets, the small but sturdy image-making machines telling their owners to move faster; together they work to lick up the final glows of the day's light. Some of the crowd has seen enough, and to avoid waiting in line, they head for the shuttle buses humming in the parking area.

"But they say the 'afterglow' really makes for the best pictures," a man says to his wife who is heading for an open door. "Well, okay, but we're going to take this tram back. She's tired. We'll see you at the room," she sighs, holding her daughter in her arms. With the orange sphere finally dropping behind the horizon, I hear a few people clapping their hands, and in a briefly contagious moment, a smattering of applause spreads among the crowd. Someone says "Bravo! Encore!" People are laughing and

chattering. Then, in orderly fashion, we climb up the stairs, line up and pack ourselves into a line of shuttle buses waiting to carry us down to hotels and campsites, cafeterias, and parking lots. And with the canyon dissolving under a night sky creeping in from the east, we bounce down West Rim Drive. I listen to a man and his daughter try to remember the names of the Seven Wonders of the World. The curled thumb on her hand shows me they've made it to four. It's completely dark outside, and I can't see through the shuttle windows. Inside, fluorescent lights now cast their yellow glow on us, turning every window pane into a looking glass. I look out the window toward the canyon to see how far we've come down the road, but the glass only mirrors our faces and bodies, shoulder to shoulder, bouncing along as crowded passengers.

5

Fantasy Trails across Popular Terrain

A photographer near Grandeur Point, who is working on a western parks feature in a national weekly magazine, says he's frustrated with his assignment. "These guys in the New York office tell me they want shots of some long, lonely road going out toward the horizon at sunset," he says, and adds, "without cars. Maybe one car or an RV. Where am I supposed to find that? All these people come in cars, and they're on the roads. People are all over the trails. I'm taking pictures of crowds. They want something that isn't here. 'Just get it,' they tell me." His job is to reproduce a conventional and familiar image of the Grand Canyon and the American West—a place for solitary encounters and open roads—for American readers, as if to assure them a dream of freedom remains waiting for them. But the difficulty he may have in creating an ideal vision of the park is also under the supervision and management of park officials.

The park service public affairs office at Grand Canyon gets several hundred inquiries each year requesting permits for filming, but actually issues about fifty.

Protection of the natural resources and the potential for interrupting visitors' experiences are main concerns when issuing permits, a public affairs officer said, giving me a copy of the park's *Filming Guidelines.* Taking photographic license (for instance, superimposing pictures) to "depict activities in conflict with the mission and goals of park management are prohibited," I read in the fourth of eleven principles spelling out the park's policy. "The NPS recognizes rights guaranteed by the First Amendment to the Constitution of the United States of persons wishing to film," reads the next principle in the guidelines.[1] "If somebody were coming out here with just a camera and doing nothing more than a visitor was doing with their own camera, we wouldn't require them to have a permit," said the public affairs officer. "What we would be concerned about is if somebody were to come out and take a picture of Grand Canyon National Park signs or emblems, and use that to promote a product. You can't use the federal government to promote your commercial product. But to use an image of the Grand Canyon on a calendar, that's no big deal." Motion picture companies present the biggest problem in terms of resource management. "We've turned many away. A lot of movies that you may think were filmed here at Grand Canyon were actually filmed out on Monument Valley or up in Utah. Like *Thelma and Louise* was not filmed here," she said, adding that she had concerns about the final scene of the film, when Thelma and Louise drive their car over the rim. "What I was concerned about was planting the seed in somebody's mind. That's just . . . a horrible thing and to depict that actually happening. . . . "

Films and television programs made in the park under park service supervision include Lawrence Kasdan's *Grand Canyon,* Howard Ramis's *National Lampoon's Vacation,* and a 1970s episode of TV's *The Brady Bunch.* Television commercials for televisions and carpet cleaners were filmed outside the park, on a section of the canyon in the Navajo Nation. Sometimes professional photographers use the canyon without asking. The August 1977 issue of *Playboy* published a pictorial of three "Playmates" on a canyon river trip. The feature, "Riverboat Gamblers," showed the topless women hiking with a male river guide over the terrain against a backdrop of sedimented cliffs, sunning themselves on rocks and showering in a canyon waterfall. "After making camp, Patti and Hope get the evening's geology lesson from a guide, who leads them through one of the many side canyons," says the caption. "Above and below, the ladies soak up some vitamin C."[2] Three months later, *Playboy* published some approving letters from readers in response to the canyon raft trip feature. "I made the trip myself with the National Wildlife Federation in 1972 but failed to see such fine specimens of 'wildlife' as photographer Richard Fegley captured on film," wrote a man from Phoenix, Arizona. "You really establish a landmark with *Riverboat Gamblers,*" wrote a man from Ohio. "I really think you managed to liberate the Grand Canyon and the people who enjoy and appreciate it once and for all."[3]

The photographer I met on the rim and the photographer who photographed the *Playboy* river trip in 1977 both put together fantasy stories of the canyon. Television programs, commercials, and movies do much the same. A park service management policy not only tries to protect "the resource," as the public affairs officer called the canyon, but protect its image as well. The mass media present a daunting force, however, compared to the park service, and no matter how many informational programs, exhibits, and maps they supply visitors, the stories people carry to the canyon begin elsewhere. "I chose to go to Grand Canyon because of its natural beauty and grandeur, which I had seen in magazines and movies," a thirty-six-year-old California man told me in a letter. "A trip out West wouldn't seem complete without visiting the Grand Canyon—one of the wonders of nature I've read about and seen in movies and on TV," echoed a fifty-four-year-old Michigan woman. Over time, the mass media have cast a spell around the canyon, as these visitors suggest. For some, media images of the canyon not only suggest a place worth seeing but also continually fuel their anticipation for their trip. A thirty-five-year-old Maryland man told me he made a special trip to Baltimore's Science Center to see the IMAX film on the Grand Canyon before heading west. "Even though part of [the film] was very scary," he wrote, "it was a great way to get psyched up for the trip."

Comments like these are fairly common. They are reminders of how visitors call upon a language of mass media to describe a sense of purpose for their travels, find media texts as a source for sustaining their enthusiasm, and casually draw from cinematic experiences as ironic frames to clarify and "certify" their visions of natural beauty. In many ways, these visitors allude to Percy's observation that the Grand Canyon has been appropriated by a "symbolic complex which has already been formed in the sightseer's mind." Percy further notes that "the highest point, the term of the sightseer's satisfaction, is not the sovereign discovery of the thing before him; it is rather the measuring up of the thing to the criterion of the preformed symbolic complex."[4]

To some extent, Percy's remarks characterize the terms of living in a mass mediated culture where people cannot but help have an image of the canyon before they arrive. The tourists I met along the rim and who wrote me about their trips suggest that these images are not necessarily an obstacle to their experience of the canyon; they provide a frame that helps them to see and appreciate the canyon.

Maps of Popular Memory

"This is the Brady Bunch trail," a twelve-year-old girl informs her mother, as she starts down the Bright Angel Trail with a bouncy jaunt. "The Brady Bunch trail?" asks her mother, who is carrying a small knapsack and a plastic jug filled with a gallon of water. "Yeah," she says. "The Brady Bunch went down this, and Alice hurt her leg." It was not the first time I'd heard such comments at the canyon and at home. "I've only been to Grand Canyon and Hawaii with the Brady Bunch," Shane, a twenty-four-year-old university student tells me. "But I'd love to really go there someday." When I mention the Grand Canyon in my undergraduate classes, students often associate it with the *Brady Bunch's* 1971 family vacation, which most of them have seen on television in syndication.

The Bradys' Grand Canyon adventure is a saccharine story stretched over three episodes with the help of regular comic mishaps, one-liners, and the constant din of a studio laughtrack. Pulling out of their driveway in a California suburb, the Bradys and housekeeper Alice appear a cohesive unit, singing old standards like "Clementine," "Down in the Valley," and "Home on the Range." They finally arrive at the canyon and stand together on a roadside lookout—no other tourists in sight—in awe of the scenery. Alice reads the canyon's vital statistics from a guidebook. The mother, Carol, informs Cindy that the Indian word for Grand Canyon is "mountains lying down," and Mike, the father, tells Peter that it took "thousands of years of running water" to make the canyon. His middle son now sees why Dad doesn't want them to leave the water running at home. Later, the family rides mules to the canyon's bottom, yet the Colorado River they saw from the rim has disappeared. After they pitch their tent in an isolated desert landscape, Alice cooks on a camp stove while Carol helps out in a salmon-colored pants suit and pumps. A final "cliffhanger" re-volves around Bobby and Cindy getting lost while looking for dinosaur fossils. An Indian boy helps them get back to the family. Jimmy, who lives in the canyon, is on the run from a grandfather who is only interested in tradition and who, Jimmy fears, doesn't understand his desire to be an astronaut. In a moment of fatherly advice, Mr. Brady encourages Jimmy to give it another try with his grandfather, Chief Eagle Cloud. The chief is so grateful he holds a ceremony to make the Bradys honorary trib-al members and gives them all Indian names. For instance, Mr. Brady becomes "Big Eagle of Large Nest." Mrs. Brady is "Yellow Flower with Many Petals." Alice gets the name "Squaw in Waiting," which only prompts her to request, "Make that a short wait." The vacation episodes end with the family dancing around a fire with Indians of no particular tribe at the bottom of the canyon. Although the Bradys' canyon is a place built on familiar stereotypes of tourists, the Wild West, and Indian traditions, it is also one that holds to a promise of the vacation as a time and place for transforma-tion. On leaving the park gate for their return home, Cindy asks the ranger if she re-members them when they arrived. "We're the Brady family," she proudly informs the ranger, only to have Bobby correct her. "You mean the Brady Braves."

The canyon rendered in the TV series is a grand invention, one that is largely ab-sent of other tourists, auto traffic, or anything else that might interrupt the family's encounter with nature. The canyon itself seems to play a cameo role. Apart from the scene showing the Bradys' arrival—with the requisite expressions of awe and venera-tion—the canyon serves as little more than a backdrop for melodrama and juvenile comedy. But by venturing there and sending episodic reports of their exploits to view-ers' living rooms (a practice that continues annually on the calendar of syndicated programming), the Bradys' Grand Canyon became mapped in the popular imagina-tion—but not for everyone. The mother and daughter hiking together are separated by a television geography that appears in an instant of recognition. They are not alone. "Were the Bradys really here?" is one of those queries park rangers amusingly file under "frequently asked tourist questions." One park public relations officer told me that she was unsure whether the Bradys actually filmed at Grand Canyon because she had not been working there at the time. It seemed to matter little to her one way or another. But for some visitors, recognizing a "Brady Bunch Trail" is only one of several "landmarks" that visitors have seen on screens at home.

"Can you show us the place where Thelma and Louise drove over the edge?" two women ask, interrupting a conversation I'm having with a tour escort who has been taking a busload of people on a tour of old Route 66. After departing from Chicago a few weeks ago, they've been following what remains of the "Mother Road," and today they've made a quick detour from Flagstaff to the South Rim. The tour escort is happy to oblige the two women, who are carrying postcards they just purchased in El Tovar.

"Thelma and Louise?" he says, with the confidence of someone who knows his way around the place. "Yeah, sure," and we move out of the shade near Hopi House and stand next to the stone wall on the rim. "It's just beyond that outcropping there," he says matter of factly, aiming his finger toward the West Rim. "That's Thelma and Louise Point right over there." They look where he tells them. "Just follow that green where the trees are, and it's right on the other side of those." I listen to his directions but can't really pinpoint the place he's describing. The women stand quietly focused, studying the rim.

"Oh," says one of the women, sounding unsure of what, specifically, she's supposed to be looking at. The other just snaps a photo in the general direction of "Thelma and Louise Point." A few of the Harvey guides told me that since the film's release, tour passengers frequently ask where the heroines, Thelma Dickenson and Louise Sawyer, drove their green Thunderbird convertible over the canyon's edge. Park guides and rangers may have their laughs over questions about Thelma and Louise, but most of them tell people the truth: that the film's final scene was actually shot in Utah's Canyonlands.

Hearing these visitors recognize canyon trails and landmarks as scenes from television and film may offer little more than an index of how the landscape circulates in popular culture and visitors' worlds, before anyone arrives on the rim. *The Brady Bunch* and *Thelma and Louise* plot the canyon with the contours of comedy and drama absent from the park maps visitors receive. Whether a desire to hike the Brady Trail or catch a glimpse of Thelma and Louise Point is an intention in anyone's visit is unclear. For the most part, it's unlikely. Instead, they reveal a geography that appears in an instant of recognition—as if hovering in the ether of popular memory—that refers and recalls another place and time when visitors occupied another form of spectatorship, in a theater or in front of a television.

Perhaps these comments are amusing because they retrieve such obviously fictionalized and invented images of Grand Canyon. To some extent, they are humorous because they recall a propensity to see tourists caught up in the machinery of mass culture, as unfortunates distanced from seeing what should otherwise be a real, authentic, and natural wonder. Yet, when I listen to these visitors (and others) discovering that they are on the Brady Bunch Trail or looking for Thelma and Louise Point, I am reminded of how much they share with other, perhaps more appropriate and sanctioned, practices of sightseeing. I imagine those tourists visiting other sites where a story, heard somewhere along the way, begins to take shape again. Today, for example, some tourist is likely looking down an old cannon barrel on a stretch of the Gettysburg battlefield, mulling over what might have gone through the mind of a Confederate soldier gulping in his last breath. In Montana, a retired couple just climbed out of their motorhome to have a look beyond a small fence at a field of scattered white markers that dissolve into the bloody bodies of Custer's Seventh Cavalry, near the Little Big Horn River. And out

on the West Rim, an adolescent boy is wandering with his parents through Hermit's Rest, Colter's imaginative dwelling built as a Harvey tour terminus, pondering the joys experienced by some hermit who presumably lived in this comfortably rustic atmosphere of bearskins and medieval wrought iron.

I suspect that someone trained in history might chafe at the comparisons between the contrived stories floating across TV and film screens and the accumulated research, evidence, and peer reviews giving ballast to the cultural narratives of Pickett's Charge or Custer's Last Stand that furrow through national battlefields. Yet, at the Grand Canyon, the fabric of history and culture has long been woven with the materials and toward the aesthetic inclinations of those who stood on its rim. The legacy of canyon views assembled by eyes, pens, and brushstrokes a century ago held their own traces of fabrication, fantasy, and synthetic sensitivities. Moran's assemblage of multiple "impressions" on the canvas he named *Chasm of the Colorado,* or Dutton's eye for architectural symmetry and Oriental nomenclature in the pages of his *Tertiary*

History, are only two strong reminders of how the Great Abyss has long been a repository for the interior fantasies of self-idealized observers. For turn-of-the-century visitors, at odds with European antiquities and hungry for the spiritual rapture glowing from a celestial city, the canyon found a public and private resonance in parallels to masterworks of art, music, and grand buildings—all reference points to worlds beyond the rim, all serving as symbols for validating the landscape before them.

The difference between one visitor who stares into the abyss, hearing Beethoven, and another who sees the Brady family is, at heart, often a matter of taste, experience, and the cultural politics that tend to divide them—at least in the mind (if not in theories of popular culture that thrive on such distinctions). Obviously, visitors who ramble over the rim today can and often do see the canyon through many eyes that tend to look in a variety of directions for some point of orientation. That a plurality of languages and visions accompanies public access is a given, and clearly apparent at the canyon when one listens closely to tourists or browses through visitor registers. The multiple canyon views any individual might acknowledge over the course of a few minutes only testifies to how its empty and open space is a contemplative sphere that cannot be easily contained by park interpreters, commercial guides, maps, or visitor center orientation programs. Contemplation "transports the dreamer outside the immediate world to a world that bears the mark of infinity," suggests Gaston Bachelard. "We do not see it start, and yet it always starts in the same way, that is, it flees the object nearby and right away it is far off, elsewhere, in the space of *elsewhere.*"[5]

However, the names given to such "elsewheres" are not entirely a matter of mutual reverence or a liberal appreciation for relativism. From the minute visitors set foot in the park, they are surrounded by markers reminding them they occupy cultural ground sanctified with the voices of scientists and poets recapitulated by park rangers, stacked on bookstore shelves, and in captions printed on posters of a canyon sunrise. The mass media also tend to reinforce ideas of the canyon as nature's expression of an artistic masterpiece. For instance, the sound tracks accompanying images of the canyon are typically classical and symphonic music, or derived from their scores. Majestic horns and cymbals often sound the arrival of sunrise over the canyon's temples. String quartets carry viewers over the canyon in shots filmed from planes and helicopters. For those who take aerial tours from Tusayan or Las Vegas, symphonic music comes to them through earphones. When the Bradys arrive at the canyon rim for their first view, the perky sound track that usually bounces them along quickly shifts to the reverential and melancholy strains of harps and violins. It is difficult not to feel the weight of this history, and often it is part and parcel of the visitor's own baggage, gathered and packed at home, and happily carried through the gate. More often than not, the push to have an awesome canyon visit finds its way to these coordinates drawn nearly a century ago. Yet, specific markers of popular culture tend not to adhere very well to the polished and sealed grain of this past. To quote Shakespeare from the rim is easily acknowledged as an act of piety. But to seek out Thelma and

Louise Point seems a case of folly and, for some, indicative of the average tourist who—in that instant—is not seeing or feeling the terms of what has become a "higher" consensus about the landscape. It is as if linking the canyon with a popular film or television program suggests a surrender to a level of banality available to anyone; they appear to render the scene in the terms of popular trivial pursuits rather than honor, as I've discussed earlier, the literary legacy that has become so sedimented in public discourse, it seems a naturalized feature of the terrain.

In many ways, the sublime hyperbole typical of early visitor accounts set the stage for looking into the canyon and finding oneself elsewhere. "The view changed at every step, and was never half an hour the same in one place," Charles Warner noted in 1891. "Nor did it need much fancy to create illusions or pictures of unearthly beauty."[6] For him, they were "illusions" and "pictures" of medieval castles and Eastern temples. Like Clarence Dutton who preceded him and others who would come later, Warner's description offered a set of symbolic reference points validating his experience with the cultural icons and images that held currency in his world. Such markers could elevate him and lend dramatic proportion to his vision, accessible to those, he said, whose "minds can rise to the heights of the sublime and the beautiful."[7] Such ideas served to separate the ideal observer from the crowd—at least on the pages of a travel account—and, simultaneously, consecrate the canyon in the terms of culture. For these contemporary visitors, the scenes made famous through television and film are points for observing and identifying a canyon traveled over by popular characters they have known elsewhere. Movie stars. Television families. Fictional events that carry significance precisely because they have been first known somewhere that is not the Grand Canyon. Recognizing them validates a knowledge they already hold about the place they may be visiting for the first time, yet seeing again. Whether it is the turn-of-the-century tourist who dreams of a celestial city, or the contemporary tour bus passenger who looks for the place where Susan Sarandon and Geena Davis drove over the rim, canyon visitors have, for the past century, mapped the landscape in a manner that defers the details of geographic specificity for landscapes populated by dramas of individual and cultural imagination. Their efforts and inclinations echo a dialectic of place and time rendered in Italo Calvino's *Invisible Cities:* "The city is redundant: it repeats itself so that something will stick in the mind. Memory is redundant: it repeats signs so that the city can begin to exist."[8] To some extent, these visitors suggest how the practice of recalling cultural symbols *allows them to exist* in a spiritual city of nature or a "real" location of a Hollywood fiction. Such texts are not divided by lines of high or popular culture as much as they fall against the criticisms of self-proclaimed pedants who tend to lay claim to a true and untainted view of nature's landscape. Historically, such claims have hinged on distinctions between "tourists" who have lost sight of the canyon for reasons of taste, education, intellectual capacity, or as evidenced by social decorum and their congregation as a crowd. In the end, however, such "purified" vantage points inevitably set the canyon as a stage, and cast the observer as a lead player in soulful and rational dramas resting in the languages of God, science, and art. Against this tradition, a seemingly infinite realm of popular discourse provides another set of reference points for visitors who are ambivalently poised toward the canonical literary and scientific authority that symbolically consecrated the canyon a century ago.

Packaged Tours

Standing near Grandeur Point one afternoon, I talk with Kenny and Betty, a vacationing couple on their way to Las Vegas. Despite the impressive view, we mostly discuss the places we have come from.

"I'm from New Jersey and my friends always kid me about how much I like going to see Smokey Bear," says Kenny. "They don't see why I want to get back to nature."

"You give me the money and I'm headed West," Betty chimes in. "I need the space. They're expecting another three million people on the East Coast in the next few years. It used to be you could drive the Garden State Parkway after 9:30 with no traffic. Now it's always crowded. Don't those people work?" Traveling from the East Coast, seeking refuge from urban congestion, they made a common journey; theirs is a familiar story of the road west leading to natural wonders, to promises of relief and renewal. I ask them to pose for a photograph, and they happily oblige. While I am changing the film in my camera, a couple of "thirtysomethings" in khaki and white wander up the trail to where we are standing. I listen as Kenny and the man, who says he's from St. Petersburg, Florida, exchange polite conversation about the canyon's beauty, how wonderful it is to stand here on the rim, how the air smells so clean and fresh like pine. They are two strangers—a black man from New Jersey and a white man from Florida—meeting at the edge of the canyon. Their conversation lulls as they admire the view. Then, the Florida visitor says something that only confirms what I've been thinking all along.

"Did you see that movie about the Grand Canyon with Danny Glover?" St. Petersburg asks Kenny.

"No, I didn't catch that one," says Kenny after thinking it over. "Which movie is that?"

"Well it's called *Grand Canyon,* actually," says St. Pete. "It's about these people from different walks of life who meet up on the Grand Canyon. It's got Danny Glover, Kevin Kline. You should see it if you can, you'd probably like it." Kenny just listens, but says nothing more except to repeat that the view is "sure beautiful." Betty, whose been chatting with Mrs. Petersburg, tells Kenny that she wants to move on. We all say good-bye, wish one another a safe trip, and shake hands. "See that movie if you can," St. Pete reminds Kenny, already a few paces down the trail. "Nice guy," he mumbles to his wife as they walk to the edge of Grandeur Point. "Seem like good people." The Florida visitor seems particularly gratified by this unexpected meeting.

After all, he and Kenny have come close to reliving a scene straight out of Lawrence Kasdan's *Grand Canyon*. In the film, however, Mack (Kline), an immigration lawyer, and Simon (Glover), a tow-truck operator, meet on the streets of Los Angeles. Mack's car has broken down in a bad neighborhood on the way home from a Lakers game. He's about to get mugged when Simon comes to the rescue. Later, while sitting on a curb in front of a service station and talking about how life in Los Angeles is falling apart around them, Simon recounts his trip to the Grand Canyon.

"When you sit on the edge of that thing, you just realize what a joke we people are," he tells Mack, who has never been to the canyon. "What big heads we got thinking that what we do is gonna matter all that much. . . . It's a split second we been here. The whole lot of us. And one of us? That's a piece of time too small to get a name." This sounds familiar. Simon seems to be rehearsing the lesson of "humility" from Ranger Karen's "Awesome Chasm" walk.[9] In Kasdan's *Grand Canyon*, people are also nagged by questions of meaning and insignificance, but the questions appear in an urban landscape split open by racial and economic fault lines, where the helicopters flying over the scene are conducting police surveillance. For Mack, Simon's good deed is nothing short of a miracle that saves his life. It is also the start of a friendship that crosses the divide between black and white, the urban professional and the working class.

Near the end of the film, Simon and Mack are shooting baskets in his driveway. Simon wants to thank Mack for setting him up on a blind date that has quickly flourished into a satisfying relationship. In the final scene, we see him offer his gift of gratitude. A van pulls into a parking lot and comes to a stop. "End of the line, folks," Simon tells his passengers, and nearly all of the film's principal characters climb out onto the asphalt. There is Claire, Mack's wife, holding a baby she's just adopted after finding him abandoned under a tree while she was jogging; Roberto, Claire and Mack's teenage son, who is named after Roberto Clemente; Jane, Simon's new sweetheart; and Otis, Simon's nephew, who has been struggling with life in the L.A. gang world. The camera shows us all of them: everyone is looking at a thing we do not yet see. "So, what do you think?" Simon asks Mack. "It's not all bad," says Mack, never taking his eyes off what Simon has shown him. Finally, the camera swings around, and we are not surprised to find them all standing on the rim of the canyon. The scene is silent, except for the cry of a raven, off in the distance. Then the camera pulls back and catapults us forward, flying directly over Simon's head, over the abyss. We hear the symphonic burst of trumpets, timpani, and then an angelic choir. Before we know it, we have left the rim and are alone, winding through empty inner canyon passages.

The canyon has long been pitched as offering a solution to the ills of the city and the malaise of everyday life, and *Grand Canyon* dutifully returns Simon, Mack, and the others to the canyon. The camera frames each of them as respectfully awestruck. Even though they are parked at Desert View, they have the canyon all to themselves for this powerful moment of reckoning. As with the Bradys' arrival, no other cars or tourists are in sight. It's a romantic ending that retrieves the mythic formulas that have long pulled people to national parks. Yet, even Kasdan's camera cannot bear to stay on the rim. It leaves these nineties' pilgrims behind for a place where none of them could really live. And we don't see them again, after the awe has worn off, back in the van on the road to their hotel, or when Claire's baby starts to cry. Films, of course, offer such idealizations. Often, they lend a comfort that is difficult to resist even as they give us models for living that largely ignore the dilemmas of those who watch films rather than appear in them as characters.

Perhaps the man from St. Petersburg found a stirring parity between Kasdan's canyon and his own. What had been a leisure walk down Rim Trail had, for an instant, become something more. He could not have planned on meeting Kenny, but their chance encounter graced him with an opportunity to feel that he was not just another canyon tourist. In fact, his life might feel richer because it connected him with a drama he had first seen as a movie. He and Kenny were more than passing strangers; they were real-life incarnations of Simon and Mack, two more men escaping the city for a soothing view of nature. If Kenny only had seen the film, he might more fully appreciate what a meeting of a black man and a white man on the South Rim could summon. But it is just as well that Kenny knew nothing of Kasdan's canyon. This would have surely doused the beam of cinematic light flashing on St. Pete. To spontaneously feel as if you are living in a movie is one thing, but to actually ask someone else to corroborate the fantasy can backfire into self-consciousness. Instead, alone with his knowledge, the Florida visitor might only hope Kenny would come home from the Blockbuster Video outlet one night with a copy of Kasdan's film. He and Betty could kick back in front of the TV in their New Jersey living room, and maybe—in the inverted logic prone to parallel universes—he would, for no apparent reason, recall a man from Florida on the edge of the Grand Canyon.

Kasdan's film wouldn't prevent St. Pete from "really" seeing the canyon as much as it might offer him a chance to find himself in a drama where, for a moment at least, his journey had taken an unanticipated turn for the better. Percy would call this an instance of "certification," where the scenes of a major motion picture paradoxically "authenticate" the events of one's own everyday circumstances. Rather than being just another tourist hoofing it along the beaten track, he has stumbled onto a role in a scene worthy of a big screen.[10] Curiously, such a scenario is in direct contrast to the taste of insignificance Simon discovered while at the rim and later conveyed to Mack as they sat on the curb in front of an L.A. towing garage. "Those rocks are laughin' at me . . . me and my worries," he'd told Mack. "It's really humorous to that Grand Canyon. I felt like a gnat that lands on the ass of a cow that's chewing its cud next to the road that you drive by at seventy miles an hour." It's doubtful such contradictions were of any bother to the Florida visitor. Despite his recommending *Grand Canyon* to Kenny, the movie he probably would have wanted him to see was the one playing in his own head. Meeting Kenny was, in the end, merely a sketch of a scene from another film in which two men of different races and from different quarters stood together on the canyon's edge, compared notes on its beauty, and felt good for doing so. St. Petersburg eventually followed Kenny down the trail, and for me, their scene had dissolved as quickly as it appeared.

Any interpretation of such events unavoidably is filled with conjecture. At the same time, it's difficult to disregard the reference points leading to the geographies of fantasy that flourish as visitors encounter the canyon and each other. This is not to concede to a purely subjective appreciation of a landscape. Places like Grand Canyon are material productions imbued with boundaries, rules, buildings, trails, viewpoints, maps, contours, and natural features. Yet, there is no way to separate the canyon's *lived social landscape* from perceptual, psychical, experiential, imaginative, discursive, aesthetic, political, economic, and existential forces at work when people arrive there. By the same token, these tourists propose how the canyon has already visited the worlds they occupy at home. Contrary to popular notions that tourists are either looking for some route to escape—or are captured by—the artificial machinations of mass media images that would prevent them from "really seeing" the canyon, visitors gravitate toward various texts and stories to orient them toward their experience of nature. Instead of running from texts and devices that might come between them and the canyon, they actively seek them out to enhance their view. Their scenes combine varying fragments of fantasy, film, literature, personal experience, and manufactured views. A visitor from Florida may find he's fallen, by chance, into a situation that feels like a scene from a film. Others who do not stumble on such circumstances may want something of the same and may make the effort to create something akin to a cinematic experience.

In Babbit's General Store, Herb, a sixty-three-year-old retired schoolteacher visiting from San Diego, peruses a display of regionally inspired music. "We're leaving the park today," he tells me, as he picks up a cellophane-wrapped cassette of R. Carlos Nakai's *Earth Spirit,* a recording of Native American flute music. "I thought it would be nice if we could listen to a tape as we drove along." Nakai isn't what he has in mind, though he has several choices: *Canyon Lifesongs* by Rita Cantu; *Canyon Trilogy* also by Nakai; and *Sounds of the Grand Canyon,* which blends natural sounds recorded in the canyon with piano, flute, and guitar. Herb picks up a copy of Paul Winter's *Canyon* and looks it over. "Do you know anything about this one?" he asks.

"I think it was recorded on a raft trip in the canyon," I say. I overheard a woman mention this while raving to her companion about Winter's music a few days ago at this very display. Her friend seemed happy to know this and bought the tape. "He's a saxophone player," I tell Herb. "He's the one who does music that sounds like whales and wolves, stuff like that." Herb's skeptical visage tells me this isn't a selling point, and he puts Winter's canyon back on the shelf.

"I'll go with this," he decides, and picks up the copy of Ferde Grofe's *Grand Canyon Suite* from the stack of cassettes that first caught his eye. "My wife will like this, I think," he says, scanning the store for her. "We're going to drive toward Desert View and then up toward Utah. It'll be nice to listen to while we go through the rest of the park . . . stop at some of the turnouts. . . . Can't go wrong with a title like that. We like classical." Grofe's 1930s symphonic portrait of sunrises, sunsets, mules on the trail, storms, and the Painted Desert had never really been a classical hit, according to critics. The Swiss composer had attempted a literal translation of canyon images into music. In the early 1960s, Grofe's *Grand Canyon Suite* was the sound track for a Disney picture entitled *Grand Canyon.* The film is largely composed of documentary footage, organized around the themes of the suite. For Herb, however, this is a spontaneous purchase, possibly a little surprise for his wife, something to augment what he was already expecting to be a pleasurable scenic drive along the edge of the canyon. He seemed gratified to make a choice. I watch him and his wife get in the checkout line. She's gathered up chips, a bag of grapes, and a bottle of orange soda in a plastic store basket, which she hands off to Herb as she studies the Grofe cassette. I don't tell him the road to Desert View is mostly lined on either side with thick stands of pine, and the canyon will be visible only in a few places as they cruise along.

"America's history is like a memory of nostalgia," Linny, a Dutch university arts director, tells me a few weeks later as we sit in the Bright Angel cocktail lounge. She and her sister, Jorina, a physician, are traveling across the Southwest with Jorina's boyfriend, who is back at camp sleeping off a hike up the Bright Angel Trail. The two tall sisters are in their late thirties, and Linny, who just told me she quit smoking a year ago, decides to roll herself a cigarette from a pouch of Drum tobacco I bought earlier at Babbit's. "The people get into kitsch, here," Linny continues. "We see the teepees and cowboys on the way here. Much of this seems . . . [like] artifice." Jorina doesn't speak English very much but, nodding in agreement, seems to understand what we're saying. Linny never tells me what she was expecting to find in the United States but loves driving through New Mexico and Arizona in their rented Dodge Spirit. "The view is big, and the [power] lines go far into the distance. We have the music from a film called *Koyaanisqatsi*. We play it over and over on our way here," she tells me. "It is like the car window is a movie screen. Have you seen this film?" I had seen Godfrey Reggio's 1983 film, which takes its title from a Hopi word loosely meaning "life out of balance." It is a visual critique of modern progress and technology that juxtaposes stunning natural landscapes (some filmed in the canyon) with accelerated images of shopping malls, freeways, television screens, densely packed city walks, neon, building demolitions, bombs exploding in deserts, and rockets blasting into space. There is no dialogue or narration, and Philip Glass's neobaroque sound track—layers of deep organ chords, trumpets, French horns, and the ethereal voices of a vocal ensemble—sets a moody tone for Reggio's images. This is the only cassette the sisters brought with them from Holland, and Linny says it puts her in a trance while they drive through much of the scenery she had seen for the first time in a Dutch movie theater.

I know little of Herb's motivations to buy the *Grand Canyon Suite* or Linny's decision to pack the *Koyaanisqatsi* sound track into her suitcase before leaving Holland, but each of them may have anticipated how the tape passing over the heads of the car's cassette player would complement, perhaps heighten, the time they spent rolling over the road. I was reminded of how often I played the Ventures' "Apache" and Neil Young's "Cortez the Killer" as I drove across the Navajo Nation between Desert View and Cameron. The opening tom-toms and staccato guitar of "Apache" could turn the rolling terrain into scenes from a Sergio Leone western. Unfortunately, the song only played about three minutes before I had to hit the rewind. "Cortez the Killer," however, is twice as long. A slow steady bass line and Young's fuzzy, wandering guitar solo guaranteed transport into a hazy dreamscape, a combination of music and high desert moving across the glass panels of my VW bus that carried me to whereabouts I'd never be able to conjure alone. Like the reflectoscopes Mary Colter had installed on The

Watchtower observation deck, the synthesis of music and the moving vehicle worked as a framing device for an otherwise insurmountable landscape, not only enhancing and individualizing a view but placing me or Herb or Linny at the center of its creation. With notes echoing through my car stereo turned up high enough to cover a grumbling engine, I could film, with or without a camera, in grainy black and white as the music projected a harsh frame around the cars and aluminum-sided tour buses parked at the souvenir stands I passed every few miles. The proverbial "surrealism" so often invoked alongside descriptions of tourism, a fascination with the alienation and recreation of the world as an aesthetic pursuit, found shape in such small but conscious efforts to give a drive across the windy Coconino Plateau the feel of a movie.

"When we are safely inside the car, behind closed windows, the external objects are, so to speak, transposed into another mode," Slavoj Žižek reminds us. "They appear to be fundamentally 'unreal,' as if their reality has been suspended, put in parenthesis—in short, they appear as a kind of cinematic reality projected onto the screen of the windowpane." This is a fairly common sensation, a "phenomenological experience of the barrier separating inside from outside," notes Žižek, where we often feel "the outside is ultimately fictional."[11] Selecting a particular musical sound track is a way toward further cultivating the fiction. Like an "establishing shot" orienting us to the scene where stories can unfold, a sound track "gives us the basic perspective, the 'map' of the situation, and guarantees its continuity, while the images are reduced to isolated fragments that float freely in the universal medium of the sound aquarium."[12] Inside our vehicles, we may create a complementary convergence of images and sounds that also reaches toward continuities with our notions of taste, previous experiences, and the internalized structures of perception common to a visual society. Grofe's symphony, scored as though it were a sound track for a film not made until decades later, appeals to what Herb sees as a taste for "classical music." Glass's alternating rhythmic current of sound synchronized to endless tracking shots, time-lapse studies of southwestern canyons and deserts, critically framed against images of destructive technologies and accelerated patterns of a dreary urban existence, actually is a cinematic sound track but one transported to a rented automobile traveling through the actual locations its passengers had first seen in a movie theatre. For Linny, who found the Southwest tourist landscape populated by kitsch, playing the music perhaps offers a vantage point toward the landscape that surpasses her stated disdain for "artifice" and any contradictions that may accompany her aesthetic inclinations. And for me, the Ventures and Neil Young undoubtedly settle in a nostalgia for TV and motion-picture westerns, and a revisionist historical tableau of Spanish conquest translated through the sentimental musings of a Canadian rock icon from the buckskin jacket hippie days (his rather than mine) whose songs I first learned to play on the guitar.

Grofe's "Grand Canyon Suite," the *Koyaanisqatsi* sound track, or my own musical staples inherently suggest that our scenic drives may be aimed toward some nostalgic effort to dwell, for a time, as an aficionado of "classical" music and landscapes, a critic of progress who envies a native connection to the earth, or a self-absorbed moviegoer who constantly gravitates toward the mythic pull of old Westerns and a sentimental recovery of his own youth. Each is an occasion of a spectator indulged in an inescapable interplay between exterior and interior landscapes. "Mental space and social realities are *in reality* inseparable," notes Victor Burgin, who rejects a prevailing dichotomy that places "fantasy" and "reality" in opposition. The perceptual, experiential, material, and imaginative space between a subjective "interior" and the concrete "reality" of an "external world" is a "mysterious realm of transaction," says Burgin, and likely "best worked out in psychoanalytic terms."[13]

This is the route Žižek follows in his diagnosis of the cinema spectator and the gaze of nostalgic film, one that also orients us toward the spectators moving through the cinematic quality of a scenic drive. The "gaze" identifies the character or object in the film "from which the subject viewing it is already *gazed at*," says Žižek. "I can never see the picture at the point from which it is gazing at me."[14] Žižek illustrates this in the western *Shane,* in which our view of the mysterious hero is mediated by the innocent gaze of the young boy. We see danger, violence, and a mythic hero through the eyes of the boy we watch on the screen. Such is the logic of nostalgic fascination in cinema, he notes. "The subject sees in the object (in the image it views) its own gaze" and to that extent "sees itself seeing."[15] Our relationship to cinematic nostalgia is split between ironic distance toward the film's narrative reality and a fascination with our own gaze. More precisely, nostalgia reveals itself as we look at the scene before us through the eyes of a spectator who comes from the past. "What we really see [when we watch nostalgic film] . . . is this gaze of the other," proposes Žižek. "We are fascinated by the gaze of the mythic 'naive' spectator, the one who was 'still able to take it seriously,' in other words, the one who 'believes in it' for us, in place of us." It is not the scene on the screen that fascinates us, but "the gaze of the naive 'other' absorbed, enchanted by it," an idealized spectator who sees and believes in our place, and who—in the end—allows us to "have the illusion of 'seeing ourselves seeing.'"[16]

Žižek essentially poses the question: Who are we, what do we see, and how do we find pleasure when we watch a nostalgic film? In many ways, the same question applies to those who make the audio-infused scenic drives that favor a sentimental retreat away from the world directly outside their moving automobiles. Intentionally carrying a sound track for a drive may offer a buffer against what, for some, might otherwise be a disappointment. While a self-chosen sound track may offer some aesthetic continuity between scene and observer, these endeavors underscore how reconciling one's place in the landscape can simultaneously be a form of fantasy production and self-fascination that occurs in cultural terms, categories, and models. The scenic drive also allows us to "see ourselves seeing" through the eyes of an ideal spectator. The music filling the car and absorbing the passengers into an unfolding drama serves as a medium for enhancing our reflection and captivation. In these instances, *Grand Canyon Suite,* the *Koyaanisqatsi* sound track, and the songs of Neil Young, and the Ventures are equivalents to what Žižek calls "the object" that looks back at us from the scene. As a point of subjective identification, the music can transpose the experience of being an automobile passenger—watching scenery pass across the window—to someone closer to a motion-picture spectator—watching a continuous flow of images framed by rhythms, melodies, and lyrics that index dimensions of taste, experience, and a creative impulse.

Seeing ourselves seeing through the eyes of an imaginary spectator, we can mystify our relationship to the landscape, the distances we travel, as we seek and enchant *natural* landscapes as sites of *cultural* production through a choice of music and the routes we follow. And all of this perhaps helps us to conceal from ourselves a more chilling recognition that we are anonymous travelers passing one another along well-worn roads. In the end, they can lead to familiar cultural territories where we may imagine feeling at home on foreign soil because, paradoxically, we can climb into someone else's skin, someone whom we admire for their vision, someone we may become, someone who, from a distance, we may fancy is much like ourselves.

"Chevy Chase pulled in here" says Kurt, a twenty-five-year-old man from Yonkers, New York, pointing his finger over the front-porch rail of El Tovar. He's having a beer with Denise, who is driving with him across the United States. His reference is to a brief scene from Warner Brothers' 1983 *National Lampoon's Vacation,* filmed in El

Tovar's circular driveway. It is all in good humor, a trivial fragment that doesn't tell me much about his cinematic tastes but merely what he's seen before. "Sparky [Chase's nickname in the film] came right in here with his dead aunt tied to the hood of the car," Kurt laughs. "Did you see that one?" I, too, had seen the film, but it wasn't nearly as memorable for me as for Kurt, who sips his beer and looks at the canyon from several directions. Kurt's tone moves toward sincerity, however, when he pulls a copy of Jack Kerouac's *On the Road* out of his day pack. He's been rereading it as they drive across the country. "Kerouac was *the man* of the road," Kurt says, and with a grandiloquent gesture hoists the book above his head. Then he flips to a page marked with a small piece of tree bark. Denise listens patiently as though she's heard this all before. "Here," he hands me the book. "This is when he came through this area." I take the book and read a few sentences in which Kerouac's narrator, Sal Paradise, recalls "zooming across the Arizona desert," swinging "north to the Arizona mountains, Flagstaff, clifftowns . . . reading the American landscape as we went along."[17]

"Does he come to the Grand Canyon?" I ask Kurt. I'd read the book several years ago and considered myself a fan as well, but I couldn't recall any mention of the canyon.

"Nah, Sal's heading east on a bus in this part," he says. "We're going west. But it was cool reading how he came through Flagstaff. I bought up all this Route 66 stuff when we were there yesterday. You can't get this stuff back east. I got one of those road signs, a bumper sticker . . . what else?"

"Magnets," Denise fills in. "Magnets for the refrigerator." Her deadpan delivery feeds his self-styled eccentricity, as I suppose it must have on other occasions.

"Yeah, magnets!" boasts Kurt. "It's tacky, I know. But I don't care. I gotta have this schlocky tourist stuff. I can't get enough of it. But Kerouac, I just love him. Sal Paradise. What a name. The Dean—Neal Cassady. I've read all his books. We're going to check out City Lights [bookstore] when we get to San Francisco. Do you like Hunter Thompson . . . Doctor Gonzo?"

Kurt wasn't the only Kerouac fan I met at the canyon. Mike, a twenty-two-year-old from Pittsfield, Massachusetts, told me he read *The Dharma Bums* "to get psyched up" for his drive across America. When I met him, he was sweaty and dirty after just completing a hike out of the canyon. He'd just finished a B.A. in American Studies and was on his first trip across the country. He left to put his backpack in his car and returned a few minutes later with a copy of an edited collection of essays and short stories, *Travels in the Americas*. "I just finished reading one by Willa Cather," he told me. "This is a great book. I read Willa Cather in Santa Fe. I really like Henry Miller, though. He's wild. *Sexus,* have you read that one? That's where he says 'What's the point of going out and not telling anyone about it?'"

"I guess that's really a big part of it," I offer. "That's a good line."

"Yeah," says Mike. "I'm going to have some stories to tell when I get back."

When I look back at the brief passage Kurt had shown me in *On the Road,* I notice that Sal Paradise had put aside a copy of Alain-Fournier's *Le Grand Meaulnes,* which he'd stolen in Hollywood, so that he could read the landscape as his bus rolled across the Southwest. "Every bump, rise, and stretch in it mystified my longing," said Sal. Romantic yearning for an open American road full of adventures is what Kerouac had named in his novel, and his work still called out to young men like Kurt and Mike for whom reading the landscape meant picking up a book rather than putting one down. Mike, in particular, who seemed to be consulting numerous authors on his cross-country trek, might have found some affirmation in Henry Miller's remarks to Anaïs Nin. "I realized that for me it is only and always the 'literary' appeal that people and places make," Miller told her, in a 1933 letter from Clichy. "The reality is void of interest. Flat. Osborn's description of Chambord and Amboise has life for me. The actual chateau had none."[18] The literary imagination has long been a tradition in popular travel, and these two canyon visitors were fully enthralled by its promise to open their journeys onto horizons full of nostalgia, romance, mystery, and aim their lives toward those writers who spoke most loudly to them. Mike may have been hopeful about having stories to tell, but both he and Kurt—with his new collection of Route 66 paraphernalia—already seemed lodged in other narratives posturing them with a wisdom of "the road." Their choice of texts offered little, if any, description of the physical geography of Grand Canyon. Instead, their books, travel guides of a sort, told them not what to see as much as who each of them might be—Dharma bums, mad drivers behind the wheel, looking for the kicks they might only know how to feel because of those who had made the passages before them.

The maps people carry on their travels are to keep them from becoming lost. But other maps may surely help them to lose themselves. It's often a fine line that separates either set of coordinates. In many ways, these canyon tourists, like those of a century ago, look for points of orientation that have little to do with the physical features of the canyon spread out before them. The models for their journeys may come from anywhere and everywhere. They lend a certain authority to visions situated between dramatic presence and reflective distance. The characters they follow on the page point toward routes that may help them claim the canyon for themselves. Kerouac, Cather, and Miller told stories about navigating roads and places far from the South Rim, yet this is of less concern for readers like Kurt and Mike. It's a unique and singular point of view, one charged with the ambiguity of a search for events and places where one might lay claim to a story that serves them in their travels. Among them, they find paths to differentiate themselves, to not become lost in the crowd, to find a landscape that possesses some continuity with a world more familiar, a sense of the past, a sense of humor, and an inherent desire to escape all of those familiarities for something else and a chance to belong differently to the world for a while. Nearly everyone wants the canyon to be their own in some way, yet it is often a desire inevitably shaped in others' accounts.

Up the road from the visitor center, I wait to pay for my unleaded inside the Grand Canyon Chevron station. The pumps are busy, and the attendant is helping someone with a flat. Outside, a man in a red T-shirt with Anasazi pictographs stenciled on the front is gassing up a white Saab. An older man in clean overalls takes a pull from a can of root beer while he fuels a motorhome stretching across one side of the fueling bay. A few cars are queued up behind them. I glance around the oily office and lock eyes with Danny Glover. He's on the cover of a *USA Weekend* magazine someone has taped to the wall near the cash register. Glover is seated on the canyon rim, walking stick in hand, throwing a big, toothy smile. In bold gold letters at the bottom, I read "Danny Glover's Grand Canyon." This is the summer travel issue. In addition to a report on Glover's canyon experience, there are several other "insider guides" to national parks. "Tom Brokaw spots elk at Yellowstone." The heavy metal-rockabilly band "The Kentucky Headhunters shine light on Mammoth Cave."[19] This is a routine formula—public testimonials from celebrities, new looks at familiar and famous places, a glimpse into the leisure pursuits of people we know mostly through their work and fame. In this case, I not only wonder how Glover's canyon will shape up but what credentials, other than his role as Simon in *Grand Canyon,* make him an "insider." According to the accompanying article, he first visited the canyon when he came here to shoot the brief final scene for Kasdan's film. I've never met Glover, but his canyon account does little to separate him from Simon. "I met different people, and we talked about the issues that confront us as we go through life," the actor said of his visit. "We were able to let go of our inhibitions and fears. . . . You surround yourself with this incredibly beautiful place. Everything else seems so insignificant." Glover's memory of the canyon essentially summarizes the theme of Kasdan's film, and the remarks of this canyon insider tend to keep him in character. Maybe this is unavoidable, an inherent dimension of describing the canyon to the public. "I felt like I was a part of something . . . that is so much bigger than you, beyond you," Glover says, elsewhere in the article. "I felt like everything past and present came together. I kept envisioning a hundred years ago how the park was used, or how people were touched by it or moved by it."[20] This is how many have described their experience of the Grand Canyon. But that "something bigger and beyond" is also the story itself and the desire to have one. It's a common story of the visitor's unique experience, one in which understanding the canyon on such personal and unnameable terms reappears throughout this century. It's the story we hear in Simon's voice when he sits on the curb with Mack, and we hear it when Glover gives his testimonial to the canyon's beauty largely because he's played Simon in the film *Grand Canyon.* And as "past and present" come together for him and the newspaper readers, they converge on "Danny Glover's Grand Canyon," reminding us of how we all want our own canyon and of the extent such desires are, in fact, already part of some other, someone else's scene.

I couldn't find an autograph on the cover of *USA Weekend* and wondered if someone at the Chevron station may have met Glover while he was filming at the canyon. Why this picture? What could Glover's canyon mean to the workers at this service station? The edge of the canyon is across the street, less than half a mile away. There are so many other pictures of the landscape to choose from. Imagining the motivation to tape this particular image to the wall carries the same difficulty as trying to decipher how items produced and directed at no one in particular—newspaper clippings, magazine articles, postcards—become attached to bulletin boards and refrigerator doors. From a steady stream of media images and commodities, "they have been chosen in a highly personal way," notes John Berger, "to match and express the experience of the room's inhabitant."[21] I begin to draw conclusions. Perhaps this is part of an inside joke about "insiders," and I imagine the employees having a good chortle late one afternoon when someone pulled out a roll of tape and smoothed the edges of the magazine cover to the wall. It's not until I see the station wrecker parked outside that I remember Glover's character, Simon, who is a tow-truck operator, and I wonder if these gas station workers find an identification or alliance with a film hero who affirms a vision of blue-collar work similar to their own.

Regardless of how I might surmise the specific intentions behind hanging Glover's picture in the gas station, the picture taped to the wall is a reminder of how people take products projected toward a mass audience and turn them toward their own horizons. Recognizing one's life as resembling a scene from a major motion picture, prying apart the packaging from a new cassette tape (or rewinding an old one) for a scenic drive, or referring to novels for the clues they may hold about their own journeys are all instances of a similar impulse. Interpreting these tourist's practices in such a manner situates them in what, over the past decade, has become a brand of cultural populism that redescribes the terms of cultural consumption as a form of cultural *production*. Rather than view people as passive recipients of texts and products that constitute them as "audiences" and "markets," numerous cultural critics, following the path of French sociologist Michel de Certeau, recognize how agency, mobility, creativity, and imagination infuse and democratize the meanings of popular culture. These tourists resemble other users of popular culture who, as Janice Radway suggests, are not interpretively constrained in a tourist landscape prepared for them but act as "free-floating" agents who create "narratives, stories, objects and practices from myriad bits and pieces of prior cultural productions."[22] Yet, it would be difficult to argue, as some critics have persistently done, that these tourists approach their landscapes in a manner prompting us to celebrate their "tactical" subversion of ideology or dominant textual meanings. For the most part, their excursions into fantasy, film, or literature are private affairs treated with indifference. Moreover, the texts that frame these tourist practices draw from quite conventional cultural modes for viewing and reading natural and social landscapes. In the end, St. Petersburg amplifies social life as a set of performances, the passengers on their scenic drives prefer to see the natural world as a movie, and Kurt and Mike are but two reminders of how once rebellious public postures have gained a cultural centrality that stands for the pursuit of individualism.

To imagine or even celebrate these tourists as engaged in semiotic combat on a politicized battlefield drawn by critics of popular culture is, perhaps, to set the stakes too high for people taking a vacation. Of course, as these examples suggest, it's difficult not to conceive of cultural terrain apart from the broader schemes and dispositions that give shape to everyday life. Seeing tourists as "nomads poaching their way across fields they did not write" in search of momentary pleasures is an appealing and appropriate analogy for a Grand Canyon sedimented with visions and meanings beckoning from the end of the last century. But the meaning of the canyon does not appear to be in question here. For each of them, the canyon is obviously a significant cultural icon precisely because of those who have described it since the nineteenth century. What is less obvious is the meaning of *who they are* as they stand on its rim, drive and walk the roads through the park, work in a place of other's leisure time, and sort through the possibilities for being and appearing in a place so often extolled and glorified as a place of freedom. This question finds many provisional and changing answers. The preceding examples point to the temporary and fleeting points of orientation tourists "read" in the landscape, texts, and themselves as they move through the park. "Reading takes no measure against the erosion of time (one forgets oneself *and* forgets)," proposes de Certeau, "and it does not keep what it acquires, or it does so poorly, and each of the places through which it passes is a repetition of the lost paradise."[23] I suspect that the original intentions of placing Glover's picture on the wall at the gas station have long been forgotten or worn thin, like the frayed edges of the cover itself. Like the tourists' comments I've quoted here, it is a vague sign holding presence and potential meanings that extend beyond its immediate appearance. Clearly, for some tourists, the events of any particular moment, when their experience is enhanced, enlivened, or cast into the recesses of intensity or reflection, are surely part of an imaginary and fantastic world destined to dissipate with time and into the cool air blowing on the South Rim. But for others, the Grand Canyon is a stage where reading its social and physical features has designs toward producing a more lasting impression of how they kept time at the edge of the great abyss.

Free Falling

Many of the visitors I spoke with aimed at desires for transfiguring and rehabilitating the significance of their presence in a place shadowed by the anonymity that falls around a cultural monument far from their homes. In varying degrees, the canyon appears as a backdrop for stories and performances pointing toward other landscapes, desires, experiential vacancies, and opportunities unrealized in scenes first grown elsewhere. This seems the case, at any rate, when I meet Tammy and Christian one afternoon after I watch her striking poses in the doorway of Hopi House. She's come in from Las Vegas, she says, and is an aspiring model. I've seen Christian around the rim on several occasions, but I'm unclear about whether or not he actually works here. Today, the two of them are doing a photo shoot, making some frames Tammy can use in her portfolio. A handful of visitors who sense something is happening here stand by and watch them. A few take pictures. Tammy and Christian appear a little self-conscious about the attention but push on like pros. Christian has a big camera with an extended flash and motordrive that fires like an automatic weapon when Tammy offers herself to his lens. She jackknifes her leg in the adobe doorway and cocks her head so a little hair falls over her eyes. She gives Christian her best sexy stuff while his flash blasts midafternoon shadows off her heavy makeup. But Tammy looks uncomfortable in her smoky nylons and stiletto heels as she walks across the esplanade to the wall on the rim.

Tammy and Christian publicly dramatize the popular practices of cultural "poaching," an analogy de Certeau employs to describe how popular readings stem from a variety of "advances and retreats, tactics and games played with the text."[24] Tammy and Christian "read" the Hopi House and other locations along the rim as a place of temporary occupation; they appropriate the rimside zone of souvenir shops and hotels, places organized around consumption and sightseeing, as locations where they recast themselves in an imaginative production organized around an image of themselves rather than the Grand Canyon. For a brief instant, her pose in the Hopi House doorway blocks the souvenir hunters and the curious. They create a spectacle of minor proportion; yet it is enough for sightseers to turn away from the scenic wonder and give the couple their attention.

Tammy's nightclub look is a stark contrast to the sportswear, T-shirts, and sandals most of the canyon visitors are wearing. In fact, she looks as though she's dropped out of a Las Vegas casino night and landed smack dab in the squinting daylight of a South Rim afternoon. I try to comprehend what they were imagining for this photo shoot when she chose her wardrobe or who she has in mind when she shakes her hair and purses her lips for Christian's camera. This is the first time I've seen Vegas chic and rustic pueblo come together in this way, and their presence stares directly in the face of romanticism's myths of nature borne in a previous century. Instead, they are heirs to the "new nature" of a twentieth-century industrial culture, which, Walter Benjamin said, had spawned the mythic power and "universal symbolism" earlier romantics hoped to find in their resurrection of ancient myths, preindustrial agrarian traditions, and the spiritual aesthetics inspiring their art and architecture. Benjamin's socio-psychological theory of modernity conceived of the urban world (for him, this proto-typically appeared in the Parisian arcades) as a dreamworld of mass culture, writes Susan Buck-Morss, where "under conditions of capitalism, industrialization had brought about a *re*enchantment of the social world, and through it a 'reactivation of mythic powers.'"[25] The rationalizing and bureaucratizing foundations structuring industrial production, institutional order, and growing markets had done nothing less than empty out and demythify social life, he observed. Rather than concede to an outright victory of rationalism and abstraction, or recover a romantic propensity to regenerate cultural mythology through art beckoning toward nature, Benjamin sought to describe the character and mood of historical experience wrought by a phantasmagoria of mass culture. In part, he rooted his critique in the spirit of the surrealists, who "viewed the constantly changing new nature of the urban-industrial landscape as itself marvelous and mythic," says Buck-Morss. "Their muses, as transitory as spring fashions, were stars of the stage and screen, billboard advertisements, and illustrated magazines."[26]

For Benjamin, this urban world of transitory and changing signs, products, and images evidenced the creative powers of industrial forces and expressed the vitality of the "threatening and alluring face"[27] of a modern mythology that had lulled people into a dream. Fixing on the distractions of a growing consumer society, Benjamin identified a pivotal and recurrent contradiction of modern urban life. Capitalist-industrial modes of production favored private life and conceived of the subject as "the isolated individual" who confronted "brand new forms of social existence—urban spaces, architectural forms, mass-produced commodities, and infinitely reproduced 'individual' experiences," says Buck-Morss. These brought about "identities and conformities in people's lives, but not social solidarity, no new level of collective consciousness of their commonality and thus no way of waking up from the dream in which there were enveloped."[28] Benjamin's project did not want to endorse the dream but instead dissolve it with the critical and historical knowledge accompanying a moment of collective awakening "in which humanity, rubbing its eyes, recognizes precisely this dream *as* a dream."[29]

Transporting observations drawn from the uncompleted critical project of a German critic wandering Parisian streets in the 1930s to the activities of these rimside tourists at play on a sunny afternoon bodes a long and seemingly tangential detour. After all, Benjamin drew his conclusions and revolutionary aspirations from a broadly historical, densely philosophical, and largely semiotic-driven assessment of the spectacular signs, arcades, and commodities flourishing in his Paris. He tended to view the "slumbering masses" from a critical and social distance. But his attraction to the surrealists, whom he feared, in the end, had become "stuck in the realm of dreams,"[30] and even his occasional experiments with hashish before strolling city streets were indicative of a larger quest—like some of these tourists—to wrestle a fresh look from a familiar scene.

"Tammy and Christian are unfortunately deep in the dream," whispers Benjamin, while I watch the couple resume their photo shoot. Yet, I am reminded that the Hopi House, El Tovar, the Kolb brothers' photo studio clinging to the canyon's edge, and all of the brochures are signs that the mythic forces of the city's "new nature" were at work amid the South Rim pines nearly a decade before he'd written a word about Paris. Early canyon tourists who immersed themselves in a phantasmagoria of simulated pueblos and hunting lodges, wrapped in Indian costumes and cowboy styles, consumed an elaborate fantasy that synthesized romantic notions of nature and pre-industrial tradition with the forces of mass culture. As I've argued earlier, their canyon poised them on the brink of nostalgia and progress. Tammy and Christian did not share exactly the same dream; they merely used the same stage and set designs. Standing in the doorway of Hopi House, Tammy seductively looks into Christian's camera as if gazing toward her own future, perhaps one holding minor regard for fossils or adobe or awe-filled gasps at the scenic wonder. This is a future of opportunity and transformation, a place for dreaming herself at center stage, despite all evidence to the contrary. Christian's camera helped record this surreal truth, one whereby the myths and private fantasies that enchanted and haunted Benjamin's "new nature" of urban life endured here on the rim, this time in Lycra, lipstick, and mascara as if reciting a modern allegory that had, indeed, become "second nature."[31]

I hear the guitars first, thinking that someone ahead of me is carrying a radio. But the sound only grows louder as I walk farther along the Rim Trail. A few yards later, I come over a rise to find four college boys, all of them strumming acoustic guitars, seated at the canyon's edge. Their song is about Los Angeles, "where all the good girls are home with broken hearts." One wearing a bandanna tied around his head like a pirate and another with a cap on backward are singing, confessing they're bad boys because they "don't even miss her," that they're bad boys because they broke her heart. With the canyon behind them, they all play and sing to the lens of a camcorder mounted on a tripod in the shade of a pine at the trail's edge. The singers want to "glide down over Mulholland" and write one of those good girls' names in the sky. And then the others join in. All of them are "gonna free fall out into nothin'"; all them are "gonna leave this world for a while."

Gerald, Todd, Mike, and Rich just graduated from Boston College, and they're driving across the country together, taking a last college-buddies road trip in Mike's Chevy Suburban before moving on with their lives. During their senior year, Gerald tells me, three of them played in a band. "We played gritty rock and roll," he says. "The Stones. Beatles. New stuff. R.E.M. Violent Femmes." I ask them about the camera aimed at them as they play. "We're tourin' around the country and playin' in different places," says Rich, the lead guitarist who shared vocals with Gerald when they performed in Boston. "We actually played in the Rockies yesterday and did the same thing."

"It's just nice to have along with us so we can remember it," offers Todd, while he checks something on the camera. "Look at the scenery behind you. It's just nice to have."

"You're only gonna be at the Grand Canyon a couple of times, maybe once, probably," Gerald says. "You'll never be able to play in front of this."

"Quite a backdrop we have for our stage," adds Rich.

"It's nothing like Boston," Gerald continues. "This is a nice refreshing change from playing in the city all the time in a hot dirty apartment. And it gives us a chance to get out. Most of us haven't seen any of the West Coast, so we're really gettin' around. We're gonna do this, ya know, throughout California and Oregon. Ever since we started this trip we wanted to videotape up on the Grand Canyon. So, this is one of our main goals we just accomplished."

"And if you come back here, you can say, 'Yeah, I played right there,' and you have it on videotape," says Todd. "We got up this morning and watched the sunrise. That was beautiful. It was amazing we got up that early."

"We pulled in at three in the morning," Mike tries to get a word in. "Slept 'til six, woke up. . . ."

"No, we got up at five," says Todd, correcting him. "We had to turn our watches back." I sense that Mike wasn't a part of the band back in Boston. In fact, he was Rich's roommate in Boston, and Rich has been teaching him to play the guitar. All four not only seem thrilled about their journey but also that I'm holding a microphone and asking them to tell me about it. Whenever they find "some good scenery," they unpack their guitars and do a few songs for the camera, they tell me collectively.

"We played in Mississippi, the Rockies, here, Chicago," reports Gerald. "We played on Pearl Street in Colorado. We're gonna play Vegas, L.A., San Francisco, Portland, Oregon."

"We're playin' Las Vegas tonight," adds Todd. "The streets of Las Vegas." I try to imagine them setting up their camcorder on the busy sidewalks of downtown Vegas or along the strip, but I find it hard to believe. "Yeah, we set up everywhere," he assures me. "Everyone always gives us funny looks but, in general, they like it, ya know? We're not hurtin' anything."

"We've gotten past our stage fright," Gerald continues. "Bein' in a band for a year kinda gives you some balls. That's why we can do this."

"Most people walkin' by they like it, ya know?" Todd says again, trading off with Gerald. "They say 'that sounds good.'"

"It kinda takes balls to get up there, though," Gerald reminds me. The most difficult place to play, they recall, was on the Pearl Street mall in Boulder, Colorado. There were a number of other street performers—magicians, jugglers, sword swallowers, musicians—and they had to compete for an audience. "The Rockies were the most difficult place to set up in, though," laughs Rich. "We set up on a little ledge on this mountain. We had to drive up this mountain and then hike a distance about from here to the parking lot," he says, pointing toward the Yavapai parking area. "But it's fun. We're gonna go home, watch 'em, and bore our friends." They ask me if I want to hear another song, and they play an acoustic version of Social Distortion's "Ball and Chain," an angst-ridden melodrama of bad hotels, broken cars, and empty booze bottles. It's a born-to-lose anthem about running with no escape, hard times getting harder. The bad boys have gotten worse, I think, as I listen through my earphones and record their tribute to empty middle-class dreams and premature wisdom gleaned from the school of hard knocks. All of this is just a few chords away from the sunny South Rim and the promise of fresh degrees from Boston College. I notice a spiral notebook filled with handwritten lyrics on the ground in front of them. When they're finished, I ask how they decide which songs they're going to sing and videotape.

"That's always the hard part," says Rich. "Usually we decide just before the camera goes on. We knew like sixty songs from bein' in the band, so it was easy to play 'em on acoustic."

"We played [Bob Dylan's] 'Knockin' on Heaven's Door' on the top of the mountain and [The Byrds'] 'Learnin' to Fly,'" adds Todd.

"Here, we did 'Free Fallin'. It seemed appropriate," Rich says.

"We did [John Mellencamp's] 'Pink Houses' in Indiana," Gerald adds to the list. "We did it in the cornfields."

"In Indiana, we played on this fence by a roadside," Todd continues, "and this older gentleman comes across the street after we finished playin' and we thought he was gonna say, 'Get off my fence, get off my land.' But he said, 'You guys just made my wife's day.' And we said, 'Why is that?' And he says, 'Well, she used to be a music teacher and she just loves to hear this type of thing.' And then he said, 'If you want some sodas or somethin', come up to the house.' We figured we'd go up there, and we played a song for her and it was really nice. And he told us another place to go and play. He had this little hill in the back of his house . . ."

"The second highest point in Indiana," Gerald and Rich say in unison, with wide grins.

"So we went up there and we played some Rush," says Todd. "Then we came back there and they had homemade angelfood cake made by, I guess, her aunt . . . an eighty-five-year-old woman made it. And we had angelfood cake and milk, and they sat us down at the table and we talked to them for about an hour. It was great. It was just meetin' people."

"The only reason we're doing this is for free food," cracks Gerald, as if trying to take the sentimental edge off Todd's story and possibly shorten the gap between their mild adventures as college graduates touring the country and their yearnings to be the kind of greasy heartbreakers who live in a rock 'n' roll "free fall" and stride in Social Distortion's tattoo toughness. Rich tells me their performances have generally been a way to make new acquaintances.

"Just by playin', bringing the guitars, we always meet people," he says. "Like we'll be playing and they'll walk up to us, just like you, and that's what I like about bringing the guitars along. We've talked to people for hours at a time. It's just because we're doing something weird like sitting here playing music. It just opens doors." While we're talking, a park service ranger rides up on a mountain bike. He's wearing a plastic bike helmet and Vuarnet sunglasses. A walkie-talkie hangs from his belt. Straddling his bike, he notes the guitars and camera and asks us what we're doing. He wants to know if this is a commercial production and if we have a permit.

"We're just playin' some songs and videoing 'em," Todd says, sounding a little nervous.

"Then this *isn't* for commercial use?" the ranger asks again, turning down the static voices coming over his radio. "Because if it is, you need a filming permit." I hope he hasn't seen my recorder. I quickly turn it off and stow the mike and earphones in my pack. I'm sure there's a permit I need and don't have.

"You've got to be kidding me," I interrupt, while the ranger talks to Todd. "Look at all the people walking around here with video cameras. Do you ask every one of them if they're carrying permits? Look at that camera," I say and point to their small camcorder on the tripod. "Does that look like this is a big commercial production?" I'm surprised by my agitated voice, and it's only after I say this and feel the attention turn toward me that I start to wonder if I really should be pushing the issue. This ranger is probably only a few years older than these college students, but I sense he doesn't like me asking him any questions or my confrontational tone.

"Look, I'm just responding to a call," the ranger says firmly, putting his hand on his holstered radio. "You'd be surprised at how many people come here and decide they can shoot commercials or movies without getting permitted or putting up a bond."

"It's that big of a problem?" I say.

"Yeah," he says. "People bring stuff up here, products they want to shoot with the canyon for scenery, and they just start setting up equipment. . . . One time people were shooting a pornographic movie . . ."

Suddenly everyone is interested in the story.

"They were trying to film out on one of the more secluded areas of the rim, but a lot of families with kids come through here," the ranger tells us. The details seem sketchy, and I have some doubts. I don't know if this is true or a spontaneous exaggeration. Is this just another canyon legend or do I simply resent the man whose query about permits seems ridiculous?

"Well, this is just for us," Todd offers politely. "It's just a video for us of our trip." Apparently satisfied that no one is breaking any rules, the ranger reports to someone on his walkie-talkie. He says he is sorry to have bothered us and wishes us a good stay before pedaling down the trail. We stand quiet, watching him until he's out of earshot.

"Now everyone take off your clothes and let's do another tune," Gerald says without missing a beat. "Todd, turn on the camera," and we have a laugh that cools all of us.

"I wish we'd had the camera on for that," Todd says, but I suspect the incident will make a better story without video support. Soon it's time to go our separate ways, and I ask the four how long they'll be staying at the canyon. Todd says they want to make Las Vegas by evening, so they'll leave as soon as they can get showers and buy some food. In Vegas, they plan to film another song before it gets dark.

"We want to play in the desert," Todd says. "In the sand, if we can find some."

"What song will you play?" I ask.

"We'll pull something together at the last minute as usual," Gerald says coolly, but he's already imagining the scene. "I think U2 for the desert, something from *The Joshua Tree*. Come on, let's play him another one before we go." They sit back down on the edge of the canyon after deciding not to videotape this song. I ask to record it on my cassette player and they seem flattered by this. "Let's play him 'Proud Mary,'" Gerald tells the others. I hold the mike at arm's length while they work their way through the Ike and Tina Turner classic, just for me. But it is also for them, I think. A last gesture on their part to impress on me the fantasy that they are, in fact, a gritty band of rockers touring the country. I nod along to their steady but too slow rhythm and listen to their voices reach a few steps short of Tina's soulful chorus. Behind the lenses of my sunglasses, they cannot see that I've closed my eyes to concentrate and keep my frozen smile from laughter. Big wheels keep on turnin' while I picture them rolling on toward Vegas and points west, Gerald at the wheel, the others bent on snoozing away the mile markers of Interstate 40.

I cannot, however, dismiss the traces of my envy for their time at the canyon and down the road, or their luck and good sense to confront these waning college days with a ritual passage. The detours they make along the way, into self-fictions and make-believe, are proportionate to a time when they are, indeed, well poised to have *the* proverbial "time of their lives." I think they suspect this. And with naïveté and cynicism, they muster the energy to do it all before the sun rises on new days. Eventually, the dawn will be a nuisance, glaring light that comes early, whacking them in the eyes, through the dirty windshield and the dark Ray Bans, as they find themselves heading east, toward Boston, home, and the life after. For now, though, it is more than enough to be howling and banging their guitars on the edge of the Grand Canyon, to sincerely say, as Gerald said to me, "This is one of our main goals we just accomplished," and for us both to believe it.

Conceivably, it's a matter of geographies, like the sharp divide between plateaus and emptiness that makes the Grand Canyon. But it's also the four easterners sitting on the brink with their backs against nothing, belting out "Free Fallin'," a song about Los Angeles. It's Christian changing his film while Tammy from Las Vegas touches up her lipstick, giving little notice to the Grand Canyon reflected in her round compact mirror. It's Mike on the Bright Angel plaza quoting Henry Miller, and Kurt with Kerouac, and Herb and Linny and me rewinding our cassettes as we drive. And it's all the others who move under this Arizona sun, through the trees, roads, and trails, seeing the Bradys, Thelma and Louise, and Danny Glover. "Here is the last stop for all those who come from somewhere else," Joan Didion said of the golden land. "Here is where they are trying to find a new life style, trying to find it in the only places they know to look: the movies and the newspapers."[32] She was, of course, writing about southern California rather than the Grand Canyon. Yet, both are places where the term "location" often refers to the ways landscapes and circumstances are fashioned into scenes and stories that might balance the weight of some emptiness or ordinary boredom.

At times, my own view of these canyon tourists finds its shape in a story about California. They account for unnameable vacancies and desires by manufacturing stories much like Nathanael West's character Faye Greener, a movie extra waiting for her big break in his novel of Hollywood, *The Day of the Locust*. When she wasn't working on some studio set, she could just spend entire days at home making up stories, she tells Tod Hackett, an aspiring set and costume designer. "She would get some music on the radio, then lie down on her bed and shut her eyes. She had a large assortment of stories to choose from," writes West. "After getting herself in the right mood, she would go over them in her mind, as though they were a pack of cards, discarding one after another until she found the one that suited."[33] Faye's daydreams are the seeds of ideas for movie plots she wants Tod to "write up" so they can become rich. Yet, her dreams are not entirely her own but inspired by movie posters and other stories. Tod cannot envision Faye apart from her interminable stock of performances. "All these little stories, these little daydreams of hers, were what gave such extraordinary color and mystery to her movements," he thought, as she spun out another tale. "She always seemed to be struggling in their soft grasp as though she were trying to run in a swamp."[34] Freedom, for Faye, meant becoming a star. She tries to impress Claude Estee, a successful screenwriter, telling him she's been buying a lot of new clothes, reciting the advice she's plumbed from trade papers and fan magazines, and relaying the legends of screen stars she's absorbed. Despite these attempts to bring the dream closer and position herself as an insider, they only show Claude the distance she lives from it.

To be sure, West offers a bleak view of behind-the-scenes Hollywood in the 1930s. His Faye Greener is, perhaps, only a despairing caricature of others who had come to live on the edge of the continent in the "land of sunshine and oranges," coming from lives where they "had slaved at some kind of dull, heavy, labor, behind desks and counters, in the fields and at tedious machines of all sorts, saving their pennies and dreaming of the leisure that would be theirs." These are the people who form the agitated crowd in West's last scene. They are the middle-aged, the old, and the families, all arriving early and filling the sidewalks so they can watch celebrities arrive for a movie premier. In the end, they've found the place of their dreams is one where "Nothing Happens. . . . What else is there?" writes West. "Every day of their lives they read the newspapers and went to the movies. Both fed them on lynchings, murder, sex crimes, explosions, wrecks, love nests, fires, miracles, revolutions, wars. This daily diet made sophisticates of them. The sun is a joke. Oranges can't titillate their jaded palates. Nothing can ever be violent enough to make taut their slack minds and bodies."[35] West tells us they simply don't know what to do with their free time; their boredom only grows, yet they keep looking, moving en masse to Kahn's Persian Palace, where they stand beneath huge, diagonal shafts of light cutting through the evening sky, signaling the premier, waiting to see movie stars exiting from limousines and making their way through the swarm of bodies and flashbulbs; here they wait together, hoping for some crumb of excitement.

At Hopi Point, camera shutters thrush and videotape runs heavy in the twilight. The setting sun cuts through a jagged western horizon and fills the canyon with shafts of gold. The Grand Canyon is a celebrity in its own right, I think, and watch the tourists break off and photograph each other next to it. Leaning against the safety rail or at the edge with no protection, their faces sometimes recall the faded Polaroids I've seen in the windows of New York City restaurants and shops where some manager with rolled-up sleeves is shaking hands with Tony Bennett, Morgan Fairchild, or Oprah Winfrey. Such images are a record of hopeful moments, pictures that many would like to believe sort out the blue ribbons from the rest of the entries. This is the hope fueling Faye Greener, even though she could never escape being an extra. West thought the milling masses at Kahn's Persian Palace knew they were extras, but that didn't stop any of them from showing up to lay their eyes on Hollywood's thin version of the Real Thing, possibly carrying away a glimpse or souvenir sharp enough to puncture their routine and let out a little of the gaseous boredom. Of course, the tourist crowds here don't seem nearly as desperate as those in West's novel. Yet, some of them do grow weary of the nature scene.

"I want TVs or radios in the lodges as it is so boring at night," I read in a visitor register. "Keep this beautiful place the way it is," wrote another. "But put in some video games." One afternoon, two gangly teenage girls proudly showed me their "I Hiked the Canyon" T-shirts near the Bright Angel Lodge. "We're sick of canyons," one of them told me. "We went on a raft trip through a canyon, and took a bus to Monument Valley." They also said they hiked three miles into the canyon and bought their T-shirts. "We get to go to Las Vegas next," the other girl said. "Finally," said the first, who said she was going to wear her new T-shirt all the way to Vegas. They'd had enough, and besides, it was raining that afternoon. Underneath the lodge awning, a group of tour-bus passengers kept dry while their uniformed bus driver entertained them by juggling three bowling pins. "We're just going to wait for the rain to stop, let them take a few more pictures, and be on our way," he told me. A middle-aged couple from Van Nuys, California, heard him say this and said they were also ready to leave. "We've seen enough, anyway," the woman added as her husband studied a road map. "I mean, you look down, you see it, now give me something to do. There was this tour-bus driver who was telling me that he was driving this whole group of Swiss around. Now they're a middle, probably upper-middle-class, well-educated group. They had *two* hours here and they said that was enough, so, you know, you can only spend so much time in a place." Few want to admit, as these comments suggest, that the canyon may become a pallid sight after a few hours, and this is when the rationalizing begins. The woman from Van Nuys was a little wary of leaving too soon, but if the smart and monied Swiss could do it, so could they. A park official rolled her eyes when she told me the average visitor's stay in the park was about four hours, but she concluded this was from a lack of facilities and overcrowding, and that people would stay longer if not for such inconveniences. I never met anyone who was disappointed with his or her first glimpse of the Grand Canyon, but this is not say they could stand in jaw-dropping awe for days on end.

It's difficult to get a reliable fix on the motives of crowds, audiences, or consumers. Tourists carry all of these labels and are, perhaps, more often a target for the anxieties, contradictions, and discontentments engendered in a modern culture of consumption. Cultural critics from the first half of this century would be quick to disparage tourists for being caught in the grind of a culture industry whose distractions were nothing more than traps of false consciousness, ways of sedating them from the real circumstances of their lives. The revolutionary critiques of Benjamin and others associated with the Frankfurt School, of course, wanted them only to wake up from the dream of mass culture. Harsher cultural observers would simply see them as truly lost to such awakening. In some ways, Nathanael West held such a view. The people who gathered in desperation at Kahn's "don't know what to do with their time," he wrote. "They haven't the mental equipment for leisure, the money nor the physical equipment for pleasure." In the past few decades, critics of popular culture would, I suppose, be prone to valorize tourists, view them through the liberal and democratic bifocals of cultural populism, see their consumption as a form of production and pleasure that cannot be harnessed or wholly understood by marketers and entertainment industries. They are already free to some extent and should be celebrated for being real people possessing creativity and imagination, for being able to decide on their own whether to take this trail or that, or—preferably—to make their own. These are broad and probably unfair summations but both positions carry their own truths. Yet, the ground settles too quickly and obviously on the critical divides of their respective, somewhat extreme, cultural politics, and I often find myself caught between them. I can easily see the college students on the rim free-falling into Jean Baudrillard's bottomless pit of media "simulacra," bouncing between songs and places as though "endlessly referring to, ricocheting from, [and] reverberating onto other surfaces," as Todd Gitlin says, again sounding the chorus of so many songs written in the name of postmodernism.[36] And I can see them as cultural "poachers" or "guerilla warriors"—Tammy and Christian are two more—advancing, retreating, and leaving invisible tracks on someone else's semiotic property. Theorizing about popular culture sometimes feels like another dash to the supermarket, an exercise paralleling the logic of the consumer society it keeps in its critical sights, choosing from among a stock of interpretive packages we only need to refine and mix for our party guests. And I suspect, for better or worse, this is why I'm drawn toward stories in which characters like Faye Greener define a modern struggle for being in a world that keeps evading them, thrilling them one minute, letting them down the next, disappearing and reappearing and disappearing again.

For all the contempt West may have shown the people who live in *The Day of the*

Locust, he did not lose sight of the ambiguities and conflicts thriving at the heart of their ambitions. Tod Hackett knew that Faye "recognized the falseness of an attitude, [but] she persisted in it because she didn't know how to be simpler or more honest. She was an actress who had learned from bad models in a bad school," writes West. "He had often seen her laugh at herself. What was more, he had even seen her laugh at her dreams."[37] The rock 'n' roll wannabes singing on the rim laughed along with Faye, even as they repositioned their camera for another number. Tammy didn't laugh about modeling in front of the Hopi House; instead, she was shy, aware of how differently she was dressed. Yet, despite any inhibitions, she stood there before the tourist gawkers and tried her best to put on a sultry show for Christian's camera.

In the endless "age of mechanical reproduction" Benjamin named sixty years ago, one Guy Debord rechristened the "Society of Spectacle" three decades later, it seems of little consequence to moralize over their endeavors. The rockers from Boston, Tammy and Christian, and many others surely look to the movies and newspapers for the stories to claim as their own. That these stories are reruns of reruns matters only if you prefer some stories over others. Behind the smoke and mirrors of their own fabulations, their pursuits are not merely drifting in a sea of relativism. Quite the opposite is true. In a world where they are confronted with endless lifestyle options, they have, in fact, made choices and are trying to live with them, inside them. They know the movies, newspapers, and magazines are not enough to keep them quiet and happily amused. They want experience for themselves and have set out to find it, regardless of how many times their tickets have been torn, how many magazine pages they've flipped, or how many songs they've played over and again. The truth of the Grand Canyon matters less to them than a truth of themselves, one they seek and sort out from a pile of cultural stories, and for a time are willing to believe holds some answer about who they might be.

The Bargain and The Modern Musketeer

I see Steve in front of the Bright Angel Lodge because he stands out. He's a beer-bellied Harley rider, complete with boots, black leather chaps, a black T-shirt with a caricature of pigs dressed like bikers, and a caption that reads "Party Animal." His long hair falls out from under a cap bearing the orange-and-black Harley Davidson shield. He's got a handlebar mustache like Doc Holliday, or maybe it's David Crosby on the *Déjà Vu* album cover. When I approach him, he's packing away an old 8mm movie camera. A few moments ago, I watched a few Japanese tourists taking pictures of him. He seemed mildly annoyed by this and aimed his movie camera back at them until they stopped.

"It happens once in a while," he laughs. "Like when I walk down to an observation point. The foreigners think, 'Hey, here's a real biker.' I had Swedes come up and ask, 'You Easy Rider?' I liked them, though; at least they *said* something. I gave them a cassette of some sixties music I had. Most foreigners don't know what to make of me. I catch 'em looking out the corner of their eye. Once in a while they just gawk. So, I just pull out my camera, and when they start gawking at me, I take pictures of them gawking. It's kind of funny when I get home and have to explain to my wife why I've got all this film of Japanese tourists and other people I don't even know." Steve comes from a small town in Texas, he says, about thirty miles south of the Oklahoma border. He's hot from riding and wants to get a beer, so we leave the sunny plaza for the dim cool cocktail lounge in the Bright Angel. He worked at the canyon in 1969 and 1970, and every time he's in the area he comes back to see if anything is different.

"I'll tell you what's changed about it," he says. "The place is full of Yuppies now." Pasty Cline is on the jukebox singing Hank Williams's "Your Cheatin' Heart"; Steve shakes his head in exaggerated disapproval. "Man, this country music, I don't know, it makes me feel like I'm back home," and he gets up to pump the jukebox with quarters. When Pasty Cline ends, Steve's songs begin to play: The Doors' "Riders on the Storm," The Eagles' "Desperado," and Crosby, Stills, and Nash's "Southern Cross." The songs added yet another layer to his guise. They shrouded him—perhaps to the point of an overstatement—in the romantic mystique of longing, living on the edge, of the sixties enchantment with mythic models of the Wild West. He tells me he's headed to the Black Hills for the annual Sturgis Rally and motorcycle races. "It's a wild time, man," he says with raucousness. "I was there the year Malcolm Forbes showed up with a big hot air balloon shaped like a Harley. I come out of a bar, I'd been doin' crank, and I call my wife. And I'm standin' in the phone booth and see this huge balloon and say, 'Baby, there's motorcycles drivin' through the sky,' and she says, 'What have you been puttin' in you? Whatever it is you better be careful.'" He laughs as he tells me this. "Man, my ole lady's alright, though," he adds. "I had some fuckin' wild nights up there, though. Believe me."

"How can you do this?" I ask. "I mean, what kind of job do you have that lets you take eight weeks off a year and ride around the country?"

"Back home I work in a paint and body shop," he says, "and the woman who owns the place likes to hear the stories and see the pictures I bring back from my trips. She knows I'll quit every summer, but she always hires me back."

"What about your wife?" I say. "What does she think about you taking off like this?"

"Well, let's put it this way," Steve says, hunkering down and sounding a bit cryptic. "I don't ask her what she's been doing and she don't ask me. That's the way it should be. But we both know where home base is." The music is loud, and I go up for another round. While I'm at the bar, I feel the flash of his camera and turn to see that he's just taken my picture. When I return to the table, Crosby, Stills, Nash, and Young's version of "Woodstock," another of Steve's choices, is playing on the jukebox. We sit, and I watch Steve scanning the lounge as if taking an inventory.

"Woodstock," he says, reminded by the song. "I was here the summer of

Woodstock and everybody that was working just left to go. All of my friends left. I didn't want to be here alone, so I took off, too, hitched up to New York." The song was a doorway back to those years, in fact, the whole place seemed wrapped in a story of returning, and we sit quietly, taking it all in.

"So the Swedes thought you were Easy Rider?" I say, trying to reboot the conversation.

"Now that's a great movie. I own the video and watch it about once a month," he says, "just to make sure I'm doing right." He's serious about this, and whether or not he views it monthly, I suspect he finds it a good compass for navigating his life. "I love ridin'," he says. "It's a way of life, they say. I'll be out there doin' seventy-five, eighty, no one else on the road. That's when I'll be gettin' it." We finish our drinks, and I ask him to show me his Harley. Out in the parking lot, we make a slow rotation around his bike. It sits low, there's a duffel strapped on the back, room enough for one rider. "It's a '76 shovelhead," he says, after I ask him about the model. "I call her 'Mona.' She breaks down every now and then, but they all do." I notice a bumper sticker on the rear fender and read it aloud: If You Don't Like The Way I'm Driving, Call 1-800-EAT SHIT. "Law enforcement usually likes that one," Steve says with a grin. We've had a good time talking and decide to exchange addresses. "After a month on the road I'll be gettin' letters from people I met and wonder 'who were they?'" I tell him I'll write anyway, and he fires up the bike. "Later, man," he says above the deep rumble of pistons, and pulls out of the lot, onto the village loop, past the stables. Out of sight, I can still hear his engine.

When I returned from the canyon, I did write. Steve wrote back and sent me the journal he'd kept during his road trip. He called it "my book," but it was really a small notepad nearly filled with entries. The day we talked at the canyon he'd told me that he'd been keeping a journal. "I like to write in the mornings," he'd said, but he didn't seem like the type who actually did. Reading his "book" gave me a different sense of the man I'd met months earlier. I discovered he'd been laid up for the previous three years due to an accident and it made him "hungry for the road." There were notations about his expenses, mileage covered on different days, and the weather. He said he liked meeting different people, seeing their ways, and he recorded the details of his days. "Just tried a halibut sandwich. Pretty good," he wrote near Hoover Dam. "Well, got me some tent stakes. Oscar had a bunch that he doesn't use anymore," he wrote while staying with a friend in Nevada. "I found out he [Oscar] used to go fishing with Doc on Gunsmoke. He showed me pictures."

In other places, his entries are an occasion for broad reflections on the meaning of his travels. "I have found since I have started the trip everyone is still searching for their own personal freedom," he noted, early after his departure from home. "For me, I have found it. And it works because it's like Dad taught me. If you have a kind word for your fellow man they will have one for you. Right on, Dad." In fact, thoughts about freedom reappear throughout his journal. "I look at my past that I have spent in these Canyon Walls and I still see the freedom which she give us," he wrote at the Grand Canyon. "She puts on a show which no man-made show could ever do. . . . People come from all over the world. I wonder how many people have found their own freedom here. Quite a few I'm sure." Nearly as often as he writes about freedom, he also affirms his spiritual beliefs and his wonder at nature, accounting for their presence on a grand scale and in minute events. "Oh, the mountains and the Plains you will always be a friend to me. The way your winds blow through the trees and the sun beats on the desert. . . . I rode my Steel horse in high country and I've rode in the Low. So just to let you know, My Soul is satisfied that you will always be there for me." At the end of the entry, Steve signs his complete name, something he hadn't done after the others. "God told me to buy that oil," he says, in an entry describing how he blew a line and was grateful to have bought three quarts of fifty-weight oil even though he really wanted the sixty weight, which was out of stock at the time.

In many ways, Steve's entries tell a story of a motorcycle rider on a quest of mythic proportion. "I am laying here in bed writing and when I look up I have my Leathers hanging on the door," he scribbles, while staying with some friends. "It's like a suit of armor waiting for me to put them back on. . . . As I lay here I feel like a pioneer searching for new land. I hope God sees fit to bring me to new adventure." What he seems to want most out of this identity is a sense of connection with a lifestyle, a fellowship with other riders. Harley riding holds such a promise for him. His obvious enthusiasm for all of its trappings expresses this continually in his entries, yet it also suggests how a complete sense of connection to the lifestyle is just beyond his grasp. This appears pointedly when he describes meeting two other riders.

"I met a couple of tramps who live on the road year round," Steve wrote from a campground in Sturgis. "Star is running [Texas] tags but stays on the road. He [is] part indian and is running an old Pan head. The other calls himself Lord Christ. He is running an old Shovelhead. I don't think I'll be able to take their pictures; [they're] not into that." He continues his account with a sense of awe for the circumstances that have brought them to a highway life. "Lord told me a story of His Wife and two Daughters. They were killed by a train twelve years ago and He has lived on the road ever since. . . . Not a day goes by that he doesn't think about them and how he wants to keep his lifestyle the way it is until the day he dies. Star was telling me how his Wife was shot point blank in the face while playing pool. He didn't seem to want to talk about it too much." As he closes this entry, he looks upon them with a sense of respect for their lifestyle and a desire to be a part of that world. "These two men are true brothers of the road. I am glad I had the privilege to meet them. They will always have a place to lay their head when they come through my area. When I meet people like this it makes me realize there is still true brotherhood left. But it is very rare. It is something that tourists cannot touch or destroy because it's in your Soul."

Steve's journal offers a remarkable testimony to the struggles for identity and individualism through travel. As I flip through his pages, I am struck by how he is always watching himself through his writing, fashioning a variety of selves pulled from other stories and fantasies, and locating himself through others' eyes. He sees himself as a source of fascination for people who gather around his bike and take pictures. Like his own narrative voice, the imaginary reader behind his entries is constantly shifting. Sometimes he writes directly to his wife, expressing his love for her, saying he misses her, and wishing she could see what he sees. He writes to God with thanks for his friends and adventures. And much of the time he writes to someone who might only understand, share, and look into the mirror he holds on himself, a reflection that might disappear if not for the writing.

"I guess I was a couple of miles from home," he notes near the end of his journal. "I pulled over and watched cars and the people in them flying by me as if I was a ghost and they didn't even see me. I started Mona up and we went on home. You know I was just as scared as I was before I left on my journey." Steve says he has doubts about returning. He wonders if he has changed, if his wife has changed, and if they would still want each other. "I felt like a little boy," he says of his homecoming. "We embraced in a Loving hold that I knew would be there forever. Then I knew I loved her. Men of the road, If you have a woman that understands your Lifestyle, Hold her like you do your scooter. Forever." Of course, Steve had already arrived home by the time he wrote down this final scene. On the road, his writing had been a way of keeping a continuity with home. Writing to his wife, God, other "men of the road," and himself, all helped create an audience who could watch him ride through his enchanted forest. Now at home, he accounts for the end of the road by looking toward it as a timeless "forever" when he will have the handlebars in his grip again, moving away from home. Writing this story, building it on the backs of so many other stories, speaking it in so many voices, he creates the only place where he can keep them both in a loving embrace while the tales of culture keep their hold on him.

Among the "blurred genres" of facts and fictions, people find and make advances toward identities, landscapes, and clearer visions of selves and lives that may evade them elsewhere. Grand Canyon tourists, like those who appear in this chapter, magnify the terms of such searches, struggles, and desires. They are constantly locating and relocating themselves in a geography illuminated by the passing sun and the seductive light bouncing from screens and pages. Both cast their shadows on the trails and roads running at the edge of the abyss, growing long, contracting, always moving toward another view. They are, in many ways, fleeting and phantomlike images of the Grand Canyon as a place of *popular* culture. This idea is often lost to those who see tourists as distracted from higher visions of nature's cathedrals and symphonies. Tourists do, in fact, recognize the canyon's grandeur in the language and images of those late nineteenth-century observers but they see other landscapes as well. Although their occasional glimpses of the Brady family's canyon or searches for Thelma and Louise's last stand may seem like acts of folly, in part, it is because few can—or are willing to—remember that the

Grand Canyon has served as a stage for the dramas and comedies audiences have found in movie theaters since the second decade of this century.

I hit the mute button on my TV because I prefer the silence over the melodramatic accompaniment recorded on the videotape copies of two silent "classics" I'm watching: *The Bargain* and *A Modern Musketeer* were both made at the Grand Canyon *before* it became a national park. *The Bargain* is a 1914 western starring William S. Hart as Jim Stokes, a.k.a. "The Two Gun Man." Hart appears on screen before the story begins. A curtain draws, and he's standing in front of the camera wearing a tuxedo. The actor bows to the camera, and before he rises up again, the film superimposes an image of him as Jim Stokes, a western outlaw with two pistols and a black hat. This technique is used to introduce all of the characters. A tuxedo-clad J. Frank Burke bows and rises as Sheriff Bud Walsh. Clara Williams wears an opera gown but transforms into Nell Brent, a prospector's daughter wearing an old sack dress. Barney Sherry turns into Phil Brent, the miner. When James Dowling bows, he rises as Wilkes, the minister, and he's atop a mule.

The Bargain begins as the camera fades from black to a view of the Grand Canyon from the rim and slowly pans across its buttes and temples. This is the landscape where much of the action takes place. Jim Stokes is an outlaw who robs the Express Company stagecoach. He gets wounded in the process and is discovered by Phil Brent, who has been out prospecting. Brent takes him back to his rimside cabin, where he falls in love with his daughter, Nell, who nurses his wound. The two get married even though she doesn't know he's an outlaw with a thousand-dollar reward on his wanted poster. In the end, *The Bargain* is a story of Stokes's redemption. The outlaw must trade his gunslinging talents for his freedom—which he does—and the film ends with Jim and Nell waving to the sheriff from the canyon's edge before going on to a new life.

The film is filled with chase scenes through the canyon, horses and men running along trails and between trees on the rim. As I search for familiar tourist landmarks, I realize I'm not supposed to find them. This isn't the Grand Canyon. Instead, *The Bargain* unfolds in a place where the canyon serves as a location for a fictional western geography. This is "Cochise County," Arizona, where the Grand Canyon is near the Mexican border; its rough terrain separates the towns of "Blue Rock" and "El Tempo." When an injured Stokes wanders the inner canyon, I read on the screen that he's escaped into the "Bad Lands." In one scene filmed on the Bright Angel Trail, I see an arrow points the way to Mexico; it reads "Border 5 miles." In 1914, the film's director, Thomas Ince, saw the Grand Canyon as a place he could transform, with editing and changing a few signs, into a rugged, western *someplace* not found on any maps, existing only on the movie screen.

Three years later, the Grand Canyon again appears as movie set in Douglas Fairbanks's 1917 romantic comedy, *A Modern Musketeer,* but this time it is a tourist's canyon.

Actually, the film begins in seventeenth-century France, with an athletic Fairbanks fencing and swinging from chandeliers as D'Artagnan, the chivalrous swordsman from Alexandre Dumas's *Three Musketeers*. After watching him fight for the honor of a young woman, the audience is asked whether heroes like D'Artagnan are forever lost to modern life. "Maybe not," I read on the screen. "Perhaps it is his spirit that actuates Ned Thacker of Kansas." In the following frames, the musketeer looks directly into the camera, as the actors do in the beginning of *The Bargain*, and we watch the sword and long mane of Fairbanks's musketeer dissolve into the clean-cut and grinning Ned Thacker. Ned is a young man in a small Kansas town who's been weaned on the musketeer stories—his mother still reads them to him—and he wants to become a modern-day D'Artagnan. "He will always be a boy," says his mother. Instead of a yellow steed, Ned's father gives him the keys to a Model T Ford, and the excitable and energetic Ned heads west in search of the chivalrous adventures he dreams about.

A Modern Musketeer transposes Dumas's old tale to the rim of the Grand Canyon.

Ned arrives there after coming to the rescue of the Vandeteer party, members of New York high society who have broken down in the desert on their transcontinental motor trip. Forrest Vandeteer is "the richest man in Yonkers," and he's taken the young Elsie Dodge and her mother on this vacation. Vandeteer wants to win Elsie's love, but the girl knows he's a lecherous scoundrel. She is on this trip only because her mother thinks the millionaire will help them get out of debt. Of course, Ned knows none of this when he comes to their aid and escorts them to El Tovar Hotel. Once at the canyon, Elsie and Ned are two tourists whose accidental meeting flourishes into a romance in a vacation setting.

I watch Ned playfully joust with Vandeteer in El Tovar's parking lot; a golf club substitutes for a sword. In another scene, Ned and Elsie attend a Hopi Dance after dinner at El Tovar. Elsie is charmed by Ned's good humor, and she laughs as he bounces a young Hopi boy on his knee while costumed Indians dance for the tourists. They leave the dance to stroll along the rim and gaze into the canyon. "Golly, what a gully," says the affable Ned. "It makes me feel so unimportant," responds Elsie. He senses she is troubled by something and asks her to confide in him. "With all this bigness, I guess my troubles don't matter," she says with forlorn eyes. "That is right," says Ned, expanding his chest and raising a pointed finger to the sky. "What was God's purpose to so rend the earth under this majestically fretted dome as to horribly shake our dispositions with thoughts far beyond the reach of our souls?" Elsie listens as he becomes the quintessential canyon tourist spouting bombastic praise. "You have a nice speaking voice," she says, shifting her awe from the scenic wonder to Ned. He doesn't know what to say, so he starts juggling three stones he pulls from his pocket. The two walk along the rim; they are falling in love, and Elsie shudders as she watches Ned try to impress her by doing handstands on the brink of the abyss.

Watching Fairbanks's modern musketeer balancing on the canyon's edge, I imagine movie audiences in nervous laughter on the night of December 30, 1917, as they attended the newly released picture. That same night, other theaters projected *The Narrow Trail,* also a new release, and audiences watched William S. Hart again play a stagecoach-robbing outlaw who reforms for the love of a woman. This time his name was Ice Harding, and the backdrop was San Francisco. *The Bargain* had been Hart's first feature film, and as Jim Stokes sat on his horse and lit up a cigarette in the Grand Canyon, audiences met the cowboy hero who would appear again and again, a gun-toting hero who could be an outlaw or minister, running through the West toward freedom, independence, and redemption; his outlaws always cleaned up themselves as they cleaned up the West. Hart was born in Newburgh, New York, four years before Powell's expedition "discovered" the Grand Canyon. The one-time Broadway Shakespearean actor made his career portraying a moral force in the Wild West for the working class who composed the bulk of movie audiences. His bow to the audience in *The Bargain*'s opening credits, where the actor in tuxedo dissolves into an outlaw, symbolized his transformation into a popular hero. When those moviegoers first discovered

Hart in *The Bargain,* the Grand Canyon had already become a national cultural symbol for Americans educated and wealthy enough to attend the theater, know of Powell's expedition, buy stereographs, attend travel lectures, revel in a nature that sounded like a symphony, and take a westbound Pullman to the South Rim—rather than go to the movies. The audience who went to see Hart's two-gun outlaw find his freedom were of a class for whom the Grand Canyon had not yet reached iconic status. What for some Americans was already cultural antiquity could for working class ticket-buyers become the rugged backdrop of a fictional West. Stokes ran from the law in a Grand Canyon that could still be turned into someplace else, with little worry that anyone watching would be distracted by this. In less than a year, however, all of it would begin to change.

In 1915, with the "See America First" campaign already underway, the Grand Canyon had more than 116,000 visitors. The dramatic increase over previous years' averages, however, was attributed, in part, to travelers who visited the canyon on their way to the Panama–Pacific International Exposition in San Francisco and the Panama–California Exposition in San Diego. The Harvey Company and the Santa Fe Railway did their best to use these expositions to promote Grand Canyon and Southwest tourism. In San Francisco, they built a three-dimensional scale model of Grand Canyon in the midway. In San Diego, they constructed a ten-acre ethnological exhibit, "The Painted Desert," designed by Mary Colter. These exhibits only mirrored the fictionalizing of the mythic West that had started in 1905 at Grand Canyon and continued to materialize. In 1914, Hermit's Rest and The Lookout, designed by Colter and financed by the Harvey Company and the Santa Fe Railway, were built on the rim. In 1915, the collaboration between these two companies was selling the canyon as a place for a "genuine Out West" experience, where visitors could wear chaps and Stetsons, and enter a world suited for their fantasies of western life. This is the canyon Ned Thacker arrived at when he appeared on movie screens in 1917. This was not only because the tourist scene there had been changing, or because increasing numbers of the population had become aware of the Grand Canyon. Surely these events were part of the story, but movie heroes, westerns, and the audiences watching them also began to change after 1914.

Between 1914 and 1918, only Charlie Chaplin held more audience appeal than movie stars like Douglas Fairbanks or Mary Pickford. Fairbanks's feature film career began in 1915, shortly after Hart's. But as audiences watched Hart's Ice Harding in *The Narrow Trail* in 1917, they saw a stoic cowboy hero whose six-guns were becoming little match for the golf clubs and boyhood fantasies of Fairbanks's Ned Thacker. Hart's characters were modeled after dimestore westerns of the late nineteenth century. Fairbanks's western tourist represented a boyish man driven by dreams of becoming a Jim Stokes. He starred in three other westerns in 1917, all of them romantic comedies. In *Wild and Wooly,* for instance, he is a wealthy modern city slicker who is a fanatic about western lore and daydreams of riding horses through Arizona deserts of cactus and sage. Unlike Hart, who was born in the East and epitomized the Wild West, Fairbanks, born in Denver, Colorado, in 1883, played a tourist who nostalgically rambles through a tamed American frontier. The two main problems facing Fairbanks's heroes are his boredom at home and work and his leisure pursuits, notes Larry May. "He admires the 'steel stamina and efficiency' of the symbolic fathers who built and rule the industrial system," says May, but "at the same time feels trapped in their creations. . . . He has luxury and urban comfort; but within his mind and soul he still wants to be self-made."[38] These are the circumstances fueling Ned Thacker's escape, and as he drove his father's Model T to the Grand Canyon, he embodied the longings of many in the movie theaters who watched him.

By 1914, working-class movie patrons were making room for increasing numbers from the middle class who were attending feature films. According to David Nasaw, trade journals reported a "newfound respectability" in the movie industry as "people who never before dreamed of entering the portals of a motion picture theater" were now being "converted to the pictures, and will, in the future, be found among 'the regulars.'"[39] White-collar managers, clerks, office workers, and people employed by large organizations were all going to the movies. As they watched Fairbanks on the screen, they often saw a mirror of their lifestyles or ones they aspired toward. "Even though his cheerful persona suggested to audiences a sense of optimism and a feeling that everything would turn out all right," suggests May, "the typical Fairbanks film would find the hero loaded with the worries of modern middle-class existence."[40]

The same year director Allan Dwan and Douglas Fairbanks blocked the scenes and stunts that filled the frames of *A Modern Musketeer,* preservationists and legislators were meeting in Washington, D.C., with other plans for the scenery. Those testifying at the 1917 National Parks Conference argued for the creation of more national parks and, in particular, the establishment of Grand Canyon as a national park. They, too, were concerned about the anxieties facing the American public who lived in cities and said that the Grand Canyon should be set aside for their recreation and education. "We need sometimes that poetry should not be drummed into our ears, but flashed onto our senses," Mrs. John D. Sherman, conservation chair of the General Federation of Women's Clubs, told the audience. "Man, with all his knowledge and all his pride, needs to know nothing but that he is a marvelous atom in a marvelous world." Like Sherman, Assistant Attorney General Huston Thompson told the audience that the American public was "caught in the throats of the great cities as they inhale and exhale our man-made civilization." Modern urban life dulled people's ears to "the still small voice of nature," said Thompson, "while man's handiwork blinds our eyes 'til it is only the shock of great altitudes or the vistas of nature in their most colossal and primeval state that can attune our ears and brush the scales from our eyes."[41] Their speeches recited the archetypal romantic sentiment of the elites who began

coming to the Grand Canyon at the end of the nineteenth century, and their voices were the ones Ned Thacker parodied from the rim.

For Ned, the canyon was a big "gully," a place where the tourist from the Midwest juggled, pretended to be a musketeer, and fell in love. Moviegoers saw the "shock of great altitudes" as the comic actor launched into a handstand on the edge of a cliff. If they did not feel nature's "poetry" on their senses or hear "the small voice of nature," it was because of their own laughter. Ned's canyon was for dreamers yearning to break free from the boredom of their small towns, the city, their routines and jobs, and dwell for a while in a fantasy life. His cinematic journey to the canyon offered an exaggerated and intensified model of escape that audiences might well have understood as they left the street and retreated into the darkened movie theater.

In the following years the Grand Canyon became a different place. The previous summer, President Woodrow Wilson signed the Organic Act of 1916 and established the National Park Service under the secretary of the interior. The new park service would be responsible for conserving "the scenery and the natural historic objects" of national parks and monuments, and "provide for the enjoyment of the same in such a manner and by such means as to leave them unimpaired for future generations."[42] By May 1918, the year before the canyon became a national park, Interior Secretary Franklin Lane spelled out the duties of the newly formed park service. In addition to conservation, it would encourage public education. "Museums containing specimens of wild flowers, shrubs, and trees, and mounted animals, birds, and fish native to the parks and other exhibits of this character will be established," wrote Lane. In developing their educational projects in new parks, the service "should seek to find scenery of supreme and distinctive quality or some natural feature so extraordinary or unique as to be of national interest and importance . . . for instance, at the Grand Canyon, as exemplifying the highest accomplishment of stream erosion."[43] The canyon that moviegoers first met through outlaws and musketeers soon fell into the hands of park planners, who scripted its scenery for the voices of geologists, botanists, archeologists, and the romantic sensibilities of the poets and preservationists who ventured toward landscapes of science and arcadia, seeking a studious and quiet distance from audiences who laughed at silent film stars.

Following their congressional charge, the park service built museums, exhibits, education programs, gathered up fossils, artifacts, and stuffed fowl and fur for the benefit of the public's eyes and minds. To leave national parks "unimpaired for future generations" has largely meant offering generations of visitors an education in earth science and natural history as if, perhaps, it were a prescription to correct their faulty vision. And since the 1920s, park planners and administrators have continued to have a clear image of the lost tourist, who remains a justification for national park service education. At an August 1995 hearing focused on the canyon's development and future funding priorities, park superintendent Robert L. Arneberger noted that only 40 percent of all visitors walked into the visitor center. "The other 60 percent probably enjoy their visit," he told the Senate Committee on Energy and Natural Resources assembled in the park's Shrine of the Ages auditorium. "But quite frankly, I think, for those of us that live here and have to deal with it, there are 60 percent that wander aimlessly, looking for the information they need and trying to learn something about the canyon."[44] Behind Arneberger's observation lies an assumption that tourists not only want the education the park service is offering but also that their inability to get it has become a nuisance, a problem of disorder. What he didn't say to the committee, yet included in his prepared statement for the hearings, is that only 3 to 5 percent of all park visitors attended the park service's guided ranger walks and evening campfire programs.[45] For the park manager, these low numbers reflect an absence of funding, staff, and facilities to "reach" greater numbers of visitors who would otherwise seek out the education they are missing.

But perhaps the matter also boils down to a question of tastes and interests, qualities typically attributed to tourists as something they are lacking. Using the park service's projected estimate of 5 million visitors to Grand Canyon in 1995 as a point of departure, Arneberger calculated that the number of visitors attending the free camp-fire programs and guided walks, supposedly to benefit and enhance their visit, would amount to approximately 150,000–250,000. When compared to the overall number of visitors, this indeed is a small group. When compared with the portion of the public who have paid to see Kasdan's *Grand Canyon* or watched the Brady Bunch go to the canyon in syndication, the numbers shrink even more.[46] Perhaps movie and television audiences offer a faulty comparison with tourists who go to Grand Canyon to see it for themselves. After all, it's unlikely those audiences are driving to theaters and video out-lets, or changing the channel to see these films because they want to see the canyon. Instead, these few films merely suggest how the canyon has been anchored in the popu-lar imagination through stories. In all of these—and many others—the canyon is the setting for some other drama audiences will find interesting, thrilling, disappointing, and, at times, an occasion for leaving one level of boredom for another. Leisure time poses questions not easily answered. Ned Thacker tried to settle a deeper set of yearn-ings by traveling to the canyon. When he arrived, the place had not yet become clut-tered with taxidermy, dioramas, fossils, and well-intentioned teachers wearing uni-forms. It's doubtful any of them would have supplied him with solutions to the riddles that tugged at him. The point of his journey was not to arrive at a definitive answer as an expert might but to have a story worth telling by living as if in a story.

Against the stock of ready answers, educational philosophies, and visitor pro-grams that now claim the Grand Canyon's tourist landscape, images of the movie out-law running over rugged terrain near the Mexican border and the modern musketeer throwing handstands on the edge laid their claim on the canyon as a place where popu-lar stories unfolded before the eyes of people looking for their own escapes and thrills. *The Bargain* and *A Modern Musketeer* are but two fossils excavated from a popular canyon, offering clues about the past and present to those who seek them out. The frustrated rangers who try to corral an aimless herd toward troughs of information, and those who cynically laugh as tourists look for scenes from movies and novels seem—despite their certainty, good intentions, and educations—to have lost sight of a Grand Canyon many tourists have come to find. These old movies carry reminders of a popular landscape that remains intact, regardless of the changes made there after these early cameras and film captured the canyon's light. After the reformed Jim Stokes waved good-bye from the canyon's rim, the final frames of *The Bargain* offered a sentimental assurance to audiences. "No Star is lost we ever once have seen," ripples across the black frame. "We always may be what we might have been." Stokes turned his life toward a new horizon at the end of the film. For an hour or so, the audience had as well, but they had made a different bargain, and would soon leave the dark-ened movie theatre to head back to work, home, or wander the city streets. The geographies of fantasy are born on movie screens and printed pages, and as others have said, they are where we look for the stories we might call our own.

Next to the maps, visitor centers, and management plans that keep the Grand Canyon for future generations, motion pictures, novels, and television programs would continue to remind the public that the canyon was a stage for their own ordinary lives, their humor and romance, and the backdrop for scenes of extraordinary adventure. Some critical theorists would be quick to tell us that the frames drawn around the scene cannot anticipate the acute and idiosyncratic "lines of flight" that continually cross and redraw the territory.[47] In their own way, tourists seem to know this well as they bounce down the Brady Trail toward the river, feel the wind against their face as they ride their steeds like D'Artagnan, and Captain America, and Billy, furiously flapping their arms while pretending to fall from the rim, and searching for the view where those two latter-day outlaws, Thelma and Louise, drove their Thunderbird past the end of the road, into a popular history, to join Jim Stokes in the "Bad Lands" of the Grand Canyon.

6

The Depths of Time

The engine in the Mercury Sable pops and creaks on the hot asphalt. It's probably been driven hard; a sticker on the rear window says it's a rental. On the asphalt below, ice cubes melt in a pool of cola. The mixture stretches from a convenience store cup—a "gusher" size—and joins a stream of anti-freeze dripping from the Sable's belly. Together they reach toward the new shade made by a Plymouth Voyager, a fresh arrival in a recently evacuated parking slot. The breeze carries a scent of diesel exhaust while a Transamerica tour bus idles and keeps the air cool beneath its stainless steel skin and tinted glass. A man in his mid-thirties wearing a New York Yankees cap cracks the seal on the Voyager and slides back the door of his land pod. "Okay, you can unbuckle, now," he tells two young daughters strapped into the bench seat. In oversized sunglasses, baggy T-shirts, and shorts, they are pale and weary life forms—like two old women shrunken back to childhood from the forces of interstates—kept alive mostly on crackers and fruity drinks sucked from foil pouches. "We're gonna look at the Grand Canyon," says Daddy. "We're here."

Vehicles fill nearly every space in the Mather Point parking lot at ten o'clock this morning. Cavalier. Escort. Taurus. Air Stream. U-Haul. Behind bug-splattered windshields, dashboards exhibit artifacts of highway life and time spent in motion. Stephen King. Clinique Total Cover Sun Block. McDonald's Styrofoam. Kodak. John Grisham. A Power Ranger is passed out on Barbie. I notice brochures for the Grand Canyon IMAX Theatre, Grand Canyon Scenic Airlines, and the Meteor Crater. Rand McNally takes cover beneath Danielle Steele's cracked spine. Here comes everybody, rolling slowly off East Rim Drive and South Entrance Road, arriving. Drivers in shades hunch over the wheel, looking for the taillights to come on. Someone is always waiting for someone. "Throw it in reverse fer Krissakes!"

I often went to Mather Point to watch Grand Canyon visitors climb from their vehicles and out onto the rim. For many, it's the first time, their first glimpse of the abyss. Here, the Grand Canyons of the mind—shaped by nearly a century of iconic images and the recent postcard views found in every gas station, Seven-Eleven, trading post and supermarket for the last two hundred miles—stand elbow to elbow, eyeball to eyeball, with the original. Tourists lean on the steel rails like passengers on the prow of a cruise ship. The ocean has disappeared, and empty space laps the stone bow below their sandals and tennis shoes. Binoculars scan the horizon and downward, looking for signs of depth and life. Shutters thrush and videotape rolls. People hand off expensive cameras to strangers and ask them to snap their poses. A camcorder trains on Mother, Amber, and little Danny, who respond with automatic waves and frozen stances before the lens leaves their faces to sweep in the panorama. The viewing area seems a continuation of the parking lot above. Tourists patiently wait for a clearing on the rail, a place to take in the scene without a wall of stiff legs and protruding butts coming between them and The Wonder. They try not to bump into one another and duck camera lenses. All of this could easily make the Grand Canyon seem an anxious place, one fraught with frustrations and anything but the patience its magnitude and geology promises. Face to face, however, almost everyone is amiable, tolerant, and polite. They laugh and seem open to each other as if mindful of private aims for this common ground.

This morning, I'm listening to a potbellied tour guide wearing a straw cattleman's hat and aviator sunglasses point out the sights to a family of three. The guide stops at the rail and pulls a penny out of his pocket. "This is for luck," he says, and tosses the penny toward a slivered outcropping about eight feet from the steel-fenced observation area. The coin lands on the rock and he chuckles, "It's my way of taking part in the Grand Canyon, I guess." The family with the tour guide cordially nod at the coin toss, but they seem tired as they follow their host to another place on the lookout. A few days ago, I watched a sixty-year-old man do the same. He held a dime and told his wife to make a wish. She closed her eyes for a few seconds, and he tossed the coin onto the rock. "Bingo!" he shouted and kissed her on the mouth.

Two women and a man from Korea, watching the guide throw his penny, rummage through their pockets and handbags when he leaves and start tossing loose change at the rock. A roving park ranger, who is walking around answering visitors' questions, spots them and hustles to the opposite rail. He taps the Korean man on the shoulder just as he's launched a nickel.

"That's pollution," says the ranger. They look startled. "That's pollution," he repeats sternly, waving his finger back and forth in front of the tourist's face. The Korean man bows his head as if he now understands he's broken some rule. He says something to the women, who nod and look at the ranger. They quietly head for the concrete steps rising to the parking lot. When they leave, I ask the ranger about throwing coins from Mather Point. "It just started happening this year," he says. "Why? You tell me. They don't understand; they could get fined. It's just like throwing paper or cans. It's pollution to the canyon." Two women, watching all of this, stroll over to where we stand talking.

"We're noticing all the coins," says one woman. "Why do they do it?"

"They don't think it's a way of polluting the environment," the ranger tells them. "They think the canyon is like a midway in a carnival," he continues. "It's like throwing a coin in a cup to win a prize on the boardwalk. They don't respect it."

"I think it's because they're superstitious," offers the other woman. "You come to this great sight and you want . . . I don't know . . . to think there's something . . . ," and her voice drifts off, unable to put her finger on it. I glance at the nameless rock sprinkled with loose change—down payments on good fortune and fate—and imagine the people who've thrown them. Mothers and fathers. Sons and daughters. Honeymooners. Germans, French, Brits, Swedes, Dutch, Koreans, Japanese thousands of miles from home. Lone travelers. People on packaged tours with adhesive name tags stuck to their shirts. Buddies wearing leather chaps, sleeping bags and duffels lashed to vintage Harleys cooling in the parking lot. Not everyone, of course; only those who notice a chance to take a shot, judge the distance and force, figure on the luck. Aiming for a target beyond the guardrails, beyond rules and rationality, they flip their pennies, dimes, and nickels, watch their coins arc and somersault over the dangerous drop, as if making the leap themselves. Polluting the environment means paper cups, cigarette butts, dented aluminum cans. This is money from the pocket. Piling up, glinting in the sun, here is opportunity, a time for banking on the *super*natural, a sudden and unexpected expression of the canyon's *Supernature*.

Here, the Grand Canyon is nothing less than what anthropologist Kathleen Stewart envisions as "a space on the side of the road" where lives and stories flourish, giving depth and dimension to the time of people in motion, people passing along the brink of a great wishing well. The ranger's admonition of midway games and carnival life is consistent with the prevailing vision of a canyon culture spoken, remembered, and written down. But the coins thrown on the rock offer another sign. They are reminders of how the canyon's tourist culture is not a preserve of ideas or preformulated packages, "but a social imaginary erupting out of a storied cultural real." This is not a view of culture that remains static and temporally fixed but is instead "ruminative and filled with density and desire; it derails into magic and threat, trauma and melancholy, playful performance and deep eccentricity," says Stewart. "It imagines itself not as a finished code but as a series of encounters and sudden eruptions of signs and action. . . . It follows a logic of gaps in the naturalized order of things and finds itself caught in latent force fields."[1]

The Grand Canyon is the Big Space on the Side of the Road, where stories and performances take shape. They are not the familiar stories of geology, nature, and history rehearsed over and again by rangers, guides, and piles of canyon literature. Instead, these stories focus on the shifts and fissures of people at leisure and seeking their freedom, the ambiguous nature of life away from home and in motion, and what might be called a "secret" or "invisible" history of contemporary tourist life on the edge of the great geological time clock.[2] In many ways, to watch visitors exercise their free time is to witness people self-consciously and unknowingly dramatize the sphere of leisure as a place of critique, compensation, escape, and fantasy. "Space is nothing but the inscription of time in the world," Henri Lefebvre notes. "Spaces are the realizations, inscriptions in the simultaneity of the external world of a series of times."[3] Perhaps this idea is most apparent in the context of leisure. At the Grand Canyon, along its trails, at observation points, in hotels and campgrounds, the domain of leisure appears as a production of temporal zones full of promise, hope, possibility, and imagination. At the same time, they are moments carrying traces of the worlds people hope to escape on their vacations.

I hear the voice of Guy Debord's announcer in his 1959 script *On the Passage of a Few Persons through a Rather Brief Period of Time.* "When freedom is practiced in a closed circle, it fades into a dream, becomes a mere representation of itself. The ambiance of play is by nature unstable. At any moment 'ordinary life' can prevail once again," says the voice. "The appearance of events that we have not made, that others have made against us, obliges us from now on to be aware of the passage of time, its results, the transformation of our own desires into events."[4] Debord's narrator seems to speak in the distance as tourists journey to the canyon and move along its rim. Their time is filled with contradictions and desires, and against the backdrop of a scenic wonder, they awaken images of selves away from home and seek to make a scene where time is measured not in terms of clocks and durations but for its capacity to offer depth, meaning, and continuity. They give way to a Grand Canyon of cultural imagination, dual landscapes full of conflicted and inverted meanings, and stories and scenes where leisure offers a sphere for critiquing and compensating for life in ways that may evade people in the everyday. But it is also a place where the modern promises of consumption, a work ethic, individual fulfillment through family and career, and lives led in cities and towns all reappear as the themes and objects of stories, comments, critical evaluations, anxieties, reaffirmations, memories, and designs for escape. Against the corpus of official representations, signs, institutional and commercial interpretive programs, park exhibits, and images suggesting the canyon's cultural significance as a national icon and tourist attraction, the canyon is also a site of personal quests for redemption and renewal, a place of a cultural poetics emerging from conflicts over meanings and ambitions, the tensions of modern experience, and fragmented displays of private life in a public setting. Those who peer into the great spectacle of geological and cosmological time may also confront their own time on the rim as equally difficult to grasp.

Between Times

Perhaps it is the dry air and clear, sunny skies, vacation optimism or the sense of arriving or, most likely, some combination of all of these, but the canyon brims with people shedding old skins and climbing into new ones. I see them in their khakis and cottons, jogging suits and sweatpants, flannel shirts and pullover nylon windbreakers, rubber Teva sandals, Birkenstocks, and hiking boots. Older men piloting motorhomes wearing coveralls with zippers up the front and lots of pockets. Stitched patches above their hearts bear brand logos or identify recreational vehicle outfitters somewhere back home. They climb out of their thirty-foot rocket ships, flip up their extra-smoked shades, survey the parking lots and campsites, and "assess the situation" for those still on board. I see women wearing new white T-shirts with flowers and vines stenciled across the front. Some wear visors to keep long hair and glare out of their eyes. Yellow and lavender bandannas are rolled and knotted around necks, along with necklaces made from piñon nuts, turquoise nuggets, and hammered silver bought on the reservation. And despite these adornments, nothing outshines the glow of new Keds bought for this trip. I see men wearing camouflage hats who are not shaving on their vacation. College boys sport T-shirts laying claim to universities, rock bands, concert tours, skateboard gear, and endless consumer loyalties. Many say "No Fear," a nation of young people with an undaunted grip on . . . whatever. And everyone is wearing sunglasses; everyone has brown or green plastic eyes outlined with chrome, wire, or synthetic tortoise shell. All signal a metamorphosis underway or already taken place; styles say "I'm here, loose, relaxed, ready to go and ready for something to happen. Come on." They are new lives born in catalogs, souvenir shops, sporting goods outlets, army surplus stores, and road movie scenes where characters stand up in speeding convertibles, punch a fist toward the heavens, and throw back their heads to howl like a coyote. I see Women Who Run with Wolves and Men from Mars who could turn into wolves, or leathery scouts, or Ansel Adams, or crystal cool Zen-Daddies, or bachelors. And many have brought their children.

"It's 2:30," says a woman, looking at her watch. She licks the vanilla trickling between her thumb and index finger while sitting with her husband on a bench outside the Bright Angel Lodge, a few feet away from me, eating ice cream cones he just bought at the Fountain. "They must be busy at work right now," she adds between licks. "I'm glad I'm missing that."

"Yeah," he nods. "Wayne and them are hauling trusses, or up on that roof. . . . It's probably done, already. They must be laying shingle by now." He spins the cone and his tongue cuts a groove into the creamy chocolate.

"What time did I hear you say it was?" I ask the woman, wondering how my morning slipped by.

"It's, uh . . . ," she pauses, looking at her watch again.

"Her watch is on Buffalo time," interrupts her husband. "We just got in last night, so they're three hours ahead, right? So that makes it," he looks to a space beyond his forehead to calculate, "about 11:30 our time. You better change your watch, Hon," he says. "She thinks she needs a watch out here," he tells me. Jan and Bill from Buffalo, New York, are on their honeymoon. Actually, the couple got married two months ago but had to wait to take this trip. She's a hair stylist, and he's a carpenter. They've been so busy at their jobs that August was their only chance to have a week off together.

"I'm just so glad to be away from there," Jan says. "I hate Mondays." Back in Buffalo, the other stylists at her shop are working on a regular group of elderly clients, she tells me. "Right now, it's probably the 'blue-hairs,' three ol' ladies who come in together. One of 'em can still drive. They just don't stop talking . . . nag on about everything."

Bill tells me about the new subdivision where he's not working today. "It's mass production," he says. "We just go, go, go. They're sweating it back there right now with one man short." He'd rather build custom homes, "but there's more work in what I'm doing. It's nice to have this break, though. I didn't think this would ever come." Jan is smiling and turning back the hands on her wristwatch when I leave, but I wondered to what extent the gesture would help them completely shake their Buffalo schedules during the long-awaited honeymoon week. This morning, at least, they found some small pleasure in reminding each other, and telling me, they were *not* working today, and people at home were. I wouldn't see them a week later, cutting hair or framing new homes on a construction site, but I could easily imagine Jan, seated in coach class and descending into Buffalo, turning her watch stem in the other direction, and giving up the three hours she happily claimed this morning.

Coping with a different time zone is, of course, a common practice for travelers. In many ways, moving a watch's hands backward and forward on vacation completes the negotiations of time already taken place—coordinating the vacation with work schedules and children's school breaks. Stopping mail and newspaper deliveries. Asking a friend to feed the cats and water the plants. Arranging for a ride to the airport. Leaving a list of phone numbers of where and when to make contact in case of an emergency. Setting timers so house lights will turn on automatically and signal to burglars, thieves, and whatever lurks "out there" at night that no one has gone anywhere. Jotting "V-A-C-A-T-I-O-N-!" across a row of calendar blocks is, perhaps, a hopeful attempt to restore a sense of the term's Latin origins—*vacatio,* meaning "freedom or exemption," and *vacare,* meaning "to be empty or unoccupied."[5] Relinquishing obedience to schedules and obligations, the promise of the vacation is to have time emptied of familiar measures and values. Despite desires to "get away from it all," orchestrating the departure means assuring ourselves to some degree that everything at home will remain the same without us.

It is difficult to entirely leave all of it behind regardless of how we plan our getaways. "She thinks she needs a watch out here," Bill had said, and noted he'd deliberately left his at home. Regardless of the gesture, he and Jan already had a two-day schedule at the canyon before moving on to Las Vegas and measured the pace of their first morning on the rim with the clocks in Buffalo. Whatever lines may get drawn or erased to portion off a week or month for leisure, Grand Canyon tourists often seem to be spinning through the turnstiles of what cultural critic David Eason has called a "Culture of Come and Go." Amid the reservations and personal itineraries, arrivals and departures, vacation time is also full of flux and ambiguity. "Coming and going," as Eason notes, "has its own time, one that has little to do with the clock or calendar."[6] For those on vacation, time becomes filled with stories and performances that give shape to the unsettled and hazy meanings of "getting away from it all." It is when people revive idealized images of self and family, try to make their freedom feel real, and grasp for lingering shadows of lives they can envision but often evade them in the currents of home, work, and daily routines. And it is also a time of seemingly paradoxical pursuits; people set out for places where their imaginations and energies may come to life in new ways but where worlds left behind often reappear.

Reading over written visitor comments collected from park registers, for instance, I often see visitors experiencing the pull of home, people, places, and other times. "This is cool!" begins an entry in a 1980 park register, ". . . too bad Bob's not here. . . . Remember: Bob-N-Machelle." Sherrilee from San Diego writes, "The Canyon's pretty okay! But the rest of this place is dead!!! It doesn't party anything like San Diego—but then nothing does. Later on . . . Paradise Hills San Diego parties hardy." They are brief entries drawing the dividing lines of presence and absence, home and away; each opens onto a larger story in which we might imagine Machelle missing Bob or a bored Sherrilee wishing she were home. During the writing exercise on Ranger Karen's "Awesome Chasm" walk, visitors similarly appeared lodged between worlds separated by time and distance. "Too many things in life are taken for granted," wrote one person. "The old saying to this experience is: *Are we working to live or living to work?* The experience of this visit is bringing back into focus the need to concentrate on life, not work." Another visitor, presumably a Louisiana state legislator, described the canyon as an occasion for clarified vision, an instance for sorting out the meaning of life and work. "The state budget has been out of balance for the past five years and I expect it will take another five years to straighten it out," begins the comment. "If I were back at the State capitol right now I'd be plugging away trying to hasten the process. I sometimes think a balanced budget is a work of art but that thought pales when I look out into the canyon. Maybe if I sat here long enough, a million years or so, I'd really learn what art work is really all about. I'm trying to figure how to move this canyon to Baton Rouge so I can gaze on it from my office window." Gazing into the natural void a few feet away, the Louisiana visitor sees a distant geography and imagines a future moment when he or she will be daydreaming about the canyon. For yet another visitor, coming to terms with the canyon offers a renewed perspective on a life lodged somewhere between past, present, and future. "The awesomeness and beauty of it all puts things in better perspective for me," the comment reads. "I am able to go home renewed and in a wonderful frame of mind feeling like I communed with nature—the vastness—the timelessness—the beautiful setting that looks like a movie setting—this is wonderful!" This passage does, in fact, offer a sense of "timelessness"; forecasting a return home, the writer anticipates a time for recalling this very moment as one of communing with a nature that is on par with a motion picture.

Each writer is literally and metaphorically *moved* by the canyon. Apart from their self-conscious humility or honoring the canyon as an artistic masterpiece or a cinematic sublime, aside from deliberating over the meaning of work or their finding and losing of perspective, despite their focus on priorities and their sense of renewal, these comments project images of landscapes and time zones far from the canyon rim. Whether they are standing in front of a visitor register or sitting on the canyon's edge writing their thoughts on a sheet of paper, each comment offers an economical illustration of divided selves grasping for continuities. To some extent, these pages open onto a view of the Grand Canyon's broader functions as a tourist landscape. Both are sites where tourists register the meanings of time spent in motion; they are temporary spaces of dwelling in reflection, imagination, and critique, and their very structure is paralleled in the stories tourists spin out along the rim.

At Yaki Point, Jerry sits under a tree drinking a bottle of Gatorade. Half an hour ago, he completed a steep, three-mile hike up the South Kaibab Trail from Cedar Ridge, where he had spent an hour or so this morning taking pictures. He hobbles to the rim and points out the steep switchback trail he's just climbed. "I was breathing pretty hard on the way up. I'm a little flabby from the trip," he says, patting a sizable paunch covered by a sweaty T-shirt and red trail dust. "I've just been sitting in the U-Haul and eating McDonald's since I left West Virginia." Jerry, who is in his late thirties, is driving to California and a job waiting for him as a penitentiary machine-shop supervisor. I ask him why he wanted to hike down on such a hot day. "Something different, you know, the challenge of it," he says. "You get out there on that rock and the wind is blowing, hitting you in the face. No one's botherin' you with nothin'. You feel free. I hate to leave this place. It's on to California and then it's all over. Got to start this job. Doubt I'll be getting a vacation anytime soon, so I'm trying to get in what I can on this move. My wife and boy drove the car out. They're staying with her aunt 'til I come, but I can't say I'm trying to break any speed records," he grins. "I've got the furniture and driving alone is really okay, but it'll all be over in a coupla days." Jerry says the new job will be much like the one he left in a West Virginia facility. "It's not bad, pays alright," he tells me. "They [the prisoners] can get outta hand now and then, but you gotta expect it. At least I can go home after my shift. I'll remember this place though, never saw nothin' like this."

His Grand Canyon trip is not a vacation per se but a brief detour from I-40 West, a singular event punctuating an "adventure in moving," as the sign says on his rental truck parked a few yards away. Jerry's excursion takes shape as a story bracketed between visions of "home," one remembered in West Virginia and one awaiting him in California. Between these two "homes," he climbs out of his truck and into the canyon, feels the wind hitting his face as if it was the sign of a temporary liberation from a road eventually leading to obligations of work and family. Travel narratives, even informal accounts like this one, often call up the past and future in a dialectical play of reversals and inversions. In Jerry's case, "home" is a point of departure and arrival, but they are not the same place. His account is a search for narrative continuities in the midst of geographic discontinuities, a grasping for familiar identity markers in the process of escaping from routine, a conceiving of "home" as it disappears in the rearview mirror, and imagining again how "home" is waiting at the opposite end of the road. "Home" is where Jerry's journey begins and ends, and it is also where this journey will, in turn, become a story. "I'll remember this place," he said on Yaki Point, anticipating the time his moving truck stops and he's asked, "How was the trip?" When and where does a journey begin and end? An idea of "home," for instance, may serve as both a real and imaginary terminus for travelers, but it is largely a designation that overlooks how meanings of "home" and "away," and the disappointments and promises of each, coexist and fuel each other in the context of travel.[7]

"I got interested in coming out here when I started learning about native life. I was reading some books about the Hopis and Navajos. It got me interested in the culture out here," Molly tells me one afternoon while seated on a flat outcropping. She is inches away from the canyon's edge, sketching on a pad. I hear a faint buzz from the Sony Walkman earphones looped around her neck. She's been listening to the Velvet Underground's *Loaded,* she says, and lifts her pencil away from her drawing of a kachina thunderbird soaring over the canyon. "I came out here to work for Fred Harvey. I'm in the gift shop," Molly says, and tells me she's a student at the School of Visual Arts in New York City, studying art therapy. "I just had to get away from Manhattan. It really started to suck, but now I kinda miss it. The city has this rhythm you get into. A tourist that goes there might go down the street and stop at every red light. But when you live there, you get into this rhythm and you just walk it, never having to stop, making all the lights. But it was just getting to be too much, so I came out here. And that's been good because it helped me to get a new look at the city. This is alright, but everything is so old. Everything back there is new, and there's a lot to do. I'm supposed to work here past Labor Day, but I might leave before that."

Listening to Molly recall the rhythmic energy of her New York was much like watching her sketch a thunderbird hovering over the canyon; they were both landscapes of invisible forces. "Must a journey always be away from home?" asks Richard Quinney. "Could not travel be a growing awareness, not of places away from home, but of the newness of home as a place?"[8] Travelers are generally "caught up in a chaotic, fragmented universe that needs to be domesticated," notes Georges Van Den Abbeele, and positing an image of *home* "demarcates one's traveling like the Aristotelian plot into a beginning, a middle, and an end . . . ," and "everything which falls into the middle can be domesticated."[9] Molly's story is less a tale of leisure travel than one of desire for an escape from life's routines. Her journey takes shape in New York, fueled by stories of native culture and the Southwest. And it is in this new place—one where an original fantasy and fascination with native spirits lingers on her sketch pad during a day off from selling Indian curios in the gift shop—that the rhythms of the city reappear with a vitality animated by reflective distance, desire, and a growing boredom already anticipating a new departure.

To some extent, travel—for all its many intentions and functions, for all its variations of pleasure and practicality—"resists any immediate perception of itself," suggests Van Den Abbeele. "No matter when I decide my trip is beginning, in some fashion it *has already begun.* Immediacy is denied by the fact that the cognition of beginning a voyage is always already mediated by the very *motion* of the voyage."[10] And it is in the flow of the journey, moving through new landscapes, crossing paths with strangers also in the flux of coming and going, that the "space on the side of the road" envisioned by Stewart flourishes as a narrative domain of projections and retrievals. It is a sometimes swampy pool of reflection in which people locate themselves in time with stories of roads traveled, places left behind, days of return; all of it drifts amid murky clues of ambition and discontent. If staying put has become stagnant and soupy, here is where a desire to move appears in stories told in the desert and high plateaus leading to the canyon.

"We're in this Jeep and I'm out in the open," Peg tells me as she picks up some popcorn from a bowl on the bar. "When I get back, I'll be in, like, this enclosed room? So, I'm totally liking driving in this Jeep. I just love the open space. It feels so free. When we stop at someone's house along the way, I just want a cup of coffee in the morning—get out of there—be someplace where we are camping in the tent again. Being inside when I'm back home, I feel like I'm in a cage. It's excellent riding in that Jeep." In the lounge of the Best Western Grand Canyon Squire Inn, Peg stops talking to order another beer for herself and her friend, Karla. They have been driving together across the country in Karla's Jeep, camping out and staying with friends. Tonight, they've pitched their tent at the Ten-X Campground south of the park entrance. The campground was boring, Peg tells me, so they drove the short distance to the Best Western to have a few drinks. This is where I met them. On my other side sits a thirty-eight-year-old commercial window washer from Louisville named Jose who is traveling alone through the Southwest on a motorcycle.

"I love riding the back roads," says Jose, and we turn to listen. "I was driving down this one road and there's this old Navajo gentleman with gray hair and the band around his head. He was wearing this old plaid shirt, and herding these sheep across the road. You know, it was picturesque. So, I turn around and go back to take his picture. When I pull up, all these dogs—about ten of 'em—surround me. All of 'em were mutts, but they all looked the same. So I pull out my camera to take a picture and then the old man runs behind this tree and won't come out until I put the camera away. So I took a few pictures of the sheep. I got one of him, though. I went into one of the gift shops out there," he says, and points to the lobby near the lounge. "This woman who works there is Navajo and she says that they believe if you take their picture, it kills a part of them. It takes a part of their soul away. . . . I hope that old man is still alive," Jose says, and laughs. "When I was on the reservation, these police stopped me because I was speeding. I think they thought I was an Indian. My mother's family is from Mexico and my stepfather's last name is German, so when they looked at my license they must've been suspicious or something. I think they thought I was an Indian and wondered what I was doing on this new bike. It seems poor out there. But they only gave me a warning in the end. I camped out there one night. It was beautiful." Jose has no particular plan for this trip; he's just wandering around for a month on his Honda Gold Wing. I ask them why they wanted to come out to the canyon. Like many tourists, they say it's just something they've always wanted to see and quickly turn their stories toward what they are getting away from.

"Most of the time, I'm hanging on the sides of buildings. I have my own business, but that don't mean I don't work. I work more than anyone else on my crew. I'm just glad to be doing something like this for a change," says Jose, and gulps from his mug. "There was this woman back home who I was seeing and we split up. I decided I just had to get out of there so I thought, 'why not take a trip and have some time on my own?' Get away from all that. But then we decided that we could maybe get back together. She wanted to move in right away, but I told her that I had this trip planned and I'm still going to do it, so I did. I put some money in my pocket and took off for a month. I was just getting sick of it all. I was married once. My whole thing was just going to work and being married. There was nothing else going on. This new relationship was going the same way. So when we split up, I decided to take this trip. But she's a good woman and when I get back home I think we'll get back together." As Jose talks, Peg listens closely, waiting for a place to jump in and tell us her story.

"I just got tired of the life I was living. I moved around a lot. Nashville. Houston. But I'm from Pittsburgh, that's where my parents are," says Peg, lighting up a Salem. "I moved in with them for a while and then I started seeing this guy who was younger than me. I'm twenty-six, he was twenty one." Karla already knows this story; I can tell by the way she nods her head as though checking off a list of details about her friend's life. "The drug scene was getting real bad with this group of friends I used to hang out with. They're good people, but everyone was into crack and coke, and I've been through that. I quit doing cocaine three and a half years ago. I don't do drugs. I'll smoke a joint every now and then or have a beer, but I've been through all that. This guy I was living with, well he was going through all that. I've done that and I just got sick of it. So, about two months ago Karla started talking about this trip, but I didn't know if I could afford it. She said, 'Well, whether you do it or not, I'm going.'"

"Oh, I *knew* you were gonna go. There's no way you wouldn't," says Karla, quiet until now.

"Well life was just getting to suck," Peg says, "I was getting sick of this guy and all the people I knew doing drugs, so I just told Karla, 'I'm going.'" Peg and Karla clink their beer glasses, give each other a high five and grasp each other's hands in solidarity like they've made the decision to go on this trip all over again. "I get antsy every spring. I got sick of this guy and I get bored real easy. My parents call me a *gypsy*. I just said I need a break to figure out what I'm going to do. You get lots of time to think when you travel. You're in a car and there's all of this way to go so you just think about what you're doing and your life. It's when you can figure some stuff out." I ask her what she'll do when the trip is over. "I *know* what I'm gonna to do when I get back home," says Peg. "*I'm going to move.* I've got to get away from those people. I thought that if I took this trip that I'd either figure out something or I never would. But I know that I'm going to move. Tomorrow we're going to hike down into the Grand Canyon, though, right?" she says, turning to Karla, who has stopped listening and is looking through her handbag.

Ironically, it is the tourist's mobility that offers an occasion for stabilizing a conception of a self through stories told to strangers. In the changing social contexts and geographies of travel, people confront continual possibilities for "authoring" a self. It is a time when the relationship among strangers is shaped through dialogue and narratives that reach for connections and explanations to the disconnected events of their lives. Mikhail Bahktin conceives of human life as based in movement, action, and speaking, where "responding to the environment, being able to answer it, is life itself."[11] Jose's and Peg's accounts of life on the road describe a time of emergent identities and provisional answers as their voices land in the ears of strangers. In the ambiguity and anonymity that come with occupying foreign terrain, travel yields the circumstances for confronting others (and "otherness") and arriving at provisional answers to fundamental questions—Who are you? Where are you going? Where have you been?—that speak to the immediacy of the journey and the broader path of a life. The Squire Inn lounge is little more than one pit stop for Jose, Peg, and Karla, but it also evokes what Bakhtin calls a chronotope of "the road," where time "thickens, takes on flesh" and "space becomes charged and responsive to the movements of time, plot and history." As a metaphor and a real location of random and accidental encounters for people who may otherwise live at social and spatial distances, "the road" is where "human fates and lives combine with one another in distinctive ways. . . . They become more complex and concrete by the collapse of *social distances*," notes Bakhtin. Time "fuses together with space and flows in it (forming the road); this is the source of the rich metaphorical expansion on the image of the road as a course: 'the course of a life,' 'to set out on a new course,' 'the course of history' and so on. . . . Its fundamental pivot is the flow of time."[12]

Accounting for the journeys that brought them to the canyon and this fortuitous meeting along the road, Peg and Jose each reckoned with life in a "culture of come and go." Their brief encounter opened onto other roads and lives, coming together and coming apart, and coming to terms with the passing of times, people, homes, and the private history each thought worth telling to a willing stranger. In different ways, both appear as prosaic and ironic figures drawn from an allegory about "traveling cultures" where, as anthropologist and cultural critic James Clifford observes, people are "more or less permanently in transit," and the appropriate question is "not so much 'where are you from?' but 'where are you between?'" When the self-described "gypsy" from Pittsburgh said, "I know that I'm going to move," it seemed less a plan for her return to Pittsburgh than a sincere account of a life she'd been living for years. A Mexican-American window washer from Louisville bearing a German surname races across the Navajo Nation on his Japanese motorcycle, pausing to photograph a traditional native hiding from a stranger's camera while a pack of curs surrounds him, only later finds that he is himself mistaken for an Indian by the authorities. Although their journeys are, to some extent, circumscribed by their gender, class, or ethnicity, Peg and Jose's tales seem distant from the potent images and the deeply conflicted dramas of immigration, exile, and escape from oppressive regimes, of people moving through "specific colonial, neo-colonial, and postcolonial circuits, diasporas, borderlands, exiles, detours and returns" that critics so often employ to stake out the terms of "culture *as* travel."[13] Compared to the sobering realities of such politicized images of displacement, Peg and Jose embody an altogether different mystery: two strangers far from home who retrieve images of home by confiding in each other in a motel lounge a few miles from the edge of the Grand Canyon. They speak a language of lives thriving beneath the surface and ambiguity of leisure. Alone with each other, they piece out the details. At this crossroads that neither could have anticipated, they describe lives holding little time for keeping track of the relationship among events, tell one another of the steady trudge through the consistently ordinary. They are better than that, they know, and that is enough reason to run from it all one day, and then turn around and head back for more of the same.

When I read visitor comments and listen to the tourists call up stories at the canyon, they often point to the simple idea that we know and value all things through contrast. Poised before a blank sheet of paper or sitting across from a stranger, they confront an emptiness and silence—as wide and free as the canyon they have come to see. Here, the many roads they've taken to the Grand Canyon can appear as a literal site and a potent metaphor for dual passages, a simultaneous discovery of a region and a self. Their journey may cut across a particular geography, but it is also a "redemptive experience occurring not in space but in another dimension, inner or spiritual," as literary critic Janis Stout suggests, with a "capacity for mirroring the inner and outer dimensions that makes possible the 'inward voyage' . . . in which movement through the geographical world becomes an analog for the process of introspection."[14] Here, tourists stand before the epochs displayed in stone—geologic time, God's handiwork—living in the cleared-out blocks on calendars and daily planners, somewhere between a departure and return, watches adjusted to local clocks, grappling with the meaning of their free time. "My most serious concerns, my daily worries, my business, my career, are really so minor," writes one visitor. "I must learn to experience & enjoy my short time on earth rather than just endure it and find that it has passed into time as the rocks of the Grand Canyon." They are brief offerings, symbolic stagings of self and a remaking of the world. "I feel so small and insignificant," writes another, "The river solved its problems. I can solve mine." Here, there is no definitive "here," apart from what marks where the land suddenly drops off for a time of dwelling in metaphors and symbols.

Upside-Down Time

Tourism is a flight from the routines and practices of everyday life. But it is also a place and time for critically reflecting on the ambiguity and dissatisfactions of daily life. Henri Lefebvre argues that leisure experience is a compensation for everyday life, providing an "inverse-image" inherently recalling—and offering a critical stance toward—the routine worlds people attempt to escape. As people seek an "end to fatigue and tension," a place for "relaxation," and what is sometimes absent or obscured in the worlds of work, family, and private life, "a 'world of leisure' tends to develop, a world which is purely artificial, ideal, and outside of daily life," he says. "But how can such an artificial world be created without constant reference to everyday life and the changing contrasts implied by it?" Such contrasts appear throughout the comments left in registers and in the conversations and anecdotes tourists share with me and one another. In many ways, they exemplify and model how a sphere of leisure can "contain in themselves a spontaneous critique of daily life," as Lefebvre suggests. "No one can leave daily life behind. The marvelous can only be maintained in the agreed upon fictions and illusions. Escape is impossible. Yet we desire to have close to us—at arm's reach, if possible—the illusion of escape. This illusion is not entirely illusory, but constitutes a 'world' both apparent and real (the reality of appearance and the appearance of reality). This illusion is something other than daily life, and yet it is as wide open and as integrated into daily life as possible." As canyon tourists actively engage the landscape, they produce visions of time and space where their lives are reframed, reimagined, and reinvented. Yet, their efforts often hinge on coordinates recasting the deep imprint of everyday life and pressing it into the contexts of leisure time.

Lefebvre's conception of leisure as an inverse image of family, work, and daily life aims toward the ways people remystify their worlds and come to inhabit fictions that may compensate for experiential vacancies and aspire toward cultural myths, ideals, ideologies, and popular fantasies. This seemed the case, at least, for a forty-three-year-old engineering professor from Michigan who sat next to me on a park shuttle one evening. "Driving west, I feel like I'm conquering the land even though I know it's been conquered," he said. "I just don't feel that way driving east," he added. His comment is a reminder, perhaps, that tourists are not lost in some realm of false consciousness about their endeavors. Rather, their journeys become a site for reviving images and growing stories, rehearsing practices and spontaneous performances, and awakening glimpses of self, family, culture, productivity, knowledge, and experience not manifested in the familiar contexts of home or work. Lefebvre points to the thousands of "Sunday painters" he sees in France as examples of how painting had become "an art of the masses." It is a leisure activity, he says, that exceeds technical skill and instead recaptures "the whole of life through a particular form of expression. Leisure then involves an original search (regardless of whether it is skillful or awkward) for a lifestyle. Perhaps, an art of living and happiness."[15] Like the Sunday painters he describes, canyon tourists appear along the rim, at campgrounds, as characters of their own stories and performances, photos and videotapes, as if painting themselves into a landscape that is both real and illusory.

At Mather Campground, domestic life reasserts itself beneath the pines. Early evening finds visitors in campsites cooking supper with portable propane stoves while others wait and read the newspaper. Now and then, I see people sitting on lawn chairs, doing crossword puzzles, reading and watching small-screen televisions. The campground is a series of loop roads with numbered sites; some have drive-through parking spaces. Other than trees or boulders, no formal boundaries distinguish one campsite from another. The placement of a tent, a camper, bicycles, or the car draw lines separating

one site from another. A retired couple staying in the site a few spaces down has a wooden sign hanging from the awning attached to their pop-up trailer. "The Calloways," it reads in cursive letters, "Henry-Margaret." A few others have written their family names on paper plates and hung them on a tree or a stick near the road.

When the German family staying at the campsite next to mine drives to Babbit's for some groceries, I stroll over and take a look around. Behind the screen door of their big umbrella tent they've arranged sleeping bags and pillows; the adults sleep in two bags zipped together, and their children's smaller bags—both covered with a fabric displaying cartoon characters—lay off to the side. Two duffel bags placed end to end in the middle of the tent make a low wall and separate the parents from the children. Outside, the pine-needle carpet of their campsite takes on a recognizable floor plan. Two vacant aluminum lawn chairs face a cold firepit. A camp stove is at one end of the picnic table. A red plastic cooler sits on the bench next to the stove, and a plastic tub with a bottle of Ivory liquid dish soap is on the other side. This end of the picnic table is the "kitchen." The rest of the table is covered with a yellow vinyl tablecloth; four stones hold down the corners. Three days ago, I watched them put it all together. The father set up the tent with his nine-year-old son while the mother and six-year-old daughter unloaded their silver Toyota Camry and set up the stove. With the tent up, she pulled out the sleeping bags and set them inside. The father and son took an empty five-gallon jug to get water. Over the past few days, the children have made friends with the children on our loop, who are from Indiana. They run through the trees before dinner. We don't speak except to say hello. We wave from our picnic tables.

Last night, my German neighbor came over with a road atlas and asked me if I knew anything about Bryce Canyon in Utah. They were going there in the morning. He had been living in Durham, North Carolina, doing a postdoctoral fellowship, and his wife, who was washing the dinner dishes while we talked, had come over with their children to travel the United States. I showed him an unpaved road, west of Big Water, Utah, that would take him to Kodachrome Basin and on to Bryce. He liked the idea of getting off Route 89 and circled the detour with a pencil. I told him to make sure he had plenty of gas and a spare tire. At first, he looked alarmed at the potential for difficulty, but his face brightened when I said that was just a precaution and assured him they would be fine if they took it slow.

"You are fortunate to be on your own," he said to me, as we pored over the route, deciding again and again he would go that way the next morning. "It must be nice to go where you want without having to take care of a family. It seems very free."

"Actually, I'm not going anywhere," I said, and told him I was at the canyon working on a book. Coincidentally, I had been watching him and his family with some envy. He was in his mid-thirties; his wife was about the same age, athletic and attractive. She spoke bits and pieces of English. The couple always seemed to be talking and laughing together with their children. Unlike their campsite, mine was empty except for my old Timberline tent. While they were eating a hot meal for dinner, I had been making my way through a bag of Doritos and a cellophaned flat of potato salad from Babbit's. His wife came over to my table when she finished the dishes and offered me a cup of coffee. I discussed my canyon project, and he showed his wife the route I recommended they take to Bryce. She nodded in agreement, and they told me about their plans to go to Yellowstone, the Grand Tetons, and then back to North Carolina. When we finished our coffee, they returned to their camp and, in lawn chairs beneath the clear night sky, talked quietly and drank wine from paper cups.

This morning, the German family is taking down their tent and packing up to leave; the Indiana family across the road is doing the same. I listen as the boy helps his father with the last of their luggage. He sounds sad to be leaving the canyon.

"Where are we going now?" he asks his father.

"To the Petrified Forest," the father replies. "Where are your friends going?" The boy tells him—to a place called "Rice Canyon." "*Bryce,*" says the father. "It's *Bryce* Canyon. . . . Well, at least you had some good times playing with them here." The boy says little as his father cinches a rope over two suitcases on top of their Bronco. With everything loaded, the family gets inside. The boy is carrying a stick he'd stripped all the bark from with a pocketknife earlier that morning. He hangs out the window and waves at the German children. The German parents wave to the Indiana parents. I hear a toot from the Bronco's horn and wave, too. Indiana grins and flashes me a hearty "thumbs up" as they pass.

After a few days, the campground loops feel like a suburban neighborhood, except everyone here seems genuinely happy. Faces become familiar, then disappear with little notice. New license plates, tents, trailers, and faces arrive. In the evenings, I smell smoke and hot dogs, steaks, and chicken broiling on grills. In the morning, I smell smoke and bacon. Without front doors to knock on or doorbells to ring, people awkwardly manage to approach strangers; they stand on the road or talk loudly to each other through trees and over bushes before they determine whether it's all right to move closer, to cross the provisional property lines. They'll notice a license plate from their home state ("What part of Texas do you come from?") or make some innocuous inquiry ("How do you like that Coleman pop-up [camper]?"), and this will break the anonymity and get the talk rolling. "It's so different here," a woman from Queens said, while we waited to fill our water jugs at the campground tap. "Don't you find everyone is so friendly? They come up to you and say hello. At home it's just rush, rush. Everyone walks past you with their head down." She voiced an awareness of a renewed social life springing up in the campground loops: an openness toward others in a public space, a peeling away of life's shields and masks, a calling up of some residual, bucolic memory of waving across the valley or leaning over the neighbor's fence. It is a space for tentative and brief encounters, often starting from a basic and unspoken premise: "Aren't we all out here managing fairly well beneath the pines without the conveniences?" Posted warnings, however, advise keeping an eye on valuables and locking cars; contact is measured, polite, and transient.

Life on the loop roads is one of mobility and change. Watching the Indiana family leave, I realized I didn't learn their names, nor those of the German family. The man strolls over to say good-bye and good luck as they get ready to drive off, and we shake hands for the first and last time. His wife stands between an open car door and the front seat, waving over the roof. "Bye," she says and smiles. An Econoline van with Maryland license plates pulls into the space just vacated by the Indiana campers. A family of six piles out, looks around the site, locks the van's doors; they all head straight for the restrooms. I wave again as the Germans drive away in their Camry. I walk through the empty campsite next to mine and see traces of where they pitched their tent. The ground holds a faint impression from the weight of sleeping bodies. Four stones lay on the picnic table, the ones they used to keep their tablecloth in place. The yellow vinyl is folded and stowed, on its way to a table in Bryce Canyon, and it no longer covers the carved and written names, initials, dates, hometowns, and countries of those who had camped here before. Except for the stones on the table, nothing remained of the German family's three-day stay.

"Camping is a temporary ordering of impermanence," writes Eric Leed. "In camping, we give our selves up to the land again. This experience makes us Americans rather than anything else. It is, moreover, the source of that 'complete wildness beneath utter regulation.'"[16] Few would argue that Mather Campground is a rule-governed and monitored facility. Many people reserve spaces in advance and others wait in line at the entry station, hoping for a cancellation or an early departure. Typically, park campgrounds are full by 10:00 in the morning. The park service has made it easy to be relatively comfortable at Mather Campground. Each site has a picnic table and firepit with a grill. Water taps are available on every loop, despite the absence of a natural source of water on the South Rim. Restrooms with flush toilets and sinks, garbage dumpsters, trash cans, pay phones, ice machines, public coin-operated showers, a laundry, a general store (with supermarket and deli counter), and a cafeteria are all within walking distance. A separate trailer park with electric and water hookups is nearby for motorhomes and trailers. Yet, apart from these amenities, the campground becomes a revolving stage where a wildness awakens in people as they build their fires. Men balance on haunches, stare into flames and smoke, and poke at burning logs; they cook animal flesh on these grills, and the dripping fat on hot coals shoots flames into the air. The surrounding forest is virtually picked clean of firewood, but campers buy bundles of split wood at Babbit's, haul it back to camp, and burn it when they are together with the family at night. Some split the wood again just to use the hatchets and axes they've brought from home. Young boys will sit alone, feverishly scraping bark from logs with pocketknives, completely focused on whittling a stick to a sharp point. Camping may be a practical and economical way to travel, but it also offers a time to pare down life to essentials, only to start fresh and put it back together again in a new shape. Laying claim to their rented patch of land and imposing order on a "wild" space, the empty campsites can seem like desert islands waiting for Crusoes from cities and suburbs.

The time people spend working in their campsites, making "improvements," and building little projects offers a way of connecting with the land quite different from the contemplative distance often associated with natural landscapes. "Someone had left all of these logs at our campsite," said Carol, a thirty-eight-year-old woman from Utah, recounting her canyon vacation. "We spent a lot of time rearranging the logs, putting them on top of each other. . . . We rolled them and made a pattern of the logs around the campfire. This was to make that spot more of a utilitarian spot. We also rebuilt the firepit during the time we were there. Sometimes I just do clean-up work, and it seems to me that we spent a lot of time doing that kind of thing." Describing her camp activities, she fastens on the value of practical efforts aimed at remaking a functional space. For many families, setting up and managing a campsite is a joint project. Everyone may, ideally, share the effort and work together to do nothing less than erect a dwelling, together, and take care of it. In many cases, these activities merely reproduce familiar gendered divisions that exist at home. For instance, men often build fires, women prepare meals and complete domestic chores, and children gather firewood, fill water jugs, help set up a tent, clean up the camp, and work side by side with a parent. Campsites are spaces of temporary occupation, arenas for mutual and ongoing performances where people revisit and reconfigure conventional and admired American values for efficiency, practicality, and a work ethic. "It changes your ideas about space and time, and how you perceive your life," Carol added. "Often when you're in a routine and you do all the same things all the time—I don't know about you—but I feel like life just carries me, and I really like to be able to go places and take the time to recenter myself." In part, Carol's reframing of space, time, life, and "recentering" means exercising some of the same old practices in a new environment to clarify the meanings of her efforts. Making a camp below the tall pines may offer some satisfaction because it provides a set of activities reuniting effort and energy toward an immediate and tangible reward. The accounts of people who leave the rim and backpack into the canyon's depths similarly suggest how hiking and camping help retrieve conventional practices, structures, and ideals that permeate daily life.

"Part of what I find enjoyable [in backpacking] is the whole process of packing and shopping and seeing how efficient I can be, and how much more efficient I can be than on the last trip," said a forty-two-year-old woman as she recounted a three-day, twenty-four-mile hike from the North Rim to the South Rim. "Like if I took an extra pot, I won't bring it this time. As far as food goes, I'll buy freeze-dried food and see if I can judge it exactly. Like on this Grand Canyon trip, we ate everything. We wasted nothing, except one bag of tortillas, which is pretty good." Lightening the load of her pack has an obvious benefit, considering that she has to carry it through the inner canyon's heat and harsh terrain. But she also notes how her skill, experience, and competence in backcountry camping are sources of pleasure because they offer a context for confirming her sense of efficiency, planning, and judgment. Many canyon hikers implied that self-reliance and personal accountability were valuable by-products of the effort and stamina they expended on hikes in the canyon's backcountry. "It's nice to know that you're depending on yourself for what you have in there [the inner canyon]," another hiker told me. "And that means blaming yourself, too."

Carrying food, water, clothing, first aid, and camping equipment through a desert environment, hikers face temperatures frequently exceeding one hundred degrees Fahrenheit. Natural water sources are nearly nonexistent, and heat stroke and hypothermia are an ever-present danger. Park service rangers respond to more than four hundred medical emergencies in the canyon each year. In 1996 alone, they performed nearly five hundred search-and-rescue operations, and approximately two hundred of those were heat-related. "We have at least one death a year because a person hasn't had enough water," said one backcountry ranger. In 1996, four people died (two were children) from complications due to heat exhaustion. "People have to realize that hiking the canyon is dangerous," he said. "Heat exhaustion is a daily event here in the summer."

For many hikers, however, the harsh environment presents a challenge registering rewards in an unmediated fashion, organically, in the body itself. "For one thing, it's very physical and your adrenaline is pumping and it feels good to work your body," noted Joan, a forty-one-year-old medical clerk who had hiked the Bright Angel Trail. "You can just let your mind go in physical work that's strenuous." My interview took place in her Salt Lake City office during a lunch break, where she suggested that the

physical effort of hiking held a sense of accountability not present in her daily job. "Daily work here is more complicated and you don't always get what you work for. You get paid, of course. But it never seems enough for what you do," she told me. "You can be using a computer to do a letter and you can lose it like that. There are headaches and little things that are beyond my control. But when I'm out in nature, and work is only physical, well, I feel like I'm more in control because I'm the only one there." Unlike the time spent behind an office word processor, hiking the canyon's trails offers an opportunity for autonomy. Joan's daily work at the office is translated into a wage, but the energy she expends on the trail offers direct and clear rewards.

Although the canyon's trails may liberate visitors from the routines and alienating dimensions of their jobs and careers, the familiar hierarchies and social differentiations may also reappear. A couple who hiked into the canyon from the Havasupai Indian Reservation, for instance, said their efforts seemed undermined by the people who rode horses and hired others to carry their equipment for them. "We packed all our own gear and food in," said Cheryl, a twenty-eight-year-old college student, "so we were feeling rather superior to the other tourists who were having the Indians carry their stuff down. . . . One group had like twenty bottles of Catalina salad dressing in their packs. You can't help but criticize." For Cheryl, such luxuries and conveniences were signs of incompetence. "We're a little bit more purist about it than that," said John, her thirty-year-old companion. "We're used to working hard at it. It seemed like most of the people that went down there were pretty amateur. We do this a lot, and it seemed like a lot of people that were there were the kind of people that would go on a cruise ship or something. . . . You kind of resent that because you're working hard to get down there, and your back is sore and your legs are tired. You're working hard so you can get to this nice place that most people don't get to," he said. The people he saw on the trail riding horses were "taking the easy way in" and probably wouldn't be able to do it otherwise. "You'd have a more solitary experience if there were not this possibility of horses taking your stuff down. If people were willing to do a little work like we were, it would be a lot nicer down there. Instead, you have all these people taking the lazy way out. It sort of infringes on our pleasure." Side by side, on horse and on foot, the value of work holds dual meanings in their story. The tourists riding horses and hiring porters he complains about are symbols of a commodified leisure, and Cheryl and John seek out a solitude that only seems to become tainted with reminders of economic exchange. They want to separate themselves from other "mere" tourists who could just as well have bought a packaged cruise. And in all of this, they lay claim to their physical abilities and a level of "work experience" that only comes from time spent refining their skills on previous hikes.

Frank, a sixty-two-year-old retired real-estate agent from Miami, equally noted how self-sufficiency, skills, and schedules were deeply tied to his canyon hiking. When I met him, he was about to begin a fourteen-day trek, starting on the South Rim and taking him to remote areas near the park's eastern boundary. He had been coming to Grand Canyon since 1970 and hiked hundreds of miles in areas where he sees "no one's footprints except my own." He said he avoided heavily used trails where most summer tourists hike. "My first time here, I did what most people do. I hiked the Bright Angel Trail—the tourist trail, that's the *corridor*. But I did it just to check and see what kind of equipment I'd be needing. That was the basis of that trip, see?" For Frank, hiking the canyon means getting away from the crowds. "It's not a glamorous thing. . . . When I get out there, I see nobody. It's not like Disney World. You can always find a crowd there. I've never been to Disney World. A lot of people take the airplanes and helicopters to see the canyon. They're happy that way, I guess. They can buy T-shirts that say 'I Hiked the Canyon,' but they may not have taken one foot down into the canyon. It's all a matter of their own values. Vanity. I think that's what they call that." Although Frank said he seeks the canyon's solitude, he most often characterized it as a place where work and pleasure went hand in hand.

"It's a beautiful feeling to get down off that rim," he said. "You go down, and you sit up and you plan. You know how it is. You plan your work and you work your plan. It's the same thing here. I keep a notebook on all the stuff I do. I do it on a time basis. The watch is very important. Most people say you shouldn't take a watch when you go into the canyon because it reminds you of civilization. But I say no. A watch is important. It tells you your progress, or if something is going wrong, or if you're slowing down, or if you're going too fast. It helps you to plan what you're going to do. You've got to hike so many miles in a day. Sometimes I'll start at seven in the morning and go until eleven at night. I'll hike in the dark, but I can do that very well. I'm experienced." Like the public campgrounds on the South Rim, where visitors remake an image of domestic life with tents and trailers, hiking into the canyon offers an opportunity to recover physical abilities, practice technical skills, and find visions of selves unnoticed or unrecognized in the flow of everyday work and life. But in these accounts, the separation between work and leisure is a blurry one and generally points to the difficulties people have in thinking of themselves outside a sphere of productivity.

Another hiker emphasized how the categories giving value to people's everyday lives also permeate the context of leisure. "Sometimes I like luxurious vacations. But my father says that he really likes vacations where you're doing as much as you can," Katherine, a twenty-two-year-old student, told me while recounting a recent canyon hike she'd made with her father. She said their trek from the North Rim to the South Rim was similar to a Hawaiian vacation with her father, when they had spent much of their time climbing volcanoes and snorkeling. "We were always doing something. I think it has a lot to do with that work ethic. You're taking a vacation, but at the same time it feels like you *have to be doing something*. I don't know how to analyze my father, but with him it seems like when we travel that we should always be doing something productive and not just 'vegging out.'" Although Katherine leveled her complaints toward her father, she eventually described similar tendencies in herself. "As far as these 'back-to-nature vacations' go," she said, referring to her rim-to-rim hike, "I enjoy them somewhat during the trip but usually more afterward. I really like cultural vacations because I really like art, history, and literature. So for me, I feel as though I'm in my element. And on those luxurious vacations, when I'm luxuriating, I usually read. And when I read, I never read junk, so I guess I'm almost always doing something productive."

A difficulty in distinguishing "vegging out" from legitimate and productive questions of taste, culture, education, and personal growth only recalls how the cultural remnants of an American work ethic have been part and parcel of "leisure time" since the nineteenth century. At face value, the merits of discipline, industry, and planning appearing in many of these comments point to an ambivalence, perhaps a sense of loss, in the idea of leisure as a distinctly separate sociotemporal space reserved for relaxation, luxury, and idleness. Leisure and work have never entirely held oppositional definitions or distinctive spheres of meaning and experience. "The idea that work offers more satisfaction than alternative pursuits can supply intensifies the problem of leisure" historically, notes Patricia Meyer Spacks in her literary history of boredom. The nineteenth-century idea of freedom from work to "pursue happiness" has little to do with "a concept of leisure as a space for recreation"; instead, it often bears on "the notion of the contemplative life as the noblest human occupation. . . . To perceive leisure as a 'problem' entails awareness of emotional danger in idleness."[17] Bourgeois reformers thought that "leisure was less the bountiful territory in which to site Utopia, than some dangerous frontier zone beyond the law and order of respectable society," argues Peter Bailey. By the mid-nineteenth century, the abuse of leisure "had imprinted itself most deeply in middle-class consciousness; in a work-oriented culture [leisure] represented an invitation to idleness and dissolution—the weakness of an ill-disciplined working class."[18] Marx's depiction of bourgeois attitudes toward leisure paint a somber portrait of pleasure and recreation, notes Chris Rojek. It is "something subordinated to production. . . . It is a *calculated* and, therefore, itself an *economical* pleasure." Leisure was essentially a debit-column entry of the bourgeois expense account, wrote Marx, and "what is squandered on his pleasure must therefore amount to no more than will be replaced with profit through the reproduction of capital."[19]

For a nineteenth-century middle class, these sentiments most often found public dissemination in self-improvement guides, manuals, and articles that placed moral virtues in a realm of economic industriousness and prosperity.[20] Prescribing the uses of free time, cultural leaders often recommended activities centered on personal growth, self-fulfillment, and a general pursuit of self-culture. Of course, the social terrain of leisure offered different possibilities and constraints for men and women of that century. Where elite men experienced a freedom to join intellectual societies or develop their physical prowess through sports and outdoor activities to fend off the effects of "overcivilization," working-class men and women of the same period saw leisure as a refuge and escape, a sphere of social opportunities, class affiliations, and mass cultural amusements more clearly separated from the context of daily labor and an ethos of personal development and productivity.[21] These campers and hikers, however, merely acknowledge how ideals of work and productivity historically permeate the sphere of leisure time. Although distant from these twentieth-century Grand Canyon tourists, nineteenth-century attitudes toward leisure remind us how a traditional work ethic promising individual fulfillment and reward also leaves absences that people seek to satisfy in their free time. Ironically, it is in accounts of people seeking landscapes absent of regulation or structure that familiar images of order, industriousness, and personal effort reappear as crucial touchstones of identity.

When the retired real-estate agent descends into the canyon, it is with the ambition to plan his work and work his plan. Over the years, Frank cached plastic half-gallon jugs of water in case of need during an emergency. "You can't fill them all the way, because they'll freeze in the winter," he said. "But if I run out, I know where they are and I'll be all set." Built into each hike is the potential return; his water cache anticipates not only the prospect of trouble but that he will be putting himself, again, into a situation where life is hard and things can go wrong. This is part of his plan, too. Frank says he roams the canyon's desolate regions summer after summer, for fourteen days at a time, only because that is the amount of time his backcountry permit allows. "I hike in the summer because I have a longer day," he says. "In the winter, it's cooler, but by five o'clock it's pitch black out and you can't do anything. What can you do at five o'clock? But, me, I have sun. It's hotter, but I can go to eight-thirty or nine in the evening. I can still move around. Set up my camp. Do something." His taking a watch into the canyon seemed less a necessity for survival than a sign of the difficulty he had living on any other terms. "If I get to my camp early, I find myself doing something. I don't know what it is, but you have this desire to read something down there. Like if you have the instructions that come with your film, you might start reading that thing over and over again. It's something to read. This is some sort of a primal instinct, this desire to read; I don't know what it is."

What Frank suspects is a primal instinct is, more likely, an incarnation of boredom and the ambiguity of being with oneself without any clear sense of obligation or purpose. Reading the directions from his film package, I suspect, was only an attempt to fill a gap in time and a one-time affair. Like Katherine, it was in response to a vague need to be productive. "This friend suggested I take a tape device to play Beethoven down there," he said. "But I'd never do that. I'm afraid I'd saturate myself with Beethoven and wouldn't want to hear it anymore. You'd hear it all the time. Besides, you can only carry so many tapes. If a guy was to take a tape player with him, he'd have to have batteries, and the dust would get in it. If something goes wrong and you can't use, it's dead weight you've got to carry. I like Beethoven, but it's not conducive to the trip. There's enough down there I can hear." Instead, Frank had started carrying a paperback edition of Shakespeare's *Richard III* on his solitary excursions into the canyon's depths.

"After hiking for so many days, my mind is clear and I can read Shakespeare cleverly," he said. "Since you're all alone, you can start spouting out loud all those lines right out of the book. No one's going to bother you, no one will laugh at you. I understand it pretty well. It's involved, of course, because it's written in the Shakespearean English, and you have to know what you're reading. One of the best is *Richard III,* because it starts out as a real tragedy and then it's comedic. This guy is such a rat, you have to laugh at him. It's lightweight and I can carry it easily. But when you're away from civilization there's an urge. And that is one of the symbols of civilization, a book. Like the library. If you go to a town and there's a library, well that's a civilized town. You can't say that about everyplace. . . . But you can really shout out loud, shout out Shakespeare out in this canyon. There's one place where you can really hear an echo. You can shout there, shout out 'King Richard'—even call yourself all kinds of dirty names—and wait a few seconds; they all come back at you. And then I say back to them, 'I'll get you for that!'" Frank said, laughing, "It's just one of those things. You do all kinds of crazy things."

Frank seems to speak for many of the canyon's campers and hikers. Whether they are towing trailers or pitching tents in Mather Campground, or hoofing up and down trails under the hot desert sun, their flight from routine lives finds them remaking and reliving features of the world left behind. Frank's decision not to haul a tape player and cassettes of Beethoven's symphonies into the canyon was, in part, a practical decision rather than an outright disavowal of a need for distractions. What he called an "urge" and "primal instinct" only recognized, in some small way, how his quest for solitude involved a desire and opportunity to make a place over on his own terms. The watch and paperback copy of *Richard III* offer a partial index to a world he will not—or cannot—leave behind. I believe part of the pleasure and meaning he finds in the canyon is in pouring himself out into the canyon, finding in it his reflection, and, in turn, having the harsh conditions and struggles of the canyon trails remake him.

Traces of everyday life run through these accounts, and it is the value of the struggles, skills, and abilities awakened in these activities that they testify to most often. These features rise to the surface in their stories (perhaps more than while undergoing the actual events), images of a self full of values and qualities that have been restored because they have undergone some difficult trial or circumstances. "You do all kinds of crazy things," Frank had said. The proverbial lone cry in the wilderness playfully sounds with both longing and satisfaction. It is the echo of his own voice, one that he could hear in no other way if not for working his plan, carrying the weight over tough terrain. He stands alone, shouting into the acoustic curve of the rock walls, speaking not only as a king but insulting himself with "dirty names" as well. These are two sides of a man who, in verbally maligning himself one moment and exalting himself the next, seems to speak for the many who put themselves out of their comforts and into the canyon's hot and dusty depths.

Every day during the summer, hundreds of people (often more than a thousand) take Bright Angel Trail into the canyon. The one-way distance to the Colorado River is nearly eight miles with an elevation change of 4,420 feet. They are in good spirits with gravity as their ally, and they laugh and joke. On the steep hike back up, each ounce they carry will seem to double in weight. The pace of those making their way out is often reduced to a shuffle. I see many of them on the trail, with crimson faces full of heat, bandannas tied around their heads and necks, half-moons of sweat beneath their armpits, wondering why they have done this. It was so easy going down. Now, they stand resting, looking up toward the rim. They'll build up a stride, go the length of a switchback, and stop again. Measure the next length of trail. Compare the distance covered with what is left to go. Take a drink of water. Begin again. For those overweight and out of shape, the physical exertion is not like anything they could have imagined. And with the end of the trail not really in clear view, hiking out of the canyon sometimes means mounting psychological pressures. They measure their lack of progress against those who pass them on the way up. They become envious and angry over their predicament. Emotions flare. "It's just around the next bend," I hear a young woman coax her mother. "Just shut up," Mother snaps back. "You've been saying this for the past mile," and she grudgingly tries again.

"It's not unusual to see people on the trail after dark, sometimes it's after midnight. There are emergency phones on the Bright Angel [trail] and this summer we've had emergency calls nearly every night," a park emergency medical technician told me. "We try to determine what state they're in because we don't have the staff to run down to everyone. Someone might call and say a member of their party can't make it up. A lot of times what they need is some food and water. Even if they are carrying it, it doesn't mean they've been drinking and eating." With a staff of approximately ten rangers available for emergency calls on the heavily used Bright Angel corridor, park personnel say they often have to sort through symptoms over the phone before determining what kind of aid is necessary. Since emergency phones were installed on the trail, the number of calls has increased. "We don't want to discourage people from getting help," he told me. "But a helicopter rescue costs a minimum of eleven hundred dollars. We don't use that as a tool, but sometimes it's necessary, and hikers have to foot the bill for that."

At the park's backcountry office, rangers try to educate hikers about the difficulties as well as the pleasures of summer hiking and overnight backpacking in the canyon. "Often, what most people need is a lot of psychological support. Hiking is very mental, especially when it is difficult like the canyon," a ranger tells the hikers who have assembled to pick up permits for their overnight trips. "There's no magic mule that's going to come and carry you out. Sometimes you'll just have to talk yourself into getting out. Think about a reservation that's waiting for you at one of the restaurants, or that favorite nonalcoholic drink you've got waiting in a cooler in the trunk of your car." Later, after the hikers picked up their permits and headed for the trailhead, the ranger told me about some of the cases they deal with on the trails. "There are some people who just aren't prepared," he said. "They'll leave the rim with a few candy bars and try to hike to the river and back in one day. When we do answer a call, we find that some of them suffer from what we call 'water intoxication.' They've had too much water but not enough food. They've flushed out their body salts and electrolytes. You have to drink water on the trail, but you also need to replenish body salts with Gatorade and trail mix." Victims of heat exhaustion and water intoxication have highly elevated body temperatures, diminished consciousness and speak incoherently. "They usually don't know where they are," said the ranger. "They think they're in their home state or maybe hiking somewhere in the mountains. They don't know what day it is. If you ask them—'Who is the president of the United States?'—they can't tell you." In an effort to warn hikers of such dangers, the park service has mounted a campaign aimed at cutting down on the numbers of people who head into the canyon unprepared. They've put educational posters with the slogan "Heat Kills—Hike Smart" throughout the park and in visitor centers and shops throughout northern Arizona. They run public-service announcements on radio stations. And on the trails, they've posted stop signs telling hikers to turn around if they are not prepared to continue. Yet, it is against a backdrop of such dangers that the canyon offers a challenge; the struggles, difficulties, and even the potential for death are what bring so many hikers to life on the trail.

"We wanted to go down into the canyon because of our adventurous spirit," recalled a thirty-eight-year-old California woman. "We had no food or water and were not prepared to go down. We didn't realize that it could be dangerous hiking down without being prepared. We were willing to take the risk." She and her companion intended to hike only a few hours, but the closer they went toward the river, the more they wanted to keep going. "We finally decided to go all the way to the bottom, even if we didn't have the necessary things to make the trip down safely. . . . Once we were there we decided to sleep there. We didn't have a permit, but that didn't bother us in the least. That night was one of the most memorable ones. The moonlight lit up the Colorado River. If I close my eyes now I can still see the picture vividly. The next day we went back up. We were hungry, thirsty, tired, dirty, and excited all at the same time because we had a fantastic experience." Her "adventurous spirit" arises in a story about confronting risks and resisting rules. Like others who describe their canyon hikes, her account outlines the obstacles and difficulties its teller has overcome and endured.

Max, a twenty-eight-year-old German medical student said, "I was quite excited, as there was nobody who could help me if I twisted my ankle or something. Timewise I wasn't sure if I could reach the river and make it back to the bus on time." Max did make it back to his bus on time and, like others, was able to tell about it. In a sense, details of potential risk and jeopardy allow for the possibility of constructing a story about perseverance. Rather than emphasizing the destination or scenery, these stories of private conquests foreground the teller's ability to face harsh conditions and emerge triumphant.

"I could just think of putting one foot in front of the other," a twenty-six-year-old New York woman said of her hike to the river. "It was still worse the next day when we had to hike up in the extreme heat. But at the top, it was like a victory. I just made it." A New Jersey man's account of the arid desert hike, filled with fatigue and futility, seems to transform him into a reptile: "This is a long, dry trip which turns excessively hot in the afternoons as the sun beats down directly on you. It is difficult to judge distance in the canyon. You see glimpses of the river at the bottom and then, an hour later, you're still not there. It can be frustrating. At rest stops I had to crawl under a rock to receive some shade and relief from the heat." A forty-year-old Oregon man described his hike in concise and painful detail. "I hiked down the South Kaibab Trail carrying approximately forty pounds. . . . It was dusty, not particularly pretty. My big toes hit the end of my hiking boots. I was in a lot of pain and ended up losing both of my big toenails. Because of the painful stress of walking, I worked double-time trying to hold back. It was exhausting."

Katherine thought "back-to-nature" vacations were more enjoyable after they were over. "One of my motivations for this kind of traveling [hiking across the canyon]," she said, "is to be able to say you've done it. So I guess I'm not a doer for the doing, I'm a doer for the bragging." In different ways, these accounts thrive on a desire to experience something that can become a story. All of them describe scenes requiring some measure of austerity. Of course, their stories vary, as do the severity of the punishments or circumstances they've endured. "To me, the canyon is a challenge," noted one visitor. "I feel a need to go inside it and face the challenges of nature—to feel its vastness and strength." A canyon hiker from Denver wrote in the register, "My first trip down to the Colorado [River] was fantastic—hiking up and down in one day. Now I can sit beside the canyon and I am at peace." Another noted that hiking the canyon "helps me know how much stronger I am as a person than I used to be." From the epic challenge of nature to the challenge of time and body, the canyon is a place of measuring one's worth. A twenty-three-year-old New Hampshire woman eating ice cream on the stone wall after completing her rim-to-rim hike told me about a couple she'd passed on her way up who "weren't having a good time." "They thought it wasn't so great down at Phantom Ranch," she said. "How could they say that? I mean, it's what you make of it. You get out of it what you put into it."

"The Grand Canyon is an equal opportunity place," Antonio tells me one night in the Phantom Ranch canteen. "It treats everyone the same way." Antonio works in the kitchen at Phantom Ranch, fixing meals for the tourists who ride mules to the bottom to spend the night in sparsely furnished cabins. Every afternoon, he watches them arrive, climb off their mules, and test their legs after a day in the saddle. Those on foot find sites at the Bright Angel Campground and then go to Bright Angel Creek to soak their bodies in the cool water. Later, a park ranger comes by to check their permits. At night, a group often assembles around a campfire pit for a ranger talk. Tonight, the ranger discusses the issues of developing access to the inner canyon. "Some people think we ought to build a tram that would make the river more accessible," she says. "It's particularly an issue for handicapped people and the elderly, who might find it too difficult to make the hike in, like you people did today. It's one of those issues that asks us how we want to regard this place. Is this really a wilderness?" We sit silent, considering her question. "Not with pay phones and cold beer," says a joker in the circle, and we laugh. I often heard people making calls from the pay phone near the campground restrooms that began, "Guess where I'm calling you from?"

After the mule riders finish their dinner at the canteen, the dining hall opens up to anyone who is staying at the bottom. Hikers wander over and sit with the mule riders, drink beer or lemonade, talk, play checkers, write out postcards to be postmarked from Phantom Ranch and carried out on a mule. It's a noisy and crowded place, and its difficult to get a seat at one of the long tables. Many people stand around trading stories and anticipating the journey back up to the rim. Despite being strangers, everyone is thrilled to be at the bottom of the Grand Canyon, and they happily affirm this for one another. Their faces are red from the heat and sun; they talk about feeling muscles they did not know they had. And although the idea of being alone in the magical darkness of a canyon night sounds romantic and enticing, the canteen has a swamp cooler and it's comfortable to be inside.

"We have famous people who come here, but they are just like anyone who comes," says Antonio, as he picks up empty cups from a table. "I met Wim Wenders one time . . . you know, the film director? He said there should be more signs in German on the trails down into the canyon. The Germans think they can hike in and out in one day without a problem." Antonio says the director made a special request to the park service about the signs, and that is why they are now written in German. "Candice Bergen came down once, and she was very nice. But that actor, Paul Hogan—you know, 'Crocodile Dundee,' with the big knife?—he was complaining there was a mouse in his cabin. He was afraid of this little mouse in his cabin." These people were not "just like anyone," as Antonio suggested. He remembers Wenders, Bergen, and Hogan. Although he may embellish the details of his encounters with celebrities at Phantom Ranch, the larger point of his story portrays the Grand Canyon as a great equalizer, always blind to the terms of status and success marking people's lives and differentiating them from others in the world above the rim. Of course, the people who hiked and carried their own supplies into the canyon often saw themselves a bit differently than the mule riders who ate their meals in the canteen and slept in air-cooled cabins. Perhaps, as Cheryl and John had said of the horse riders and Indian porters on their way to Havasupai, they were self-consciously "a bit more purist about it than that." But whether hiker or rider, everyone who came down into the canyon could surely see themselves as different from the tourists who lined its edge at the top and looked down into the depths. Many go with a basic plan: leave the tourist crowds behind, walk beyond the postcard views, and seek out the "real" Grand

Canyon. Those who travel the corridor to Bright Angel camp or Phantom Ranch, however, know they will not be alone.

Permits for an overnight stay at the bottom of the canyon typically require a five-month advance reservation. Bright Angel Campground has a capacity for ninety people each night, although rangers tell me they generally "overbook" the campground because they know that some people will cancel or not show up. In 1997, the park service instituted a new backcountry permit-processing fee of twenty dollars and an impact fee of four dollars per hiker per night. The funds raised from the permit processing fee allow the park service to send a twenty-two-minute videocassette, *Hiking the Grand Canyon,* to each permit holder. The park lodges take reservations for Phantom Ranch nearly two years in advance, and it is generally booked to capacity six to eleven months in advance. But for those who go, the institutionalized process of permits and reservations is a small obstacle compared to the canyon's steep trails and heat.

Returning hikers arrive on the plaza outside Bright Angel Lodge during the late morning and afternoon. They are covered with dust from the trail, hot, sweaty, shuffling toward the Fountain for ice cream and soft drinks. This is a daily drama played out on new faces. The trails of the aptly named "Corridor" bring to mind the stark scenery of Beckett's *Waiting for Godot,* of Estragon struggling with his boots: "We always find something, eh," he tells Vladimir, "to give us the impression we exist."[22] And I don't think I'm alone in seeing such drama. Those who do not go down into the canyon sometimes watch the hikers making their way up. They sit perched on the rim daily, looking through binoculars and telescopes at the hikers and mule riders below on the trail, measuring their progress against the canyon's immense stage. Like ancient mythological gods looking down from Olympus, they speak among themselves, witnessing and judging the antlike figures in the course of their journeys. "Wait until they get to the steep section, that will be a surprise," I hear them say. "She'll never make it out before dark at the rate she's going." It is a simple yet deeply rooted drama of descent to a bottom—natural, physical, mental, social—and rising up again, despite the obstacles. And whether the view is from the rim or on the trail amid others making their way out, "nothing exists except in the absolute, there is no symbol, no allusion, everything is presented exhaustively," as Roland Barthes said of the wrestling match. The canyon is an arena of excess gesture, clarity, and passion, an "age-old image of the perfect intelligibility of reality," where finally setting a victorious foot at the top conjures the self-satisfaction and euphoria of men and women who have been "raised for a while above the constitutive ambiguity of everyday situations and placed before the panoramic view of a univocal Nature, in which signs at last correspond to causes, without obstacle, without evasion, without contradiction."[23]

"What a day," says a thin and weary man near me on the stone bench. It is late afternoon, and he has been silent for the past fifteen minutes, legs crossed like a worn-out Buddha, sipping a Mountain Dew. Noticing the red dust covering his tennis shoes, I ask him if he's hiked into the canyon. He pauses and furls his brow as if my question didn't even begin to fathom what he'd just accomplished. "Yes, yes, I did," he says, collecting himself at the edge of his emotions. "And boy, do I feel it. I can barely walk now. I'm just trying to stretch out. I was doing fine when I got to Indian Gardens, and I thought that I may as well try to make the river. But that was a mistake. It's a lot tougher going out." He is a computer-systems analyst in Texas, and this is the end of his one-week vacation. "I pretty much work alone, and it's a stressful job. I'm sitting all the time and . . . I guess I was thinking this hike would be, you know, an adventure, the high point of the trip. Probably should've done some training to get ready. It's my last day, and I thought 'why not?' I've seen people come up who are older than me. I'm going to need a vacation after this vacation," he says, shaking his head over the hackneyed paradox of a vacation that exhausts, of anticipating a high point to the trip that only sends him down. It's a tough hike, I tell him, and say his legs would feel better in the morning, even though I know otherwise. He quietly smokes his pipe, taps the soda can on the bench, and stares off into the memory of his afternoon. "They ought to have a register down there, at the river," he says. "So you can kind of check in."

"Like a book, so you can sign your name?" I say.

"Yeah, so your name would be there," he says. "Wouldn't matter, though. No one would look at it, ever. But I would . . . kind of be there for posterity." When I leave the bench, I am hoping he will buy himself one of the "I Hiked the Canyon" T-shirts. There is, in fact, a register at the bottom in the Phantom Ranch canteen just across the river, where he rested before turning around to start an eight-mile hike back up to the rim, but I don't have the heart to tell him this. Besides, he'd soon be in Texas and undoubtedly telling his story—not yet fully grasped or formulated—to any audience he could find.

Listening to the Texan describe his pursuit for an adventure only reminded me of how such experiences do not receive the applause of a crowd as much as reveal a sense of self and desire hidden in much of daily living. To the extent hiking down to the canyon is an "adventure" really says more about the "adventurer" than anything else. The Bright Angel and Kaibab trails are well traveled. Park service personnel patrol them, and hundreds of people either walk or ride mules down them each day. Instead, self-described "adventures" depict people trying to "restore values which have been worn thin by domesticity," as Paul Zweig writes. "Sometimes we feel that we have paid too high a price for our comfort; that the network of relationships and names which we have become does not leave us room to breathe. The limits which define us for others then seem like prisons. And we suspect, momentarily, that we live in exile from the best part of ourselves."[24] This is the appeal, in part, of walking into the desert with a load of food and water biting against the shoulders. Some leisure endeavors may look and feel like work, but they also provide measures of self-worth that other struggles and hardships in daily life cannot adequately name or bestow. "We try to heal the fractures in our existence in many different ways and on many different levels," observes Adrian Moulyn. "We go through valleys of suffering courageously and heroically in order to lead a worthwhile life. When we succeed in what we set out to accomplish, sometimes to a lesser, other times to a greater extent, we reach a state of bliss as the capstone of the painful period which now lies behind us. . . . Suffering is the *conditio sine qua non* and it is the hallmark of our striving for these values."[25]

Conceiving of leisure as a time of self-imposed work, productivity, hardship, and an occasional opportunity to seek out new ways to physically suffer may surely go against conventional ideas about vacations as time for relaxation and rest. Yet, as these hikers describe their ventures into the canyon, I hear them cast a subtle doubt on the conventional myths that work and career are guaranteed avenues toward personal fulfillment and affirming identity. "With a growing emphasis on the individual's control over his or her own identity, the institutional ways of engineering personal transformations have lost much of their power," notes folklorist Roger Abrahams. "For such socially sanctioned transformation to occur, we must believe in the power of those vested with authority to mark these changes for us. But in many ways such authority has been undercut because of our belief that we should do such changing on our own."

Feats of endurance and magnitude—like hiking the Grand Canyon—become ways of authenticating a self through *experience;* they become part of an "economy of experiences," a form of social currency and "personal resources" that help establish identity in our exchanges with others. Such "experience" appeals to wisdom and skill. "I'm experienced," Frank said proudly when he described his canyon hikes. And it is the curious sense of elation that comes when the hiker says, "We were hungry, thirsty, dirty, and excited all at the same time because we had a fantastic experience." Although the term *experience* may be used to describe ordinary actions, "we expect the more intense occasions to have a point, even to carry a message," says Abrahams. "Somewhere between experience and the Big Experience we impose a frame on the activity by calling attention to its extraordinary character." Like Lefebvre, who sees leisure as an "inverse-image" of daily life, a time and space of compensation and critique, Abrahams considers the coexistence of ordinary and extraordinary experience. "What do we contrast with what in developing our notions of the 'real'?" he asks. Activities calling "for us to act and react together at a high pitch can become a Big Time for us, valued for itself and used in some cases as a baseline against which everyday activity is judged," he notes. "In so doing, the breaks in the routine order of the everyday world come to provide the measure of whether life is being lived to the fullest. Ever greater importance is placed, then, on those experiential departures into the higher and deeper registers of feeling that emerge in rehearsed events and that break our routines by encouraging us to get 'deep.'"[26] The stories of those who go down into the canyon remind us how extreme experiences are ways to fix oneself in a landscape, idealize a self and an identity, and recall how the structures of daily life may fail to confer similar values.

In some ways, the canyon's natural edge serves as a threshold to a time when people can discover a self and yield values that do not come with more conventional symbols of status, paychecks, or benefits packages. Anthropologists have long described life on such borders as places of "liminal" experience. Territorial passages through magico-religious lands often required entry through symbolic and ceremonial portals. "To cross the threshold is to unite oneself with a new world," observed Arnold van Gennep, pointing to the threshold itself as a zone of purification rites for uncontaminated passage across sacred terrain.[27] They are liminal zones of cultural performances, notes Victor Turner, separating people from daily life, putting them in an unfamiliar "limbo," and returning them "changed in some way, to mundane life." Liminal experience is a reflective and reflexive domain where images of society are magnified, reformed, inverted, minimized, and recolored, and where routine ways of ordering the world, society, and self experience a rupture. "The same person(s) are both subject and object," notes Turner. "The 'self' is split up the middle—it is something that one both is and that one sees and, furthermore, acts upon as though it were another."[28] It is this divided self—one who does and one who watches the doer—that comes to life in the stories told by those who climb in and out of the canyon.

Though the hike itself may be a feat of effort, the story told afterward is equally a performance. Cultural performances require "a coherent, consensually validated set of symbols and social arenas for appearing," wrote anthropologist Barbara Myerhoff. They can reflectively display an accumulation of knowledge where we may "watch ourselves and enjoy knowing what we know" but also offer a reflexivity where we are "at once actor and audience" and see ourselves as "heroes in our own dramas."[29] The potential risk of failing on a canyon hike is important only because it allows for some relative measure of success or a self-display of perseverance, fortitude, and mettle that we might feel is worth reporting to others. The inner canyon becomes a stage in this way for alternating expressions of how people grasp for power in a place that asks them to recognize their powerlessness.

Postcards from the Underworld

"I always get reflective on trips because the routine is broken," says Carol. "I always do my best thinking then. Prioritizing, making decisions, those type of things, and the Grand Canyon was one of those trips." Divorced for three years and a thirty-eight-year-old mother of three children, Carol began a new relationship with a younger man only to find her "ex-husband had decided that he made a really poor choice and wanted to come back." These were the circumstances surrounding her as she and her new companion went camping at the canyon. "I was trying to come to terms with what was there . . . what was the best decision to make," she says. "Should I start this new life with this new person, or should I go back to my ex-husband and start a new life with him? Those were the kinds of things I was working on at the Grand Canyon." She describes the trip as a "romantic adventure." They made camp, hiked along the rim, cooked meals over a fire, poked around the souvenir shops, and admired El Tovar's architecture together. "We didn't communicate a lot," she says. "Neither one of us were very verbal. Everything had more to do with these kinds of little rituals we'd do around camp. We could go for hours without saying words but we were incredibly close while we worked. It was like another form of language, being able to do something together without a lot of talk. Every place we'd go, I'd leave a circle of rocks or a pile, and just leave markers. No one will ever know I left them, and I'll probably never go back there. For instance, one day I started to take all of these little rocks and we made a little model of the Grand Canyon with them. When we left the place, we left it there. You know, you say good-bye to places, and you kiss the ground. It's a part of the respect you have for the good times you have when you just change your environment."

In retrospect, Carol says the trip with her young lover was a product of "some faulty decision making" on her part. "There was a time during the trip when I thought I had made the decision to stay with this person," she says. "Let's get married. Let's do it. Life's really simple when it's just the two of us. We had adventures. We had fun. The thought of staying on vacation has always been a wonderful idea to me, but coming back and trying to make decisions about the reality of everyday life and the reality of the vacation was difficult. Looking back on the trip now, after not getting married to this person and getting back with my ex-husband . . . well, it was a great time, it was romantic, we had decided to get married, and then we got back to town and it was a different situation." With responsibilities of children, school, and work awaiting her return, Carol says her trip was a time when "I basically checked out" and "left behind all the things that were important to me as an adult." She doesn't offer any more details about deciding to remake a life with her former husband, but near the end of our interview she offers an anecdote suggesting the extent to which she had immersed herself in her new relationship and projected herself into its future. "They had all these benches on the trails and people had carved their names on them. You could see marks with dates like '1940.' To think that you could come back here after that amount of time and see it. Think of all the people that sit here. So I carved my initials in it. My initials are in there, but so are the initials of the man I was with," she laughs. "If I ever go back, I guess I'll do it without my husband."

Carol's story tells of a time when another life of possibilities emerges as seductively perfect and entirely plausible. I imagine her return to the canyon (as she does herself) with husband and children, sitting on the bench, running her fingers over the initials gouged in the wood, recalling a life when she spoke in symbols—"another language" without speech, she said, now secret and dreamy, a kissing of the ground to honor what comes when you "change your environment," a gathering and piling of stones to monumentalize their time in a place made sacred as they built a Grand Canyon together. If the chasm of the inner canyon calls people to its depths to recover selves and fill vacancies distant from the routines of everyday life, Carol's story offers an equally powerful image of how people dwell in an imaginary sphere where they refashion identities, pursue images of self and family, and grasp at ideal reflections of their relationships as they move across the terrain of a culturally sanctified place. Carol's model of the Grand Canyon is, perhaps, a fitting memorial to all those who arrive at the canyon and strengthen ties, rediscover images of companionship and continuity, exist together as family in the same place at the same time, and experience the world in a manner that binds them to one another in new ways.

In Babbit's store, El Tovar souvenir shop, and other stores in the park, I see copies of Francis and Helen Line's *Grand Canyon Love Story* for sale. The book is a memoir of the couple's enthusiastic relationship with Grand Canyon for more than fifty years. "It subtly helped to draw us together before marriage," they write, and it "has been a golden thread woven through our married life; we have had a combined total of one hundred and fouteen year's [sic] acquaintance with it."[30] Married on May 1, 1928, the Lines have made numerous descents into the canyon, returning year after year to celebrate their wedding anniversary by hiking to the bottom. Their book is an account of how their marriage is intertwined with their relationship to the canyon. For instance, the couple hiked to Phantom Ranch on their fiftieth anniversary. On returning, they sent word to their friends and family of the event in a letter. "A 50th wedding anniversary, we discovered, is symbolically similar to the Grand Canyon, where we spent ours in an exciting hiking adventure," they wrote. "This important milestone has given us a new breadth of vision, and a new depth of experience, which we just did not have before. Like the Canyon, we have been subjected to maturing forces. Grand Canyons and 50th anniversaries both are charged with elements of depth and vision, and experiences of climbing." Their letter provides details of the hike, people they passed along the way, and a story of a dinner at Phantom Ranch when, after announcing their anniversary to others, everyone applauded and a pack of Boy Scouts on an overnight came up to shake their hands. After their dinner, they walked out beneath the stars and recited their marriage vows on the banks of Bright Angel Creek. "There is something so special about fifty years of togetherness that just can't be measured," they write. "It's a part of the great intangibles of living. We felt it, perhaps more fully, due to our trip through the spaces of this marvelous Grand Canyon, where we had literally dropped through ages of time, through two billion years. Our lives unrolled as we slipped down the trail. It is something like seeing a movie of your life run backward. The memories crowd in and you measure them against the agelessness of the Canyon."[31]

The Lines's canyon book is a public story of how private life intersects with a cultural icon. Moving through the geologic and symbolic space of the canyon that endures the ages, they find a metaphor for their physical and temporal endurance. And as they move through the canyon, the canyon moves through them, providing reference points and biographical coordinates for their identity. The canyon's trails are where they mark the development and meaning of their relationship, emphasizing not only where they have gone geographically but also how they have lived together. While *Grand Canyon Love Story* offers a published, sentimental account of one couple's seemingly inexhaustible devotion to each other and the canyon, it only magnifies how many find the landscape a backdrop for their relationships.

A retired sixty-eight-year-old Iowa woman said that an important part of her marriage was an annual hike into Grand Canyon with her seventy-one-year-old husband. "For us, coming back year after year gives us a feeling of confidence in ourselves, exercise and a challenge to keep ourselves in condition to do this each year," she wrote. Their annual hikes included Christmas celebrations, family reunions, and like the Lines, wedding anniversaries. Another woman told me how her canyon hike offered her a means to develop a "strong camaraderie" with her friend. "I don't think we'd necessarily be as close if we hadn't done these kinds of things," she said. "We have these great common experiences—hiking Grand Canyon and climbing Grand Teton— and they give you a common bond to look back on, to reminisce over. . . . I was away on the East Coast for about five years and we weren't establishing many new common experiences and things to reflect on. The fact that we had these things that were really physically challenging . . . were important because they gave us an esprit de corps." The quest to climb in and out of the canyon is a time for sustaining relationships and a means to forge a common past that can carry across changes in life. "The most significant part of the trip is being able to share it with my hiking buddy, Geza!" a thirty-five-year-old Indiana man wrote in a letter. "Geza is an older gentleman of sixty-seven-years young," and he "has become my 'adopted' dad since my father died twelve years ago. Geza has been able to do and share many experiences which I had hoped my father would have loved to do." A forty-seven-year-old Wisconsin woman said the canyon marked a transition into a new life. "My first trip to Grand Canyon in 1984 was different because I traveled as a single person for the first time," she wrote. "I chose to go to Grand Canyon because the river trip was sponsored by the College of Wooster and a planned, guided trip was the sort of thing I needed on my first solo vacation as a widow. That alone made it important in my life—a landmark of sorts."

To some extent, all of these stories suggest how the canyon becomes "a landmark of sorts," a navigational device for people to find their way through the discontinuities of life and toward a time when they redeem private relationships and selves on public, cultural terrain. Undergoing a challenge like a canyon hike or a river trip may be occasion for dramatizing a common bond, but the vacation is also when people seek to renew their family connections. Numerous cultural observers say that American families have increasingly less time to spend with one another. "Half the population now says they have too little time for their families," notes economist Juliet B. Schor. "The problem is particularly acute for women: in one study, half of all employed mothers reported it caused either 'a lot' or an 'extreme' level of stress. . . . And growing numbers of husbands and wives are like ships passing in the night, working sequential schedules to manage their child care."[32] As Schor points to leisure hours diminishing in the face of increasing work time, sociologist Arlie Hochschild notes a reversal of traditional values taking place between the sphere of work and home. In an age when many couples find themselves "time-poor," home has become an arena of stress rather than the refuge from a harsh world it is often thought to be, she argues. At home, parents often feel underappreciated, and there is a constant barrage of unfinished duties. "In this new model of family and work life, a tired parent flees a world of unresolved quarrels and unwashed laundry for the reliable orderliness, harmony, and managed cheer of work," says Hochschild. "Some people find in work a respite from the emotional tangles at home. Others virtually marry their work, investing it with an emotional significance once reserved for the family, while hesitating to trust loved ones at home."[33] In contrast to the "time binds" experienced by many Americans, the vacation is often an opportunity to try and settle the score by reserving an extended period when they may reinvest in their relationships. "Most people, most of the time, seem to muddle through using available resources as ontological sandbags to shore up the realities of identity and meaningful relationships," writes Donald Redfoot, and they often rely on "the private sphere as an ontological anchor amidst the uncertainties of modern life." In contrast, the vacation is "likely to be experienced as a liberation from the private sphere, a time . . . to do what they wish, where they wish," he says. "Most importantly, it is a time that can be devoted entirely to family and friendships as the core of what is most importantly real."[34]

Mary, from Santa Rosa, decided to go to the North Rim in anticipation of her daughter, Jackie, going away to college. "We viewed the canyon and made photographs, including a self-timed one of both of us with the canyon in the background. We optioned against dinner in the lodge dining room and instead bought a cafeteria meal which we brought outside to eat on the verandah as the sun set. Pretty special!" she wrote in a letter. "Now she is away at school and probably won't move back home when she graduates. We had a wonderful time and had time to talk. . . . And we have this common experience to which we refer often, and find photos or news articles to share with each other about the places we saw." Mary made her first visit to Grand Canyon at age thirteen and again when Jackie was in preschool. On this trip, the canyon is a backdrop—as in the self-timed photo she describes—for a life transition. The last time Mary came to its rim, she was a young mother. Returning years later, she watches the sunset with the same daughter, now ready to leave home for good. Lynne, a thirty-eight-year-old divorced mother from San Francisco, wrote about her canyon trip as a time to overcome the distances separating her from her children. Her daughter lived with her, but her son lived with his father in Boston. "It was a good trip for the three of us. The kids camped pretty well and traveled well in the car, and although they did their usual rivalry thing . . . , I still felt happy and close to them. I liked sleeping between them in the tent. It seemed so natural, and I realized how rare it is that we're so physically close and peaceful," she wrote. "Though I did feel pretty alone sometimes. I certainly didn't see any other women alone with kids at campgrounds. . . . It took a lot of energy to keep us together and safe, and when the kids were fighting or when I had a flat tire in the 110 degree heat outside of Joshua Tree [California], I wished for some adult company. But, as usual, it worked out, and I managed."

In different ways, these women suggest how the miles traveled on the vacation may offer routes for spanning the gaps in lives led at home. While Mary describes making a "common experience," one she and Jackie return to in their correspondence, her letter also tells how being together in this fashion—mother and daughter, alone on the road—is an *uncommon* feature of their lives. For Lynne, physical closeness to her children in the car and on the road seems a natural, yet comparatively rare event. Both of their letters not only describe traveling to Grand Canyon but also how those journeys are times when they see their image as mothers with a particular, perhaps self-conscious, appreciation for their efforts to connect with their children. Obviously, these women write with the benefit of hindsight and reflection. Like all travel stories, they show how the tellers' sense of meaning, significance, and value becomes fixed in the journey, the tales of good luck and pleasures that come their way, and the obstacles they've encountered and managed to get through.

Inevitably, travel stories are occasions for expressing an identity, a relation to others and how one has moved through the world. Mary and Lynne note the significance of their trips as details—a photograph of mother and daughter, a dinner at sunset, listening to the radio in the car, sharing a space when they bed down at night—that could just as easily appear in stories about life at home. But as they seek the hopeful benefits of quality time and the recyclable memories of common experience, they do so in a place of cultural import; it is as if the cultural authority of the landscape invites them to ceremonialize their lives and relationships for themselves. The vacation is a rite of passage in which "the ordinary and extraordinary coexist," to borrow from Abrahams; it comes with a set of conventions that "permit the framing and stylizing of activities, calls attention to the participants, and encourages a spelling out of the meanings and feelings carried within these activities."[35] Mary's photo with Jackie and Lynne's recollection of sleeping peacefully with her children at her side are but two examples implying how vacations are rituals with simple satisfactions that can emerge as lucid expressions of desires to live with a wholeness and continuity. They are times when people search for signs of a family and self often veiled by the demands and distractions of everyday life. Mary and Lynne tell stories of having seen such signs. For those who visit the canyon, however, the search is ongoing, appearing as brief eruptions of conversation and postures revealing an expansive gap between worlds experienced and envisioned.

"I'm going to walk over to that trail a little bit," I hear a husband tell his wife. They've only parked their car a few minutes ago and are now looking over the rail at Mather Point with their daughter and an older woman who is either his mother or his wife's

mother. He's trying to break away from the pack, go off by himself for a few minutes. "Can you *just stay here*," says his exasperated wife. "I mean, so we can try to . . . *try* to be a family, or at least look like one." In silent resignation, he takes his daughter's hand, walks to another place along the rail, and stares into the canyon. Later, on the observation area below The Lookout gift shop, I watch another family. Two brothers, about seven and nine years old, are fighting for control of a set of binoculars. The boys' parents are trying to make them cooperate for a family photograph while another tourist stands by focusing the father's camera.

"It's my turn to use them, Dad," says the older boy, as he tries to wiggle the binoculars loose from his brother's hands. "He's being a wimp." Unfazed by their little battle, the father separates the boys by moving the younger one over to the mother.

"Daniel," he says to the son who has just called his brother a wimp, "it helps to have lots of categories if you want to use superlatives." The boy gives his father a puzzled eye; this isn't the time for a translation. "Now look at the camera," his father says in clipped control. "Let this man take our picture."

"Ready?" asks the man behind the camera. The mother takes off her sunglasses and brushes her hair back from her forehead. The two boys straighten up, and the four smile as the man presses the shutter. "Got it," says the man, and hands the camera back to the father while the older son advances toward his brother, who still holds the binoculars.

The promise of the family vacation and the experience of living through it show clefts and fissures. Offhand remarks and split-second performances beckon toward fantasies of self and family. The inherent pushes and pulls that inevitably accompany actually spending an extended time together can quickly dissolve and reconstitute on vacation. "Can we at least try to look like a family?" a wife says, frustrated. I watch the instantaneous retrieval of postures and smiles, a fatherly hand placed on a son's shoulder in the pause before the camera shutter opens and lifted off when it closes. Such moments flash light into the gaps between the lived and imagined, illuminate a canyon of divided selves, a ritualized dwelling in double consciousness, and a time for seeing with split vision. Tourists tack back and forth, managing not only the disparity between the ideals and realities of their vacations but also the selves and families who live in each. In the struggle to keep it all together, they shape-shift into a "possible family," resurrected by the rites of vacation time and the occultlike power of photo opportunities. And in this pursuit of the vacation as an ideal family time, one for making and collecting material fictions, desires not only get expressed but continue to flourish. For some, the quest for freedom may become encumbered by the very weight carried in expectations for the journey.

One afternoon, I meet three women viewing the canyon near El Tovar. Helen and Donna are in their fifties; they are sisters. The third, Kathy, is in her late twenties, and Helen's and Donna's niece. "My grandmother took all of us here for a vacation," Kathy tells me. "She wanted to have three generations of Campbell women take a trip together before she got too old. Grammy's not feeling too well, though. It's the altitude I think, she's up in the room taking a nap." Helen thinks that her mother will feel better after a day or so, but the important thing is that the women in the family can spend this time together. Kathy says she is glad she's come along, particularly since her own mother couldn't make this "reunion." Donna says nothing. She just looks at me with caution. "It's great to be here together," says Kathy. "Oh, yes," Helen agrees. "This is probably one of the few times we'll ever get to be together like this." Seated together on the bench, they are the dream of a woman napping upstairs.

Later that night, I run into Kathy and Helen again, this time perched on bar stools in the El Tovar lounge, eating salted nuts from a bowl and drinking vodka tonics. "Where are your aunt and grandmother?" I ask Kathy.

"They're up in the room, thank god," she says, rolling her eyes at Helen. "They're both such a pain in the ass, . . . complain about everything . . . don't want to do anything. How long are we going to be here? A week?" Helen nods.

"She *is* difficult, honey," says Helen. "Donna has been miserable all her life. She's such an old maid. I wish she had married but . . . well . . . who would want to? She's so negative. But you can't imagine how happy your grandmother is that you came. She's so excited we're all here together. We'll just have to make it through the best we can." They clink their drinks to seal their pact as Kathy orders another. Their disappointment only hinted at how much energy had been expended on the notion of redeeming an ideal of family togetherness and welding a bond across three generations. If the canyon serves as a site for such dramas, it also reveals its glimpses of a backstage.

Kathy, Helen, Donna, and Grammy might collect themselves for a few photographs out on the rim, but listening to them in the bar only reiterated how entirely different worlds can exist side by side. As Kathy aired her complaints and consoled herself with drinks, Helen became an ally, reminding her this was all for the sake of the family matriarch. The premise behind this "reunion" of three family generations spoke to a dream of continuity and cohesion, yet the dream had its rough edges and cracks; their vacation script preceded the journey, and these scenes didn't easily fit the story cooked up at home.

Standing outside on El Tovar's porch beneath a cool Arizona night, I look through the window into the lounge. The piano player is working through Billy Joel's "Piano Man," and I see Kathy and Helen huddled at the bar, laughing. Grammy and Donna were the brunt of some joke between them, I guess. In their own way, they suspected that the reunion idea was as much a fiction as full of constraints and sacrifices, something to "make it through" the best they could, anything but a time of unchecked fun and freedom. And while the prospect of three generations renewing family ties may have become, for the moment anyway, a distant mirage, the aunt and her niece were certainly fortifying their own bond—stitching together a subplot, identifying scapegoats—that might get them through the trip and the unanticipated conflicts inherent in spending this time together. Family vacations are not only an institutionalized cultural ritual but idealized interpretive spaces where people play out the "family" in a volley of advances and retreats. Putting the principles of kinship to test, they sometimes pass, sometimes fail, but the vacation remains open to indeterminate forces and actions. As a temporal sphere where people aspire to idealizations of selves, relationships, and places, the vacation can easily symbolize liberation from daily life's limitations. But symbolic ideals, at the time of their declaration, also sow the seeds for tensions or alternatives that arise as expressions of desire and freedom, assertions of a self *against* the symbolic conventions elevating the vacation as an ideal domain.[36]

At the end of the trail that runs from the visitor center to the rim, a young couple and their two daughters tape a short story for their vacation home video. The mother has given the camera to the girls, probably about nine and eleven years of age, who make up their story on the spot. Mother stands behind them, off the trail and smiling, as she watches them direct their father through a set of shots to make a scene easily titled "Dad Falls into the Grand Canyon." Their first shot shows Dad taking in the view. He climbs up on a rock, puts his hand on his hips, and admires the scenery while the girls film him from behind. Their next shot is a close-up of his tennis shoes slipping from the place where he stands.

"Okay, now get back on there and pretend like you're falling," one of the girls tells Dad. She is delighted with how the scene is going. The other girl is serious, waiting for directions from her sister. Their mother looks over at me as I watch, smiling and shaking her head.

"Like this?" he asks, and undulates his torso while making big circles with extended arms.

"Yeah, that's it," says the girl directing. "Keep doing it." And he does until they finish their shot. They move back to the place of the first shot and take some footage from the original angle, except he's no longer in the scene. Off to the side, the father watches them tape the empty viewing place where he just stood. For the final scene, the girls direct him to get below the rock and climb up. His baseball cap tilts sideways, his sunglasses hang across his nose and forehead, he looks disheveled—as he should after falling into the canyon—and throws apish arms up on the rock, pretending to climb back to the place where he stood in the first take. The daughter who has been directing beams over the performance as her sister carefully keeps the camera on their father.

"How'd I do?" he asks, after finishing the scene and walking toward his wife. He brushes himself off (although there's really nothing on him) and readjusts his cap and sunglasses.

"Stop taking the picture, Sherri!" cries the older daughter. "You'll ruin it!" Even though the scene is completed, her sister has kept the camera on him, capturing their father's return from the fall and his exit from the frame of their story.

"I guess they don't have to worry about you picking up any Academy Awards," his wife tells him as he moves toward her. The girls give the camera back to their mother, and they continue down the rim trail, laughing about the scene they've just made. I hear one of the girls say she can't wait until they get home so they can watch the video on their TV. At such a young age, their facility with the conventions of visual storytelling, with long shots, close-ups, and internal editing, is clearly impressive. I did not see the final version of their home movie; I could only watch them set up each shot and imagine what was in their viewfinder. Regardless of the production qualities, the disjunction between these two scenes—a family in the middle of their vacation and a mininarrative of the vacation that takes shape when the children are given the camera—shows the boundary and tension between social narratives of family. The girls' contrived scene is literally one of inverted and excess meanings. In the midst of family sightseeing, and presumably collecting home video footage in which the children pose while mother and father frame the ideal vacation memory through their camera, the girls take an opportunity to document the vacation on their own terms. Like a Saturday morning cartoon or a TV sitcom, their father reappears as foolish and uncoordinated under his daughters' direction. Given the chance to script the vacation, the children's first response is to throw Dad over the rim in a comic video play that only underscores their new, albeit temporary ability to direct the day's events.

Clearly, there is little that is overtly malicious or hostile in their endeavor. Quite the opposite. Their father happily obliges their requests; he willingly participates in much the same way that celebrated public figures sit next to a podium as they are "roasted" by their friends and colleagues. But as the girls become so passionately animated in their efforts, it is difficult not to see this scene as a homegrown version of a carnivalesque impulse, that performative rupture of popular life Mikhail Bakhtin recognized as a time for realizing the relativity of "established authority and truth." Carnival reframes the world in a populist utopian vision, he noted. It is a festive critique celebrating "temporary liberation from the prevailing truth of the established order; it marks a suspension of all hierarchical rank, privileges, norms and prohibitions."[37]

Although far from the proportions of carnival Bakhtin described, the girls' video shows traces of a popular tradition for temporarily turning authority upside down. As Dad plummets into their canyon fiction, they stand at the top, laughing, holding his camera. Of course, this is all an emergent and spontaneous play of the girls' creativity and imagination. But it also expresses a symbolic challenge to the structure of their relationship and the conventions of their vacation. Although vacations remove people from the rule of everyday life, they carry their own inherent rules, hierarchies, and authority. Watching the girls make their video is like watching them tell a joke and cross a line between order and chaos, convention and parody, structure and subversion. As they depict father losing his footing on the canyon's edge, they invoke the classic structure of the joke—a quick slip from control into bedlam. It is a gesture toward a freedom that comes when the predictable is upset by chance.

Jokes offer a moment when "the unconscious is allowed to bubble up without restraint, hence the sense of enjoyment and freedom," writes anthropologist Mary Douglas. The amount of energy expended "monitoring our subconscious" appeals to formalized perceptions of social order and control. In comparison, the "joke, because it breaks down the control, gives the monitoring system a holiday." Given this interpretation, the girls' home video creates a symbolic vacation in the midst of their family vacation, a gap in the "naturalized order of things," as Stewart calls it. Clearly, Douglas's understanding of jokes is grounded in a Freudian vision of that subdued underworld lurking inside us. Jokes release energy, she says, "for they allow the subconscious itself to be expressed. . . . Something which might have been repressed has been allowed to appear, a new improbable form of life has been glimpsed."[38] I would prefer not to diagnose the girls' video production as a case of repressed hostility toward the father, although it surely invites such an interpretation. Instead, their joke offers an enlarged glimpse at the lines dividing freedom and restraint, the possibilities of leisure to uncover private dreams, desires, and imaginary worlds hidden within the flow of the everyday. Their playful video scene is a postcard from a place real and invented, an alternative landscape where different forces and forms of life exist and dwell—counter to the family vacation they are having—and materialize only as they spin out their story.

On another day, in the very same location where the girls put Dad into the canyon's depths, a older couple and a younger couple approach the rim. Later, I learn this is a family outing; a retired couple from Phoenix is visiting a son and his wife at their new home in Flagstaff. All of them had been to the canyon before. They talk and laugh together as they follow the trail, paying attention to little else except their conversation, and pause when the canyon comes into view.

"Hey, will you look at that!" says the older man, exaggerating disbelief, "You'd think we were at the Grand Canyon." He takes his Instamatic from the black covering case hanging around his neck while his wife moves closer to the rim. She tells him she wants to get a view away from the trees. "Hey, Doris, a few steps closer," he says, the brushing motion of his hand urging her to the edge.

"You'd miss me, Joe," she says with a chuckle, not turning toward him. She looks carefully where she's placing her feet.

"Come on, go closer," he says, winking to his son. "Your insurance policy is all paid up."

Like the girls making the video, the man's joke about his wife falling into the canyon is a case of folly, a friendly rub against the value of their relationship, this family outing, and life itself. Such jokes are told everyday at the canyon by tourists and tour guides. I recall listening to two middle-aged men in the Bright Angel Lounge one afternoon having a few cocktails. "Another drink?" asked the bartender, sweeping up their empty glasses and wet napkins. "Sure. A gin and tonic and a Jack on the rocks," one replied. "But we've got to go after that. Gotta hike that trail." The bartender threw him a cockeyed glance, thinking, perhaps, they shouldn't be on the trail after drinking alcohol. "Going into the canyon?" she said, filling fresh glasses with ice, gin, and Jack Daniels. "Until we fall, I guess," he grinned back. "Hey, that's what one of the tour guides told me," said his friend. "Keep your videocorders on because if you fall over the edge you'll get the best twenty seconds of footage you'll ever have in your life."

Such jokes may express unspoken fears about the dangers looming beyond the canyon's rim, a fear of falling over its edge. But perhaps they intimate a caution toward the other direction as well, one where routine, control, restraint, and codes of social propriety reign most of the time in daily life and on vacations as well. These jokes are little sparks energizing a borderline separating a world of order and expectation from another world where the unpredictable is recovered as a gesture toward freedom from all of it, to be taken in stride, and sanctioned by laughter. Whether it is the girls having Dad pretend to fall, or the retired man's tongue-in-cheek plan to collect on his wife's insurance policy, or the cartoon caricature of the tourist who keeps the tape rolling before smashing into the canyon floor, these jokes narrate landscapes emerging at the brink of a social imaginary rooted in desires which fly against the smooth grooves of monotony and complacency that seem unavoidable in daily life and recur even during the vacation. The imaginary landscapes of children's videos and tourists' jokes do not offer legitimate alternatives to the worlds people occupy when they spontaneously call them up. Instead, they are glimmers of what is left over and left out: uncontained impulses, temporary, frivolous expressions of freedom, imaginary landscapes people envision only because they have secure footing on firm ground. These fleeting dramas and sketches of life depict people looking below the surface and over the edge, recognizing not only the potential danger and death looming beyond the rim but the forces of life springing from the depths of shadowy places. Against the composed and rational face of order and routine, those on vacation find the time to teeter on the brink of a world that is difficult to see but takes a shape through these sorts of photographs, video plays, and jokes.

"Do you find people dream differently when they come here?" Maxine Hong Kingston asks one morning in the aisles of Babbit's store. She and her husband, Earll, who does the weekly solo performances of John Wesley Powell at the Shrine of the Ages, were shopping for groceries. I could have expected such a question coming from the author of *The Woman Warrior: Memoirs of a Girlhood among Ghosts,* her 1976 novel about divided identities, family myths, and powerful storytellers. "I've been noticing that I have different dreams when I stay here," she says, and owes the change to some quality in the landscape. Her question about tourist dreams was in response to a story I'd told Maxine and Earll about Jill and Stanley, a couple from Orange County, California, I'd met the previous day while walking the Rim Trail. They were two drama teachers absorbed in a mix of philosophies brought to life for a New Age. They came here often and hiked numerous trails over the years. "It's a spiritual home for us," Jill said, and her husband Stanley urged her to tell me a story they called "Chasing Ghosts in the Grand Canyon."

We were off the trail, and I was asleep, and in the middle of the night I sat up because there was a young man standing there. I can still see him. He was wearing a Pendleton shirt and he was sandy-haired. I imagine he would be in his twenties, and he had a knapsack in his hand. He was just looking at me very benevolently, and it was beautiful. And I woke up Stanley. I said, "Stanley, there's somebody here. There's someone there. He's looking at me." Stanley got up, took the flashlight, and went out to look, but there was no one there at all. The next day, Stanley got up, and there were no footprints anywhere. So he thought maybe it was a dream. I said, "No, it was not a dream." I knew that. When we got up, I went to the restroom, and there was a young woman in the bathroom and I told her about my experience. And she said, "Once it's happened to you, it will happen again." Quite a few years went by, and then at home one night, I had the same visitation with the same young man. Nothing was said, but he was there. It was a feeling, very calming. It was a beautiful, beautiful experience. . . . It was magnificent. And then I took a class one time in shamanism, and I went on a guided meditation. And after I had gone on through into the Underworld, I was asked what did I see. And it was the same young man, and he was offering me his knapsack. And I didn't open it or anything, he was just offering it to me. After the meditation, when I was brought out of it, the shaman guide asked me about my experience. The shaman told me the young man with the knapsack was offering me knowledge. That's how it was interpreted. But he hasn't come back, and I'm still waiting.

Maxine seemed fascinated by this story of dreams and ghosts, and suggested it would be interesting for me to collect accounts of the dreams people had when they slept at night near the canyon. This topic had not come up in my interviews, but in a different way, I felt I had captured some of their waking dreams, the phantom traces of other lives appearing and disappearing as I listened to people expound on their vacations, and as I watched them enter and exit an imaginary stage of performances mimicking their lives and giving shape to self-fictions. Jill's story about chasing ghosts in the canyon may have seemed fanciful at first, but it was a story that fit neatly with a larger view of a world she and Stanley lived in.

"The thing it relates to," Stanley explained after Jill ended her story, "is that she has Blackfoot heritage and I have Cherokee on both sides. So the experiences we've had have been like visitations of guardian angels. For example, butterflies will come and land on my finger. When we're out in the desert, butterflies will come and land on us or come and kiss us. We were in the French Alps one time, we were standing together, and both of our jeans were covered with butterflies." I listened and looked for traces of the Blackfoot and Cherokee, but I could see nothing of their family bloodlines, nor beyond Stanley's gray beard and Jill's blond hair, silver-rimmed sunglasses, and walnut tan. "It's something that happens to us. It's something that we cannot explain. . . . It just occurs. It's just sort of a blessing, or a protection, or some sort of a guidance beyond us." Jill told another story, lending further evidence to their "blessing" and potential to witness these extraordinary events. "One time, I was visited by a huge black bird. I think it was a raven, but it was larger than Stanley," she said, and described how the raven had a baby bird under its wing and it was caught. So she helped free the baby. "Just before the big raven left, it came and touched me on the lips with its beak, and then it went away."

In their own right, Jill and Stanley seemed friendly ghosts, contemporary incarnations of those nineteenth-century canyon visitors who testified to their awe on the canyon's brink, the great pull of its mystery, and sublime ecstasy. "You feel incredible energy," Jill said of the canyon. "I sometimes become emotional—that seems so superficial to become emotional about the energy—but you become part of the universe, part of God, if you will." Their metaphysics, however, were stitched together from many sources. "The canyon just has that spiritual pull," Stanley said. "The Hindu influence in the canyon is very appealing. You're dealing with upper chakra levels simply by being here and taking in the ambiance. That's another thing. It's, it's, uh, pantheistic. It's appeal is . . . the Indian. The universality. God is all. This is a manifestation of God on Earth, 'cause this is the most physically grand. I know it's a cliché, but it is. Nothing compares to the Grand Canyon. It is a spiritual magnet that keeps bringing us back. It's *our* vortex. We've been to three of them, incidentally," he added. "Stonehenge, Kauai, and Sedona. The other one is the Bermuda Triangle, but we haven't been there yet."

The couple from Orange County spoke comfortably about ghosts and knew a world of vortexes and forces where people channeled voices living in the heavens and other planets. Among other canyon tourists, however, apparitions from other times and lives appeared in broad daylight, without ceremony or sleep. For instance, Frank, the retired real-estate agent from Miami, told me about his passion for exploring Anasazi ruins he found on his treks deep into the canyon. "Up there in Lava Canyon, there's this Indian ruin and I saw where they put on the adobe," he recalled. "The Anasazi smeared the adobe to hold the rocks of their dwelling together. In this one area, you could see how he's run his fingers through, and they left an imprint. I reached over there very gently and I put my hand right on his hand. I was going back to the days of the Anasazi, back over eight hundred years ago. That guy left his hand prints and I put my hands over his. It was a strange feeling. And every time I go back there, I do the same thing. This guy was a short guy and had very narrow fingers, could've been a woman, probably was a woman. My presence doesn't even represent civilization in this Grand Canyon. My presence is temporary. I'm moving on. That's the whole thing." Feeling a presence from another age, the mud wall is a site of memory where Frank revives an ancient inhabitant and simultaneously acknowledges his own passing presence through the same terrain.

"Travel (like walking) is a substitute for the legends that used to open up space to something different. What does travel ultimately produce if it is not, by a sort of reversal, 'an exploration of the deserted places of my memory?'" writes Michel de Certeau. "There is no place that is not haunted by many different spirits hidden there in silence, spirits one can 'invoke' or not," and the "hints of what is known but unrevealed are passed on 'just between you and me.'"[39] Frank tells of conjuring an old ghost, of shaking hands with the Anasazi woman who left her tracks on the space where he stands centuries later. In different ways, other tourists find the imprints of those who lived in other times as they travel the canyon.

"We grew up together and became, well, like brothers to each other," Art told me one night at Phantom Ranch. Now living in Sonoma, California, Art was on his third annual canyon hike with his friend, Tom from San Jose. They had spent their youth in a San Francisco neighborhood, each an only child. Now in their forties and living in different cities, the canyon trails provided a road into the past. "Not many people have friends that go back this far," said Tom. "Most of the time we just walk around and reminisce about our childhood days, growing up together, and that kind of thing. Sometimes I think we could be anywhere, but I really like coming down here into the bottom. . . . So we'll probably keep coming back here for a few years." Their hike on the canyon trails offered a route to another time and geography; it was a place to resurrect past lives of people who once dwelled in an entirely different locale.

Standing on the West Rim with a tour group, our driver points to mule riders below us, descending into the canyon. "My grandmother promised me when I was sixteen that we would take the mules down," I hear a woman in her late sixties say to her husband. "But then the war came, so of course we didn't get to. I'd still really love to take those mules down." At Mather Point, an elderly woman from Ohio tells me it's been fifty years since she'd been to Grand Canyon. "The last time I was here they had tents for the tourists, and the only restaurant was the Bright Angel, I think. We had breakfast there. It used to be you could eat and look out on the canyon. It's a real disappointment how they've changed it." For a retired couple from Massachusetts, traveling across the country involved an itinerary of places that had significance earlier in their lives. "When we go through Texas, I plan to go up to Wichita Falls and see the place where I was trained before I went overseas," Joe told me when I sat with him and Kaye on the rim one afternoon. "We were in San Diego, and I took Kaye to see the place where I shipped out to Okinawa. I said, 'There it is. I was there in '46.' So I want to see if that training station is still there in Wichita Falls." The ghosts of their pasts wax and wane along the roads they travel. One woman sees the girl who never rode the mules. Another sees a family vacation at a Grand Canyon that has irrevocably changed. Joe points to his younger self, a man in 1946 about to face battle, as if he were a tour guide pointing out a landmark to Kaye.

In the coin-operated laundry near Mather Campground, a man in his early sixties sits silent and alone, watching his clothes spin in a dryer. I sit quietly next to him, watching the tangle of my own clothes go around and around. Finally, trying to strike up a conversation, I ask him where he's from. "South Dakota," he says, and that is all. I try again with my usual follow-up question: "Is this your first time here?" He remains still for a moment and then looks at me with a tired eyes. "No, I've been here before," he says solemnly. "Me and my wife used to travel around here quite a bit. She loved this place, the whole area around here. She died last year. Cancer. It happened pretty quick." I tell him I'm sorry, and he continues. "We have a trailer—one of the old Airstreams—pulled it all over the place. She really loved it here. It's a lot different coming back alone. Maybe I shouldn't have come this way. Just couldn't figure out where else to go, I guess." Later, after we carry our clothes out to our cars, I say goodbye and wish him well. He is solemn as he drives away, pulling the old Airstream behind his Dodge pickup, the space on the passenger side filled with a basket of clean and folded clothes.

Although sight is a celebrated faculty in a tourist world, these stories—with all of their nostalgia, sentimentality, and melancholy—describe a world of presences *appearing* in absences. "In a culture seemingly ruled by technologies of hypervisibility, we are led to believe not only that everything can be seen, but also that everything is available and accessible for our consumption," notes Avery Gordon, who looks to ghost stories as material expressions pointing to "the dialectics of visibility and invisibility" as "a constant negotiation between what can be seen and what is in the shadows."[40] To hear these tourists summoning ghosts is not to find them "haunted" (although some may be) by their past. Instead, they "reveal a desire to overcome absences created when the past is necessarily left behind," as Janna Jones notes in her analysis of narratives from patrons and workers of a historic picture palace. "The desire to literally journey to the past is impossible for mortals, yet we frequently try, compelled by wanting to 'get the past right,' to better understand the present, or to simply take pleasure or feel the anguish of past thoughts. . . . We may only sense our pasts peripherally, but the absences and gaps of our personal histories are at times a seething presence. Even in the periphery, the traces are impossible to ignore, and at times, we may attempt to lure them into the spotlight so that we may relish them."[41]

As I walked the rim trails watching and listening to these tourists, I sometimes imagined their performances constituting a world in its own right, self-enclosed and cut off from any traces and signs of their lives at home, a place of fleeting images and stories where all of the symbols, metaphors, laughter, memorable geographies, ghosts, dreams, and the fictions of selves and families existed in toto, a universe unto itself thriving on potentials, aspirations, longings, and where hopes were channeled through these vacation rituals as if calling on spirits from elsewhere. For all the canyon photographs and videotapes poised toward a future where people might remember themselves as happy families at the Grand Canyon, the vacation did not satisfy all of their wants and expectations. "I'd like to come back here when I've got more time," a plumber from Oregon said one afternoon after he and his family hiked up from the three-mile rest house on the Bright Angel. They'd made it halfway down before deciding to abandon their plans to camp overnight at the bottom. "Maybe we can try it next year when the kids are older," he sighed. While some may resurrect a past, others may look hopefully toward those spirits from the future, the "potential selves" they have set out to embrace but instead taunt them with the real constraints of time.[42]

Maxine talked of special dreams at the canyon as if the land had something to do with it. Jill and Stanley were convinced this was the case. The San Francisco Peaks, some forty miles south of the South Rim, is the place where Hopis direct messages to "kachinas," spirits from other planets and stars, noted Frank Waters in his *Book of the Hopi*. During the late 1950s, Waters traveled the Hopi reservation about a hundred miles east of Grand Canyon Village to study the complex cosmology of Hopi tradition and ritual. He called them "mystery plays," an annual cycle of religious ceremonies dramatizing the Hopi Road of Life and the story of their emergence from the First World. Kachinas are respected spirits who manifest themselves on earth every six months through ritual dances held at Hopi pueblos. The ceremonial masks worn by kachina dancers are invested with unearthly powers. They symbolize numerous spirits who emerge from the Underworld during ceremonies in circular chambers, or kivas. Kachinas are "the inner forms, the spiritual components of the outer physical forms of life," wrote Waters. "They are the invisible forces of life—not gods, but rather intermediaries, messengers," and their annual arrival is aimed at renewing life for those on earth. During the kachina dances, the masked men who impersonate these spirits lose "their personal identities" and become "imbued with the spirits of the beings they represent," he said, and described the endless flow of the masked dancers he saw, as he sat in the kiva, appearing in groups, yelling, singing, shaking rattles to the rhythm of drumbeats. "One is swept away by it all in a queer, momentary illusion" that is "projected so powerfully on the unconscious by the grotesque imagery of these strange and indescribable figures," he wrote. "Spirits temporarily embodied in the flesh themselves, they remind us all of our own brief roles on this transient earth. . . . They keep coming—a swelling host of *kachinas,* the spirits of mineral, plant, bird, animal, and human entities, of clouds and stars and all the invisible forces of life." At the heart of Waters's account is a story of how rituals opened onto a dual world, affirming a past and future, and ultimately a "cosmic drama" where a "whole multi-world universe is its stage; the cataclysmic epochs of geological change provide the props; and its characters are the Hopis themselves, masked as the races of mankind." For Waters, this was enough to hold his attention, for "seldom has any cast attempted to play simultaneously two different roles—that of the cosmic spirit of mankind and that of temporal man."[43]

Waters's translation of the Hopi myths and religious structure does not suggest some correspondence between native ritual and the modern tourists who come to Grand Canyon. But his descriptions of beings and spirits invoked through annual ceremonies certainly caught my attention as I watched people arrive at the rim and remake themselves as ideal families, call forth hidden selves, and search for connections between the worlds they knew and the ones they suspected were out there. In some ways, *Book of the Hopi* is a story of a lost world, of migrating peoples, symbolically remembering and reinvesting themselves in what some call the Promised Land. "The premise of Hopi life then and now," Waters said, "is the ideal of unifying at their permanent homeland, the Center of the Universe."[44] Perhaps this is the only thing the cosmography of Hopi tradition shares with the private quests of these canyon tourists, a contemporary cycle of modern "mystery plays" grasping toward a life both real and imaginary, with seriousness and humor, a story of brief emergences of lives from an underworld, one beneath the orders of daily life, lurking beneath the skin, and appearing as fleeting spirits and masks guided by constellations of past and future.

Out of Time

An hour before the Grand Canyon sun punches out for the evening, weird shadows pass over the stage near the Hopi House. Bob and Mike, in black pants and shirts, rainbow suspenders and greasepaint faces, waddle and mug for parents, children, and people just strolling up after dinner. A sign on an easel, "Mime in the Canyon," captions a space once reserved for Hopi dancers performing for tourists. Considering their code of silence, the mimes have an ambitious plan: an interpretation of a Grand Canyon vacation. In a hushed portrayal of the journey from home to canyon, the mimes caricature scenes of life on the rim; they are white-faced silhouettes who stand for each member of the audience watching them.

At center stage, a stunned mime wakes from his slumbers. The alarm on Bob's face tells us a clock is ringing, signaling the start of a work day. Bob rushes frantically to wash his face, brush his teeth, put on a tie, and then make a panicked drive to work. When he finally arrives, I assume he's a supermarket clerk, since he appears to be checking out groceries. Maybe it's an assembly line. Maybe there's little difference, but I believe Bob has studied scenes from Chaplin's *Modern Times*. All of his motions are mechanical and hurried, as though he's a machine about to overheat or blow a gasket. He argues with an invisible boss. This mime hates the job, the boss, and the customers, I think. We know he is off the clock when his necktie comes off; it's a signal the vacation has started. It helps to have Mike flashing a cardboard sign that reads "Work/Vacation." Bob packs his suitcase and gets in the car, and we watch another lengthy episode of wild and hectic driving. In fact, he is still at the wheel when Mike picks up another cardboard sign reading "Welcome to the Grand Canyon."

But the canyon is only full of more frustrating routines. Bob's anxious expressions and postures tell us there's a leaky dividing line between work and vacation, and he's doing more of the same at every turn. He has difficulty finding a parking spot and elects to pull into a place where Mike stands frozen, holding a symbol of a wheelchair on a board reading "Handicap Zone." Bob parks anyway, only to get a ticket from a ranger who appears when Mike puts down the sign and puts on a ranger's hat. Mike takes off the hat and picks up another sign—"Shuttle Bus"—and we watch Bob bounce along as a passenger. In another context, he could easily appear as a New York subway rider. Without Mike's signboards, it would be difficult to know exactly what is taking place on Bob's vacation. We know the mime is finally seeing the canyon when Mike holds up a sign reading "Hopi, Mohave, and Pima Points." We watch Bob perform "looking off into the distance," and with one eye squinting, he looks through a frame formed by his thumbs and index fingers to snap pictures of a canyon only he can see. I hear smatterings of laughter, but much of the audience is quietly watching and waiting, just like the mime they see portraying a tourist "waiting in line." A few people sit on the edge of the real canyon and view the show from a distance. The mimes have taken on a formidable task, and frankly, they're not getting away with it. When the show finally ends, the small crowd politely applauds and quickly scatters down the esplanade, toward hotels, cars, and the evening ranger program. A few linger to soak up the last traces of the sun's aura on the horizon. The mimes gather up their signs and props. They are sweating through their makeup, and Bob's eyeliner runs like black tears on his white face. Bob says something to Mike about improving tomorrow's performance. They have worked hard to put on this show, but I think they sense the audience's indifference.

Perhaps the theme was a problem. Their act had drawn from a limited reservoir of tourists' physical behaviors and covered most of the bases. Driving. Looking. Waiting. Riding the shuttle. Taking pictures. They might have been better off working some of the old chestnuts like "walking into the wind" or "the man trapped in a glass box." Instead, their silent comedy reduced the canyon vacation to a black-and-white index of robotic gestures and flattened features. The mimes' rendering of vacation time certainly held a kernel of a truth tourists knew and could laugh about. They know they are balancing on a thin line between work and leisure. For an audience who lived the wait–ride–circle the parking lot–look–snap the photo-repertoire first hand, the mimes' effort to translate tourist banalities into Art merely seemed another request for patience. Besides, there was much more to it than these surface images and impressions.

"Landscapes can be deceptive," notes John Berger. "Sometimes a landscape seems to be less a setting for the life of its inhabitants than a curtain behind which their struggles, achievements and accidents take place. For those who, with the inhabitants, are behind the curtain, landmarks are no longer only geographic but also biographical and personal."[45] The Grand Canyon may offer a backdrop for many tourist dramas, yet they are often hidden behind a curtain we call *tourism*. The canyon's tourist landscape, made of viewfinders and observation points, scenic roads and trails, museums and gift shops, guided tours, maps, and interpretive programs, is deceiving to the extent it shrouds and blankets the lives of the people they are made for. The manufactured and prefabricated products and landscapes of mass culture offer a convenient, though faulted, set of clues for critics of the crowds, the audience, or the tourists who pay the admission prices, line up, sit down, and live stranded on the black-and-white surfaces of a consumer society. To see the Grand Canyon—or any other tourist site—on such terms is to sit on one side of the curtain of mass culture, either naïve or unwilling to see and acknowledge other geographies emerging as individual lives intersect with cultural productions, narratives, fantasies, and territories mapped for anyone. Behind the curtain of mass culture, beyond the mimes' sunset performance, lay numerous geographies of tourists who make the canyon over in ideal refractions of their lives. In the end, spatial references seem less compelling than watching and listening to these tourists make the scene, and make meaning out of time.

In many ways, the tourists' Grand Canyon is similar to what cultural critic Dick Hebdige has called an "impossible object," where people strive for a real and material embodiment of an ideal that seems beyond their grasp. "It is impossible not because it encapsulates an unattainable dream," he writes, but "because it serves so many different (symbolic) functions, supplies so many diverse needs. . . . It is a screen on to which so much inchoate yearning and desire are projected that putting them into words is impossible. That investment of energy, that projection of desire exceeds rational description—in a word, it is sublime." This is not the same "sublime" that awestruck and enraptured Grand Canyon tourists from an earlier age described as nothing less than a beatific vision. Instead, these canyon tourists stress the aesthetic excesses and desires of lived culture where the concrete and impalpable coexist, where the invisible becomes visible in symbolic gestures, and their actions and stories underscore "the primacy of that vital point," as Hebdige notes, "where the individual and the biographical meet the collective and the historical."[46]

Long after the sun had passed below the horizon, and the mimes and tourists and everyone else are in their slumbers, I am unable to sleep. With the canyon covered in darkness, I drive along the roads of Grand Canyon Village with an idea to make a photograph of Mather Point when it is empty and free of tourists. Every time

I have gone there to make this photograph (which has become an obsession of sorts), I find the place occupied with people lingering after sunset or waiting for dawn. I have bought new batteries for my camera's flash attachment, and I decide to wait until after midnight to ensure I'll find what I'm looking for—the empty viewpoint rolling out into darkness and nothing—an image of the time when there is no canyon to see. Creeping along the roads, I see the garage and lot where drivers park the Harvey tour buses at day's end. Now empty and quiet, they huddle together, giant aluminum-and-glass beasts with empty bellies, taking a respite from their work of parceling time and vision. Above their windshields I read yesterday's and tomorrow's destinations: Sunset Tour. Bright Angel Tour. Hermit's Rest. And the ever so vague and paradoxical "Special."

I go around the village loop road, park and walk up to El Tovar. Hopi House is dark, and the slab stage where the mimes performed is now empty. Inside the hotel, a clerk stands behind the counter shuffling through receipts and punching numbers on a calculator. The chairs in the cocktail lounge are upside down on the tables, and I hear a vacuum cleaner. I stroll down the esplanade toward Bright Angel Lodge. A dishwasher from the Arizona Steakhouse sits on the wall with the dark canyon poured out below him. He's wearing gray and white houndstooth checkered pants, greasy Converse high-tops, a T-shirt, and an apron. A cigarette hangs on his lower lip as he listens to a Walkman. Whatever he hears, it must be an upbeat rhythm. His hands hold invisible drumsticks, and he's banging on the cymbals and tom-toms of a drum kit only he can see. Air drumming. Someone has left a light on in the gift shop, and I see silhouettes of souvenir kachina dolls lined up on shelves like a small army of mysterious aliens. Inside the lodge, an Asian man is asleep, sitting upright on a bench. Another clerk stands behind the front desk, writing names on a schedule sheet; she doesn't look up as I walk through and out, into the parking lot and back to my car parked near the historic train depot.

I drive out to Yaki Point, and the parking lot is empty. I climb out and walk along the rim trail for a few minutes and find a place to sit. The sky is black, clear, and bright with many stars. To the east, I see a thin crescent moon. My flashlight finds the canyon's edge; beyond it is only darkness, and I hear a stiff breeze rushing through the trees. The canyon feels like a powerful presence here with the wind churning up out of the abyss, particularly after I turn off my light and just sit with all of it. I discover I'm self-consciously trying to see and feel the canyon in some new way. I'm fearful I have only grown weary of it, taken it for granted because of the time I've spent here. I wonder if I've missed or am incapable of experiencing that sense of awe and insignificance so many have testified about in their accounts. Suddenly, I hear the sound of another car and stand up to get a look back toward the parking lot. It's a park ranger's cruiser, and its driver turns on the high beams and the flashing emergency lights mounted on the roof. A ranger gets out and walks around my car with a flashlight, looking in the windows. My heart races a bit as I watch all of this from the trees. I haven't done anything wrong, I think, but the flashing lights on an official vehicle only bring to mind ideas of crime scenes and accidents. Then I finally realize that through the ranger's eyes, my lone car in the parking lot could be a sign of just that— a crime, an accident, a person in trouble, someone who has come here to jump.

"This is how it begins," a Coconino County Sheriff Department detective told me one afternoon in his Flagstaff office. "Rangers find a car where people don't usually park. They take note of the time and license plate. Twenty-four hours later they'll tow the car and find a suicide note, then try to contact the family." The detective told me he'd investigated more than twenty-five suicides during the past five years. "The ones who come here to do it are really driven," he said. "They are not looking for attention. No pills, no cut wrists. The canyon is a very effective means of suicide. The bodies look like a rag doll. All the bones break, but nobody comes apart. The skin can withstand a lot. I'm certain it's an instantaneous death when they hit." In all of his investigations, he'd found no common denominator among them. "Look at it this way," he said. "A city of five million people will probably have a certain number of suicides every year. You get five million people, and some loose ends are gonna show. The canyon has about five million visitors a year, so the number of suicides is probably not that disproportionate. There are a lot of people there on vacation so it's different from a city, but not everyone goes on vacation happy."

After a few minutes had gone by, the ranger shut off his lights and pulled away. I was alone again on Yaki Point and remembered that some people had chosen this place to jump. In 1989, it was a twenty-one-year old man from the Midwest who left home to go on a self-searching journey. "You'll hear from me when I find myself," he told his parents. Instead, they heard about him from Coconino County deputies a few days after they found his car parked at Yaki Point and, later, his body. In 1993, at the South Kaibab trailhead I had passed on the access road to Yaki Point, a California man in his early twenties drove his car over the rim. A hiker who had just come up the trail told park rangers he saw the man in a white car slowly circle the parking lot. The driver waved to him and drove out of the lot. A few minutes later, the hiker said, the same car came back into the lot and this time it was going more than thirty-two miles per hour, heading straight for the rim. It clipped a tree and went over the edge. It never slowed down, the hiker recalled. The engine was still roaring, pedal to the floor, even after the car left the ground.

If canyon visitors collectively formed a city, as the detective said, reading reports from the sheriff's office and Arizona newspapers had shown me some of its dark quarters.[47] Most often, there are no witnesses to canyon suicides. Instead, officers piece together clues allowing them to ascertain whether a death is a result of foul play, accident, or intentionally self-inflicted. But in the end, the "case-closed" determinations of officers investigating suicides seem a pale conclusion when I read through what remains in the aftermath. Instead, the reports of people stumbling onto evidence and clues that "something is not right here" call up a greater mystery of lives taken to the edge of worlds filled with disappointment and despair, friends and families who could not understand, failed plans and divorces and drug abuse, and haunting images of people confronting their final days, hours, and minutes. The victim was "seen last Thursday night, sitting in his parked car near Grand Canyon Village with the dome light on, writing," says one report. "The car was four days overdue and had been rented for use in Nevada only," says another. "Some empty beer cans and some Marlboro cigarette butts were on the ground near the vehicle." A suicide note found in another victim's vehicle said he "was despondent about being gay and the way his family could not accept it." Another file tells of a sixteen-year-old from South Dakota who, following a meeting with his high-school vice principal over declining grades, took his mother's car to the Grand Canyon. According to his mother, her son had become lazy regarding schoolwork over the past year and a half, a change she attributed to her separation from her husband. Five days after he left home, park rangers found his body near the Mather Point Overlook. "The victim held clutched in his right fist a small six inch in length twig," said the report, and "clutched within his mouth was a gold colored crucifix which he held in his teeth [and] was worn on a gold colored chain around his neck." Officers found the boy's car unlocked with the keys in the ignition. Inside, they retrieved a black folder with poems about death and immortality but nothing specifically resembling a suicide note. They found a Winchester 12-gauge pump shotgun, a Smith and Wesson .357 revolver, a Smith and Wesson .38 special revolver, and ammunition for all the weapons in the trunk.

Despite gathering and sorting through the clues and evidence for motives and conclusions, these reports follow a trail to the edge of Grand Canyon that remains, in the end, inexplicable and puzzling. Some of them have come great distances to end their lives here. In 1993, a recently divorced thirty-seven-year-old woman from Texas drove to the canyon and tried to drive over the rim at The Abyss, a place just west of the Mohave Point scenic turnout, but her Chevy Suburban came to a stop when it got hung up on a large boulder at the canyon's edge. According to park service and sheriff's department investigators, she climbed out of the Suburban and jumped but landed on a talus slope fifteen feet below the rim. She could have stayed on this ledge but instead crawled to the edge and jumped again. This time, she fell another twenty-five feet and landed on a second ledge. Officers found a small crucifix and a blue coat on the second ledge. Again, she chose to jump, and this time fell forty-five feet to a small shelf where her body was recovered. A detective contacted the woman's former husband to report the Suburban they found on the rim and that there had apparently been a suicide. "Did she drive the Suburban into the Grand Canyon?" the ex-husband asked the detective. He said his ex-wife had been depressed and suicidal since their divorce. "She was infatuated by the movie *Thelma and Louise*," he told the officer, and had kept renting the film—more than fifty times—according to information he had from the video store. As chilling as her persistent effort to kill herself may seem, it is also a story of how some of these Grand Canyon suicides are final performances. No one can know the extent that the final scene from *Thelma and Louise* offered a model for her suicide, but reading the report brings to mind an instant when the cinematic freeze-frame of her movie suddenly broke—like film getting stuck in the projector, the image melting into a hallucinatory globule on the screen and leaving everyone stunned in the darkness—and real life rushed to the surface with extraordinarily concrete choices.

A suicide report about a thirty-four-year-old man from Pennsylvania suggests that he arranged the events of his death as a kind of macabre theater. Two days before the man jumped from Hopi Point, he took a scenic flight on Grand Canyon Airlines and took aerial photographs of the canyon which he had processed and mailed to his parents on the following day. Sometime after mailing the photographs, he leaped from Hopi Point. Officers recovering the body noted the victim was wearing black combat boots, cutoff jeans, and a black T-shirt reading "Over the Edge" (although the autopsy report says the T-shirt had the phrase "Out of Body Back in Five Minutes" printed across it). The jumper's brother cleaned out his dead brother's desk at his former place of employment two weeks later and found a suicide note with a cartoon depicting a man falling, the report said. The note was written as a poem and made reference to "falling" and a "suicidal shooting star." Another report from January 1995 describes the ritual-like scene of a twenty-five-year-old man who jumped from the rim near the Powell Memorial. Swiss tourists found a set of footprints (visible in fresh snow) leading to the canyon's edge with no returning footprints and contacted park rangers who investigated the scene. They found the victim had drawn large initials—nearly two feet in size—in the dirt and an arrow pointing to the canyon's rim. Near the initials, the man had set up an artificial rattlesnake on a ledge. "The victim took the time to draw the initials, set up the rattlesnake on a ledge and pack dirt around it to make it look real," says the report. Near the rattlesnake, they found a watch on a small rock. He had ceremoniously crushed the face of the watch with a stone in the moments before he jumped. The investigating deputy filing the report interpreted the initials and arrow as a symbol that the victim went this way, over the rim, and met death. The rattlesnake was a symbol of death, he wrote, and the broken watch indicated he had run out of time.

Beneath the starry skies over Yaki Point, the sound of the wind whipping up and over the canyon's rim is unsettling. I am not considering jumping, only thinking about those who do, maybe because the ranger's cruiser had come and checked my car. Maybe because jumping is a choice I am not making, and it only brings to mind the alternative. "We don't know what the limit of tolerance is in any human being," M. F. K. Fisher wrote in a meditation on the urge to jump from high places. "I know this pull well, and I have no feeling of impatience or anything but tolerance for the people who jump. There *must* be those places. There are those places." Fisher was describing how San Francisco's Golden Gate Bridge called up such feelings. "I felt an urging toward oblivion, I suppose, toward peace," she said. "I do not believe it was bad. I do feel the Golden Gate Bridge is a place of great beauty, where many people merge with that beauty into a kind of serenity, a compulsion to get out of this world and into a better one. And that is not evil at all." The Grand Canyon is one of those places where desires and disappointments from other places find some relief, satisfaction, or continue to haunt the people who come here. Fisher acknowledged, however, there were "many evil things that lurk in the minds of all people who are left after the suicide of somebody they love," yet she seemed to understand how people could feel compelled to take their lives into their own hands.[48]

Those who come to Grand Canyon for a final leap must surely drop a heavy measure of sadness into the lives they have left behind. Their last notes and gestures seem like messages sent from beyond the grave, accounts of people feeling the press to leave one world for a better one, standing at the turning point, deciding, and acting. Few people talk about suicides at the Grand Canyon. It is one of those subjects that appears as a small newspaper item now and then. Yet, everyone who comes here can feel the awesome potential beyond the edge; I hear it in the jokes and wisecracks and shrieks of those who roam the trails, sit in the bars, and grab for their children's hands as they stray toward the rim. Those intent on leaping remain a mystery at the end of the day. They have thrown the tourist's terms of escape beyond proportion, often beyond the ken of comprehension for the rest of us who return to the comparatively minor dreads, boredom, and routines of our jobs and lives. I cannot celebrate or defend those who jump from places like Yaki Point where I sit now, alone. But I can understand the desire to escape from oneself and the world. It takes shape every day here at the canyon, as I watch tourists walk into the canyon's depths, make their campsites, and adjust themselves for photographs. They are existential performances, ways of marking time in a powerful landscape, reconciling the divisions between who we are and how it all might be.

At two o'clock in the morning, I arrive at Mather Point and I see no other cars in the parking lot. With camera and flash, I walk out to the scenic overlook. My hand follows the railing through the darkness and down the concrete steps. Finally, I have the place to myself, I think, and I can make the photograph I have only imagined. I gaze up at the big smear of the Milky Way, and across the canyon, I make out the dim lights of the lodge on the North Rim. It is so dark, I can barely see my own hand when I hold it to my face, and I suddenly realize that I will not be able to focus my camera. I will just have to aim toward the canyon, shoot, and hope something will come of it. Then, I hear their voices. "I think I'll go back for one more year and then decide if I should get out of the relationship," I hear a woman say. "I'm a loyal person. I give everything to the people I love. It was that way with Gary, but he didn't see it at the time." Someone else is here; people are sitting and talking, but I cannot see them. I wonder if they know I am here or whether it matters. I stand quietly and listen as the woman tells her companion, a man with a German accent, about her past relationships and how they have come apart. "I'm really a good person. I'm committed, devoted, but people just don't see that side of me," she says. "Yes, yes, yes, you are," I hear the man say, reassuring her again and again. "That is true of you. You are like that. . . ."

7

Making and Breaking the Scene

On a cold and damp November afternoon, I can see clouds hovering in the canyon below the rim. The thunderstorm has passed and the sun is breaking through, illuminating distant buttes and plateaus, and leaving shadows on inner canyons. The clouds below the rim rise like smoke drifting up from hell. "That *is* stunning. It's so huge, much bigger than I imagined it. This is the first time I've seen this," I tell my friend Nancy, who stands next to me. "It's beautiful," she says. "Look at the colors . . . the light." We speak quietly, not so much in reverence but not to disturb the others around us, who silently gaze at the scene. "Did you see this over here?" I say, and we turn to look at a canyon's sulfur walls bathed in sunlight. "Look at those two guys on that overhang," I say, pointing to the tiny figures in the distance. "Oh," says Nancy, "and look, you can see the steam coming from . . . what are those? . . . geysers? He really had an eye for details." This is the first time either of us has seen Thomas Moran's *Chasm of the Colorado* (1873–1874) and the *Grand Canyon of the Yellowstone* (1872). The enormous canvases are hung opposite each other in one room of the National Gallery of Art in Washington, D.C.; they are part of a major retrospective exhibition simply titled "Thomas Moran."[1]

We turn back to Moran's painting of the Grand Canyon in Arizona. I move up close to see the brushstrokes and look for the traces of the man who painted the scene so many nineteenth-century Americans saw in reproductions and woodcuts before tourists even started coming to the canyon. We listen to others gaze in awe at this original. "Oh, my," a woman says to a companion. "It's breathtaking." He nods in silence, hands on his hips, head bent back and looking up at the canvas nearly covering the entire wall. "Yes, it is," he says, "but this doesn't capture all of it. If you go there, you'll see." A man with a ruddy face, wearing biking shorts tells his girlfriend, "I've been there," as if he just rode in from Arizona. I wonder if they know this "there" is really only found *here*, that Moran invented this view from sketches and photographs made at different locations on the North Rim in the first decades of the 1870s. They know it's a painting, yet everything they say aims toward someplace else where they might feel like they feel now, standing before these oils and pigments Moran spread on the canvas more than a century ago. This is how Americans have been urged to see the national parks. I recall finding a 1967 Rand McNally guide in my parents' basement. "Visiting the national parks is truly an art, requiring time, training, patience," it said, echoing observers who stood on the rim in 1899. "Walking through a gallery, the man who has learned how to look at pictures perceives deeper than eye level. He absorbs with his mind and senses; so, too, should it be with national parks."[2] But in all of the trips we took to national parks during my childhood, I never recall my parents taking such advice too seriously. My father bought the Rand McNally for its road maps and lists of campgrounds. We knew little about how to properly see works of art, but we could sometimes feel the land stir our hearts and bodies nonetheless.

People move through the exhibit wearing headsets connected to tape machines slung over their shoulders. They listen to an audio tour as they look for the depth of Moran's vision. In the next room, two counters on opposite walls have mounted stereoscopes with stereograph cards. People stand in line behind each station and wait for their turn to sit down in a wooden chair, put the hood up to their brow to close out the milling crowd in the gallery, and focus to see a three-dimensional West. Nancy and I look at Moran's painted landscapes and note how much of their drama comes from the mist of clouds, stormy skies, breaking thunderstorms, and the sunlight shining on monuments and valleys as if coming from heaven. In addition to all of his talents, we decide that the painter was a good weatherman for many in the nineteenth century, particularly those who had grown weary from the optimistic but hollow forecasts of progress as they looked out their doors to drifting industrial smoke and an urban life that could feel equally weightless. It was raining when we took a cab to the National Gallery. Our driver sped along the avenues Pierre L'Enfant had designed in 1791; Washington D.C. was the first city in America planned by a "trained professional," a Frenchman who combined Philadelphia's grid plan with the diagonal avenues, vistas, and monuments of Versailles.[3] But when we head back to the Hyatt Regency, where we are attending an American Studies conference, the steel-gray sky is clearing, and clouds give way to golden shafts that light the sides of buildings. "Ah, we have a 'Thomas Moran Sky,'" says Nancy, collapsing her umbrella, as we pass up the cab drivers, choosing instead to find a way back on our own.

At the end of the Moran exhibit, on a cart where people placed their audio-tour headsets, I found a visitor comment book and read a few entries. "Such a breathtaking journey," said one person. "Is it any wonder America took on mythic proportion to European as well as Eastern citizens who vacationed in the West. This is the country of 'Dances with Wolves.' This is the eden our progress transformed." "Splendid scenery," wrote someone else. "Thank you for this majestic view." "Having been to many of the places Moran painted it is wonderful to see his unspoiled views of those magical places," said another. "I would have liked to have seen some of the more factual information gathered by the *scientific* expeditions that went into these areas where the paintings were made," wrote someone who seemed less than willing to absorb Moran's paint on its own merits. They are grateful and appreciative to whoever put this exhibit together and placed this book for them to sign. They understand an American West made of myths and symbols and the machine in the garden.[4] They mix fantasies with realities; they are romantics and skeptics. Their comments wander in directions far from the gallery's walls and toward landscapes mapped with past and present, ambition and desire, loss and redemption.

These exhibit visitors' comments sound much like those I've read from visitors at the Grand Canyon who speak of unspoiled, magical Edens as they gaze from the rim. "Looking at these wide expanses I wonder why people (the human race) has the need to argue. We are such a small part of this universe, let us cooperate." The canyon "really makes me wonder why everyone in the world can't 'get along' (Why are there wars, murders, etc.?)," wrote someone else. "I think if everyone could come and view the canyon and all of its 'vastness' and 'beauty' mankind may take a different perspective of themselves." The canyon prompted another visitor to imagine a divide between a human intolerance and an essential humane nature. "It is apparent that people, wherever they are from, have the same basic wants, needs, and desires," but "in looking at such a sight, it makes one wonder about the bigotry of man." Somone else saw the canyon as a prescription for resolving global conflict. "Place all the leaders of all governments that are at odds with one another at the bottom of the canyon," the writer advised. "Don't let them out until they feel the greatness of nature and sublimate their petty gripes."[5] As optimistic, naïve, or nostalgic as they may appear, both the painting in the museum and the canyon itself offer screens on which people project possibilities for alternative visions of life, society, and culture as they index contemporary problems, disappointments, and conflicts. Each scene—in the museum and in Arizona—inspires hopes for some place better.

Oscar Wilde once remarked that "a map of the world that does not include

Utopia is not worth glancing at," and in many ways, these visitors' comments imagine awesome landscapes of perfection and harmony. The literal meaning of "utopia," of course, is "nowhere"; it is an imaginary destination one arrives at through writing and reading. Historically, "utopia" has been a genre giving form to a social and cultural imagination, argues Paul Ricoeur, which critically examines the legitimacy of an ideological symbolic order. "Utopia introduces imaginative variations on the topics of society, power, government, family, religion," he says, and suggests that the "nowhere" of utopia is a symbolic counterpart to the concept of ideology. "The nowhere puts the cultural system at a distance; we see our cultural system from the outside precisely thanks to this nowhere," writes Ricoeur. "What is ultimately at stake in utopia is not so much consumption, family, or religion but the use of power in all these institutions. Is it not because a credibility gap exists in all systems of legitimation, all authority, that a place for utopia exists too?" The cultural function of literary utopias, he says, is to "expose the credibility gap" in systems of representation which sustain social order that surpass "both our confidence in them and our belief in their legitimacy."[6]

For Ricoeur, ideology and utopia are processes of a "reproductive" and "productive" cultural imagination. On the one hand, ideology stages "a process of identification that mirrors the order" of social life; its reproductive capacity provides an integrative "picture" of society that "has a function of preservation [and] conservation." Utopia, on the other hand, suggests how "imagination may have a disruptive function; it may work as a breakthrough . . . an imagining of something else, the elsewhere."[7] Whereas ideology reproduces a justifiable social order through repeated representations, utopia has the productive capacity and "fictional power of redescribing life."[8] More's sixteenth-century *Utopia,* L'Enfant's eighteenth-century blueprint for Washington D.C., the early nineteenth-century Saint-Simonians' socialist tracts, Fourier's plans for a "new industrial world," and the late nineteenth-century images of a "celestial city" that observers superimposed on the Grand Canyon are all fueled by reformist visions, at once real and imaginary, echoing the redemptive and evaluative "glance from nowhere" Ricoeur sees in literary utopias; it is a glance emerging from a "credibility gap," from cracks and fissures in a legitimatized social order and the contradictory experiences of modern life.

What binds Moran's *Chasm of the Colorado* with the Grand Canyon in Arizona is a vision of nature reaching from the end of the past century to the end of this one. It is a way of seeing that inspires utopian images—glances toward elsewheres—but these images remain as discursive fantasies that do not often materialize in any other form because of an ideology that, ironically, reproduces and preserves an idea of the canyon as a painting of a premodern Eden. The Grand Canyon should not change; this is the creed of preservationists and the park service. They hold tightly to a deeply sedimented history of unbroken paeans to insignificance and awe even as they see themselves surrounded by manufactured viewpoints, museums, gift shops, hotels and theme-park Indian dwellings, telescopes, asphalt trails, daily mule trains, and scenic helicopters and airplanes taking to the air nearly every minute of every day. If the Grand Canyon's physical, geographical, and cultural landscape appears to have changed little over the past century, it is because of these watchful custodians. But those who are inspired toward dreams of an *elsewhere,* or come to the canyon in an effort to redescribe life, sometime expose the dividing line between ideology and utopia, preservation and disruption, integration and a new order. Let me offer a few illustrations from the past three decades of this century.

During June 1967, for example, Coconino County Sheriff Cecil Richardson asked the governor to put the Arizona National Guard and Arizona Highway Patrol riot personnel on alert due to reports of an expected hippie "love-in" at the park. "Richardson said informants have told him there is a chance 20,000 to 50,000 hippies will invade the Grand Canyon area for a 'love-in' session beginning June 26 and lasting through the July 4 weekend," reported Bill Nixon in the *Arizona Republic.* "No confirmation could be obtained yesterday of any such plans among the hippie groups, which are generally loosely knit organizations that do not have the resources to move the numbers of people estimated by law enforcement officials." In preparation for the event, the FBI organized a special two-day seminar to advise county and national park law enforcement agents on the terms of their "arrest powers in a national park and the legal and physical problems that could arise in a love-in of hippies," and focused on laws regarding theft, narcotics, prostitution, indecent exposure, littering, and disturbing the peace. "We doubt if there is a precise date on which the hippies will descend on us 10,000 strong, but it is pretty certain they will come," Park Superintendent Howard Stricklin told the press. "Some of them already have been here in ones, twos, and threes."[9] However, the mass gathering never came to pass, and by June 25, the day before the love-in was to have started, the *Arizona Republic*'s coverage of the story had dwindled to a small news item. "Authorities said yesterday they had a group of twenty-five hippies under surveillance at Grand Canyon National Park and hoped they are not the vanguard of a large congregation," the Associated Press reported, and word out of "San Francisco has been that the 'love-in' was canceled."[10]

It's not easy to imagine a Grand Canyon where people would come by the thousands not just to take in a view of a spectacular natural wonder but also to be with each other. During the late 1960s, such a scene was beyond the ken for many who saw loose threads of America's social fabric unraveling everywhere. Obviously, the planned love-in only revealed the extent the Grand Canyon had remained a precious American icon since the end of the last century, a symbolic space to retreat from the chaos and disorder of culture. The call to arms over the advancing hippies showed an otherwise invisible frame surrounding the scene. The few eager hippies arriving early for the love-in surely knew they were in the sights of park authorities. Even though they came in "ones, twos, and threes," like any American shareholder of a national park, standing out at the Grand Canyon—or anywhere for that matter—was part and parcel of the politics of the late–1960s counterculture movement. There could have been no better place to assemble than the Grand Canyon for youthful rebels who pursued their utopia through sentimental images of harmonious native tribes and vision quests, who showed up on city streets wearing buckskin jackets, beads, long hair and head bands, whose desire to abandon the myths of one America meant adopting the myths of an America from a previous century, and who—despite their desires to "drop out" and "get off the beaten track"—continually sought conventional public arenas for dramatizing their resistance.

"Subculture forms up in the space between surveillance and the evasion of surveillance; it translates the fact of being under scrutiny into the pleasure of being watched. It is hiding in the light," observes Dick Hebdige. "Since the 1950s, the 'politics of youth' in this country has been played out, first and foremost as spectacle: as the 'politics' of photogenic confrontations, of consumption and 'life style.'"[11] In hindsight, the canyon's spectacular scenic divide perhaps offered an appropriate backdrop for a spectacle of an increasingly divided American culture. If anything, the prospect of hippies collecting themselves on the canyon's rim retrieved the persistent myths of the American West as the "childhood of the nation," the place where an antimodern imagination sought what Emerson called an "original relation to the universe," and where contemporary incarnations of Twain's Huckleberry Finn could still "light out for the territory."[12] But they also showed how these traditions aroused another West, one that had become bureaucratized, heavily managed and policed, and how quickly the sandbags and barbed wire could be thrown into place against anything threatening the ideal of a collective American vision of the Grand Canyon—a place supposedly free of politics and unencumbered by a particular point of view apart from one's individual gaze. The hippies wanted to come to bask in their sunshine daydreams with the childlike innocence prone to a nostalgic West, but it was difficult to see the canyon as anything beyond the masterpiece framed in gold and hanging on the museum's walls. They were not alone in finding that the canyon's freedom had limits or that pursuits of the imagination and identity were chained to aesthetic conventions trailing back a hundred years.

In September 1980, Los Angeles stuntman Dar Robinson drove a white sports car at high speed off a ramp on the rim, soared into the Grand Canyon, and parachuted to safety while his vehicle smashed on the canyon floor below. The stunt was filmed for a television episode of *That's Incredible*. Park officials denied Robinson a permit to perform the stunt within park boundaries, but he was granted permission for his feat by tribal administrators on the Hualipai Indian Reservation, eighty miles west of the national park. A newspaper article reported the event was a "callous desecration of the Grand Canyon for the sake of entertainment . . . staging and filming such a stunt in the Grand Canyon cheapens one of the scenic glories of the world."[13] In 1986, French aerialist Philippe Petit sought permission from officials to temporarily suspend a one-inch cable across the Colorado River in the canyon's inner gorge. Petit, who once walked a tightrope between the twin towers of the World Trade Center in New York City, said he wanted to produce "the most immense theatrical event ever made . . . a kind of aerial opera in the Grand Canyon." Petit said he envisioned himself balancing on the cable over the gorge while musicians performed an opera he would compose for the feat, and he also was negotiating with television networks to broadcast the event. "I am a theatrical person," said Petit, "looking for a place to write and direct and act." The park service, however, was "philosophically opposed" to his plans, said a spokesman. "We're charged with the protection and enjoyment of our visitors, not their demise."[14] The *Arizona Daily Sun* stated a similar view. "Petit's proposed stunt would be dangerous and the preparation of the cable and the assemblage of musicians, camera crews and spectators could forever mar some of the canyon's splendor," an editorial read. "The Park Service should tell Petit thanks, but no thanks for his art show. We'll all continue to enjoy the beauty of the canyon more without such publicity stunts."[15]

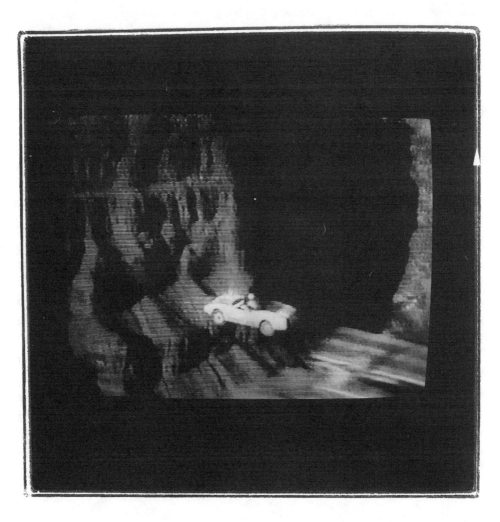

In part, our cultural views of Grand Canyon do not change because it remains under the eyes of observers who sought to anchor themselves against the uncertainties of national identity and the ambivalent atmosphere of change at the end of the nineteenth century. Their quest was for culture, and that meant places like the Grand Canyon became the equivalents of great artworks that were to be admired from a silent and contemplative distance. Dar Robinson and Phillipe Petite imagined scenes closer to something we might find at a circus—a man shot out of a cannon, a tightrope walker, a trapeze artist, a lion tamer. Robinson and Petit sought to star in dramas pitting humans against the forces of nature and fate, sensational displays of courage and daring that dramatize, as historian Paul Johnson notes, "the noise and physicality of working-class recreations."[16] The stuntman driving over the edge and the tightrope walker ask us to celebrate the individual over the canyon. But this role has typically been reserved for the scientist and the artist.

It's worth noting that one year before Robinson went over the edge, and seven years before Petit publicly announced his plan for an "aerial opera," the park service granted a permit for a piano concert near Maricopa Point on the South Rim. On September 18, 1979, pianist Marden Abadi played selections from Debussy, Gershwin, Chopin, and Grofe's *Grand Canyon Suite* before several hundred people. The park service would not allow the use of a helicopter to lower the one and a half ton, $30,000 rosewood grand piano below the rim. Instead, like a group of ants, a team of about forty people carried the piano and placed it rather precariously by the canyon rim. "The bench was right at the edge," Abadi told me, "and during the middle section of Chopin's *Grande Polonaise* in A flat, when the piano thunders, the bench started to shift. I quickly jumped off or I would have gone over. I had to start the piece again." The concert was taped and televised by CBS. "It was a real *cultural event*," said the pianist. "The park service people didn't think it would come off, they thought it was crazy, but they gave us permission and were quite pleased by the result. The acoustics were marvelous, just unbelievable. It was like playing in a great auditorium rather than outdoors, where sound sometimes does not carry well." Seventeen years after Abadi's concert, on September 18, 1996, President Bill Clinton sat at a desk carried to the canyon's edge—and placed near the spot Theodore Roosevelt stood ninety-three years earlier—to recite another classic. "You cannot improve upon it," said Clinton, wearing khakis, cowboy boots, and quoting Roosevelt's speech. "What you can do is keep it for your children, your children's children, all who come after you." And with a stroke of his pen, Clinton created Canyon of the Escalante National Monument, 1.7 acres of red-rock country in Utah, under the Antiquities Act of 1906. A few hundred spectators attended the event, which took place during Clinton's reelection campaign tour, and a *New York Times* reporter noted how the scene had, in fact, been improved for the president's appearance. "In an era of supreme attention to campaign visuals, the stop also provided Clinton with a breathtaking backdrop—and the branches of trees behind him had been tied back and down with yellow nylon cords to make sure the television cameras could record the full panorama."[17]

Playing Chopin can be dangerous; it depends on where you sit at the piano. Sometimes you can bend a branch so it does not break; it's a matter of judgment and force. In the end, what is at stake in all of these examples centers less on questions of damaging the environment or protecting lives. If this were the case, the daily mule trains to Phantom Ranch would end; the rivers would be free of spirited vacationers wanting to ride the rapids; the propellers on the planes and helicopters flying over Grand Canyon would stop turning; and guardrails would surround the canyon. What is really at stake is damaging a vision of the scene that remains lodged in a nineteenth-century frame, a potential vandalizing of the masterpiece.

A recent attempt to temporarily scandalize a view of the Grand Canyon comes from a fifty-four-year-old former California building contractor named Nicolino. His project is called "Bras Across the Grand Canyon," and he traveled the United States trying to collect ten thousand brassieres to make a one-mile chain stretching from one rim to the other. The spectacle, which he says would hang for a month, is aimed at drawing attention to a cultural obsession with how breast size relates to women's self-esteem and the potential physical harm caused by artificial breast implants. Nicolino thinks the identity issues raised by his plan are important enough to warrant a permit for the use of public lands. However, national park officials do not agree and will not give him permission to use the park for his project. "We have pretty much told him it's not going to happen," said a public affairs officer at Grand Canyon. "It's not an appropriate event for the park. . . . To put it in artistic terms, it's like painting a mustache on the Mona Lisa."[18] Nicolino has also been denied permission to use sections of the Grand Canyon on the Navajo Nation and in Glen Canyon National Recreation Area. "The Navajo people are a matrilineal society holding womenfolk in utmost reverence and stature," said the Navajo Nation's director of parks and recreation, Clarence Gorman, in a letter to Nicolino. "We therefore feel the project will denigrate and embarrass our people and desecrate our tribal values." The Department of the Interior told Nicolino that his "proposal directly conflicts with the management of this area by impairing the visitor's opportunity for peace and tranquillity in a natural setting" and that the "construction of the sculpture has a high potential to cause irreparable damage to natural resources and would be in direct conflict with the daily visitor's float trips within the inner canyon."[19] Despite official support, Nicolino has remained committed to his plan to stage the event. "Besides being so well known, the Grand Canyon symbolically represents cleavage," he told me. "On another level, it also represents the rift between normal behavior—what I would suggest is a consensus about normal behavior around body—and the rift between that, and obsessive behavior. So the canyon is symbolic in many ways. Those are two of the most prominent ones. In other words, symbolically, it became a cultural canyon separating those two places—normal behavior and obsessive—and with these donated bras—over ten thousand of them from women all over the world—I'm using those bras to make a statement by linking them all together and spanning that rift, that cultural canyon."

The letters Nicolino collected from people who heard of his project suggested it would take more than a string of undergarments to bridge the divisions existing among members of the public who heard of his plans through newspaper and radio reports. "You creepy degenerate pervert," wrote a Lakewood, Colorado, man who said he was "sick of lazy misfits like yourself taking the deserved spotlight away from *true artists* just to get yourselves in the public eye. . . . You will probably label me a philistine or something for writing this but my God has something in store for people who do things such as you." A woman from Arlington, Texas, told Nicolino that he might want to consider another line of work. "Maybe a park maintenance man would be appropriate for you," she wrote. "You might even learn to appreciate natural art rather than man-made horrors." A man from Grand Junction, Colorado, wrote that "a national park is not the place to hang out underwear" and suggested the project would be "much better placed in New York City, say between the World Trade Center buildings. The city has been entirely destroyed and a few more pieces of underwear floating across its skyline certainly would not be any worse of an intrusion to any already fouled earthspace."

Supporters of the project represented a variety of public and private interests. "Art reflects the social climate of the times, say something, send a bra," said the February 1994 newsletter for Women Informed Now, a Las Vegas–based information and support network for women with breast implants. "I would be honored if you would include my bra in your artwork," wrote an Arvada, Colorado, woman. "I am anticipating the day when women will be free from the 'subservient message' of lace." An Albuquerque woman wrote, "I've got plenty of these barbaric restraint devices that I'd be delighted to put to good use for once." And a woman from Livermore, California, said she wanted to donate her bras to "represent those women like me, who are less well endowed."

Nicolino's art project may never materialize, but his idea alone held the potential to animate a public life that is more often silently affirming an existing set of views. "A certain kind of public life can be nurtured through triangulation," suggests Ronald Fleming, "setting up some third element—an activity, a work of art—that ignites a conversation between people."[20] In some ways, the responses he's received from federal and state agencies, the Navajo Nation, and people across America did probe beneath the surface of the canyon masterpiece, like chipping away the oils and pigments of a painting to discover other images have been covered over. I found a similar phenomenon at Grand Canyon as I read through comments left in a visitor register from the early 1980s, pages full of loose coordinates toward other imagined landscapes reflecting a fragmented public vying to have others see the canyon and nature from their point of view. "Earth must be protected for *her* sake, not for the people who live on her bounty," wrote a February visitor. "If she is not, she will be transformed into another form of energy, frightening to 'man.' 'Man' is destroying her, and 'man' will not survive. Women are the natural protectors and nurturers—let *them* form the strategies, tend the earth as they did in the past and life will last." On another page I find a plan for equalizing the canyon's accessibility through technological improvements. "I'd like to see a carefully located tramway to the bottom so the handicapped and the aged could enjoy *all* of the Grand Canyon," wrote Jack from Wisconsin. "Install a chairlift part way down the mountain [*sic*] to enable people to walk further into the canyon, not just along the top (P.S. Not too expensive)," wrote another.

Filling in the blank space on the pages of a park register, these tourists recreate a critical observation point that looks out toward a transformed society and a democratized geography. They have not found a utopia in the canyon but suggest how the canyon might more closely resemble one. I envision these critics stepping up to the register and, for an instant, putting down a few sentences contributing to what reads like a disjointed but collective map of an imaginary canyon, an idealized geography where the canyon's conventions and ideologies publicly appear as privately recognized absences and exclusions. "Let everyone know that the flood in the Book of Genesis created this canyon 5 thousand years ago," writes a visitor in March 1982, one of several criticizing the park's bias for geology exhibits. "This is a very interesting place. But you should have more on The Indians," reads a comment signed by April (who adds that she is a Hopi). Another person also criticized an exhibit devoted to Indian life. "The recording is very unclear when the Red Man speaks. When the White man speaks, a voice clear and in control leads the way," wrote a December visitor. "I want to know what the Red Man has to say. Don't drown him out [even] if you have to rerecord it." Taken together, their inscriptions map a canyon where patriarchal dominance is corrected by an ecological feminism, a place where technology equalizes public access to the natural resources and nature's treasures, where science and religion find balanced representation, and where all can freely speak for themselves and be heard by everyone.

The park register where I found these comments merely anticipates current public debates focused on questions of multiculturalism, diversity, and representation. A 1994 *National Parks* magazine article, "Designing for Diversity," reported that African Americans accounted for 1.5–2 percent of park visitors, and Latinos accounted for 4.7 percent of visitors arriving in cars. The article advocated the development of programs "to make parks more accessible to lower-income people and other underrepresented groups." The problem with low numbers of minorities and ethnic groups was not necessarily a question of resources or a desire to travel, wrote author Jack Goldsmith, but that "minorities simply do not see themselves mirrored in Park Service employees. Like the rest of the federal government, NPS has been wrestling with how to provide a workforce that, as President Clinton says, 'looks like America.'"[21]

Goldsmith's article offers a curious statement in an age when overcrowding at national parks is a continual topic of public debate. He seems to recognize certain groups have decided not to go to places like Grand Canyon and there is something wrong with that picture. Subsequent responses to Goldsmith's article offered an occasion for a public display of divergent views over his plan for a diverse population enjoying the scenery. "To modify the National Park System to lure ethnic minorities would be a disaster and one more facet of our country that would be changed to please a few, ignoring the desires of the majority. Bringing more minorities into the parks would probably raise the crime rate," says a letter from DeLeon Springs, Florida. "Many of us look to the parks as an escape from the problems ethnic minorities create. Please don't modify our parks to destroy our oasis." A letter from Grand Junction, Colorado, stated, "It is obvious that the activities and environment in the National Park System, which many of us deeply appreciate, are not of great interest to most blacks and Latinos. They prefer other activities. . . . Bringing in blacks and Latinos from the ghettos will only contribute disproportionately to vandalism and other criminal activities, including robbery, murder, drug trafficking, and gang activity."[22]

In different ways, these letters beckon toward the attitudes of those who saw the Grand Canyon as a celestial city reserved for the eyes of a special class whose "minds could rise to sublime heights" and could appreciate the view. In 1967, hippies had posed a similar threat to the scene. Daredevils and performance artists similarly draw up aesthetic reminders trailing back to the nineteenth century. "Only a horizon ringed about with myths can unify a culture," wrote Friedrich Nietzsche in 1872, and the Grand Canyon has always appeared on such a horizon.[23] A mythic scientific unity of nature and the transcendent aesthetic unity of the sublime landscape helped compose the larger myths of American culture that might overcome divisions, transformations, and fragmentation. The Grand Canyon known to Americans since the nineteenth-century has always been understood through images of a transparent scientific gaze and a sense of culture that equated the landscape with paintings, symphonies, and majestic architecture, as if they were authentic avenues toward a world in which everyone silently affirms that "this is how it should be." In an age when moral, social, and scientific consensus is shattered by the divergent practices of various interest groups, tourist sites stand out as cultural landmarks that point to moments and places where knowledge, history, and aesthetics *seem* to be in fundamental harmony, notes Jonathan Culler.[24] Places like the Grand Canyon have invoked such an image for more than a hundred years, and it is continually sustained through metaphors equating culture and civilization with natural scenery.

Behind all of this is a fear that the canyon will become unreal or inauthentic. Perhaps the greatest perceived threat is that people would lose faith in the power and value of nature and see the canyon for what it has largely become—a heavily populated tourist attraction. In part, this is why the image of the masterpiece is continually invoked. Revered art objects suggest authenticity, antiquity, a culture's sense of common values, and a persistence of some truth that withstands time and change. I went to see Moran's painting at the National Gallery for many reasons, but mostly because it was an original in a world of reproductions, and I stood before the painting with a moderate feeling of awe in confronting a key element in a story I had been coming to understand about history, vision, American culture, and aesthetic experience. I was not surprised or disturbed to leave the exhibit and find the gallery gift shop had lines of people buying the usual souvenirs—wall calendars, notecards, books, and canvas bags with "Thomas Moran" printed on the side. Perhaps it was no accident that on another floor of the National Gallery was a retrospective exhibit of the works of M. C. Escher. The gift shop carried its souvenir tribute to him as well, and it somehow seemed appropriate to have these two artists come together like this in the shape of commodities that would land in homes on coffee tables, desks, refrigerators, and offices. Both artists were masters at managing vision, opening up our eyes to landscapes that played tricks on us, and carried our minds to places our bodies could never go. I doubt that anyone who put down their credit card for one of these items would have difficulty distinguishing between the heavily guarded Escher or Moran they saw on the walls of the National Gallery and the souvenirs they carried out onto the street. Yet, the fear of the reproduction and the mass-produced constantly plagues our ideas of tourists and nature; it is a fear I sometimes heard expressed by the official guardians of Grand Canyon.

One night I sat at Ranger Rick's evening program and listened as he tried to reinforce the idea that Grand Canyon was *the* genuine article. The ranger's talk was entitled "Gee . . . This Place Is Just Like Disneyland," a visual travelogue of the similarities between the famous theme park in Anaheim, California, and the Grand Canyon, a quarter mile from the towering pines of Mather Amphitheater, where we looked at slides projected on a screen. Ranger Rick showed us pictures of Goofy, Mickey Mouse, and Donald Duck and then drew a parallel to the wildlife we could see at the canyon. We watched theme-park visitors in Disney's Adventureland crammed into the cockpit of an artificial log canoe and splashing down a water chute. The canyon had something similar, he said, and he projected a slide of rafters blasting through rapids on the Colorado River. Disneyland had its Frontierland, so did the canyon, and he drew our attention to these parallels for nearly an hour. His performance was, of course, tongue in cheek, and by the end of the talk, he said he had become convinced of the similarities between the theme park and the canyon. But then he came to his senses, he told us, when he returned to the canyon after visiting the theme park and found himself watching the sunrise over the chasm.

"I found myself screaming to no one in particular that this place is *not* like Disneyland!" he screamed at us, and then he related his epiphany to all of us seated in neat rows on benches. "To compare Grand Canyon to anything man-made—Disneyland or otherwise—would be to trivialize what this canyon is all about. It's so special, that there's a special name for it. It's called *Grand Canyon National Park*. It's so special, we protect it. The goal of the National Park Service is to protect and preserve the national scenery, the wildlife here, and keep it for future generations. We try to protect this place from the influence of man, and that's another reason why I think this place is not like Disneyland. Disneyland is a tribute to man and what man can do. Grand Canyon is a tribute to nature, and what nature can do." Ranger Rick told us we were free to think about all the similarities between Grand Canyon and Disneyland, and said he hoped all our dreams and fantasies would come true while we stayed in the park. But before he ended, he asked us to do him a favor. "The favor is this," he said, speaking to us like we were all good buddies and now cued to his insights on the Disney/Canyon confusion. "As you enjoy the Grand Canyon, look around and if anyone in earshot says anything to the effect of 'Gee, this place is just like Disneyland,' what I need for you to do for me is to grab 'em and shake 'em and say 'I understand how you can make that statement in your head, but you know, this place is *not* like Disneyland and I'm gonna tell you why right now.' So tell 'em why, and *I think you know why.* So will you do that for me?" A few people say "Yeah" and a few others politely applaud, but this was not enough for Ranger Rick. "No. No. No. I say, *Will you do that for me !?*" he shouts into the microphone like he's an evangelist. This time the audience cheers, *"YEAH!"* and applauds louder than before. "Thank you," says Ranger Rick. "I think if you react in any less of a way than that to that statement, well, I think you're being Mickey Mouse about it. And on that note, I want to thank you for coming to the evening program and have a great night at Grand Canyon National Park." Again, the audience bursts into exuberant hand claps, and Ranger Rick bows.

A century ago, the vision that most haunted antimodernists was of "a docile mass society," notes Jackson Lears near the close of *No Place of Grace,* in which people "somehow had to choose between a life of authentic experience and the false comforts of modernity." It was as if they had to choose between Christ and Dostoevsky's "Grand Inquisitor," writes Lears, and quotes from a passage in which the Grand Inquisitor, forecasting his rule of the earth, tells Christ, "They will marvel at us and will be awestricken before us, and will be proud at our being so powerful and clever. . . . Yes, we shall set them to work, but in their leisure hours we shall make their life like a child's game. . . . And they will be glad to believe our answer, for it will save them from the great anxiety and terrible agony they endure at present in making a decision for themselves. And all will be happy, all the millions."[25] A hundred years later, Ranger Rick stood by his campfire, seeming to conjure up the ghost of Walt Disney as if he were a modern incarnation of the Grand Inquisitor. The ranger performed an exorcism of sorts, drawing out and crushing the spirits from a world of fabricated distractions and illusions, and held up the lantern on the path to the Promised Land. In some ways, the yearnings for authentic and real experience have changed little, and the antimodern impulse Lears described at the end of the nineteenth-century still provides a reference point for many in contemporary America. At Grand Canyon, a bureaucratized and institutionalized society often appears as the foil for imagining a "real" nature. Places like Disneyland incarnate our worst fears of a mass society that has grown unreal and phony, and Ranger Rick's evening performance offered a solution in the mystical experience of a canyon sunrise. His final gesture was to make us part of that scene, deputizing each of us with the charge to preserve and maintain the scenic wonder, and straighten out those who could not tell the difference between plastic and a ponderosa pine.

A year after I listened to Ranger Rick at the evening campfire, park administrators meeting to develop a general management plan for the next century would not find it so easy to dispel the ghost of Disney. "We are concerned with sort of the lowest common denominator," the Grand Canyon Trust's president, Geoffrey Barnard, told the audience gathered at the Shrine of the Ages, but "we do not think the Park experience should incorporate . . . sort of a Disneyland type experience. We think the parks have a higher standard than that." Barnard had another analogy in mind. "The Sistine Chapel is open for everyone to see, but only a certain number of people can see it any given time," he said, "and the Grand Canyon, in a sense, is the Sistine Chapel of the United States."[26] On the table were the issues of an overcrowded park, transportation problems, proposals for higher fees, a reservation system, and a new transportation system that could close off much of the automobile traffic that clogged park roads built decades earlier. The question before them seemed a choice between the Sistine Chapel or Disneyland, authentic experience or modern comfort, the late nineteenth century or the late twentieth century, Christ or the Grand Inquisitor. I would hear an answer some two years later as Park Superintendent Robert Arneberger spoke to an audience at the National Building Museum in Washington, D.C. on November 11, 1997. The biggest problem was the number of vehicles. Seventy-five percent of the visitors arrived in cars, and there were more than thirty-two thousand commercial bus tours in the park each year, he said. The automobile was the primary reason for a "diminished park experience," as some sixty-one hundred cars went through the south entrance each day in the summer and competed for about two thousand parking spaces. Arneberger told the audience the solution was to separate people from their automobiles. It was a solution he had broached two years earlier, in 1995, at the Shrine of the Ages. "I do not want to compare the Grand Canyon to Disneyland, but you do not drive into the middle of Disneyland," he said. "You park on the outside, and then you are efficiently conveyed to the site, and then once you are in there you are also efficiently moved within."[27] In Washington D.C., on the podium with park administrators from Yosemite, Yellowstone, and Acadia, Arneberger offered a slide show of the Grand Canyon in the twenty-first century, pictures of light-rail trains taking people to a Mather Point transit center from a staging area in Tusayan. In one slide I see the front of a futuristic train with "Grand Canyon" displayed as its destination. In another slide, I see an artist's rendering of the new Grand Canyon with the roof of El Tovar still rising above the pines. Below the hotel, I see the old steam locomotive that carries people to Williams. And in the foreground, the new train appears in sleek aerodynamic design, arriving at the South Rim from a new terminal in Tusayan, and points as far away as Anaheim and Orlando.

Breaking the Scene

I'm tired of Grand Canyon, I think, walking up the hill toward El Tovar; it's time to head back. The car I've rented for the month is due in Tampa on July 1, and if I leave tomorrow, Saturday, June 27, I can make it with a few days of steady driving. I've been staying at Mather Campground because I've been lucky enough to get a site. It's been hot all week. There's a shower near the camp, but I'm ready to get back to a real bed and home and a refrigerator with food, even though I know Florida's humidity will be a shock after a month on the South Rim. Tonight, I'm meeting Earll Kingston for a drink in the El Tovar lounge. It may be the last time I see him, since I doubt I'll be coming back to Grand Canyon for a long time. Tonight, he's been doing the John Wesley Powell show at Shrine of the Ages and said he'd be here by 9:30 or so. It's dark and people are coming back from the sunset at Hopi Point, retrieving their cars or waiting for a shuttle to a lodge or the campground. The canyon has come to feel like a routine for me. Nothing changes, except the weather and new tourist faces arriving everyday. *Bang.* I hear the sound ring through the night air. Someone's car is back-firing; it's so loud I imagine a muffler exploding. Below me, on the Village Loop road, I barely make out a car going about eighty miles per hour, headed west toward the Bright Angel Lodge. Then, I see three ranger vehicles, lights flashing, going just as fast, chasing the speeder in the white car. *Bang. Bang.* Someone better have their distributor looked at; I saw a flame flash from the muffler that time. *Bang.* That doesn't sound good.

Earll is already seated in the lounge when I arrive. His face is a little red after washing off Powell. This summer he's grown a beard so he doesn't have to glue on a fake one for the performance; he looks a little like Ahab, though not nearly so driven. We sit and talk about the usual stuff. He's frustrated by the attendance of his show tonight at the Shrine of the Ages. He makes a convincing Powell, I tell him; he makes the nineteenth-century adventure come alive. And we talk about writers we admire. I mention Richard Ford, Don DeLillo, and Walker Percy. He tells me of his admiration for the poet Gary Snyder. We share stories about our fathers, our childhoods, and growing up. He tells me Maxine will be coming to the canyon soon. I tell him I'm leaving in the morning. By eleven o'clock, it's time to say good-bye, and we exchange addresses, as in other years, and promise to write. Outside El Tovar, there's a nice breeze, and the air is cool enough for me to put on a jacket. Earll gives me a hand-shake and a strong hug before he heads back toward his cabin. We've become good friends over the past few years, even though we've only met each other a few times to talk. Before I go to my campsite, I decide to drive into Tusayan and buy some snacks for tomorrow's drive. I want to get an early start in the morning, and Babbit's is closed. I really don't feel tired enough to sleep, anyway.

Lights are flashing near the park entrance as if there's been an accident. My headlights fix on a ranger who signals me to stop, shines a light on my face quickly, and waves me through with a flashlight baton. Through my passenger window I don't see a wreck but an unexpected and eerie scene. Men in fatigues carry automatic rifles, moving in slow motion, spread out in line. Flashlights play through the trees; they are a search team. At the Stix Canyon Food Mart in Tusayan, I ask the clerk if he knows what is going on at the park entrance. "It's that escaped con. They think he's in the park," he tells me. "Some cops came in here and said that's what it was. They think it's Horning." I vaguely remember reading an article in this morning's *Arizona Daily Sun* about Danny Ray Horning. He escaped from the Arizona State Prison, a maximum-security facility in Florence, last May. The article said he'd robbed a retired couple's cabin in Pine, Arizona, while they were on vacation in Oregon. Horning stole clothes, shoes, a .22-caliber rifle and bullets, a chainsaw, a thirteen-inch color TV, food, sleeping bags, a toolbox, and the owner's 1980 Chevy four-wheel-drive truck. A Department of Public Safety officer spotted Horning driving the Chevy on Sunday, June 21, and chased him through the woods south of Flagstaff. But he ran from the truck and got away, and no one had seen him since. In the Chevy, Horning had left a note for the man he'd robbed—a polite apology for inconveniencing him.[28]

When I get back to the park's south entrance, a roadblock is already in place. A sheriff's deputy stops me, shines a light on my face, and tells me to proceed with caution. I ask him what's going on, and he just says they're looking for someone. At my camp, I can't imagine climbing into a tent and sleeping with all the action going on. Instead, I walk over to the Yavapai Lodge. At night, they convert the cafeteria into a disco. It's dim inside, and there's a mirror ball spinning. The place is nearly empty, but loud with heavy metal. A few off-duty cafeteria workers are having drinks. On the dance floor, two stout women in blue jeans and silky blouses are trying to decide if they can dance to the power guitars. Neither the bartender nor the lone patron seated at the bar knows anymore than I do about what's going on outside. I order a beer and take a seat at the table. Shards of light rotate over everyone. The two dancers give up and sit at a cafeteria table. This place could easily win the "most boring nightspot in all of Arizona" award on this Friday night, but with everything happening in the park beyond the walls of this grim makeshift nightclub, there is no chance I will leave the canyon in the morning.

"There's so many weird things that can go on here," Frank, the retired real-estate agent had said of his journeys into the canyon. "But I have to be careful who I tell about these things. They'll think I've been out in sun too long. I think the most weird was when I was at the Tanner Rapids. It was a miserably hot day and I heard a rock split open. I'll never forget it. It was like a shot. No one else was around. I ran around looking, and I found where a rock had split from the immense heat." Frank said people were skeptical when he told them this story, and, I admit, so was I. But he added that scientists told him such events were common in the canyon, even though he'd only witnessed it once in all his years of hiking. Frank's story of a rock splitting under heat came back to me, though, as an image of what occurred during the seven days before the Fourth of July, 1992. I did not realize it at the time, but the sounds I heard as I walked up to meet Earll at El Tovar—thinking a car was backfiring—were gunshots. And as they echoed through an otherwise pleasant night on the South Rim, they signaled an unexpected series of events at Grand Canyon that cracked open the entire landscape. Between June 27 and July 4, the park became the site of the largest and longest manhunt in Arizona history.

On Thursday, June 25, forty-three-year-old Adam Lakritz drove his white Taurus, a company car, from Phoenix to Flagstaff to replace a piece of computer equipment at a Jack in the Box fast-food restaurant managed by thirty-nine-year-old Kathryn Falk.[29] It was Kathryn's day off, but she was there anyway doing some paperwork. Adam and Kathryn were not really close friends but "business associates," as Kathryn described it. Adam wanted to buy a pair of cowboy boots, and the two headed over to the Circle Q Western Wear shop on Santa Fe Avenue, part of old Route 66. It was almost five o'clock when they arrived, and they spent about ten minutes in the store. Adam didn't find anything, so they went back to the car. A red van had boxed him in, so he had to jog his Taurus back and forth to get it out. Suddenly, someone rapped on his window, and he turned to see a man in a white T-shirt showing him a gun stuffed in his pants. They both started to get out of the car, but the man pulled out the gun and stuck it in Adam's ribs. "Get in the car," he yelled. "Get back in the car." They did, and the man climbed into the backseat, ducked out of view, and put the gun through the front armrest area back into Adam's ribs.

"Pull out and head toward the freeway," the man said, and Adam followed his orders. Adam saw a green Bronco in his rearview, with red and blue lights on the grill, driven by an officer of some kind, and he told this to his new passenger. "They made me," the man said. "The police've made me. Keep driving. Act normal." The gunman told Kathryn to rip the vanity mirror from the car's visor so he could see through the back window. She tried, but couldn't get it off. When they got to the freeway entrance, the gunman told Adam not to get on, and he kept driving until they came to Black Bart's Trailer Park, and he pulled off the road. With no one following them, the man sat up and told Adam to pull into an empty space behind a trailer. "Shut off the car and give me the keys," he said, and Adam did. "Do you know I am?" he asked them. "My name is Danny Ray Horning. . . . Now do you know who I am?" Adam said he had heard about him from the news, but Kathryn didn't know who he was. "You guys really saved my ass. The cops would have nailed me if they knew it was me. I thought they made me back there, that's why I had to take you guys. I've been in the woods for a while. I'm sorry I stink and look so bad."

With Adam and Kathryn in the front seat and Danny in the back seat holding a pistol on them, the three sat in Black Bart's Trailer Park, and he told them he'd escaped from the state prison in Florence, where he was serving four consecutive twenty-five-year sentences. "I'm a nonviolent person and I've never done violent crime," he said. "I never killed anybody and anything you might've heard on the news is total garbage spread by the police." He said he was involved in a child molestation case, but there was no penetration and there was nothing to it; it wasn't as bad as it sounded. "I'm a bank robber," he said. "That's what I do for a living. I don't feel bad about it. It's what I like; it's the lifestyle I've chosen." Danny said he had a wife he married when she was sixteen years old. He had children, and a brother in Monterey, California, who was a policeman. They'd grown up poor, he said, and he didn't like his in-laws. He'd told the judge who sentenced him to the "joint" in Florence that he'd escape within a year. "I missed it by two days," he bragged. "I'm gonna make a name for myself and in five or ten years I'll come back and talk with Phil Donahue on TV and expose the penal system for what it is." He apologized to Adam and Kathryn for inconveniencing them, but the cops had messed up his plan and he had to get out of the area. Adam and Kathryn were going to help him get out, he said, and as long as they did what he told them, nothing bad would happen to them. "If one of you tries to escape," he said, "I'll kill the other one then come after you." He asked Adam if he knew anything about handguns. Adam said he didn't. "Well, this is a .44 Magnum and if I shot you at close range it would take your head off." After listening to Horning threaten them, Adam and Kathryn were terrified and told him they were scared. The gun made them nervous. Cooperation was the key to their survival, he said, and instructed them to leave the trailer park so he could retrieve a bag of supplies he'd stashed off Humane Shelter Road outside downtown Flagstaff. Soon after, Adam turned his car onto Route 180 and drove up to Grand Canyon.

At the south entrance gate of the park, the ranger was closing up for the evening, and he didn't charge them to enter. The ranger gave Adam a park map and a copy of the *Guide,* and they drove up to Mather Point. With the sun setting on the canyon through their windshield, Adam and Kathryn listened as Danny hatched his scheme from the backseat of the Taurus. He wanted to find a big RV with a family who had children. He was going to take them as hostages, demand a million dollars ransom, and the release of his brother, Jerry, who was also serving a prison sentence in Florence. The RV would allow him to keep an eye on the hostages, he said, and remain mobile. They sat at Mather Point for about half an hour before driving around the park to scout out potential targets. But Danny did not see an RV that suited his plan, and night was falling. Adam and Kathryn said they were tired. Adam had driven up from Phoenix that morning; they told Horning they wanted a hotel room for the night.

Adam and Danny had to wait in line at El Tovar's front desk. Kathryn sat outside in the car, but Danny took the keys. He reminded her he'd kill Adam if she tried to run. The lobby was busy; people milled around and made phone calls. When they finally got to the desk, only one room was left, and Adam took it. Adam said he was hungry, and Danny went over to the maitre d' to order room service. "You have to order room service by phone," the man said, "and you better hurry because you need to order before ten." The lobby phones were all being used and Danny got agitated. He walked up to a man who was on a phone and said he needed to order room service in the next few minutes. The man gave him the receiver and Danny ordered himself a steak with extra sour cream on the baked potato, then gave the phone to Adam who ordered steaks for himself and Kathryn.

Danny didn't like Room 6478 at the El Tovar. It was a big and expensive suite with a verandah, a sitting room, an eating table, and a separate area for sleeping. "There's too many windows," Danny complained to Adam and Kathryn, "and I don't like those doors going out to the balcony." Then room service arrived, and Danny hid in the bathroom with his gun drawn. He told Adam not to let the waiter in the room. Danny listened through a cracked door and came out to watch Adam sign the dinner bill (which came to $76.84, including the tip). After they finished their steaks, Danny decided to take a bath. Adam and Kathryn were happy about this since he smelled awful. He brought them into the bathroom so he could keep an eye on them as he bathed. Adam sat on the toilet seat while Danny filled the tub and stripped down to the bike pants he wore under his trousers. He asked Kathryn to turn around so she wouldn't see him naked. She sat on the stoop in the doorway while he washed and put his bike pants back on. After his bath, he washed his clothes, which were so filthy the tub couldn't drain.

It wasn't easy to sleep that night. Kathryn and Adam had the only bed in the room. Adam was going to use a rollaway cot, but Kathryn asked him to sleep in the bed with her since she was so frightened. Danny moved some of the furniture to block the doors to the balcony. He told them to move around on the bed so he could get an idea of how it might sound if they tried to leave. Danny used the rollaway cot to barricade himself near the closet at the foot of the bed and slept on the floor. He set his wristwatch to go off every hour. Every time the alarm sounded, Danny would get up and walk around the room and light up a Camel. This annoyed Adam and Kathryn; they didn't fall asleep until early morning.

The next morning, they ordered room service for breakfast. Danny wanted some supplies so he and his brother could hide out after he sprung him from prison. They left El Tovar and drove to Williams. By ten o'clock, they were at the First Interstate Bank, and Adam took a $1,500 cash advance on his American Express card. Danny didn't want to go back to Flagstaff, so they drove a hundred miles west to Kingman, and went shopping at K-Mart. Danny bought a backpack, duct tape, rope, freeze-dried food, camping equipment, a microcassette recorder, and lots of batteries. At one point, he got into an argument with a clerk in the sporting goods department over a pair of binoculars. The manager came over to smooth the waters and made sure Danny was happy with the purchase. Since they were spending so much money—their bill came to more than $500—they had several employees trying to help them. At one point, Kathryn tried to mouth the words "call the police" to one of the sales clerks. "Excuse me, ma'am?" said the clerk, not understanding. Danny was close by, so

Kathryn just said, "Nothing, thanks." After K-Mart, they went to the McDonald's drive-through for lunch. At J & J Sporting Goods, Danny talked to the cigar-smoking proprietor about Uzis, grenades, and handguns, and discussed methods for converting semiautomatic weapons into fully automatic weapons. Danny picked up a mummy sleeping bag, a knife, and a few camouflage T-shirts. Before leaving Kingman, they bought $139 worth of freeze-dried food at a supermarket and, with the car loaded with supplies, turned east on I-40 to go back to the park.

Adam and Kathryn surely must have been terrified by all that happened during the past twenty-four hours. But some of that fear seemed to lift for a moment as they drove along the interstate toward Williams and Grand Canyon. In addition to every-thing Danny bought for his big caper, he also purchased three different hats and sev-eral pairs of sunglasses to use for various disguises. Kathryn took a fancy to a black hat Danny bought and was wearing it in the car. "I hope you don't think you're getting this back," she told him. "If you like it that much, go for it," he said. This was about the time they all started talking about how this would be a good story for a made-for-TV movie, something like *Danny Ray Horning's 45-Day Adventure.* "Who do you want to play you?" one of them asked Danny. "Well, you know, I think the guy that plays Billy the Kid on *Young Guns.* With his little personality, I think he'd be perfect for it," Danny said, thinking of himself played by Emilio Estevez. He asked Katherine and Adam who they wanted to play them in such a movie, and they said they would play themselves. Part of this was a joke and part of it was the truth. As far as Kathryn was concerned, she was already in a movie. When they searched for potential hostages at Grand Canyon later that night, they would look for people they could imagine as characters fitting the plot of their movie—a real-life drama that was scary and dreamy, real and unreal, all at once.

It was after six when they returned to the canyon that evening. In Babbit's park-ing lot, Danny tried to put together his supplies but was unhappy about the equip-ment he bought. They went inside the store, and Danny saw all the top-line equip-ment in the sporting goods section. He got angry that he'd settled on a pack from K-Mart. He found a model he liked better and also bought a new pair of Danner hik-ing boots, more dried food, candy bars, beef jerky, and some lip balm. They returned to the car and he dumped everything out of the K-Mart pack and put it in the new one. Adam suggested they start looking for a hotel room for the night. Danny said he didn't want to go through that again; besides, he had already picked out an RV and a family he wanted to kidnap. It was a 1992 Dodge van from Texas towing a Fleetwood trailer, and it was parked in the corner of the lot away from the other vehicles. Adam parked the Taurus near the Texas RV, and they waited for the family to return. According to his plan, Adam and Kathryn would pose as newlyweds, strike up a con-versation, tell the owner they were interested in buying a trailer, and ask to see the in-side of the Fleetwood. But before they carried this out, there was one more thing to do. They all got back in the Taurus, and Danny pulled out the tape recorder he bought in Kingman. Adam and Kathryn listened to him dictate his demands for the people he would take hostage.

"Testing—one—two—three," he said in the microphone, and paused. "Good morning Vietnam. This is Danny Ray coming at you via cassette tape directing towards Lieutenant Baldwin, Winslow Police Department. I know you're not gonna be in charge of this case, the FBI will take it over, but still I want you to know—once again I hold you responsible for the outcome. . . . I'm gonna let you know that if anything goes wrong here—you better hope I don't survive it—because if I do I'm coming for you first, at least, or somewhere down the line. So make sure you emphasize to your fellow comrades—even though they're incompetent—that, uh, your life depends on the fact that my demands on this tape are met. . . . I have now left Flagstaff where the last sighting of me was, and I have kidnapped six people. Once again—I have now kidnapped six people. I'm graduating. The school of hard knocks has really taught me a lot; I do appreciate the education you've given me. For the safe return of these hostages, you will have to meet the requirements that I'm going to verbally—on this tape—point out to you. I want one *million* dollars in cash—well-circulated bills." Danny gave precise figures for how many of each denomination.

"They are not to be marked. No ink bags, and no tracing devices please. In order to see to it that you keep your side of the deal, we're gonna throw in a little bonus, and that bonus is my brother, Jerry Dewayne Horning, D-O-C number five-six-zero-one-eight. You are to release him with the one million dollars in cash inside an army duffel bag." Danny repeated his demands again, including the denominations and how many of each. "You have until six, thirty—sixth month, thirtieth day—which is June 30 at 3:00 P.M. to have both my brother and the money sitting on a brand-new Nissan or Toyota four-by-four pickup—red in color, paperwork still on the windows—sitting in front of the Circle K across the street from the hardware store where the old Safeway used to be, right there in Winslow." Danny spelled out his plan into the recorder. His brother would wait an hour, then drive to Payson where he'd make a phone call to Danny. He was not to be followed. When he made the first call, Danny would then give him a new phone number and time to call.

"I'm gonna know that he is being followed. So, in that case, I will shoot one half of the hostages. . . . So if you want to play with the hostages' lives, that's six people that you will be costing the lives of—and I'll tell you right here and now—one of the six will survive for the simple reason that I would want that one person to notify the media and the families of the other four—excuse me, the other five—that you played games with the hostages' lives, thinking that this was TV where the cops always win. Well, this isn't TV and you're not Clint Eastwood, so let's not play no games." Danny said when he received the money and his brother, he would send the police a tape telling them where to pick up the hostages. "They will be hungry and they will be thirsty, and very uncomfortable I might add—I'm not the DOC—I don't have the money to house people like you do—so let's not play no games. They're nice people and they deserve a fair shake," he said. "But if you do not do exactly as I say, well then I will do as exactly as I told you I would do. . . . If these hostages do not work out— and you play games—and I run out of hostages, I can easily go get more. Hell, the United States is full of hostages—and we can do it again and again and again. . . . It's time consuming and these are innocent people. They don't deserve it, so in the meantime . . . I'm gonna start sniping off your cops while they drive down the highway, while they're inside of their gun towers in the prisons, whatever it takes, lawyers, cops, judges, DAs, whatever I can get, uh, my sights on, I'm taking out. If I have to burn down your forests in different locations of this state, I'll do that as well. If I have to blow up your bridges, I will do that. If I have to derail your trains—whatever it takes to get you to do what I say—I'm gonna do it. I have no limitations, nor do I have anything to lose, so . . . you have no choice. . . . You either do it—and if it isn't done by the time that I said—you will receive a telephone call telling you where a tape is, telling you where your body bags need to be brought. Think I'm bluffing? Try me." Danny made his demands into the cassette for nearly twenty minutes, continually repeating the details. When he finished, Adam and Kathryn knew they were in trouble.

Manuel Norman, his wife Sylvia, their son Manuel Jr., and Sylvia's brother, Wilford Hudson, who they called "Sonny," were having sandwiches by their van when Adam, Kathryn, and Danny walked up and asked to see their trailer. Kathryn and Adam had talked to the couple earlier, while Danny was working on his pack, and Manuel had said hello to Danny on his way to get some ice at Babbit's. They seemed friendly, he thought, and he and Sonny took them back to see the trailer. Sylvia and her son stayed in the back of the van to eat their sandwiches. Five of them went inside the trailer, and Danny told Adam and Kathryn to sit down on the couch. They sat, frozen, while Danny talked to Manuel and his brother-in-law.

"Do you know who I am?" he asked, and Manuel said he didn't. "I'm Danny Ray Horning," he said, but this meant little to Manuel. "We're from Texas," he said. "We've been on vacation for a while. I don't know . . ." Danny pulled out his revolver and pointed it at them. "I'm Danny Ray Horning and I'm an escaped fugitive," he said, "and I'm going to take you and your family hostage for the next four days." Manuel looked at Danny and said, "Are you kidding? Man, I've got to go to work on Monday." Danny said, "I don't think you'll have to worry about them missing you at work. Now get your wife and boy." Manuel was about to comply, but Sylvia already sent her son back to the trailer to see what was taking so long. Manuel Jr. arrived and saw Danny pointing the gun at his father. "Come here," Danny said to the boy, but he didn't listen and just started backing up, looking at his father and Danny's gun. "Wait a minute, I'll get him," said Manuel. "Come here, son." And he moved between the gun and his child. The boy kept backing up until he was at the front of the van, and then he bolted. "He's got a gun," the boy screamed, running toward Babbit's. "He's got a gun." That's when all hell broke loose.

"Get out! Get in the car," Danny yelled to Adam, Kathryn, and Sonny, and tried to herd them to the Taurus. Manuel Sr. ran away. Danny kept yelling and pointed the gun at Sonny, telling him to get in. Sonny told Danny he couldn't get in because there was too much camping gear in the car. Adam jumped in the front seat of the Taurus on the passenger side and Kathryn got in the backseat. In all the confusion, Sonny broke away and just ran. It was about 9:15 when park ranger Don Miller pulled into Babbit's parking lot as part of his regular evening patrol. "You have to stop him," Manuel Jr. said, as he ran up to the officer. "He's got a gun." The boy pointed to the east end of the parking lot and Miller drove over. Danny stood behind the Taurus, and Miller got out of his cruiser. He asked Danny to come around to his side of the vehicle so they could talk. Danny ignored him, and Miller asked again. This time, Danny raised his pistol and pointed it at the ranger. The officer ducked and got into his car. Danny got behind the wheel of the Taurus and sped out of the parking lot. Miller followed and called for backup units.

Traffic was a bit heavy this time of night, but Danny barreled across Village Loop Drive, over into the visitor center parking lot and toward the Shrine of the Ages. Kathryn sat in the back and tried to get her seatbelt on. Danny yelled at Adam for directions, but he didn't know where to go. They pulled onto Village Loop Drive, and Danny headed west toward the lodge area. Two park rangers answering Miller's call came up from the opposite direction. Danny stuck his gun out the driver's window while steering with his left hand and fired a shot at the cruiser. "I'm just trying to scare 'em," Danny told Adam. "Just trying to slow 'em down." He drove like a crazy man, yet he didn't hit anyone walking along the road. Danny kept yelling, his adrenaline was pumping, and he told Kathryn he was thirsty. "The sodas are all in the trunk," she said, but Adam said there were some six-packs in the back seat. She found them and gave Danny a soda which he drank while he drove. As the car sped past El Tovar, it's doubtful that Danny or Kathryn or Adam noticed me walking up the hill toward the hotel on my way to meet Earll. It was dark, and they were busy and afraid.

"I need to slow these people down," he yelled. "Kathryn, duck your head and plug your ears." She got down, and he fired his pistol through the back window. "I'm trying to scare them," he said, fired another round, and all of the glass shattered. By now, Kathryn was on the floor. "Grab the pack and throw it out," he told her. "It's too heavy," she said. "I can't lift it." He told her to find his holster, and Danny reloaded his pistol as he drove. Suddenly, they were heading toward the West Rim barricade. If the road is barricaded, thought Adam, it surely went straight to the canyon's edge, and he feared Danny was going to drive right over. With three ranger vehicles chasing them, Danny turned up West Rim Drive. He fired another shot through the rear window and told Adam to take the wheel and slow down so he could jump out. Adam tried, even though they were going about fifty. They passed Hopi Point and out of sight of the cruiser.

When Miller came around the bend, the Taurus's brake lights were on, and it had stopped. The ranger saw Danny get out of the driver's side and pause, then disappear into the woods on the other side of the road. Two more park ranger vehicles arrived to where Miller stood in tactical position, behind his cruiser, gun drawn on the Taurus. Danny watched them from the trees on the other side of the road. He moved behind the patrol cars and saw the rangers take Kathryn and Adam from the Taurus as if they were felons. It wouldn't take long to figure out they were not accomplices but his kidnap victims. In Danny's terms, he had not taken any hostages because he'd never delivered the tape asking for ransom. He dropped Adam's wallet and the tape recorder on the ground, and made his way down through the cover of trees. He saw the barricade he just smashed through. Park rangers checked people and vehicles. Soon, Adam and Kathryn sat in the park's Ranger Operations office, telling their story to Coconino County sheriff's department detectives, Flagstaff police, and FBI agents. Search units arrived at the park. Roadblocks went up. Back near the hotels, Danny tried to hot-wire a maroon Chevy convertible. He couldn't get the car started, but he got a change of clothes, and started working on a new plan.

I drive around the park on Saturday morning in an effort to take the pulse of a Grand Canyon where everyone's heart is beating a little faster. News crews from Phoenix with mobile broadcast units were in the park. More than two hundred agents and officers assemble from the FBI, the Coconino County and Gila County sheriff's departments, the Flagstaff Police Department, the Arizona Department of Corrections and the Department of Public Safety, the National Park Service, the U.S. Border Patrol, and a Las Vegas SWAT team. Canine units with tracking dogs arrive. Multiple checkpoint roadblocks spring up at the south and east entrances to the park, and along highways into Flagstaff and Cameron. On KFGC, the local Grand Canyon radio station, I listen to a special news bulletin from an otherwise nonexistent news desk. "Escaped fugitive Danny Horning has been located on the West Rim Drive between Mohave and Hopi Points," an anxious-sounding announcer reads. "He is considered armed and dangerous. The West Rim Drive has been closed. Roadblocks have been set up at various locations throughout the national park, and long delays are expected. Horning was last seen wearing a black IOU T-shirt, black windbreaker, and black jeans with hiking boots. He is a white male, five foot, nine inches tall, one hundred forty pounds, blue eyes and brown hair, and he's thirty-five years old. If you see someone fitting this description, do not approach him. Contact the National Park Service immediately at 911. Danny Horning is considered armed and dangerous. Officials are initiating a massive manhunt to locate Horning." When the announcement ends, the music comes back in the middle of a song about playing hide and seek. *"Well fee-fi-fo-fo-fum, look out baby now here I come,"* a man sings. *"Ready . . . Get ready,"* echoes his backup.

By Saturday afternoon, everyone has the news. A desk clerk at El Tovar says he was partying in the woods with some other employees last night during the chase. "We saw this guy running in the brush," he tells me. "I think it was him. It was dark;

THE COCONINO COUNTY SHERIFF'S DEPARTMENT
Post Office Box 39 • Flagstaff, Arizona 86002 • (602) 774-4523

Joe Richards
SHERIFF

SPECIAL BULLETIN

ESCAPEE FROM ARIZONA STATE PRISON

SUSPECT I.D:

HORNING, Danny R.
aka CONNELLY, Shaun
aka COOPER, Steve

White Male 5'9 140#
Blue eyes, Bro hair, med
tan complexion, thin
build, 35 yrs old, scar
on left shoulder blade
and a 5" scar on left shin

POB: Salinas, Ca.
DOB: 8-13-56
SSN: 527-17-0731
FBI: 694238V10
SID: 08942790
ADOC: 085897

Last Seen Wearing:
Black T-shirt with White
logo "IOU Fashions"
Black pants
Navy Blue baseball cap
"Food Distributors"
Dark Blue Windbreaker
WEAPON: .44 Mag
Suspect is clean shaven
except for a mustache.

Last seen on 6-26-92 at approximately 2130 hrs on West Rim Drive at the South
Rim of the Grand Canyon...Suspect did shoot at a Park Ranger putting a bullet
hole in his vehicle..no injuries.

BELIEVED TO BE ARMED AND EXTREMELY DANGEROUS!!! DO NOT APPROACH!!!

If any information, Please contact the Coconino County Sheriff's Dept.
at 1-800-338-7888 IMMEDIATELY!!

I can't say for sure, though. Showing up in Grand Canyon with all these visitors, it's almost like he wants to be chased. He just must like the thrill of it. I can't imagine someone who's running so hard wanting to show up in such a public place. That's something a lot of us have been talking about that we can't figure out. But he sounds pretty slick. He's got bloodhounds on him and they can't catch him. I think he's got to be caught. He did some things that were wrong. I'm not sure what, but if he did the crime, he's got to do the time." He says that people staying at the park are nervous and want answers, but he can't give them any information because no one knows anything. "The front desk at El Tovar was jammed this morning. All the front desks in the park had the same thing. But as nervous as people are about all of it, there's very few cancellations in the park today. Very few. Maybe just two or three early check-outs, which is basically normal. It didn't seem to bother any of the hikers. The Bright Angel has about as much traffic as it always does."

At The Pub, an employee bar with a pool table located across the street from Ranger Operations, I talk with Dale, who works for Harvey. Today is his day off, and he's camped out at The Pub to keep tabs on the action. "I've been living at the Grand Canyon for seven years, and I've been following this story since he escaped from Florence," he tells me. "I kind of got to like the guy. The cops can't catch him. But something changed, something snapped in him psychologically and he decided to take some hostages. So now, I feel like I'm a hostage in my own home, but I still like the guy. I just hope he doesn't hurt anybody." I ask him why he likes Horning, and he says it's because he can't be caught. "He's his own man. He leaves thank-you notes. He steals your shit and leaves you a thank-you note. You don't feel like you've been ripped off . . . if you like him, that is. I love the guy. Last night they had a shoot-out on the West Rim. He kinda got forced into shooting at some police because they got too close. That's what he does. It's the wild, wild West. That sums it up. Three words. Wild. Wild. West. He's an outlaw, and we need a modern-day outlaw because everybody conforms. It's the same reason we need a [Ross] Perot. Horning's an outlaw. I don't think they're gonna catch him alive. These guys are gonna shoot 'em. These guys have been chasing 'em too long and I think they want to kill him. I hope he turns himself in alive because it will be a great movie." Dale shared his opinions about the heavy search effort as well. "I think the stupidest move they made is to let the train come up from Williams. There's six hundred people on that train. If you want some hostages, there you go," he said. "They're using infrared devices on the helicopters. I asked a Department of Corrections guy about this, about how sensitive the infrared was for picking stuff up. He told me they spotted something in a tree from fifty feet. It was a porcupine. It picks up cattle, deer, elk, coyotes, small rodents. Horning is a bobcat. I love it. I think he's miles from here by now."

In the following week, the search for Horning grew larger every day, with more than three hundred agents drawn from a variety of state and federal law enforcement agencies. Anyone who arrived at Grand Canyon could not look into the abyss without thinking of Danny Ray Horning. Everyone seemed to know some detail about the chase for a thirty-three-year-old escaped convict, serving a one-hundred-year sentence for armed robbery, aggravated assault, kidnapping, and burglary, who had walked past prison guards on May 12, disguised as a medical worker. Law-enforcement officers reminded everyone that Horning was not only a convicted bank robber but also a suspect in a grisly murder case. Authorities in San Joaquin County, California, wanted to extradite him to stand trial for killing Sam McCullough, a forty-year-old catfish farmer and alleged marijuana dealer who, they say, Horning shot in the head, execution-style, dismembered his body with a serrated kitchen knife in a bathtub, put the body parts in plastic bags, and threw them in a river near Stockton, California, where they were found by local fishermen.

But as search helicopters flew in and out of the canyon and along the rim, as federal and state law enforcement agents brandishing automatic weapons walked trails and stood at viewpoints with tourists carrying videorecorders and cameras, Horning became a source of public fascination. Dale was not alone in his appreciation for Horning's ability to run from the law. By July 2, Horning's escapade through the Grand Canyon had become national news on television and radio and in newspapers across the country. "This guy is good," Bernie Lawrence, an Arizona Department of Public Safety officer, told reporters. Reputed to be Arizona's best tracker, Lawrence said he advised search teams to hunt Horning "like you would an animal." The biggest problem facing the agents, he said, is that Horning is "in great physical shape. . . . He gets a lead on them and then he basically outwalks them. By the time they get lined up, he's miles ahead. He seems able to go from one mountain range to the next without breaking a sweat."[30] Rumors began circulating that Horning had been trained by the military as a Green Beret with special survival skills. "An Army veteran with training in reconnaissance, Mr. Horning is an expert in surviving in the wilderness," reported the *New York Times*. "He has evoked comparisons with the movie character Rambo."[31] Rodney Horning, Danny's brother in Stockton, California, said the comparisons to Rambo were "a bunch of garbage" and that he was not the survivalist the press made him out to be. "He was only in the Army for a year in Europe. He never received any kind of special recon training," he said. "But he is a pack mule and in good shape. I just think he is smarter than all those people looking for him."[32] This may have been a gesture of loyalty toward his brother, but Rodney was only saying what many people were thinking.

The unfolding events became a weird drama drawing up the dividing lines between freedom and conformity. One afternoon I noticed a UPS truck in front of the search headquarters. In the dust on its side someone had written "Run Danny Run." It was a small sign marking the growing public image of Horning as a folk hero. "In the comfort of our air-conditioned offices and homes, we think about the desperate fugitive and, perhaps, feel the cops breathing down his neck as he lives the stuff of our own nightmares," Paul Brinkley-Rogers wrote in the July 2 issue of the *Arizona Republic*.

"This country was founded by outlaws, people who revolted against king and crown—people who settled the West," the Tucson writer Ray Ring said in the article. "The notion of personal independence is very strong out here. . . . As that notion of personal independence gets crushed by the modern world, people still hold on to it in the hope that they can survive the system. Some people see that in Danny Ray."[33]

During the week of the chase, I'd heard employees at The Pub talk about Horning like he was a brother. He symbolized an "outlaw life" for some of these workers, who wanted to identify with him. One night, a few Harvey employees told me they were glad Horning was running through the park and hoped the search would last a while. "Actually, it's been great to have all the rangers out on this search. They're leaving us alone," one of them said. "Usually you can't even have a beer without feeling like they'll pinch you for public intoxication. I'll hate to see what happens if they don't catch him by Wednesday. Wednesday is payday, and the rangers are usually out in full force. This has been nice, lately. They're laying off on us." Over the years, I'd heard other Harvey employees remark about feeling singled out by Park Service law enforcement. When I asked rangers about this, they typically assumed I'd heard an isolated comment. "Who's saying we single them out?" one ranger said. "The ones who are getting arrested?" The park employs about sixty law-enforcement rangers, who make approximately four hundred arrests a year in the park. The offenses they investigate include homicide, drunken driving, assaults, and burglaries. Recently, they have had to deal with a rising number of gang-related crimes. In addition to the nearly thirty thousand visitors who come through the park each day in the summer months, the rangers handle domestic disputes and have even been conducting undercover drug investigations among the community of about three thousand people who live and work in the park. Increasing numbers of confiscated weapons in national parks across the nation have prompted many of the rangers to wear bulletproof vests and replace their standard-issue revolvers with semiautomatic 9-millimeter and .45-caliber pistols.[34]

The more than three hundred agents and dogs and high-tech search equipment were no match for a single man running through the piñon and juniper, relying on his determination and wits. Horning taunted the law. In his ransom tape, he told the officers chasing him to "take up needlepoint" because they were poor trackers. "I'm the great escape," he said, and called himself a "freedom fighter." To make matters worse, after six days of unsuccessfully searching the canyon, the FBI set up a toll-free number, thinking that Horning might turn himself in. "We need to give him [Horning] the vehicle to reach out," said an FBI agent. "Hey, you never know. Some people get tired and want to toss it in."[35] The hotline seemed laughable to many at the canyon who saw the whole operation as an expensive and embarrassing show by federal and state law agencies. If anyone was getting tired or wanted to throw in the towel, no one thought it was Horning.

"I see your book is writing its own last chapter," Earll says, when I bump into him in the parking lot at Babbit's General Store on Monday morning. Everything had started while we sat in El Tovar last Friday night talking about writers and their tales, telling our stories as we'd told them before. "I thought I'd see you again," he says. "You couldn't have asked for a better ending." Despite all the urgency, hysteria, and warnings circulating through the park, we both knew we had landed in the middle of a different and more exciting Grand Canyon. The events surrounding the manhunt for Horning had put a new frame around the scenery. A wild tale was sprouting among the neat rows of careful and well-rehearsed stories that make and remake the Grand Canyon salient and safe for public consumption. The escaped convict had upset the tables in a place where meanings, values, and public order are largely a matter of consensus, and rules are followed more often than they are broken. In a strange way, the man few people actually saw (except on the wanted posters throughout the park) had altered how everyone saw the canyon. Suddenly the canyon had become energized; people were asking each other questions, coming up with theories, looking at one anothers' faces to see who they were really talking with. Horning had disguises. The latest report was that he was not the dark-haired man we saw on the posters but had dyed his hair strawberry blonde. He could be anyone among us. Horning was everything we did not know or see. His presence in the park was an assumption. "I don't even think he's still here," Dale told me as he stood in the doorway of The Pub. The only thing anyone could say for certain was that Danny Ray Horning had punctured an enormous system, and a display of force rarely seen all in one place had come together to plug that hole. His absence from a cell in Florence on May 12 had grown to a magnitude beyond comprehension, and out of that absence poured a small army of men and weapons, barking dogs, helicopters, news cameras, legends, and myths.

Unlike those who came to Grand Canyon to escape the crowds, Horning had run into the crowd and put its anonymous mask to work for him. In return, everyone at the park could, perhaps, somehow feel a little more authentic because the canyon had become a real place where something of TV news proportion unfolded before their eyes. No one could have planned this when they left on their vacations or anticipated this opportunity for a genuine "you'll-never-believe-what-happened-on-our-trip-to-Grand Canyon" story to carry home. I thought of Milan Kundera's novel *Immortality*, in which he speaks of "the wild joy of the photographer who had been bored watching the banal spectacle and suddenly saw that luck was falling his way from the sky in the shape of a burning airplane!"[36] The Horning chase was not nearly so spectacular. Instead, it dragged on for days. Someone would spot him, a road would close, and we would wait to see him brought in. But nothing happened. On Monday, June 29, he stole a yellow station wagon from Zoeneck Kel and Janna Cerny, a couple from Oregon, at a picnic area near Moran Point. At gunpoint, he told them to get in the car. Zoeneck told Danny, "you'll have to shoot me first," and ran away from him with Janna. The next day, helicopters found the yellow station wagon near Grandview Point. These little pieces of information came down the line every day or so. A burning airplane hits the ground sooner or later, but the chase just lingered over the canyon with a strange energy. Anything could happen, but nothing did often enough. It was an atmosphere like an accident, a mistake, a crack, or a gap in the routine that suddenly put everything and everyone in new light, with a heightened, excited sense that was not evident before the car chase on Friday night.

A few people suffered the terror of the escaped outlaw while he ran through the canyon. Adam, Kathryn, the Norman family from Texas, and the couple from Oregon had all found themselves in that gap where the world no longer felt real—"you've got to be kidding me"—and then felt more real than ever. They told stories of Horning filled with fear, survival, and how life felt like a movie. But none of it prompted a mass retreat from the park. In fact, the twenty thousand visitors who were expected for a Saturday and Sunday in June or July showed up as usual. Within a few days, park administrators noted a 10 percent lapse in normal visitor numbers.[37] However, the park's nine hundred and seven hotel and motel rooms were filled every night, for nearly two hundred rooms had been rented to law-enforcement officers involved with the search. By July 2, Babbit's reported a loss of about seven hundred customers a day. The Yavapai curio shop reported a heavy decline in photo-processing requests. Campfire programs and tours were canceled. Roads closed on the East and West Rim Drive as search teams shifted their attention to new leads and sightings.[38] The place where people had come to escape their routines had suddenly become one of strict order, procedure, surveillance, and paranoia. Against this backdrop, an invisible man was running for freedom, and his efforts exacted a price from anyone who came to look into the Big Absence.

"I've taken more pictures of the FBI than I have anything else," a man tells his wife while they wait for a park shuttle. He aims his videocamera toward his five-year-old son, who is standing next to three FBI officers dressed in camouflage pants, black T-shirts, and holding rifles. "Our vacation pictures are going to be full of FBI agents and weapons," he shakes his head, and she laughs. At the Bright Angel curio shop, two middle-aged women from New Hampshire tell me Danny Horning keeps reorganizing their plans. "First they closed the West Rim and we couldn't go out there for a sunset tour we planned," one of them says. "Then he's on the East Rim. So they close that and we can't take the Desert View tour. We've been planning this trip for six months. So, now we've decided, 'Hey, let's go have a few drinks,'" she says, and strolls off with her companion. Outside on the plaza, a man who arrived yesterday from California is laughing and shaking his head with mock disbelief. "I just came from Los Angeles. On Sunday we had the biggest earthquake in forty years," he says. "Now there's a guy running around here. I'm just waiting to see what happens next."

I am hoping the "what happens" will hurry up a bit. My car is due back in Tampa today. A new, more expensive rental rate is kicking in, I remind myself, while I walk to El Tovar. I run into Kelly, a Harvey waitress, on the esplanade and she's excited, even though it's eight in the morning. "Did you hear about it?" she says. Horning is captured, I think, but before I can speak Kelly says, "I waited on Tony Danza and Patrick Swayze last night. They're staying at the E.T. I think they're going down to catch a raft at Phantom. I'll bet they're still there." That's where I'm headed, I tell her, thanks for the tip.

I walk through the lobby and grab a cup of coffee from the big urn put out for the hotel guests every morning. Then I spot Swayze walking into the hotel newsstand and I follow him, trying to play it cool, like I don't know who he is. He's wearing a baseball cap, sunglasses, and faded black jeans with a pack of Carleton cigarettes stuffed in the front pocket of his pants. He's holding up a day pack and water bottle to the man behind the counter, asking him to fix something. "Are you going down the trail?" I say. "Yeah," he says. "Staying at Phantom Ranch?" I try again. He's kind of jumpy, but answers anyway. "I'm going down. But I don't know where. We're a group. We get on a raft somewhere down there," says the movie star. "Do you know how this goes?" He hands me his water bottle and I attach it to the pack. "Thanks," he says, and buys a pack of gum. I watch him head into the lobby. He looks nervous; he probably doesn't want to be recognized, but he darts around looking for someone. Finally, an attractive woman on the couch sees him and says, "Honey, over here." They go into the dining room for breakfast.

I walk out to sit on the front porch of the hotel and drink my coffee, and I'm surprised to find the rest of Swayze's celebrity party. Tony Danza is pacing back and forth near the front steps, wearing a small black fanny pack with "Who's the Boss?" written across the front in white letters. On the front step, Tony Robbins, the motivational speaker I've seen marketing personal success tapes on late-night infomercials, is laughing as Danza tries to call Swayze with a small megaphone. Off to the side, Pat Riley, coach of the L.A. Lakers, leans against the rail. "Hey, Tony," Tony Robbins says to Tony Danza. "Who *is* the boss?" He's making fun of the pack and Danza's efforts to get their hike on the road. "Hey, the show didn't run that long," Danza grins. "These gifts are important." A few other people who aren't famous stand around, too, and watch Danza clown around with the megaphone. "They're still eating breakfast in there," he says, through the bullhorn into El Tovar's lobby. "We'll never get going." Everyone is waiting for Swayze, and Robbins cracks up at Danza's antics. Two young boys with crew cuts come up to Danza and ask for a photo. He kneels down with them, then gets up and turns them around so they are in the sun. "It'll make a better picture if we get in the light," he says, and kneels with them while the father snaps a photo. Riley sits quietly through all of this. Hair slicked back, black shades, he seems patient or is wondering how he got booked on this trip. Other people like me watch the stars wait on the steps. Except for the two boys who asked for a photo, we all keep a safe and polite distance.

That afternoon, a woman who just hiked up tells me she saw Patrick Swayze riding a mule down into the canyon. "People were coming up to him on the trail to say hello and ask for pictures. I think a lot of those famous people lead sad lives," she says.

"Patrick Swayze can't even get on a mule without people making a big deal out of it. Tony Danza from that TV show was there, too, but he was walking. And so was that other guy, that coach. . . . What's his name?" "Pat Riley," her husband fills in the blank. "He was walking with Tony Danza," she says. "Patrick Swayze has bad knees or he would've walked, too. He used to be a dancer. We walked; it's not that easy coming back up." She didn't mention Tony Robbins.

"Have you noticed everyone is looking at you?" a man from Louisville asks me in the laundry near Mather Campground. "Every man in the park between thirty and forty years old is getting looked at. I've got a mustache and I'm his height. I seen this lady in the laundry while I'm waiting for my clothes and she's just staring at me." I know how he felt. I had been getting looks from people as well. Twice I had undercover agents approach me and strike up a conversation. Each time they were on mountain bikes. It happened the first time while I was making a phone call near the post office. The line was busy, so I stood by the phone waiting to try again. A man on a mountain bike watched me the entire time and came over to ask me if I was going to make a call. I said there are plenty of phones that work if he wanted to use one. Then he asked me what I was doing in the park. I was approached again right outside the laundry, before I met the man from Louisville. Another man on a mountain bike asked me how my trip was going. Then I realized he was riding a new bike, with the same kind of new handlebar pack as the first guy, same new helmet, windbreaker, and bike shorts, too.

The day after I see the celebrities, I talk with a family near the old Kolb photo studio about how their vacation is going, given that the manhunt is in full force. "It's fine," says the father. "There were some lines we had to wait through on the way in. But once we got here it's been okay. I'm just keeping a closer eye on her," he says, pointing to his daughter. "They say he's using disguises and coming up to tourists." Then he pulls a copy of Horning's wanted poster out of his front pocket, unfolds it, and holds it up to compare with my face. "Let's see here," he says. "Not a bad resemblance." He laughs and hands the poster to his daughter. She studies Horning's face, looks at me, and then at the poster. "What do you think?" I ask. "Think I look like him?" She thinks it over. "No," she says, "you're not him." I am slightly relieved by her decision, but realize I've grown wary of talking to tourists. It had always been so easy to strike up a conversation with someone at a lookout area or on the trail. People were on vacation; they were open to meeting strangers. Now, everyone seemed a little suspicious, and for good reason. Horning was showing up at scenic lookouts and in parking lots using a similar technique. In a place where I had spent so much time looking at tourists, I found the tourists had started to look back at me, and with caution. Since the search started, I had been saying that I was a journalist doing an "independent story" on the manhunt. It was not entirely a disguise—even though I didn't have any press credentials—and given all the reporters on the scene, assuming this role made it easier to hold up a microphone and ask law-enforcement officers or park rangers questions about the chase. But on July 3, all of this suddenly changed.

Walking across Babbit's parking lot, I see a K-9 patrol officer come out of the store. I walk over to ask him how the search is going. "Are the dogs working out?" I say. "I hear he's got the dogs running in circles." I try to be friendly, make a little joke; he says nothing and just keeps walking toward his truck. Then I just start laughing. "You guys are pretty serious," I say, trying to let him know I'm laughing at him for blowing me off. He just looks at me and gets inside. I shake my head and keep laughing, hoping he's watching, and he sits in his truck. On the bench in front of the post office, I sit down to write out a few postcards. A few minutes later, I notice a cruiser pull into the parking lot. It's followed by two more. Then I see three officers coming my way; they are sneaking up cautiously, hiding behind posts. I feel a little nervous. I just keep my pen on the postcard, not looking up, but notice their movement through the corner of my eye. All at once, they are standing in front of me. There's a park ranger and two Coconino County sheriffs with hands ready on their weapons, but they haven't drawn them.

"Do you have some I.D.?" one of them asks. Across the parking lot, the K-9 officer watches from a distance. I can't believe this is happening. I reach for my backpack to get my wallet, and they move closer. "Go easy there," says the officer. "Go nice and slow."

"I have to get my wallet out of my pack," I say. "What is this? I'm just trying to do a story. I'll bet that guy over there called you because I was asking him questions. Is that why you guys are here?" I'm very nervous, and my mouth feels dry. I don't know how to act with them standing here, and I notice that the people coming out of Babbit's with grocery bags are stopping and watching what is happening—which is me. I am what is happening at this instant. "You guys are making me nervous," I tell the officer, and I stand up to give him my driver's license.

"Whoa, there," he says, holding out the palm of his hand, directing me to remain seated. "Why are you so nervous?" he says. "You *know* who *we* are. Now just relax."

"Yeah, that's the point," I say. "I know who you are and you're making me nervous." I also hand him my university identification card. For some reason, I think this might carry some privileges. Another ranger takes both cards and calls in on his radio. He tells the voice on the other end my name and driver's license number, and I wait for a response.

"Hi, Mark," a voice says behind me, and I turn around to see Rachel. She runs a cash register at Babbit's, and I interviewed her a day ago. "What's all this?" she says, and walks right past one of the officers and sits down next to me on the bench. "These men think I'm Danny Ray Horning and they're checking out my I.D." She laughs, and the ranger looks at the sheriff's deputy. *"He-e-e-e's not Horning,"* she drawls with a big grin. "He's a writer or something like that, uh, . . . a professor. He's writing a book about the park." I appreciate Rachel's vouching, but her word holds little sway with the officers. It's just nice to have a person who knows me without the benefit of an official identity check. We sit for only a few minutes, but it seems longer. Finally, the officer returns with my identification and hands them back.

"He's okay," he says to the others. "He checks out." The three officers just walk away; they don't say anything else to me. They walk over to the K-9 officer and then look back over toward me and Rachel. All of them wear aviator sunglasses. The ranger rubs the back of his neck while the four talk and look around the lot. I am another false sighting. They are edgy and tired of the manhunt. Everyone's nerves seem a little raw, and I still feel uneasy about getting detained. I'm not the only person who has been stopped by officers. Just yesterday, a clerk at one of the gift shops said everything was getting out of hand. "I saw two of those FBI guys with automatic rifles lead a young man away at gunpoint," he said. "They had rifles on him. The guy gave his father the video camera before they took him. His father videotaped the whole thing. The FBI guy was pointing his rifle at the young man and then turning around. When he did, he was aiming his rifle at the father. That's dangerous. I watched the whole thing. Another day, I saw three National Guard walking throughout the Bright Angel gift shop looking for people," he told me. "They had their rifles out, fingers on the trigger. I told 'em, 'Don't you think you ought to put the safety on?' Imagine that. They didn't have the safety on while walking through a crowded gift shop." I had taken such stories with a grain of salt, signs of how people were hostile toward the military presence visiting the park. Now, I believed all of it.

"Are you all right?" Rachel says, sensing I'm still shaken by the officers. "Here, I got you something after our interview yesterday. I was hoping I'd run into you. It's funny it happened like this. They say there are no coincidences." She opens up her pack and pulls out a paperback copy of C. S. Lewis's *Mere Christianity*. On the front page she's written me a note. "This book changed how I see the truth. In reading this it is my hope you will not only find some answers, but also more questions. Remember, God finds those who seek Him. Be well—Rachel." We had a long interview yesterday, and she had told me about her past and how she'd been born again. C. S. Lewis was a key influence in her rebirth. She was from the Midwest and was working this summer as part of a Christian youth group. I told her I was raised a Lutheran, but I stopped going to church when I went to college. Over the years, I flirted in spiritual pursuits—Quaker, Episcopalian, Unitarian, and Zen—but nothing ever stuck with me, or I didn't stick with any of them long enough. I thank her for the book. "I hope you get a chance to read it," she says. "I've got to go back to work. See you around Mark. . . . I mean, Danny." She laughs as she walks around the corner.

I stay on the bench in front of the post office for a long time, thinking about what to do next. Horning had been running through the park for a week now, and it didn't look like anyone could catch him. There wouldn't be any tidy or convenient ending to this chase—a capture at the end of the week. Tomorrow was the Fourth of July, and the park would likely be busy despite the lines, roadblocks, and ongoing manhunt. I fan the pages of *Mere Christianity* and find a small blue envelope tucked behind the back cover. It was a little card from Rachel, and I read it. "While reading in Psalms last night, I stumbled over this passage—'Great are the works of the Lord; they are pondered by all who delight in them.' So why do people visit the Grand Canyon? Everyone has a different story, but we are bound together in that we all have the same Author. C. S. Lewis said (and this is a poor paraphrase) that until he found God his life was crammed onto the title page of his story, but when God came into the picture, chapter one began. What is your story, Mark?"

Good question, Rachel. I spent a lot of time listening to other people's stories; the prospect of excavating my own never really came up. Maybe this was a defense mechanism, as a good friend once suggested; listening to others was a way of not traveling through some of my own shadowy canyons. I always enjoyed the summers I spent at Grand Canyon because I felt free to do anything I wanted, when I wanted. I liked meeting people and listening to how they were spending their vacations, but I often heard more about their lives at home. Horning had said that the United States was full of hostages. People at the canyon sometimes admitted they felt trapped by mortgages, jobs, and routines, yet few truly seemed willing to give it all up and spend the rest of their days camping in a tent, staying in a hotel room, or living in an RV. I wouldn't either. I wanted to go home, but I knew that after returning to Tampa I'd soon want to leave again and come back to the West. I thought Danny Ray Horning's run through the park would make a good story or, as some were already suggesting, a movie. Admittedly, I was seduced by the whole "outlaw" myth surrounding him. It seemed like an epic tale of freedom that only took on a strange and ironic character against the backdrop of Grand Canyon. It was a story I could make *my story* only by the pure luck of having been in the right place at the right time. Some of the tourists complained they came here at the wrong time, but I knew otherwise. This was a singular moment, and I seized it for that potential. Such stories are a hope of anyone who takes a vacation. And I admit turning a deaf ear to the murder accusations leveled against Horning. I preferred he be the "freedom fighter," running from institutional authority, running toward Mexico with his brother Jerry, hauling a duffel bag loaded with a million dollars. I was on his side, like many people I had met, only because he represented a sense of being free and betting against the odds at all costs. He didn't have anything to lose. But all this changed when I got stopped by the officers a few moments ago. In a matter of seconds, the stakes Horning played with seemed real and heavy. My freedom was only in question for a few minutes while the deputy checked my identification. Only in that brief moment could I begin to imagine the escaped convict's life beyond the outlaw legend and exciting myths. His story was one of ruthless action. My story was far less exciting. I was an observer, an interested bystander, a witness to the events around me. I ask people how they're living, and I take notes. My story hinges on what someone else is doing, and it's easy to romanticize and fantasize from a scenic observation point.

I walk aimlessly along the rim trail for the rest of the afternoon. In the forest near the visitors center at the rim, I see a family talking to a ranger. The family is sniffing the bark of a ponderosa pine. "See, it smells like butterscotch," the ranger tells them. On the trail ahead of me I see two men in camouflage scanning the terrain as they carry rifles across their chest. Law enforcement is everywhere. Last night I locked my car doors and slept in the backseat at the campground because I thought it would be safer than in the tent. It was hard to sleep in an economy rental, and today I'm tired. I walk down to the Bright Angel Lodge and then turn around to go back to the Babbit's parking lot, where I've left my car. It's late afternoon when I return, and I notice that the East Rim Drive is closed off due to another Horning sighting. I wait for a while, but nothing happens and I decide it's time to leave. I'm sick of waiting and head into the Yavapai cafeteria to get a good meal before I hit the road. I settle on a chicken-fried steak, mashed potatoes, green beans, and coffee, and carry my tray to an empty table. The place is busy, and a group of Italians on a chartered tour comes and sits down. Paula, their perky tour escort, sits across my table and says her group just arrived. Paula is Italian but speaks English well. Some of her passengers look over as we talk and eat.

"The people on my bus watch me all the time to see what I do," says Paula. "Like that man in the cafeteria line. I see him looking at my bowl of chili. He had the spaghetti, but tomorrow he'll be eating chili. I tell them to try these different things. You know about this root beer float?" I nod, and tell her I know of the root beer float. "It tastes terrible, like throat medicine, but it does not help your throat. Who thinks of putting these things together? The root beer and the ice cream? It is terrible to taste this, but it is an American thing so I make sure they try it. And the baked potato with sour cream? That's another thing I make them try. I love this food. When I'm in Italy I can't have this. So I tell them to try this and this and this. That's how I show them America," she laughs. "The root beer float, chili, and the baked potato with sour cream." I ask Paula if she's had to study American history in order to lead the tours. "Sometimes I do some studying the night before we go through someplace," she says. "You should see my suitcases. Full of books and notes and papers. I tell them about Grand Canyon geology. I say the names of different rocks and the millions of years, but there are so many that it is confusing. It doesn't really matter what you say. Sometimes when we are on the bus I'm supposed to tell them about the history of the place we are going through. But if I don't know it, I'll make it up. Like I'll say, 'Oh this is the place where Brigitte Bardot met Dwight Eisenhower in 1959' or something like that," she laughs. "They don't know." Paula's bus driver, Chuck, joins us and says when they get to San Francisco, he lets the tourists walk across the Golden Gate Bridge. "They love the walk," he says. "Oh no," says Paula, "not this group. We have two dwarves. It will take forever for them to get across."

I finish my meal and say good-bye to Paula and Chuck. She asks if I'll be around the canyon for a few days, but I tell her I'm driving back to Florida. Walking to my car, I laugh to myself over Paula's words. The whole place is dissolving before my eyes.

It's a good time to leave. Just then I see Mike, a hotel maintenance worker, and a few of his buddies walking out of Babbit's. Each of them is carrying a case of beer. I wave to them. I saw them at The Pub earlier this week and we shot a few games of pool. I remember he talked about going to Lake Powell for the Fourth of July weekend. I guess they're just stocking up on supplies for the drive.

"We're gonna go find Horning," he shouts to me, and I walk over. "We're the Harvey corps, and we're gonna get ourselves a $25,000 ree-ward." They're all laughing. "Hey, did I tell you about my bumper sticker idea?" he says. "It's gonna say 'Honk If You're Horning.'" Mike's friends crack up. "I got a T-shirt I'm planning," snickers Carl, his friend, "It's gonna say 'I Hiked the Day with Danny Ray.'" They all laugh again and load one case of beer into a big cooler they filled with ice at one of the lodges. The other cases they stow in the trunk. "Off to Desert View," Mike says, trying to sound like cowboy-movie character. "Make sure yer loaded boys. He's a dangerous fugitive," and they drive off. Bumper stickers. T-shirts. Beer and the Fourth of July. They are men with a plan, and they follow a well-traveled road along the edge of Grand Canyon. I wave good-bye, hoping they'll see me in their rearview. They do. Mike toots the horn as they hang a right and head east, the direction I'll be heading in minute.

Danny Ray Horning left the park late the next morning.[39] He kidnapped two British tourists, Caroline Young and Sally Edmonds, who were sitting in the front seat of their red Nissan Sentra rental car in the parking area at Desert View. Danny walked up and pointed a gun at Sally. He said he wanted a ride to Grand Canyon Village, and he climbed in the backseat. "My name is Danny Horning," he said. "That's H-O-R-N-I-N-G," and told them he'd escaped from prison. They already knew who he was. "If you try anything crazy," he said, "I'll fire a hole in the gas tank," and showed them his gun. He said it was safe as long as it wasn't cocked, but then he cocked the gun. Sally and Caroline were terrified. At the intersection for Village Loop Drive, Danny told them to go south toward the park gate. Now his hair and mustache were dyed blonde. He wore a straw Panama hat, sunglasses, and a white T-shirt with "Fun Run" written across the front.

When they reached the first checkpoint, an officer tried to stop them, but Danny told Sally to keep her foot on the gas. In her rearview mirror, she could see the annoyed policeman, but she just kept going. Both women sensed Danny was tense in the backseat, and they couldn't see where he was pointing the gun. At the second roadblock, right at the park gate, the officer stopped their car. Caroline and Danny looked at pages in her diary, pretending to be preoccupied, hoping no one would say or do anything. The officer looked inside the car and then asked Danny to roll down his window. "Would you remove your hat and sunglasses please?" asked the officer, standing about three feet from Danny's face. Danny took them off and looked into his eyes. "Is everything all right, officer?" he said. The policeman gave him a good look. "You're not the guy I'm looking for," he said, and waved them through. Five minutes later, they reached a third and final roadblock. Again, an officer stopped the car but this time only asked Sally to pop open the trunk. After looking inside, he let them go. Earlier, Danny wondered if he could fit in the trunk, and now he was happy he didn't make that choice.

After refueling, they drove toward Williams. Danny talked about a friend who lived north of Williams who could help him, an army buddy from two years ago when he was in the service. He searched the terrain looking for his cabin but could not remember where he lived. Just outside of Williams, Danny told Sally to turn down a dirt road and said he was going to take their car. They asked him if they could keep their things. They had passports, luggage, plane tickets, and traveler's checks. He thought about it for a minute and decided they could. He found a piece of rope while they unloaded the gear, and told them to sit down, face to face, wrap their arms around a tree, and he tied their hands together. They were afraid he was going to shoot them, they told him, so Danny took the bullets out of his pistol and put them in his pocket. He found fifteen dollars in cash in one of their wallets, and instructed them to wait thirty minutes before trying to get up and walk out. As he drove off, they sat bound to the tree with all their belongings on the ground around them. It was about half past noon when Danny left in the Sentra, and it took Sally and Caroline about fifteen minutes to untie themselves. They got back on the dirt road, and by 1:30 they had flagged down a ride into Williams and contacted the police.

I was south of Albuquerque on I-25 South, listening to the Mutual Broadcasting System's hourly radio news when I heard that Danny Ray Horning was captured. There weren't many details on the broadcast, but it was repeated hourly for much of the day. I later learned that Department of Public Safety officers spotted him in the Sentra on I-17 south of Flagstaff. They chased him to an exit, and Danny fired a shot at one of them through his side window. He wrecked the car while trying to make a turn at a hundred miles an hour. Then he jumped out and ran. An officer grabbed a 12-gauge shotgun from his cruiser and fired a round at Danny as he ran into the woods, but it didn't hit him. At about 9:30 that night, a resident of Oak Creek Village, near Sedona, spotted a man drinking from a garden hose in a neighbor's yard and called the Yavapai County Sheriff's Department. Law officers and bloodhounds were soon searching the area. They captured Danny at 2:13 A.M., on Sunday, July 5. He had burrowed beneath a neighbor's gazebo. He didn't struggle when they caught him. Danny told the Coconino County sheriff it had been a "really fun chase and that he enjoyed it." He walked into the Coconino County jail wearing handcuffs and shackles, and seemed to like the attention from the reporters and photographers gathered outside. "How does it feel to be captured?" someone shouted. "I would have liked to have prolonged it," said Danny, wearing a T-shirt bearing a logo for Tri-State Greyhound Racing with the silhouette of a running dog.[40] And all of this seemed strangely sad, as I drove through Texas that Sunday, and passed the towns and cities where people were shaking off last night, sweeping up, still coming to their senses on the day after the Fourth of July.

The Time of My Life

My family, friends, and colleagues often joked about my summer trips to Grand Canyon. Most said I chose a great research subject because it had a built-in vacation. They didn't believe I grew tired of the scenery after a few days or that I spent my time gathering notes, interviews, and photographs, or sat in the study collection at Grand Canyon and in libraries in Phoenix and Flagstaff. I thought my last day at the canyon would have been July 3, 1992, and that Earll Kingston was right and my last chapter was writing itself. There would be little more to say. But I went back to the canyon over the next two summers. The thought of missing something has always nagged me, so I flew to Phoenix each time—in 1993 and 1994—rented a car, and drove up to camp out for another month in Kaibab National Forest south of the airport, off an old forest service road where the pines open into a clearing, near the same old tree that was hit one time by lightning. No one ever camped there. I just put down a tarp and my bright orange sleeping bag, and slept under the stars on most nights. Sometimes, usually in the hour before dawn, I heard coyotes howling nearby. In the early morning hours, I lay in my bag looking up at the sky as if it were the ceiling of my bedroom. Scenic tour planes flew over, and I imagined passengers pointing me out, maybe even snapping a photograph. When the sun rose enough to bathe me in brightness and it became too hot to lie there another minute, I got up, packed my sleeping bag and tarp in the trunk, and followed the service road back to the main drag through Tusayan. On my way to the canyon, I'd stop at McDonald's for coffee, flash my entrance fee receipt at the park gate, and head to Babbit's to find a parking place before it got too busy. It was something of a routine, but a better one than I was accustomed to most of the year.

Sometimes I drove around the area looking for signs from past years at the canyon. One night I accidentally ran into Cosy Sheridan. I'd met her my first summer at the canyon in 1988, when she spent a week singing at the Bright Angel Lodge cocktail lounge. She was in her early twenties and drove an old pickup truck when I first met her. She played bluesy songs by Bonnie Raitt and a few of her own. When I ran into her years later, she had recorded two CDs and her career as a songwriter was taking off. We drove down to Flagstaff one afternoon, and I asked her how she knew she wanted to live on the road, playing clubs, how she could have decided on singing and writing and not look back. "I just went with plan A," she said, "and there's no plan B." I've always envied her for having such a good answer at such a young age.

Apart from some of the park rangers, and Earll and Maxine Kingston, most of the people I met one summer at the canyon were not there the next. Harvey workers sometimes got hired and disappeared within a month. During my first week at the canyon in 1988, I met a cook who called himself "Dodger." He came to the canyon after his motorcycle broke down outside of Phoenix. He was running from a marriage that suddenly fell apart and came to the canyon looking for work. We shot pool in

Tusayan one night, and I listened to his wild stories. He said he was married to a former *Playboy* centerfold model. He got the name "Dodger" because he used to be a bag man for dope deals in Chicago. He said he ran an X-rated novelty shop in Los Angeles, and often sold porno tapes and sex toys to a whole slew of TV actors and rock stars whose names I best not mention. As a teenager, he said he was taken in by Louis L'Amour, the famous western novelist, and lived on his ranch. He told me all of this in a few hours one night. Each time I went back to the canyon, I hoped to meet him again, in person or in someone else's face, but I never did. I didn't believe his stories then as much as I do now, only because I now know better.

I drove through the Navajo Nation east of the park every summer and looked for Jake, the Sioux who stood by the side of the road waiting to pose for tourist photographs. Instead, I found construction crews had widened and repaved the road winding from Desert View through the Navajo Nation to Cameron. Some of the old souvenir stands were abandoned and new ones had sprung up. I never saw Jake again. But one morning, while driving to Flagstaff to buy some film, I picked up Jerry, who was hitchhiking to the bus station. A heavyset Navajo who carried a beat-up bedroll, Jerry said he'd climbed out of the canyon after spending the night with some friends down there drinking some strange mixture of corn and whiskey boiled over a fire. Then, he just walked up and out in the darkness. He saw snakes and lizards all over the trail, and was still a little drunk when I picked him up. While we drove toward Flagstaff he asked if I'd ever been in a war. Jerry fought in Vietnam, and his glazed eyes stared straight through my windshield, all the way to Southeast Asia, where gunfire crackled, bombs exploded, and he lay in jungle mud surrounded by dead men. He would take the Trailways bus to Tuba City and talked of a friend who was also a veteran. "This man from Tuba went to see the Vietnam soldiers' wall one time," said Jerry, "and he saw his own name on the wall. He got wounded in Vietnam but he didn't die. He asked the United States government to take his name off the wall and they told him they couldn't do that. They paid him twelve hundred dollars, but he couldn't tell anyone about it. His name is still on the wall. Everyone who sees it thinks he's dead. He got twelve hundred dollars." I dropped Jerry off at the bus station and later discovered he dropped his knife in my car. It had a yellow bone handle and was the size of a steak knife. I think of Jerry, the Grand Canyon, and Vietnam every time I pull it from my kitchen drawer to slice off a piece of cheese or quarter an orange.

I heard many stories at the Grand Canyon. Those told by rangers didn't change much over the years. In fact, several of the full-time rangers told the same stories in their evening programs year after year. They were professionals, and each time they sounded fresh, as if it were the first time. I kept going back because I sought the stories few people heard, those told by people who were between places, tales of who they were, how things were going at home and on the road, what they wanted to do, why they couldn't do it, the places they wanted to see before they died, the places they knew they'd never see, and whatever else they might want to tell me. The Horning manhunt only showed how a story could expand and grow at the canyon over a short period. Once in custody, Horning said the media had blown him and the chase way out of proportion.

"I never [told] the media and them out there that, you know, I'm this Rambo with all this Army experience," he told a judge. "They [the Department of Corrections] built this up into what it is. . . . They won't admit that all I did was walk out. . . . They gotta cover up their incompetence by making it look like I'm some big hotshot Rambo MacGyver all rolled up into one. . . . Sure, I *am* a problem, and when I get back out—which I will—there's gonna be some problems, all right . . . but I am not the person, the young man, that they describe me as."[41] As far as Horning was concerned, his expert survivalist image was a fiction of law-enforcement officers who needed an alibi to cover themselves for taking so long and spending so much money to catch him. Despite his protests, his folklore status seemed entrenched for some of the people who recalled his great escape.

"The problem wasn't Horning," a Harvey employee told me in 1994. "It was these *children* they sent up here to catch him. The National Guard. They caused more trouble than anything." I had talked to this same man during the chase, and two years later he told the same story about men carrying rifles through the gift shop with the safety off and FBI agents taking a tourist at gunpoint while his father videotaped the event. "Horning was an ex-Green Beret and they sent the National Guard to catch him," he said. "That's the problem. He drove right through their roadblocks. The only reason they caught him was because he gave up. He was tired. The only reason he was running in the first place was to protest his prison sentence. He wasn't any Boy Scout, but giving him four life sentences for a bank robbery? That's why everyone got behind him like they did. We all knew he got a bigger sentence than he deserved. That's why he became a hero. It's the American way; we get behind the guy who hasn't been treated fairly. A guy with his kind of talent ought to be rehabilitated. Don't you think the government could have some use for a man with his kind of skill?"

A taxi driver I met in 1994 at the Denny's restaurant in Tusayan also remembered Horning, but his version of the chase had stretched out over the years. "That guy was a master of disguises. He stole five rifles from the army, drove their vehicles. He had cops chasing 'em for three months," he said, as we drank coffee and ate the breakfast special at the counter. "Well, they chased him for a month through the park and still couldn't catch him. He had to give his self up. He walked right up to these police who were standing there and asked 'em if they thought that convict was still in the area. Danny said, 'How close do you think he is?' And the cops said, 'We don't think he's around here.' And then Danny walked over to a water tap and washed out his hair and came back to 'em and said, 'Is this the guy you've been lookin' for?' He just turned his self in. They couldn't get 'em." They built their stories on Horning's independence and a view of institutional incompetence; they were tales of the underdog winning over the giant. It's a familiar plot of summer blockbuster movies, and the stories turning up about Horning depicted him as nothing less than an action figure waiting for another season.

For seven days, the predictable postcard scene had been torn in half, and suddenly everything became possible. It's difficult to say whether the people who waited in lines at roadblocks or turned their cars around because of the potential threat felt this way. But I do know that people I met at the canyon then seemed thrilled to be on hand for the chase. I recall sitting with some Irish tourists and drinking beer on the back porch of the El Tovar. One of them held a pair of binoculars to her eyes and followed the FBI agents patrolling the trails. "Oooh, look at them," she mocked. "They don't quite look like they could catch 'em, now, do they?" She said this each time new agents passed and laughed from deep in her belly. It was a strange tournament, and she became a self-appointed commentator for the rest of us at the table. They were going to stay until Horning was caught or left the park; that's all there was to it. "It's so much better than the movies," said one of the men, "and I *like* American movies." The world became a richer place because the familiar maps of the canyon had fallen apart for a few days. "Here's hoping you're alive at the end of the world," one of the men laughed and hoisted his glass, toasting all of us and a world that, in fact, suddenly felt more alive.

It is nearly impossible to see the Grand Canyon apart from the way it has been appropriated by a "symbolic complex which has already been formed in the sightseer's mind," wrote Walker Percy. "Seeing the canyon under approved circumstances is seeing the symbolic complex head on," he said, and asked his readers to consider if it is possible for the sightseer to "recover the Grand Canyon" apart from the ways it is already mediated. Percy's question did not stem from a particular interest in the canyon but from broader concerns over the character of modern life, where "sovereign experience" is often "surrendered to a class of privileged knowers, whether these be theorists or artists," who parcel and package experience for consumers. Was is it possible to know and feel anything in the modern world apart from preformulated meanings that eventually became stale and cliché? Some might try to "get off the beaten track" only to find others who have had the same idea, that the backcountry maps and back roads are rutted from the traffic. "I kind of get mad at all of these [backcountry] hiking books," a canyon hiker told me. "It's sort of a paradox. I mean you're happy they wrote 'em because you can find some of these new places, but so can everybody else. So it makes it worse." Others who spend energy trying to avoid becoming part of the beaten track can find themselves mired in self-consciousness about their efforts. For instance, this is how one man described his attempt not to look like a "typical" tourist: "It's really hard to describe what I do. I guess I'm trying to be me, but that's not very informative. It's mostly defined in terms of what I'm trying not to be. . . . You know, people stand out there and gawk and say things like 'Oh, wow!' and 'Oh, neat!' and they say it out loud a lot. So instead you say [calmly], 'That's nice.' You try to be cool about it. You try to be competent. . . . It's being in control." In attempting not to become a "typical" tourist, he only brings on a self-conscious awareness of his own performance. "I'm just trying to be me," he says. Even though he's traveled some distance to gaze into the canyon, he adopts a posture of cool indifference.

Percy imagined the unanticipated subversion of expectations as a possible route out of the dilemma, as in the case of an "accidental encounter" or a moment when the symbolic order of a place broke apart.[42] This seemed to be the case when Danny Ray Horning ran through the canyon. He was the "accident," a monkey wrench thrown in the gears of the canyon's "symbolic machinery," and despite all the agents, blood-hounds, helicopters, and infrared devices, no one—not the rangers, police, the Irish tourists who watched from El Tovar's porch, or anyone who came to the canyon with a suitcase full of expectations—knew how any of it would turn out. Yet in the face of it all, they pulled the ambiguous and inexplicable event back onto familiar territory. Horning became an outlaw, a Billy the Kid, a Rambo, and the world seemed like a movie. The empty abyss has always been a rich site for generating myths and metaphors, for mirroring the hopes and tensions of the times—a celestial city, the great divide, the earth's womb, a textbook of the earth's history, a sermon in stone—and with Horning it was much the same.

Few events at Grand Canyon captured the public's attention like that manhunt in 1992. Like everyone, tourists live in a time rife with expectations that are ordinarily sated in predictable routines of consumption. Amid the advertising slogans like Burger King's, which says they're "Keepin' it real," and the onslaught of reality-based TV programming like *Cops,* and all the new genuine-leather bomber jackets floating through the malls, tourists hit the road for places like the Grand Canyon hoping it may offer some way out from under it all. But as easily as Horning's jaunt through the park made the canyon disappear and offered an enticing allegory for freedom and escape from the most pressing of routines, the whole thing ended with an equally dramatic return to life in an unbearable cage. In a landscape where all seems mapped and photographed beyond proportion, and little seems to change, if only to reinforce the dream of an authentic bulwark against market playgrounds, suddenly something unimaginable appeared and disappeared on the horizon, and the mystery held a presence that invited attention, engagement, and awe for the way it shook an otherwise settled ground. We have always expected as much from the Grand Canyon, but rarely had I seen it delivered with such intensity. Lessons large and small, and new light can sometimes come from the cracks, the accidents, and the unexpected confrontations.

One summer, I left the canyon for a few days, drove to Phoenix, and flew to San Diego to visit some relatives. I opened up a copy of *USAir Magazine* from the seat pocket in front of me and read an article about a painter I had never heard of, Mark Tansey. The Los Angeles County Museum of Art was holding a retrospective of his work, but what immediately caught my eye was a photograph of his painting *Constructing the Grand Canyon* (1990). The small magazine reproduction didn't show much detail, but I was intrigued by a quote from the artist below the image.

"Deconstruction, the dominant art theory of the '80s, held that all the world's a 'text' to be deciphered," said Tansey. "An extrapolation of this might suggest that, were it true, nature would be text and the Grand Canyon would be a grand deconstruction project."[43] I knew I had to see his painting, and after a day in San Diego, I drove up to L.A. and found the canvas hanging on a panel in the middle of the exhibit.

The walls of Tansey's *Grand Canyon* are made of text—lines and lines of sentences, piled one on top of the other. Workers in T-shirts with jackhammers, shovels, sledge, and chisel smash off big blocks of text, split them open, and let them fall into piles of scattered words and phrases. In the foreground, at the bottom of the canyon, a group of seven with hammers pulverizes pieces of sentences into dust. A man pours the ore into an open mining cart sitting on railroad tracks. Behind him, someone takes a measure to see how deep they've gone with their work. Off to one side, an athletic climber scales the face of a rock made from text; he can only climb it because he is too close to read it. (Later, I learn that Tansey painted an entire canvas magnifying this image of the climber, *Close Reading*, 1990.) At the opposite end of the canyon, there is smoke from an explosion. Workers are blasting rock. Cranes, with ropes and pulleys, are mounted on one rim. On the other rim, two bison peer down. Everyone is breaking into a sweat as they hammer away on sentences, phrases, and words. Perhaps the most surprising aspect of the painting are the people Tansey has painted in the center of the scene. Harold Bloom, Paul de Man, and Geoffrey Hartmann stand there, overseeing all of the busy workers. Jacques Derrida is nearby. Off to the left, Michel Foucault sits alone on a big block of text.[44]

Tansey's canyon exhilarated and disturbed me at the same time. His painting captured a Grand Canyon I had, at different times, been imagining all along. But as I looked at all the busy workers chipping away the text and trying to "master" it, I realized their eagerness to "deconstruct" it meant that soon there would be nothing left. The bison grazing on the rim, watching all the blasting and hammering, suddenly seemed sad creatures. The canyon was being erased before their eyes, and I understood how they might feel.[45] My time at the canyon left me with little of the Grand Canyon I first saw when I was fifteen years old, driving across the country in my parent's Ford Fairlane. Taking stock of the years that followed, I realized I had spent most of my thirties in the Grand Canyon. When I wasn't driving out to Arizona or camping in Kaibab Forest and walking the trails and talking to tourists, I was trying to write about what I had seen, heard, and learned on the rim. People like John Wesley Powell, Clarence Dutton, Mary Colter, Thomas Moran, and even Danny Ray Horning had all spent some portion of their thirties in the Grand Canyon. I would not presume to draw any comparisons between their efforts and my own, but I recognized they all had a sense of direction and purpose, working toward some vision or running from some place of captivity. "The greatest mystery is not that we should have been flung at random amid the profusion of life and the stars," wrote André Malraux, "but that in what Pascal calls our prison, we can draw from ourselves images powerful enough to deny our nothingness."[46] In one way or another, Powell, Dutton, Colter, Moran, and Horning all seemed to know this. Each had come to the canyon to tell some version of an American story. But to some extent, mine was a story that began on foreign soil and, like many at the end of the nineteenth century, my sense of American culture began on the other side of the Atlantic. Tansey's painting held many European monuments and landmarks I knew well. My canyon guidebooks, translated from the works of French and German critics, provided an archaeology of knowledge, power, and panoptic pessimism; they pointed me to the stratifications of cultural formations and hegemonic blocs, and I imagined a thousand plateaus where nomad subjectivities wandered rhizomatic trails. Tansey's *Grand Canyon* brought all of this into focus; it seemed to say everything because it said the canyon's "grand canon"—the accumulation of more than a century of texts and images, stories and voices—could be turned into rubble at the hands of the busy deconstructionists wielding their hammers. Every generation who had come to the canyon in Arizona seemed destined to make the scene with the terms of their times, and the time of my life was no different.

But as I walked around the Los Angeles museum looking at more of Tansey's paintings, I found a painting that captured what could easily be another view of the Grand Canyon. One holding a different promise, offering another truth. On this canvas, a couple has stopped their sedan on the side of the road, and the front passenger door is open. The driver, a woman, waits behind the wheel with her hand on the stick shift. A crack runs across the highway and beneath the car. Perhaps there has been an earthquake somewhere and the aftershock has put a rift in the road. Her companion has left the car to investigate the crack in the pavement. He stands on one knee in the middle of the highway and reaches his hand to feel this break in the surface. Surely he could have seen it from his passenger seat. But this was not enough. They have stopped the car, and he's climbed out to put his fingers into the gap to feel it for himself. The painting, *Doubting Thomas* (1986), was another side of Tansey's *Constructing the Grand Canyon* hanging on the wall in the museum.

The original Thomas couldn't believe the stories of a man returning from the dead until he felt the miracle with his own hands, the ancient book tells us. In the 1920s, Charles Lummis seemed to retell the tale with a voice welding American culture to forces of divine magnitude. "See it for yourself," he said, in the pages of magazines and railroad brochures. "The Grand Canyon Bids You! . . . Come—and penitent—ye of the United States, to marvel upon this chiefest Miracle of our own land!" In the end, the America he imagined still held its doubts, and perhaps the Grand Canyon might offer some salvation and faith for a culture the public could hold as its own. Today, little seems to have changed as we stand on the edge of the chasm. Here, the dream of an ageless scene can melt into air, as Shakespeare and Marx each said of dramas still playing before us, and all that seems solid could be swept away to a canyon of fictions where we stand listening to hearts beating beneath the flesh and bone.

But this is not the whole view from the South Rim, where the tourists stand together and alone, watching the sun rise from the east, arc across the sky, and draw the curtain of night as it descends in the west. They see and know with more than eyes, and they are neither captured nor entirely satisfied by pictures, postcards, theories of the beginning, or the stories recited by the vigilant guards who claim to know. They pass along the rim for a brief time, and their hands feel both the heat on the stone and the comforting steel of the safety rails. I have watched them drag their planets in and out of this great tear in the plateau, this fissure of time. Many know that the answers they find in the Grand Canyon cannot entirely sustain them when they drive away at the end of the day toward other divides and chasms at work and home. The stories springing from the canyon offer few assurances, but it is a place where we witness and speak the terms of nature and culture to those at our sides, and where we can return— as many do—to wrestle with questions of faith and doubt; laugh at presumptions of certainty; seek out challenges of mind, body, and spirit; feel the jolt of a lightning bolt snapping across the sky; and grasp for some glimmer of a truth we sense laying beyond the flatness surrounding the abyss. I have watched them cast themselves into the great empty space for a time that waits at the end of the paved roads, so distant from the places where they work and love and sleep, to participate in a mystery none of us can solve, and walk away haggard, weary, laughing, crying, and quietly embracing a scene echoing experience and uncertainty with the many languages of life.

Notes

Introduction

1. Some key studies of the American West as a landscape of cultural politics, fantasy, and imagemaking include Frederick Jackson Turner, *The Frontier in American History* (New York: Henry Holt, 1920); Henry Nash Smith, *The Virgin Land: The American West as Symbol and Myth* (Cambridge: Harvard University Press, 1950); Wallace Stegner, *Beyond the Hundredth Meridian: John Wesley Powell and the Second Opening of the West* (Boston: Houghton Mifflin, 1954); Earl Pomeroy, *In Search of the Golden West: The Tourist in Western America* (1957; reprint, Lincoln: University of Nebraska Press, 1990); Frank Waters, *The Book of the Hopi: The First Revelation of the Hopi's Historical and Religious Worldview of Life* (New York: Viking Penguin, 1963); Leo Marx, *The Machine in the Garden: Technology and the Pastoral Ideal in America* (New York: Oxford University Press, 1964); Howard R. Lamar, *The Far Southwest, 1846–1912: A Territorial History* (New Haven: Yale University Press, 1966); Roderick Nash, *Wilderness and the American Mind* (New Haven: Yale University Press, 1967); G. Edward White, *The Eastern Establishment and the Western Experience: The West of Frederic Remington, Theodore Roosevelt, and Owen Wister* (New Haven: Yale University Press, 1968); Alfred Runte, *National Parks: The American Experience* (Lincoln: University of Nebraska Press, 1979); Alan Trachtenberg, *The Incorporation of America: Culture and Society in the Gilded Age* (New York: Hill and Wang, 1982);

Richard Avedon, *In the American West* (New York: Harry N. Abrams, 1985); Patricia Nelson Limerick, *The Legacy of Conquest: The Unbroken Past of the American West* (New York: W. W. Norton and Company, 1987); Richard White, *"It's Your Misfortune and None of My Own": A History of the American West* (Norman: University of Oklahoma Press, 1991); P. N. Limerick, Clyde A. Milner, and Charles E. Rankin, eds., *Trails: Toward a New Western History* (Lawrence: University Press of Kansas, 1991); Jane Tompkins, *West of Everything: The Inner Life of Westerns* (New York: Oxford University Press, 1992); James R. Grossman, ed., *The Frontier in American Culture* (Berkeley: University of California Press, 1994); Scott Norris, ed., *Discovered Country: Tourism and Survival in the American West* (Albuquerque: Stone Ladder Press, 1994).

2. David Bottoms, "An Old Hymn for Ian Jenkins," in *Under the Vulture-Tree* (New York: Quill Press, 1987), 29–30.

3. E. Burton Holmes, *The Burton Holmes Lectures: The Grand Cañon of Arizona*, vol. 6 (New York: McClure, Phillips and Company, 1905), 139–41.

4. Clarence E. Dutton, *The Tertiary History of the Grand Cañon District*, U.S. Geological Survey, monograph no. 2 (Washington, D.C.: U.S. Government Printing Office, 1882), 141.

5. Holmes, *Lectures*, 117–18.

6. For excellent and indispensable resources on the history of Grand Canyon, see Wallace Stegner, *Beyond the Hundredth Meridian;* J. Donald Hughes, *In the House of Stone and Light: A Human History of the Grand Canyon* (Grand Canyon, Ariz.: Grand Canyon Natural History Association, 1978); and particularly Stephen J. Pyne, *Dutton's Point: An Intellectual History of the Grand Canyon,* Grand Canyon Natural History Association, monograph no. 5 (1982). Pyne's *Dutton's Point* has been expanded in Stephen J. Pyne, *How the Canyon Became Grand: A Short History* (New York: Viking, 1998). See also Barbara J. Morehouse, *A Place Called Grand Canyon: Contested Geographies* (Tucson: University of Arizona Press, 1996).

7. James M. Houston, "The Concepts of 'Place' and 'Land' in the Judeo-Christian Tradition," in *Humanistic Geography: Prospects and Problems,* ed. David Ley and Marwyn S. Samuels (Chicago: Maaroufa Press, 1978), 225. Houston is one of many cultural geographers who have informed this work. Others include Yi-Fu Tuan, *Topophilia: A Study of Environmental Perception, Attitudes, and Values* (Englewood Cliffs, N.J.: Prentice-Hall, 1974); J. B. Jackson, *The Necessity for Ruins and Other Essays* (Amherst: University of Massachusetts Press, 1980); Douglas C. D. Pocock, *Humanistic Geography and Literature: Essays on the Experience of Place* (London: Croom Helm, 1981); Denis Cosgrove, *Social Formation and Symbolic Landscape* (London: Croom Helm, 1984); Denis Cosgrove and Stephen Daniels, eds., *The Iconography of Landscape: Essays on the Symbolic Representation, Design and Use of Past Environments* (Cambridge: Cambridge University Press, 1988); Edward Soja, *Postmodern Geographies: The Resurrection of Space in Critical Theory* (New York: Verso, 1989); Rob Shields, *Places on the Margin: Alternative Geographies of Modernity* (London: Routledge, 1991); Alexander Wilson, *The Culture of Nature: North American Landscape from Disney to the Exxon Valdez* (Cambridge, Mass.: Blackwell, 1992); James Duncan and David Ley, eds. *Place/Culture/Representation* (New York: Routledge, 1993); and Patrick McGreevy, *Imagining Niagara: The Meaning and Making of Niagara Falls* (Amherst: University of Massachusetts Press, 1994).

8. Freeman Tilden, *The National Parks: What They Mean to You and Me* (New York: Alfred A. Knopf, 1951), 18–19.

9. Roland Barthes, *Mythologies*, trans. Annette Lavers (New York: Hill and Wang, 1972), 142–43.

10. Raymond Williams, *Problems in Materialism and Culture* (London: New Left Books, 1980), 39.

11. Wai-Teng Leong, "Culture and the State: Manufacturing Traditions for Tourism," *Critical Studies in Mass Communication* 6, no. 4 (1989): 356.

12. Mark Neumann, "Tourism and American Culture: A Study of the Meanings of Leisure Travel at Grand Canyon National Park," (Ph.D. diss., University of Utah, 1991).

13. I have used pseudonyms for most of these people because I told them I would. I was more interested in their stories than anything. In some cases, I have used real names either drawn from public records and newspaper reports, or because it would be a disservice or an impossibility to conceal their identity.

14. Alexander Wilson, "The View from the Road: Nature and Tourism in the Postwar Years," *Border/Lines,* no. 12 (summer 1988): 10. For other studies of tourism, see Louis Turner and John Ash, *The Golden Hordes: International Tourism and the Pleasure Periphery* (London: Constable Press, 1975); Valene L. Smith, ed., *Hosts and Guests: The Anthropology of Tourism* (Philadelphia: University of Pennsylvania, 1977); Paul Fussell, *Abroad: British Literary Traveling between the Wars* (New York: Oxford University Press, 1980); Eric J. Leed, *The Mind of the Traveler: From Gilgamesh to Global Tourism* (New York: Basic Books, 1991); Dean MacCannell, *Empty Meeting Grounds: The Tourist Papers* (New York: Routledge, 1992); and Caren Kaplan, *Questions of Travel: Postmodern Discourses of Displacement* (Durham: Duke University Press, 1996).

15. See T. J. Jackson Lears, *No Place of Grace: Antimodernism and the Transformation of American Culture, 1880–1920* (New York: Pantheon, 1981), 4–58.

16. See, for example, Jean Baudrillard, *For a Critique of the Political Economy of the Sign,* trans. Charles Levin (St. Louis: Telos Press, 1981); Fredric Jameson, "Postmodernism, or, the Cultural Logic of Late Capitalism," *New Left Review,* no. 146 (1984), 53–92; Jean-François Lyotard, *The Postmodern Condition: A Report on Knowledge,* trans. Geoff Bennington and Brian Massumi (Minneapolis: University of Minnesota Press, 1984).

17. See Marshall Berman, *All That Is Solid Melts into Air: The Experience of Modernity* (New York: Penguin, 1988).

18. In 1997, visitor attendance at Grand Canyon National Park was expected to surpass five million. The most popular national park in the United States is Great Smoky Mountains National Park on the Tennessee–North Carolina border, with annual visits averaging ten million.

19. James Clifford, *The Predicament of Culture: Twentieth-Century Ethnography, Literature, and Art* (Cambridge: Harvard University Press, 1988), 9.

20. See Daniel Boorstin, "From Traveler to Tourist: The Lost Art of Travel," in *The Image: A Guide to Pseudo-Events in America* (New York: Harper and Row, 1961).

21. See Dean MacCannell, *The Tourist: A New Theory of the Leisure Class* (New York: Schocken, 1976).

22. Henri Lefebvre, *The Production of Space,* trans. Donald Nicholson-Smith (Cambridge, Mass.: Blackwell, 1991), 224–25.

23. John Berger, "The Enigma of Appearances," in John Berger and Jean Mohr, *Another Way of Telling* (New York: Pantheon, 1982), 128. Berger reminds us that a photograph "cuts across time and discloses a cross-section of the event or events which were developing at that instant." If that cross-section is wide enough, it can allow "us to see the interconnectedness and related co-existence of events. . . . A photograph which achieves expressiveness thus works dialectically: it preserves the particularity of the event recorded, and it chooses an instant when the correspondences of those particular appearances articulate a general idea" (120–22).

1. The Nostalgic Theater of the West

1. Christopher Lasch, *True and Only Heaven: Progress and Its Critics* (New York: W. W. Norton, 1991), 100.

2. James F. Muirhead, *America, The Land of Contrasts* (London: John Lane, 1902), 38.

3. James W. Carey, *Communication as Culture: Essays on Media and Society* (Boston: Unwin Hyman, 1989), 142–72. See James A. Ward, *Railroads and the Character of America, 1820–1887;* and Robert H. Weibe, *The Search for Order, 1877–1920* (New York: Hill and Wang, 1967).

4. Alan Trachtenberg, *The Incorporation of America: Culture and Society in the Gilded Age* (New York: Hill and Wang, 1982), 19.

5. T. J. Jackson Lears, *No Place of Grace: Antimodernism and the Transformation of American Culture, 1880–1920* (New York: Pantheon, 1981), 4–5.

6. John Muir, "The Wild Parks and Forest Reservations of the West," *Atlantic Monthly,* January 1898, 15–16.

7. For a more detailed account of the Santa Fe/Harvey association, see James Marshall, *Santa Fe: The Railroad That Built an Empire* (New York: Random House, 1945); James David Henderson, *"Meals by Fred Harvey": A Phenomenon of the American West* (Fort Worth: Texas Christian University Press, 1960); and Keith L. Bryant Jr., *History of the Atchison Topeka and Santa Fe Railway* (New York: Macmillan, 1974).

8. Marta Weigle, "From Desert to Disney World: The Santa Fe Railway and the Fred Harvey Company Display the Indian Southwest," *Journal of Anthropological Research* 45, no. 1 (spring 1989): 133. Weigle's study provides an excellent summary of the commodification of Native American culture throughout the Southwest between 1882 and World War II.

9. See Alfred Runte, *National Parks: The American Experience* (Lincoln: University of Nebraska Press, 1979).

10. Susan Stewart, *On Longing: Narratives of the Miniature, the Gigantic, the Souvenir, the Collection* (Durham, N.C.: Duke University Press, 1993), 23.

11. Edwin Burrit Smith, "As Seen by a Layman," in *The Grand Canyon of Arizona: Being a Book of Words from Many Pens, about the Grand Canyon of the Colorado River in Arizona* (Chicago: Passenger Department of the Santa Fe Railway, 1902), 63, 65.

12. See J. Donald Hughes, *In The House of Stone and Light: A Human History of the Grand Canyon* (Grand Canyon: Grand Canyon Natural History Association, 1978), 42–63. I am indebted to Hughes's overview of early tourist development of the Grand Canyon throughout this book.

13. Mrs. M. Burton Williamson, "A Visit to the Grand Canyon," *Historical Society of Southern California* 4 (1899): 200.

14. John Muir, "The Grand Cañon of the Colorado," *Century Magazine,* November 1902, 107.

15. Dwight L. Elmendorf, "Grand Canyon of Arizona," *Mentor,* October 1, 1915, 1.

16. Lasch, *True and Only Heaven,* 92.

17. *Grand Canyon Outings* (Chicago: Henry O. Shepard, 1915), 2–3.

18. Michael Kammen, *Mystic Chords of Memory: The Transformation of Tradition in American Culture* (New York: Alfred A. Knopf, 1991), 167.

19. *Grand Canyon Outings,* 2.

20. W. J. Black, *El Tovar: Grand Canyon of Arizona* (Chicago: Norman Pierce Company, 1909), n.p.

21. Ibid.

22. Ibid.

23. Lasch, *True and Only Heaven*, 84.

24. Black, *El Tovar*, n.p.

25. Ibid.

26. See Janet Wolff, *Feminine Sentences: Essays on Women and Culture* (Berkeley: University of California, 1990), 12–33.

27. This brief summary is drawn from Lears, *No Place of Grace*, 103–67.

28. Elliot J. Gorn, *The Manly Art: Bare-Knuckle Prize Fighting in America* (Ithaca: Cornell University Press, 1986), 187. The final decades of the nineteenth century saw the rise of college football, rowing, professional baseball, boxing, tennis, golf, body building, and increasing numbers of athletic clubs. "Athletic strife grew especially important to a society that was rendering life soft with material comforts and empty with religious skepticism," says Gorn. "Sports taught valuable lessons to young men from prosperous families, showing them how to suppress their social and spiritual doubts with bursts of vigorous energy" (188).

29. Lois W. Banner, *American Beauty* (New York: Alfred A. Knopf, 1983), 142–43. Physical exercise, Banner notes, was a response to the "accepted social Darwinian theories of women's inferiority, arguing that any inferiority was the result not of innate factors, but of women's restrictive clothing and their lack of exercise" (143).

30. Lasch, *True and Only Heaven*, 94.

31. Richard White, *"It's Your Misfortune and None of My Own": A History of the American West* (Norman: University of Oklahoma Press, 1991), 620.

32. Lasch, *True and Only Heaven*, 98–99.

33. Richard Slotkin, "Nostalgia and Progress: Theodore Roosevelt's Myth of the Frontier," *American Quarterly* 33, no. 5 (winter 1981): 614–15.

34. *Grand Canyon Outings*, 2. Note that in the nineteenth century, tan skin was a mark of laborers who spent days outdoors and pale skin a sign of wealth that allowed one to remain indoors, away from harsh natural elements.

35. Theodore Roosevelt, *The Strenuous Life* (1905; reprint, Bedford, Mass.: Applewood Books, 1991), 12.

36. Gorn, *The Manly Art*, 188–89.

37. White, *"It's Your Misfortune,"* 627–28.

38. G. K. Woods, compiler, *Personal impressions of the Grand Cañon of the Colorado River near Flagstaff, Arizona, as seen through nearly two thousand eyes, and written in the private visitor's book of the world-famous guide Capt. John Hance, guide, story-teller, and pathfinder* (San Francisco: Whitaker Ray Company, 1899), 52.

39. Ibid., 63.

40. Lesley Poling-Kempes, *The Harvey Girls: Women Who Opened the West* (New York: Paragon House, 1991), xvi-xvii.

41. Ibid., xiii.

42. *The Harvey Girls*, Metro-Goldwyn-Mayer (1945).

43. Jane Tompkins, *West of Everything: The Inner Life of Westerns* (New York: Oxford University Press, 1992), 44.

44. Walter Benjamin quoted in Richard Wolin, *Walter Benjamin* (New York: Columbia University Press, 1982), 71.

45. James Clifford, "On Ethnographic Allegory," in *Writing Culture: The Poetics and Politics of Ethnography,* ed. James Clifford and George E. Marcus (Berkeley: University of California Press, 1986), 119.

46. As quoted in Henderson, *"Meals by Fred Harvey,"* 30.

47. Black, *El Tovar,* n.p.

48. Vine Deloria Jr., *Custer Died for Your Sins: An Indian Manifesto* (New York: Macmillan, 1969), 2.

49. Ibid., 81.

50. T. C. McLuhan, *Dream Tracks: The Railroad and the American Indian, 1890–1930* (New York: Harry N. Abrams, 1985), 19–20.

51. *The Grand Cañon of Arizona: Through the Stereoscope,* ed. Frederick S. Dellenbaugh (New York: Underwood and Underwood, 1904), 31.

52. P. C. Bicknell, *Guidebook of the Grand Canyon of Arizona, with the only correct maps in print* (Kansas City: Fred Harvey Company, 1902), 78.

53. Miner R. Tillotson and Frank J. Taylor, *Grand Canyon Country* (Stanford: Stanford University Press, 1929), 27.

54. McLuhan, *Dream Tracks,* 20.

55. George A. Dorsey, *Indians of the Southwest* (Chicago: Passenger Department, Atchison, Topeka and Santa Fe Railway, 1903), 176.

56. Byron Harvey III, "The Fred Harvey Collection, 1899–1963," *Plateau* 36, no. 2 (fall 1963): 36.

57. This brief biographical sketch of Colter is drawn from Virginia L. Grattan, *Mary Colter: Builder upon Red Earth* (Flagstaff, Ariz.: Northland Press, 1980), 1–19.

58. William C. Tweed, Laura E. Soulliere, and Henry G. Law, *National Park Service Rustic Architecture, 1916–1942* (Washington, D.C.: U.S. Government Printing Office, 1977), 8.

59. Grattan, *Mary Colter,* 21.

60. Tweed et al., *National Park Service Rustic Architecture,* 11.

61. *Grand Canyon Outings,* 3.

62. Harold D. Mitchell, "Architecture in America: Its History up to the Present Time," *California Architect and Building News,* February 1882, 29.

63. David Gebhard, "Architecture and the Fred Harvey Houses," *New Mexico Architect,* January-February 1964, 18.

64. Dean MacCannell, *The Tourist: A New Theory of the Leisure Class* (New York: Schocken, 1976), 8–9.

65. Mary Jane Colter, *Manual for drivers and guides descriptive of the Indian Watchtower at Desert View and its relation, architecturally, to the prehistoric ruins of the Southwest* (Grand Canyon, Ariz.: Fred Harvey Company, 1933), 11–12.

66. Fred Kabotie and Bill Belknap, *Fred Kabotie: Hopi Indian Artist* (Flagstaff, Ariz.: Northland Press, 1977), 49–62.

67. Colter, *Manual for drivers and guides,* 12.

68. Sallie Saunders, "Indian Watchtower at Grand Canyon Is Dedicated by Hopi Indians," *Santa Fe Magazine,* July 1933, 28.

69. Ibid., 31.

70. Listen to Bob Dylan (or Jimi Hendrix's version), "All Along the Watchtower" (Dwarf Music, 1968).

71. Mitchell, "Architecture in America," 29.

72. Kammen, *Mystic Chords of Memory,* 294–95.

73. "Einstein Is 'Great Relative,' Hopis Decide on His Theory," *New York Times,* March 2, 1931, 5.

74. "Einstein Sees Lack in Applying Science," *New York Times,* February 17, 1931, 6.

75. Richard White, *The Roots of Dependency: Subsistence, Environment, and Social Change among the Choctaws, Pawnees, and Navajos* (Lincoln: University of Nebraska Press, 1983). "Implicit in [Navajo] injunctions to hard work and the general concern with maintaining one's property and herds was a fear of poverty," argues White. "This fear, however, was coupled with a distrust of riches and rich men. . . . The goal of hard work and thrift then was not riches; it was security and respect" (240–41).

76. Richard White, "Frederick Jackson Turner and Buffalo Bill," in James R. Grossman, ed., *The Frontier in American Culture* (Berkeley: University of California, 1994), 29.

77. Dean MacCannell, "Tradition's Next Step," in *Discovered Country: Tourism and Survival in the American West,* ed. Scott Norris (Albuquerque: Stone Ladder Press, 1994), 162.

78. James Earl Fraser's design for the Indian Head Nickel (also called a "Buffalo Nickel") was minted as U.S. currency from 1913 through 1938.

79. D. H. Lawrence as quoted in Keith Sagar, ed., *D. H. Lawrence and New Mexico* (Salt Lake City: G. M. Smith, 1982), 64.

80. Ibid., 2.

81. Kammen, *Mystic Chords of Memory,* 400.

2. A Cultural Abyss

1. John F. Sears, *Sacred Places: American Tourist Attractions in the Nineteenth Century* (New York: Oxford University Press, 1989), 137.

2. Susan Stewart, *On Longing: Narratives of the Miniature, the Gigantic, the Souvenir, the Collection* (Durham: Duke University Press, 1993), 71.

3. For example, see William Culp Darrah, *Powell of Colorado* (Princeton: Princeton University Press, 1951); Wallace Stegner, *Beyond the Hundredth Meridian* (New York: Houghton Mifflin, 1954); and William H. Goetzman, *Exploration and Empire* (New York: Alfred A. Knopf, 1966).

4. John Wesley Powell, *Exploration of the Colorado River of the West and Its Tributaries* (1875; reprint, Garden City, N.Y.: Doubleday, 1961), 80.

5. Stegner, *Beyond the Hundredth Meridian,* 96.

6. Dante, *The Inferno,* trans. John Ciardi (New York: Mentor, 1954), 223.

7. Paul Zweig, *The Adventurer: The Fate of Adventure in the Western World* (Princeton: Princeton University Press, 1974), 24.

8. Powell account of August 18 in John Cooley, *The Great Unknown: The Journals of the Historic First Expedition down the Colorado River* (Flagstaff, Ariz.: Northland Press, 1988), 165.

9. Powell, *Exploration of the Colorado River,* 194.

10. Cynthia Eagle Russett, *Darwin in America: The Intellectual Response, 1865–1912* (San Francisco: W. H. Freeman, 1976), 3.

11. Sumner account of August 9 in Cooley, *The Great Unknown,* 147.

12. Eric J. Leed, *The Mind of the Traveler: From Gilgamesh to Global Tourism* (New York: Basic Books, 1991), 202–3.

13. Gillian Beer, *Darwin's Plots: Evolutionary Narrative in Darwin, George Eliot, and Nineteenth-Century Fiction* (London: ARK, 1985), 44–45.

14. Russett, 3. The following brief discussion of evolutionary theology is largely drawn from Russett, *Darwin in America,* 25–45.

15. Rev. James H. McIlvaine, "Revelation and Science," *Bibliotheca Sacra* 34, nos. 133–36 (1877): 260.

16. Lyman Abbott, *The Theology of an Evolutionist* (Boston: Riverside Press, 1897), 15.

17. John Wesley Powell, "Prehistoric Man in America," *Forum 8* (January 1890).

18. John Wesley Powell, *Selected Prose of John Wesley Powell,* ed. George Crossette (Boston: David R. Godine, 1970), 72.

19. Stegner, *Beyond the Hundredth Meridian,* 248–49, 15–18.

20. Charles F. Holder, "The Great American Abyss," *Country Life in America* 14, no. 2 (June 1908): 151–52.

21. United States Federal Railroad Administration, *Grand Canyon National Park, Arizona* (Chicago: United States Railroad Administration, 1919), 11.

22. Stegner, *Beyond the Hundredth Meridian,* 343.

23. Charles A. Higgins, *Grand Cañon of the Colorado River* (1892; reprint, Chicago: Henry O. Shepard Co., 1893), 14.

24. Connie Rudd, *Grand Canyon's Young Adventurer* (Grand Canyon: Grand Canyon Natural History Association, 1985), 5.

25. Sears, *Sacred Places,* 42.

26. Charles Taylor, *Sources of Self: The Making of Modern Identity* (Cambridge: Harvard University Press, 1989), 297–99.

27. Ibid., 416–17.

28. Little has been written about Dutton, and my brief discussion of his work is indebted to Stegner, *Beyond the Hundredth Meridian,* 158–74.

29. Quoted ibid., 142.

30. Clarence E. Dutton, *The Tertiary History of the Grand Cañon District,* U.S. Geological Survey, monograph no. 2 (Washington, D.C.: U.S. Government Printing Office, 1882), 139.

31. Ibid., 58–59.

32. Wallace Stegner, "C. E. Dutton—Explorer, Geologist, Nature Writer," *Scientific Monthly* 45 (July 1937): 82–85.

33. Paul Shepard, *Man in the Landscape: A Historic View of the Esthetics of Nature* (College Station, Texas: Texas A&M University Press, 1990), 251.

34. Ibid., 253.

35. Ibid., 132.

36. Don D. Fowler, *The Western Photographs of John K. Hillers* (Washington, D.C.: Smithsonian Institution Press, 1989), 55.

37. See Stephen J. Pyne, *Dutton's Point: An Intellectual History of the Grand Canyon,* Grand Canyon Natural History Association, monograph no. 5 (1982), 41–44; and Stephen J. Pyne, *How the Canyon Became Grand: A Short History* (New York: Viking, 1998), 96–101.

38. See Joni Louise Kinsey, *Thomas Moran and the Surveying of the American West* (Washington: Smithsonian Institution Press, 1992).

39. Dutton, *Tertiary History,* 141.

40. John Ruskin, *The True and the Beautiful in Nature, Art, Morals, and Religion* (New York: Merrill and Baker, 1858), 250.

41. John Ruskin, *Modern Painters,* vol. 1 (New York: Wiley and Putnam, 1847), xliii.

42. Moran cited in George Sheldon, *American Painters* (New York: D. Appleton and Co., 1881), 125.

43. Dutton quoted in George Wharton James, *In and Around the Grand Canyon: The Grand Canyon of the Colorado River in Arizona* (Boston: Little, Brown, 1900), 86.

44. Ralph Waldo Emerson, "Chapter VII: Prospects," from *Nature* (1836), in *The Complete Works of Ralph Waldo Emerson,* vol. 1, ed. Robert E. Spiller and Alfred R. Ferguson (Cambridge: Harvard University Press, 1971), 40–43.

45. Ralph Waldo Emerson, "Nature," from *Essays: Second Series* (1844), in *The Complete Works of Ralph Waldo Emerson,* vol. 3, ed. Joseph Slater, Alfred R. Ferguson, and Jean F. Carr (Cambridge: Harvard University Press, 1983), 104.

46. Arnold cited in Williams, 115, 118.

47. Alan Trachtenberg, *The Incorporation of America: Culture and Society in the Gilded Age* (New York: Hill and Wang, 1982), 155–56.

48. Raymond Williams, *Culture and Society, 1780–1950* (1958; reprint, New York: Columbia University Press, 1983), 43.

49. Charles Dudley Warner, *Our Italy* (New York: Harper and Brothers, 1891), 181.

50. Warner, *Our Italy,* 195–96.

51. Roderick Nash, *Wilderness and the American Mind* (New Haven: Yale University Press, 1967), 67.

52. Warner, *Our Italy,* 193.

53. Ibid., 195–96.

54. John Muir, "The Wild Parks and Forest Reservations of the West," *Atlantic Monthly,* January 1898, 28.

55. Harriet Monroe, "The Grand Cañon of the Colorado," *Atlantic Monthly,* December 1899, 818–19.

56. John Muir, "The Grand Cañon of the Colorado," *Century,* November 1902, 108–9.

57. Michael H. Cowan, *City of the West: Emerson, America, and Urban Metaphor* (New Haven: Yale University Press, 1967), 74–75.

58. Higgins, *Grand Cañon,* 10.

59. Muir, "The Grand Cañon of the Colorado," 111.

60. Warner, *Our Italy,* 190–97.

61. Mrs. M. Burton Williamson, "A Visit to the Grand Canyon," *Historical Society of Southern California Quarterly* (1899): 203–4.

62. John L. Stoddard, *John L. Stoddard's Lectures,* vol. 10 (Boston: Balch Brothers, 1898), 81.

63. Ibid., 100–101.

64. Ibid., 102.

65. Kenneth Burke, *Permanence and Change: An Anatomy of Purpose,* 3rd ed. (Berkeley: University of California, 1984). Burke noted, "The gargoyles of the Middle Ages were typical instances of planned incongruity. The maker of gargoyles who put man's-head on bird body was offering combinations which were completely rational" (112). He offers James Joyce as an example of "blasting apart the verbal atoms of meaning, and out of the ruins making new elements synthetically, [and producing one of] our most striking instances of modern linguistic gargoyles" (113).

66. Charles Darwin, *The Origin of Species* (New York: W. W. Norton, 1970), 122.

67. Monroe, "The Grand Cañon of the Colorado," 820.

68. T. J. Jackson Lears, *No Place of Grace: Antimodernism and the Transformation of American Culture, 1880–1920* (New York: Pantheon, 1981), 179.

69. William James, *The Varieties of Religious Experience: A Study in Human Nature* (New York: Modern Library, 1936), 396, 414.

70. Russett, *Darwin in America,* 43.

71. Charles S. Gleed, "The Canyon by Dark and by Day," in *The Grand Canyon of Arizona: Being a Book of Words from Many Pens, about the Grand Canyon of the Colorado River in Arizona* (Chicago: Passenger Department of the Santa Fe Railway, 1902), 66.

72. James MacCarthy, "A Rhapsody by 'Fitz-Mac'," ibid., 92–96.

73. Ibid., 96.

74. Burke, *Permanence and Change*, 104.

75. George Wharton James, *In and Around the Grand Canyon: The Grand Canyon of the Colorado River in Arizona* (Boston: Little, Brown, 1901), 331–32.

76. Dwight L. Elmendorf, "Grand Canyon of Arizona," *Mentor*, October 1, 1915, 2–3.

77. See Peter De Bolla, *The Discourse of the Sublime: Readings in History, Aesthetics and the Subject* (Oxford: Basil Blackwell, 1989), 12–14, 33–39.

78. John C. Van Dyke, *The Grand Canyon of the Colorado: Recurrent Studies in Impressions and Appearances* (New York: Charles Scribner's Sons, 1927), 4–5.

79. Ibid., 218.

3. Framing the American Masterpiece

1. Charles F. Lummis, *A Tramp across the Continent* (New York: Charles Scribner's Sons, 1892), 244–45.

2. Charles F. Lummis, "The Greatest Thing in the World," *Land of Sunshine* 3 (1985): 197. Lummis's essay was reprinted in Charles A. Higgins, *Titan of Chasms: The Grand Canyon of the Colorado* (Chicago: Passenger Department of the Santa Fe Railway, 1902), 2–9, beginning in 1902. Higgins's *Titan of Chasms* was reprinted again and again in the first two decades of the twentieth century; each new version was updated with information about additions to the lodging and tourist facilities at the South Rim of the Grand Canyon.

3. Joaquin Miller, "A New Wonder of the World," *Overland Monthly*, March 1901, 786–90. The essay was reprinted in *The Grand Canyon of Arizona: Being a Book of Words from Many Pens, about the Grand Canyon of the Colorado River in Arizona* (Chicago: Passenger Department of the Santa Fe Railway, 1902), 58–60. Miller knew the power of fashioning an image. His own poetry received little notice until he moved to London in the early 1870s, published *Songs of the Sierras,* and reinvented himself in the romantic image of a flamboyant cowboy who wore boots, a sombrero, smoked three cigars simultaneously, and nipped at the ankles of debutantes. See *Benet's Reader's Encyclopedia*, 3rd ed. (New York: Harper and Row, 1987), 650–51.

4. Edward Hungerford, "A Study in Consistent Railroad Advertising," *Santa Fe Magazine*, March 19, 1923, 44.

5. "The Canyon in Art," *Mentor*, October 1, 1915, n.p.

6. Thomas Moran, "American Art and American Scenery," in *The Grand Canyon of Arizona: Being a Book of Words from Many Pens, about the Grand Canyon of the Colorado River in Arizona* (Chicago: Passenger Department of the Santa Fe Railway, 1902), 86–87.

7. Albert Bushnell Hart, "See America First," *Outlook*, December 27, 1916, 933.

8. Charles F. Lummis, "A Cosmic Intaglio: An Appreciation of Grand Canyon National Park," *Grand Canyon National Park* (U.S. Railroad Administration pamphlet, ca. 1920), 4.

9. Ned J. Burns, *Field Manual for Museums* (Washington, D.C.: U.S. Government Printing Office, 1941), 8, 315.

10. "Race Differences Declared Inborn: Dr. Davenport Tells Academy of Sciences the Results of Tests," *New York Times*, November 22, 1928, 8.

11. See Alfred Runte, *National Parks: The American Experience* (Lincoln: University of Nebraska Press, 1979), 106–37.

12. "Outdoor Museums" (editorial), *New York Times*, November 27, 1928, 30.

13. Robert Sterling Yard, "Our Educational Parks: Organizations Working to Bring out Value of National Reserves," *New York Times*, December 15, 1928, sec. B, 20.

14. John C. Merriam, "The Unity of Nature as Illustrated by the Grand Canyon," *Scientific Monthly* 33 (September 1931): 228–29.

15. Burns, *Field Manual for Museums,* 2.

16. Frank A. Waugh, *A Plan for the Development of the Village of Grand Canyon, Arizona* (Washington, D.C.: U.S. Dept. of Agriculture, Forest Service, 1918), 12.

17. Ansel F. Hall, "Studies for Museum Development in Grand Canyon National Park," November 15, 1934, 2–20.

18. Tony Bennett, "The Exhibitionary Complex," *New Formations* no. 4 (spring 1988): 73–76.

19. The preceding account is largely drawn from Ken Parks, "Shrine of the Ages: Proposed Chapel at Scenic Shrine Will Be Place of Worship for All Men," *Arizona Highways,* August 1955, 8–15.

20. Bradley quoted in "Shrine of the Ages," *New York Times,* June 3, 1956, sec. 2, 37.

21. Kundali Dasa, "Escaping the Reality Illusion," *Back to Godhead,* February–March 1988, 21–24.

22. Steven A. Austin, ed., *Grand Canyon: Monument to Catastrophe* (Santee, Calif.: Institute for Creation Research, 1994), 9.

23. Kurt P. Wise, quoted from the video documentary *Grand Canyon: Monument to the Flood* (Santee, Calif.: Institution for Creation Research, 1995).

24. Rev. Charles W. Gilkey, "The Spiritual Uplift of Scenery as Exemplified by the Grand Canyon," in *Proceedings of the National Parks Conference* (Washington, D.C.: U.S. Government Printing Office, 1917), 140–43.

25. Merriam, "The Unity of Nature," 227–34.

26. For examples, see William Graham Sumner, *What Social Classes Owe to Each Other* (New York, 1883); *The Challenge of Facts and Other Essays,* ed. Albert G. Keller (New Haven: Yale University Press, 1914); and Theodore Roosevelt, "Social Evolution," *The Works of Theodore Roosevelt,* vol. 13 (New York: Charles Scribner's Sons, 1926), 223–41.

27. "Race Differences Declared Inborn," *New York Times,* November 22, 1928, 8.

28. This physical geography is translated through what Gilles Deleuze and Félix Guattari describe in "10,000 B.C.: The Geology of Morals," in *A Thousand Plateaus: Capitalism and Schizophrenia,* trans. Brian Massumi (Minneapolis: University of Minnesota Press, 1987). For our purposes, physical strata of the canyon literally serve as a site for "deterritorializing" and "reterritorializing" stratifications of language. "The strata themselves are animated and defined by relative speeds of deterritorialization; moreover, absolute deterritorialization is there from the beginning, the strata are spinoffs, thickenings on the place of consistency that is everywhere, always primary and always immanent," they write. "That which races or dances upon the plane of consistency thus carries with it the aura of its stratum, an undulation, a memory or tension" (70).

29. Ortega y Gasset quoted in Martin Marty, *The Public Church: Mainline-Evangelical-Catholic* (New York: Crossroad, 1981), 95; also see Belden C. Lane, *Landscapes of the Sacred: Geography and Narrative in American Spirituality* (New York: Paulist Press, 1988), 16.

30. Walker Percy, *The Message in the Bottle: How Queer Man Is, How Queer Language Is, and What One Has to Do with the Other* (New York: Farrar, Straus and Giroux, 1975), 9.

31. Kenneth Burke, *Permanence and Change: An Anatomy of Purpose,* 3rd ed. (Berkeley: University of California, 1984), 272.

32. Mark C. Taylor, *Erring: A Postmodern A/theology* (Chicago: University of Chicago Press, 1987), 88–89.

33. Ibid., 90.

34. Henri Lefebvre, *The Production of Space,* trans. Donald Nicholson-Smith (Cambridge, Mass.: Blackwell, 1991), 189.

35. Lennard J. Davis, *Resisting Novels: Ideology and Fiction* (New York: Methuen, 1987), 98.

36. Hans-Georg Gadamer, *Truth and Method,* trans. G. Barden and J. Cumming (New York: Seabury Press, 1975), 164.

4. Managing a View

1. See Daniel Boorstin, "From Traveler to Tourist: The Lost Art of Travel," in *The Image: A Guide to Pseudo-Events in America* (New York: Harper and Row, 1961).

2. Charles Dudley Warner, *Our Italy* (New York: Harper and Brothers, 1891), 178.

3. Frederick Law Olmsted, "Preservation for All," in *Mirror of America: Literary Encounters with the National Parks,* ed. David Harmon (1865; reprint, Boulder, Colo.: Roberts Rinehart, 1989), 117.

4. See Robert Weyeneth, "Moral Spaces: Reforming the Landscape of Leisure in Urban America, 1850–1920" (Ph.D. dissertation, University of California, Berkeley, 1984), chap. 2, cited in Lawrence Levine, *Highbrow/Lowbrow: The Emergence of Cultural Hierarchy in America* (Cambridge: Harvard University Press, 1988), 186.

5. Olmsted cited in Levine, *Highbrow/Lowbrow,* 183.

6. Ibid., 145–46.

7. Mrs. M. Burton Williamson, "A Visit to the Grand Canyon," *Historical Society of Southern California* 4 (1899): 203.

8. P. C. Bicknell, *Guidebook of the Grand Canyon of Arizona, with the only correct maps in print* (Kansas City: Fred Harvey Company, 1902), 25.

9. Ibid., 33–34.

10. John Kasson, "Civility and Rudeness: Urban Etiquette and the Bourgeois Social Order in Nineteenth-Century America," *Prospects* 9 (1984): 148, 162.

11. Pierre Bourdieu, *Distinction: A Social Critique of the Judgement of Taste,* trans. Richard Nice (Cambridge: Harvard University Press, 1984), 56–57.

12. Henry Van Dyke, "Daybreak in the Grand Canyon of Arizona," *Scribner's Magazine,* September 1913, 275–78.

13. Levine, *Highbrow/Lowbrow,* 164.

14. Harriet Monroe, "The Grand Cañon of the Colorado," *Atlantic Monthly,* December 1899, 818.

15. John Muir, "The Grand Cañon of the Colorado," *Century Magazine,* November 1902, 110–11.

16. Ford Harvey, "The Public and the Grand Canyon," *Proceedings of the National Parks Conference* (Washington D.C.: U.S. Government Printing Office, 1917), 323.

17. J. Donald Hughes, *In the House of Stone and Light: A Human History of the Grand Canyon* (Denver: University of Denver, 1985), 85–94.

18. Enos Mills, "The National Parks for All People," in *Proceedings of the* 1917 *National Parks Conference* (Washington, D.C.: U.S. Government Printing Office, 1917), 43.

19. Harvey, "The Grand Canyon," 324–26.

20. Ibid, 325.

21. Albert Bushnell Hart, "See America First," *The Outlook,* December 27, 1916, 933–34.

22. Walter Benjamin, "The Work of Art in the Age of Mechanical Reproduction," in

Illuminations, ed. Hannah Arendt, trans. Harry Zohn (New York: Harcourt, Brace and World, 1968), 220–23.

23. Susan Sontag, *Against Interpretation* (New York: Dell, 1969), 297.

24. Rob Shields, *Places on the Margin: Alternative Geographies of Modernity* (London: Routledge, 1991), 4–5.

25. Leroy Jeffers, "Our Newest National Park: Nature's Wonders Await the Tourist at the Grand Canyon," *Motor Life,* September 1919, 40.

26. John C. Van Dyke, *The Grand Canyon of the Colorado: Recurrent Studies in Impressions and Appearances* (New York: Charles Scribner's Sons, 1927), 159–60.

27. Annette Thackwell Johnson, "Silence," *Independent,* September 22, 1922, 96–98.

28. John T. McCutcheon, *Doing the Grand Canyon* (1909; reprint, Grand Canyon, Ariz.: Fred Harvey Company, 1922), 1–3.

29. John Berger, *About Looking* (New York: Pantheon, 1980), 35.

30. Dale King, "Scope and Function in the Interpretation Program of the Southwestern National Monuments," in *Report of Custodians, Southwestern National Monuments* (Washington D.C.: U.S. Government Printing Office, 1940), as quoted in Barry Mackintosh, *Interpretation in the National Park Service: A Historical Perspective* (Washington D.C.: U.S. Government Printing Office, 1986), 84.

31. Douglas Hubbard and William W. Dunmire, *Campfire Programs: A Guide for Leaders of Campfires in the National Parks* (Washington, D.C.: U.S. Government Printing Office, 1968), 3–8.

32. Struthers Burt, "Where's the Canyon?" *Saturday Evening Post,* July 13, 1929, 26, 146.

33. Mills, "The National Parks for All People," 38.

34. Kenneth L. Nyberg, "Some Radical Comments on Interpretation: A Little Heresy is Good for the Soul," in *On Interpretation: Sociology for Interpreters of Natural and Cultural History,* ed. Gary E. Machlis and Donald R. Field (Corvallis, Ore.: Oregon State University Press, 1984), 152.

35. Albert Mauncy, *"Say, Ranger . . .": Or, How to Perform in the Information Center* (Washington D.C.: U.S. Government Printing Office, 1968), 3; Arthur Deikman, *A Guide to Implementing the Receptive Mode* (Washington D.C.: U.S. Government Printing Office, 1976), 2.

36. National Park Service, *Interpreter's Training Manual: Grand Canyon National Park* (1988), 162.

37. Ibid., 5–7.

38. Ibid., 7.

39. John Dewey, *Individualism Old and New* (1929; reprint, New York: Capricorn, 1962), 34–149.

40. Ibid., 126.

41. Ibid., 151–52.

42. Ibid., 159–68.

43. James W. Carey, *Communication as Culture: Essays on Media and Society* (Boston: Unwin Hyman, 1989), 88.

44. Edwin Corle, *Listen, Bright Angel* (New York: Duell, Sloan and Pearce, 1946), 235–36.

45. McCutcheon, *Doing the Grand Canyon,* 5.

46. Mary Jane Colter, *Manual for drivers and guides descriptive of the Indian Watchtower at Desert View and its relation, architectually, to the prehistoric ruins of the Southwest* (Grand Canyon, Ariz.: Fred Harvey Company, 1933), 65.

47. Benjamin Brooks, "Over Night at the Edge of the Grand Canyon," *Scribner's Magazine,* May 1905, 615–26.

48. Wolfgang Schivelbusch, *The Railway Journey: The Industrialization of Time and Space in the Nineteenth Century* (Berkeley: University of California Press, 1986), 192–93.

49. Jonathan Crary, *Techniques of the Observer: On Vision and Modernity in the Nineteenth Century* (Cambridge: MIT Press, 1990), 150.

50. Jonathan Crary, "Unbinding Vision: Manet and the Attentive Observer in the Late Nineteenth Century," in *Cinema and the Invention of Modern Life,* ed. Leo Charney and Vanessa R. Schwartz (Berkeley: University of California Press, 1995), 47.

51. McCutcheon, *Doing the Grand Canyon,* 5.

52. Bicknell, *Guidebook of the Grand Canyon of Arizona,* 55–56.

53. *Grand Canyon Outings* (Chicago: Santa Fe Railway, 1915), 3–4.

54. This brief account is based on William C. Suran, *The Kolb Brothers of Grand Canyon* (Grand Canyon, Ariz.: Grand Canyon Natural History Association, 1991); and J. Donald Hughes, *In the House of Stone and Light,* 72.

55. Frederick S. Dellenbaugh, *The Grand Cañon of Arizona: Through the Stereoscope* (New York: Underwood and Underwood, 1904), 7.

56. Crary, *Techniques of the Observer,* 124–32. Crary (124) cites Hermann von Helmholtz, *Handbook of Physiological Optics,* vol. 3, trans. George T. Ladd (New York: Dover, 1962), 303.

57. *National Park Overflights Act of 1987,* 100th Congress, 1st session, Senate Report 100-125, July 24, 1987 (legislative day June 23, 1987), 1–2.

5. Fantasy Trails across Popular Terrain

1. These quotes come from a two-page copy of *Filming Guidelines: Grand Canyon National Park* I obtained from the park's Public Affairs Office. The guidelines note that all "commercial operations at Grand Canyon National Park are regulated by Title 36 of the Code of Federal Regulations. National Park Service Guidelines state that a filming permit, issued by the Public Affairs Office, may be required for filming in Grand Canyon National Park. The National Park Service (NPS) understands the desire of many to film in areas of Grand Canyon National Park. In addition to entertainment and other values that may be communicated using visual information, the NPS recognizes that many of the films produced in parks also may carry an environmental and educational message to the public."

2. Richard Fegley (photographer), "Riverboat Gamblers," *Playboy,* August 1977, 81–85.

3. "Dear Playboy," *Playboy,* November 1977, 11–12.

4. Walker Percy, *The Message in the Bottle: How Queer Man Is, How Queer Language Is, and What One Has to Do with the Other* (New York: Farrar, Straus and Giroux, 1989), 47.

5. Gaston Bachelard, *The Poetics of Space,* trans. Maria Jolas (New York: Orion Press, 1964), 183–84.

6. Charles Dudley Warner, *Our Italy* (New York: Harper and Brothers, 1891), 196.

7. Ibid., 176.

8. Italo Calvino, *Invisible Cities,* trans. William Weaver (New York: Harcourt, Brace, 1974), 19.

9. As discussed above in chapter 2, "A Cultural Abyss," and chapter 3, "Framing the American Masterpiece."

10. This discussion is indebted to Walker Percy's *The Moviegoer* (1960; reprint, New York: Ballantine, 1988), 53.

11. Slavoj Žižek, *Looking Awry: An Introduction to Jacques Lacan through Popular Culture* (Cambridge: MIT Press, 1992), 15.

12. Ibid., 40.

13. Victor Burgin, *In/Different Spaces: Place and Memory in Visual Culture* (Berkeley: University of California Press, 1996), 28–31, 38. Drawing particularly from the work of Henri Lefebvre, Jacques Lacan, Guy Debord, and Walter Benjamin, Burgin argues that the "distinction between the social and the psychical" with regard to the production of space "is itself an abstraction, a fantasy." The interconnections between mental and social space, fantasy and reality, are a "'mysterious' area of transaction," that inevitably leads back to the theoretical importance of the surrealist movement. "The leading surrealists," Lefebvre observed, "sought to decode inner space and illuminate the nature of the transition from this subjective space to the material realm of the body and the outside world, and thence to social life" (quoted in Burgin, 31). For Burgin, this passage not only suggests Lefebvre's kinship with Lacan (both born in 1901 and living through a similar moment of French surrealism, as Burgin points out) but also how a psychoanalytic perspective is at the heart of understanding, and dissolving, a dichotomy between "fantasy" and "reality" in the realm of spatial production.

14. Žižek, *Looking Awry,* 125.

15. Ibid., 114.

16. Ibid., 112–14.

17. I didn't note which edition of Kerouac's book Kurt was reading. But I later found the passage in Jack Kerouac, *On the Road* (New York: Penguin, 1991), 102.

18. Henry Miller to Anaïs Nin, July 28, 1933, in *A Literate Passion: Letters of Anaïs Nin and Henry Miller, 1932–1953,* ed. Gunther Stuhlmann (New York: Harcourt Brace Jovanovich, 1987), 197.

19. *USA Weekend,* May 22–24, 1992, 1.

20. Ibid., 4.

21. John Berger, *Ways of Seeing* (New York: Penguin, 1972), 30.

22. Janice Radway, "Reception Study: Ethnography and the Problem of Dispersed Audiences and Nomadic Subjects," *Cultural Studies* 2, no. 3 (1988): 363.

23. Michel de Certeau, *The Practice of Everyday Life,* trans. Steven F. Rendall (Berkeley: University of California Press, 1984), 174.

24. Ibid., 175.

25. This discussion of Benjamin is drawn from Susan Buck-Morss, *The Dialectics of Seeing: Walter Benjamin and the Arcades Project* (Cambridge: MIT Press, 1991), 253–62.

26. Ibid., 256.

27. Benjamin cited in Buck-Morss, *The Dialectics of Seeing,* 254.

28. Ibid., 261.

29. Benjamin cited in ibid., 261.

30. Ibid.

31. Buck-Morss (68–70, 396) attributes the idea of "second nature" to George Lukacs, *History and Class Consciousness,* trans. Rodney Livingstone (Cambridge: MIT Press, 1971).

32. Joan Didion, *Slouching towards Bethlehem* (New York: Pocket Books, 1981), 20.

33. Nathanael West, *Miss Lonelyhearts and The Day of the Locust* (1950; reprint, New York: New Directions Publishing, 1962), 104.

34. Ibid., 104, 106–7.

35. Ibid., 177–78.

36. Jean Baudrillard, "Simulacra and Simulations," in *Jean Baudrillard: Selected Writings,* ed. Mark Poster (Stanford: Stanford University Press, 1988), and Todd Gitlin, "Postmodernism: Roots and Politics," in Ian Angus and Sut Jhally, eds., *Cultural Politics in Contemporary America* (New York: Routledge, 1989), 350.

37. West, *Miss Lonelyhearts,* 104.

38. Larry May, *Screening out the Past: The Birth of Mass Culture and the Motion Picture Industry* (Chicago: University of Chicago, 1983), 109–11.

39. David Nasaw, *Going Out: The Rise and Fall of Public Amusements* (New York: Basic Books, 1993), 205.

40. May, *Screening*, 110.

41. Mrs. John Dickinson Sherman and Huston Thompson, as quoted in *Proceedings of the National Parks Conference* (Washington, D.C.: U.S. Government Printing Office, 1917), 47, 50.

42. *Organic Act of 1916*, signed by Woodrow Wilson on August 25, 1916 (39 Stat. 535), U.S. Code, title 16, sec. 1.

43. National Park Service, *Annual Report, 1918*, quoted in Horace M. Albright (as told to Robert Cahn), *The Birth of the National Park Service: The Founding Years, 1913–33* (Salt Lake City: Howe Brothers, 1985), 69–72.

44. Robert L. Arneberger, Superintendent, Grand Canyon National Park, August 28, 1995, *Priority Needs of the Grand Canyon National Park: Hearing before the Committee on Energy and Natural Resources, United States Senate* (Washington, D.C.: U.S. Government Printing Office, 1995), 12.

45. "Prepared Statement of Robert L. Arneberger, Superintendent, Grand Canyon National Park, National Park Service," ibid., 14.

46. According to gross box office revenues, approximately 6.6 million people bought tickets to see Lawrence Kasdan's *Grand Canyon*. In excess of 20 million people have seen Harold Ramis's *National Lampoon's Vacation* in theaters or on home video. Since 1994, more than 33 million people have seen Richard Donner's *Maverick*. The audience estimates for all of these films are conservative and not statistically valid. The estimates for movie theatre audiences is based on an average ticket price of five dollars, the national average according to *Variety* magazine, divided into the gross revenue figures for each film. Gross revenues on video rentals and sales were divided by four dollars.

47. Gilles Deleuze and Félix Guattari, *A Thousand Plateaus: Capitalism and Schizophrenia*, trans. Brian Massumi (Minneapolis: University of Minnesota Press, 1987), 9; see 3–25.

6. The Depths of Time

1. Kathleen Stewart, *A Space on the Side of the Road: Cultural Poetics in an "Other" America* (Princeton: Princeton University Press, 1996), 63–64.

2. My idea of a "secret history" is indebted to Greil Marcus, *Invisible Republic: Bob Dylan's Basement Tapes* (New York: Henry Holt, 1997), which says much about culture and nothing about the Grand Canyon.

3. Henri Lefebvre cited in Eleonore Kofman and Elizabeth Lebas, "Lost in Transposition: Time, Space, and the City," introduction to Henri Lefebvre, *Writings on Cities*, trans. and ed. by E. Kofman and E. Lebas (Cambridge, Mass.: Blackwell, 1996), 16.

4. Guy Debord, "On the Passage of a Few Persons through a Rather Brief Period of Time," in *Situationist International Anthology*, ed. and trans. Ken Knabb (Berkeley: Bureau of Public Secrets, n.d.), 30–32.

5. These definitional terms for *vacatio* and *vacare* are from *New Shorter Oxford English Dictionary*, 5th ed. (New York: Oxford University Press, 1993).

6. David L. Eason, "Editor's Note," *Critical Studies in Mass Communication* 5, no. 2 (June 1988): n.p.

7. See Georges Van Den Abbeele, "Sightseers: The Tourist as Theorist," *Diacritics* 10 (winter 1980): 9–10.

8. Richard Quinney, "A Traveler on Country Roads," *Landscape*, no. 1 (1986): 25.

9. Van Den Abbeele, "Sightseers," 9.

10. Ibid.

11. Katerina Clark and Michael Holquist, *Mikhail Bakhtin* (Cambridge: Harvard University Press, 1984), 64–66.

12. Mikhail Bakhtin, "Forms of Time and the Chronotope in the Novel," in *The Dialogic Imagination: Four Essays by M. M. Bakhtin,* ed. Michael Holquist, trans. Caryl Emerson and M. Holquist (Austin: University of Texas Press, 1981), 84, 243–44. Others have noted the motel as a chronotope of travel and culture. See Meaghan Morris, "At Henry Parkes Motel," *Cultural Studies* 2, no. 1 (1988): 1–47; and James Clifford, "Traveling Cultures," in *Cultural Studies,* ed. Lawrence Grossberg, Cary Nelson, and Paula Treichler (New York: Routledge, 1992), 106.

13. Clifford, "Traveling Cultures," 108–9.

14. Janis P. Stout, *The Journey Narrative in American Literature: Patterns and Departures* (Westport, Conn.: Greenwood Press, 1983), 13.

15. Henri Lefebvre, "Work and Leisure in Daily Life," in *Communication and Class Struggle: Capitalism, Imperialism,* ed. Andre Mattelart and Seth Siegelaub, trans. Mary C. Axtmann (New York: International General, 1979), 137–40. Originally published in the forward to the second edition of Lefebvre's *Critique de la Vie Quotidienne* (Paris: L'Arche, 1958).

16. Eric Leed, "Why We Camp," *New York Times,* August 10, 1991, sec. 1, 19.

17. Patricia Meyer Spacks, *Boredom: The Literary History of a State of Mind* (Chicago: University of Chicago Press, 1995), 17–20.

18. Peter Bailey, *Leisure and Class in Victorian England: Rational Recreation and the Contest for Control, 1830–1885* (London: Routledge, 1978), 170. Cited in Spacks, *Boredom,* 17.

19. Karl Marx, *The Economic and Philosophic Manuscripts of 1844* (New York: International Publishers, 1964), 157.

20. Chris Rojek, "Leisure and 'The Ruins of the Bourgeois World,'" in *Leisure for Leisure: Critical Essays,* ed. Chris Rojek (New York: Routledge, 1989), 95–98, suggests that Benjamin Franklin's "Project of Moral Improvement" is indicative of an emerging bourgeois class consciousness. Franklin's list of thirteen virtues—temperance, silence, order, regulation, frugality, industry, sincerity, justice, moderation, cleanliness, tranquility, chastity, and humility—were "intended to act as practical aids in the day-to-day management of life. . . . For example, under *Order* he wrote 'Let all your Things have their Place. Let each Part of your Business have its Time' . . . [and] under *Industry,* 'Lose no Time. Be always employ'd in something useful. Cut off all unnecessary Actions.'" Like Franklin, Samuel Smiles's 1859 *Self Help* equally recommended cautious restraint in the pursuit of leisure. "Amusement in moderation is wholesome, and to be commended; but amusement in excess vitiates the whole nature, and is a thing to be carefully guarded against," wrote Smiles. "The maxim is often quoted 'All work and no play makes Jack a dull boy'; but all play and no work makes him something greatly worse."

21. In *Eight Hours for What We Will: Workers and Leisure in an Industrial City, 1870-1920* (Cambridge: Cambridge University Press, 1983), Roy Rosenzweig argues that for the working-class men, whose time and labor was sold for a wage and monitored by a boss and time clock, leisure provided a haven from a ruthless sphere of individualism and offered a context for articulating class consciousness, conflict, solidarity, mutual aid societies, and male privilege. Working-class women, writes Kathy Peiss in *Cheap Amusements: Working Women and Leisure in Turn-of-the Century New York* (Philadelphia: Temple University Press, 1986), found that the pursuit of leisure "did not lead them to . . . the traditional domain of workingmen . . . but to emergent forms of commercialized recreation, such as dance halls, amusement parks, and movie theaters" (5). This is in contrast to Janet Wolff's study of bourgeois women's experience of leisure during the same period. Bourgeois women experienced leisure time as increasingly

privatized through much of the nineteenth century, notes Wolff. Women were expected to devote their time to activities such as flower arranging, cookery, dressmaking, and generally keeping clear of any public places of leisure for fear they would be taken for prostitutes or members of a working class. See Janet Wolff, *Feminine Sentences: Essays on Women and Culture* (Berkeley: University of California Press, 1990), 22–23; also Rojek, "Leisure and 'The Ruins of the Bourgeois World,'" 107.

22. Samuel Beckett, *Waiting for Godot* (New York: Grove Press, 1954), 44.

23. Roland Barthes, "The World of Wrestling," in *Mythologies,* trans. Annette Lavers (New York: Hill and Wang, 1980), 24–25.

24. Paul Zweig, *The Adventurer,* 229, 239.

25. Adrian C. Moulyn, *The Meaning of Suffering: An Interpretation of Human Existence from the Viewpoint of Time* (Westport, Conn.: Greenwood Press, 1982), 10.

26. Roger Abrahams, "Ordinary and Extraordinary Experience," in *The Anthropology of Experience,* ed. Victor W. Turner and Edward M. Bruner (Urbana: University of Illinois Press, 1986), 52–67.

27. Arnold van Gennep, *The Rites of Passage,* trans. Monika B. Vizedom and Gabrielle L. Caffee (1908; reprint, Chicago: University of Chicago Press, 1960), 17–25.

28. Victor Turner, *The Anthropology of Performance* (New York: PAJ Publications, 1988), 24–25.

29. Barbara Myerhoff, "Life History among the Elderly: Performance, Visibility, and Remembering," in *A Crack in the Mirror: Reflexive Perspectives in Anthropology,* ed. J. Ruby (Philadelphia: University of Pennsylvania, 1982), 104.

30. Francis R. Line and Helen E. Line, *Grand Canyon Love Story: A True Living Adventure* (1984; reprint, Irvine, Calif.: Wide Horizons Press), 190–97.

31. Ibid.

32. Juliet B. Schor, *The Overworked American: The Unexpected Decline of Leisure* (New York: Basic Books, 1992), 11–12. "A major problem is that children are increasingly left alone, to fend for themselves while their parents are at work," says Schor. "Local studies have found figures of up to one-third of children caring for themselves. At least half a million preschoolers are thought to be left at home part of each day" (12).

33. Arlie Russell Hochschild, *The Time Bind: When Work Becomes Home and Home Becomes Work* (New York: Henry Holt, 1997), 44–45.

34. Donald L. Redfoot, "Touristic Authenticity, Touristic Angst, and Modern Reality," *Qualitative Sociology* 7, no. 4 (1984): 306.

35. Abrahams, "Ordinary and Extraordinary Experience," 70.

36. Stewart notes that "the problem of *ideals . . .* is not that of a simple tension between a notion and its always incomplete realization, or between the ideal and the real, but a split born with the dialectical structure of the notion itself. . . . The internal split, or gap, in *ideals* creates the possibility, if not the necessity, for complex appropriations, resistances, and excesses" (*A Space on the Side of the Road,* 187–88).

37. Mikhail M. Bakhtin, *Rabelais and His World,* trans. H. Iswolsky (Cambridge: MIT Press, 1968), 10, 109.

38. Mary Douglas, "Jokes," in *Rethinking Popular Culture: Contemporary Perspectives in Cultural Studies,* ed. Chandra Mukerji and Michael Schudson (Berkeley: University of California Press, 1991), 294.

39. Michel de Certeau, *The Practice of Everyday Life,* trans. Steven F. Rendall (Berkeley: University of California, 1984), 106–8.

40. Avery Gordon, *Ghostly Matters: Haunting and the Sociological Imagination* (Minneapolis: University of Minnesota Press, 1997), 16–17.

41. Janna Jones, "The Downtown Picture Palace: The Significance of Place, Memory and Cinema,"(Ph.D. diss., University of South Florida, 1998).

42. Hochschild develops the concept of the "potential self" as it becomes characterized through stories of an ideal future. "A potential self is a set, not of imagined present alternatives—activities one 'might have done' or ways 'one might have been'—but of imagined future possibilities. . . . They were fantasy creations of time-poor parents who dreamed of being time millionaires" (235).

43. Frank Waters, *Book of the Hopi* (1963; reprint, New York: Penguin Books, 1977), 165–73, 27.

44. Ibid., 122.

45. John Berger and Jean Mohr, *A Fortunate Man: The Story of a Country Doctor* (New York: Pantheon, 1967), 13–15.

46. Dick Hebdige, "The Impossible Object: Towards a Sociology of the Sublime," *New Formations* 1 (spring 1987): 47–76.

47. These accounts are drawn from suicide reports on file in the Coconino County Sheriff's Department in Flagstaff, Arizona, and a file of newspaper clippings titled "Accidents-Deaths" that I found in the Grand Canyon Research Library at Grand Canyon. I have tried to protect the anonymity of the victims and their families by not using specific names or referring to case numbers.

48. M. F. K. Fisher, "Jumping from Bridges," *Paris Review* 37, no. 134 (spring 1995): 293–95.

7. Making and Breaking the Scene

1. The Thomas Moran retrospective exhibition was on display at the National Gallery of Art from September 28, 1997, through January 11, 1998.

2. Michael Frome, *Rand McNally National Park Guide* (Chicago: Rand McNally, 1967), 13.

3. See Witold Rybczynski, *City Life: Urban Expectations in a New World* (New York: Scribner, 1995), 95–97.

4. See Henry Nash Smith, *Virgin Land: The American West as Symbol and Myth* (Cambridge: Harvard University Press, 1950); and Leo Marx, *The Machine in the Garden: Technology and the Pastoral Ideal in America* (New York: Oxford University Press, 1964).

5. This exercise is discussed at length in chapter 3, "Framing the American Masterpiece," 117–26.

6. Paul Ricoeur, *Lectures on Ideology and Utopia,* ed. George H. Taylor (New York: Columbia University Press, 1986), 17–18.

7. Ibid., 265–66, xxviii.

8. Ibid., 309–10.

9. Bill Nixon, "Grand Canyon Park Awaits Threatened Hippie Love-In," *Arizona Republic,* June 9, 1967, sec. B, 1–2; Howard Stricklin is quoted in "Riot Force Suggested for Love-in at Canyon," *Arizona Republic,* June 14, 1967, sec. B, 2.

10. "Hippies Show up at Grand Canyon," *Arizona Republic,* June 25, 1967, sec. B, 2.

11. Dick Hebdige, *Hiding in the Light* (New York: Routledge, 1988), 35.

12. See Christopher Lasch, *The True and Only Heaven: Progress and Its Critics* (New York: W. W. Norton, 1991), 92–100.

13. "Grand Canyon Stunt," *Brunswick News,* October 8, 1980, sec. A, 4.

14. "Aerialist Planning Canyon Cable Walk," *Arizona Daily Sun,* July 15, 1986, sec. A, 2.

15. "Just Say No to Aerialist," *Arizona Daily Sun,* July 20, 1986, sec. A, 22.

16. My analysis of these events is indebted to Paul Johnson's study of the early nineteenth-century daredevil, Sam Patch, who jumped waterfalls in the eastern United States. See Paul Johnson, "'Art' and the Language of Progress in Early-Industrial Paterson: Sam Patch at Clinton Bridge," *American Quarterly* 40, no. 4 (1988): 438.

17. "Clinton Protects Utah Land," *St. Petersburg Times,* September 19, 1996, sec. A, 1, 8.

18. Kathleen Donnelly, "Grand Canyon or Bust," *San Jose Mercury News,* May 2, 1994, sec. C, 8.

19. Personal correspondences to Nicolino from Clarence Gorman, May 15, 1995, and from the National Park Service, Glen Canyon Recreation Area, May 8, 1995.

20. Ronald Fleming quoted in "Whatever Became of the Public Square?" *Harper's,* July 1990, 53.

21. See Jack Goldsmith, "Designing for Diversity, *National Parks,* May-June 1994, 20.

22. Letters to the editor, *National Parks,* September-October 1994, 6.

23. Freidrich Nietzsche, *The Birth of Tragedy and the Genealogy of Morals,* trans. Francis Golffing (New York: Anchor Books, 1956), 136.

24. Jonathan Culler, "Semiotics of Tourism," *American Journal of Semiotics* 1, nos. 1–2 (1981): 139–40.

25. T. J. Jackson Lears, *No Place of Grace: Antimodernism and the Transformation of American Culture, 1880–1920* (New York: Pantheon, 1981), 300. Lears cites Fyodor Dostoyevsky, *The Brothers Karamazov,* trans. Constance Garnett (New York: Signet Classics, 1957), 239.

26. Geoffrey Barnard, quoted from *Priority Needs of the Grand Canyon National Park: Hearing Before the Committee on Energy and Natural Resources, United States Senate,* 104th Congress, August 28, 1995 (Washington D.C.: U.S. Government Printing Office, 1995), 38, 58.

27. Robert L. Arneberger, quoted ibid., 17.

28. Andrew Faught, "Horning Left Calling Card," *Arizona Daily Sun,* June 26, 1992, 2.

29. I have based this account on several sources: investigative reports and evidence transcripts filed by detectives with the Coconino County Sheriff's Department, and court reporter's transcripts from sworn testimony by Katherine Falk, Don Miller, and Manuel Norman given on July 27, 1994, and by Danny Ray Horning given on August 26, 1994, in the Superior Court of California, San Joaquin County (*The People of the State of California* v. *Danny Ray Horning,* No. 55917).

30. Bernie Lawrence quoted in Mark Shaffer, "Top Tracker Impressed by Escapee," *Arizona Republic,* July 2, 1992, sec. A, 10.

31. Dirk Johnson, "Fugitive Kidnaps Two and Eludes Search," *New York Times,* July 5, 1992, sec. 1, 12.

32. Clint Williams, "Auto Found, But Con Still Free," *Arizona Republic,* July 1, 1992, sec. A, 8.

33. Paul Brinkley-Rogers, "Our Heroes Have Sometimes Been Outlaws," *Arizona Republic,* sec. E, 1. Ray Ring is quoted on the same page of the article.

34. See Jim Robbins, "A Day in the Life of the Grand Canyon," *USA Weekend,* May 22–24, 1992, 5. According to Alexandra Bandon, "Crimes against Nature," *New York Times Magazine,* July 24, 1994, 30–31, nationwide crime statistics for national parks across the nation for 1992 show approximately 2,400 disorderly conduct offenses. The number increased to 5,200 in 1993. There were approximately 1,600 weapons confiscated in the entire park system—often fully automatic machine guns—during 1992. That number increased to 3,000 in 1993.

35. Clint Williams, "FBI to Con: Call Us," *Arizona Republic,* July 2, 1992, sec. A, 1.

36. Milan Kundera, *Immortality,* trans. Peter Kussi (New York: Grove Weidenfeld, 1990), 30.

37. Clint Williams, "Two Hundred Track 'Rambo' at Canyon," *Arizona Republic,* June 28, 1992, 12; Eric Malnic and Mary Tolan, "Convict Eludes Grand Canyon Search," *Los Angeles Times,* July 2, 1992, sec. A, 2, 29; and "Manhunt for Horning at Park" *Grand Canyon News,* July 2–8, 1992, 1, 4.

38. Williams, "FBI to Con: Call Us," 1, 10.

39. This account is drawn from officers' reports provided by the Coconino County Sheriff's Department and the sworn testimony of Caroline Young and Sally Edmonds given in the Superior Court of California, San Joaquin County on July 29, 1994. For a newspaper report of the Young and Edmonds kidnapping and Horning's escape from the Grand Canyon, see Amy Pyle, "Convict Kidnaps Women, Flees Canyon," *Los Angeles Times,* July 5, 1992, sec. A, 3, 19.

40. Sources for this account include officers' reports from the Coconino County Sheriff's Department; Dirk Johnson, "Prison Escapee Is Caught after Two-Month Manhunt," *New York Times,* July 6, 1992, sec. A, 8; Tina Daunt and Laura Laughlin, "Escapee Captured after Seven-Week Chase," *Los Angeles Times,* July 6, 1992, sec. A, 3, 19; and "Elusive 'Rambo' Finally Captured," *St. Petersburg Times,* July 6, 1992, sec. A, 1–2.

41. Danny Ray Horning, July 22, 1992, Case #17410/17423, "Oral Argument on Defendant's Motion for Change of Custody," Coconino County Court, transcripts by Marilyn Taylor, court reporter, 20–21.

42. Walker Percy, "The Loss of the Creature," in *The Message in the Bottle: How Queer Man Is, How Queer Language Is, and What One Has to Do with the Other* (1975; reprint, New York: Farrar, Straus and Giroux, 1989), 47–50.

43. Judith Bell, "Illusions and Allegories," *USAir Magazine,* August 1993, 43.

44. The Mark Tansey retrospective was exhibited at the Los Angeles County Museum of Art, June 17–August 29, 1993. See Judi Freeman, "Metaphor and Inquiry in Mark Tansey's 'Chain of Solutions,'" *Mark Tansey* (exhibition catalog) ed. Judi Freeman (Los Angeles: Los Angeles County Museum of Art, 1993), 29–33.

45. Freeman, ibid., 30–32, notes "'sous rature' (under erasure) is perhaps Derrida's most familiar coinage, often employed to describe the deconstructionist method of printing texts and striking through them. Many of Tansey's painted texts are themselves 'under erasure'; Tansey takes pages of published text, which he has underscored, crumples them, and then silk-screens them onto his canvases."

46. André Malraux, *Lazarus,* trans. Terence Kilmartin (New York: Holt, Rinehart and Winston, 1977), 103.

Index

Mark Neumann is associate professor of communication at the University of South Florida. He has published articles on ethnographic studies of tourism, documentary, gambling, and bootleg music recording in various journals and edited collections.